7

0996 N - Karolyn
130 RN - Johanna
4116 OR - papote

Lawrenceville Press

An Introduction to Computing Using ClarisWorks®

version 4

Bruce Presley
Beth Brown
Elaine Malfas

Copyright © 1996
by

Third Edition

ISBN   1-879233-81-9   (softcover)
ISBN   1-879233-82-7   (hardcover)

Printed in the United States of America

All orders including educational, Canadian, foreign, FPO, and APO may be placed by contacting:

Lawrenceville Press, Inc.
P.O. Box 704
Pennington, NJ 08534-0704
(609) 737-1148
(609) 737-8564 fax

This text is available in both hardcover and softcover editions.

16 15 14 13 12 11 10 9 8 7 6 5 4 3 2 1

First Edition published 1994

P Preface

We believe the best way to introduce students to computing is with an introductory course that gives them considerable "hands-on" computer experience. This objective is best accomplished with an integrated software package such as ClarisWorks that allows students to use a word processor, database, and spreadsheet. We also believe that an introductory course should include discussions about the roles computers play in modern society as well as a brief history of computing. These goals are accomplished by this text which is designed to serve the needs of students who will complete only an introductory course, as well as those who will go on to take subsequent computer courses. The emphasis of this text is on the concepts of computing and problem solving so that students learn how computers can be applied to a wide range of problems. The text is written to be used either in a one or two term course by students with little or no previous computer experience.

Designs and Features

Format: Each chapter contains numerous examples and diagrams printed in a two color format to help students visualize new concepts. Important commands are listed on the first page of each chapter. ClarisWorks menus are displayed in the margins for easy reference.

Objectives: An outline of the significant topics that should be emphasized is presented at the beginning of each chapter.

History of Computing: Before learning to use the applications software, Chapter One introduces students to a history of computing and covers the vocabulary needed to understand the concepts presented in later chapters.

Concepts of Applications: Each of the application areas begins with an introductory section which describes the application and its uses. In this way, students are taught the purpose of the application without being overly concerned with the specific software. If the student then goes on to use another software package, he or she will fully understand the general concepts behind each application.

Hands on Practice: In the applications chapters each new concept is presented, discussed, and then followed by a hands-on Practice which requires the student to test newly learned skills on the computer. The Practice sections also serve as excellent reference guides to review applications commands.

Chapter Summary: At the end of each chapter is an outline that briefly discusses the concepts covered in the chapter.

Vocabulary: A vocabulary section which defines the new terms used is given at the end of each chapter.

Review Questions: Numerous review questions are presented keyed to each section of the chapter, providing immediate reinforcement of new concepts. Answers to all review questions are included in the *Teacher's Resource Package* described below.

Exercises: Each of the applications chapters includes a set of exercises of varying difficulty, making them appropriate for students with a wide range of abilities. Answers to all exercises are included in the *Teacher's Resource Package* described below.

Graphics and Desktop Publishing: Chapter Twelve offers an introduction to desktop publishing using the draw and paint tools. Various methods of emphasizing documents are discussed. Students are also taught how to import a previously created graphic.

Social and Ethical Implications: Because computers play such an important role in modern society, Chapter Thirteen discusses the social and ethical consequences of living in a computerized society. Advances in computer-related technology that will impact on the student's world are also discussed. Telecommunication is explained and the ClarisWorks communications application introduced.

Careers in Computing: It is hoped that many students will become interested in careers in computing based upon their experience in this introductory course. A section in Chapter Thirteen outlines different computer careers and the educational requirements needed to pursue them.

Appendices: Summaries of ClarisWorks functions, System commands, and keyboarding skills are presented in appendices at the end of the text for easy reference.

Teacher's Resource Package

When used with this text, the Lawrenceville Press Teacher's Resource Package provides all the additional material required to offer students an excellent introductory computer applications course. These materials place a strong emphasis on developing the student's problem-solving skills. The Package divides each of the chapters in the text into lessons that contain the following features:

- **Assignments** – Suggested reading and problem assignments.

- **Teaching Notes** – Helpful information that we and our reviewers have learned from classroom experience.

- **Discussion Topics** – Additional material that supplements the text and can be used in leading classroom discussions.

- **Transparency Masters** – Diagrams of the different topics that can be copied onto film.

- **Worksheets** – Problems that supplement the exercises in the text by providing additional reinforcement of concepts.

- **Quizzes** – A short quiz that tests recently learned skills.

P

In addition to the material in the lessons, other features are included for each chapter:

- **Tests** – Two sets of comprehensive end-of-chapter tests as well as a midterm and final examination. Each test consists of multiple choice questions and "hands-on" problems that require work on the computer. A full set of answers and a grading key are also included.

- **Answers** – Complete answers for the review questions and exercises presented in the text.

Master Diskettes, included with the Package, contain the following files:

- **Data files** – All files the student needs to complete the practices and exercises in the text. These files allow students to work with large amounts of data without having to type it into the computer. Also included are the files needed to complete the worksheets, quizzes, and tests in the Package.

- **Tests** – The tests are also provided in word processing files so that they can be edited.

- **Answer files** – Answers to the practices, exercises, worksheets, quizzes, and tests.

Student data diskettes can be easily made by following the directions included in the Teacher's Resource Package. Student diskettes are also available in packs of 10.

As an added feature, the Package is contained in a 3-ring binder. This not only enables pages to be removed for duplication, but also allows you to keep your own notes in the Package.

Our Works Texts

The previous editions of our Works texts have established them as leaders in their field, with more than one million students having been introduced to computing using our "hands-on" approach. With this new ClarisWorks edition, we have made significant improvements over our earlier Works texts. These improvements were based on the many comments we received, a survey of instructors who are teaching the text, and our own classroom experience.

This text presents material for ClarisWork's word processor, database, and spreadsheet in introductory, intermediate, and advanced chapters. The word processing chapters discuss such topics as footnotes and paragraph indents. The database chapters cover such topics as queries and reports. The spreadsheet chapters include charts. Other chapters cover desktop publishing, telecommunications, and the Internet.

As an additional feature the softcover edition now has an improved sewn lay-flat binding which keeps the text open at any page and gives the book additional strength.

Thousands of instructors have found the Teacher's Resource Package and its accompanying diskettes an integral part of their instructional materials. The latest edition includes new worksheets, tests, and quizzes.

As active teachers, we know the importance of using a well written and logically organized text. With this edition we believe that we have produced the finest introductory computer text and Teacher's Resource Package available.

P

Acknowledgments

The authors are especially grateful to the following teachers and their students who classroom tested an early version of this text as it was being written. Their comments and suggestions have been invaluable:

Dr. Mary K. Adkemeier, Fontbonne College, St. Louis, MO

Judy Boyd, Sanford H. Calhoun High School, Merrick, NY

Mary Ann Dougherty, South Brunswick High School, NJ

Dr. Cindy Emmans, Central Washington University, Ellensburg, WA

Calvin Gates, Lebanon High School, Lebanon, PA

Neil Hall, Bedford Community Schools, Bedford, IA

Joanne Prell, College of DuPage, Glen Ellyn, IL

Sherry Reinking, IKM Community School, Manilla, IA

Walter Vestal, Ridgewood High School, Norridge, IL

Thanks are due Rick Dunn and Linda Stumpf of Courier Book Companies, Inc. who supervised the printing of this text. Rachel Stern designed the imaginative cover. The new graphics for this edition were produced by John Gandour.

The success of this and many of our other texts is due to the efforts of Heidi Crane, Vice President of Marketing at Lawrenceville Press. She has developed the promotional material which has been so well received by instructors around the world, and coordinated the comprehensive customer survey which led to many of the refinements in this edition. Joseph DuPree and Robin Van Ness run our Customer Relations Department and handle the many thousands of orders we receive in a friendly and efficient manner. Michael Porter and Richard Guarascio are responsible for the excellent service Lawrenceville Press offers in shipping orders.

Jodi McMasters, the newest member of our staff, has edited this text and did much of the research needed for the database chapters. We appreciate her efficiency and thoroughness.

Carol Esser has edited this text and is an author of the accompanying Teacher's Resource Package. Carol currently teaches computer applications. We appreciate her professionalism and positive spirit.

Finally, we would like to thank our students, for whom and with whom this text was written. Their candid evaluation of each lesson and their refusal to accept anything less than perfect clarity in explanation have been the driving forces behind the creation of *An Introduction to Computing Using ClarisWorks*.

P | About the Authors

Bruce W. Presley, a graduate of Yale University, taught computer science and physics at The Lawrenceville School in Lawrenceville, New Jersey for twenty-four years where he served as the director of the Karl Corby Computer and Mathematics Center. Mr. Presley was a member of the founding committee of the Advanced Placement Computer Science examination and served as a consultant to the College Entrance Examination Board. Presently Mr. Presley, author of more than twenty computer textbooks, is president of Lawrenceville Press and teaches computing applications.

Beth A. Brown, a graduate in computer science of Florida Atlantic University, is director of development at Lawrenceville Press where she has co-authored several applications texts and contributed in the development of several programming texts and their Teacher's Resource Packages. Ms. Brown currently teaches computer applications and computer programming.

Elaine Malfas is a graduate of Hartwick College and earned an M.S. in Technical Communication from Rensselaer Polytechnic Institute. Ms. Malfas has co-authored and edited a number of computer texts and their accompanying Teacher's Resource Packages. Currently Ms. Malfas teaches computer applications and desktop publishing.

P

An Introduction to Computing Using ClarisWorks

T | Table of Contents

Chapter Three - Manipulating Text with the Word Processor

T Chapter Four - Advanced Word Processor Techniques

Chapter Five - Introducing the Database

Chapter Six - Manipulating Data with the Database

Chapter Seven - Reports and Advanced Database Techniques

Chapter Eight - Introducing the Spreadsheet

Chapter Nine - Manipulating Data with the Spreadsheet

Chapter Ten - Advanced Spreadsheet Techniques

Chapter Eleven - Integrating the Word Processor, Database, and Spreadsheet

Chapter Twelve - An Introduction to Desktop Publishing

Chapter Thirteen - Telecommunications and the Social and Ethical Implications of Computing

Appendix A - ClarisWorks Functions

Appendix B - System Commands and Backups

Appendix C - Keyboarding Skills

Chapter 1
An Introduction To Computers

Objectives

After completing this chapter you will be able to:

1. Define what a computer is.

2. Discuss the history of computers.

3. Understand how computers work.

4. Name the components of a modern computer system.

5. Understand the advantages of using a computer.

6. Describe what software and hardware are.

1

This text is about computers: their history, how they process and store data, and the role they play in modern society. We will use a popular computer program named ClarisWorks to teach you about word processors, databases, spreadsheets, graphics, and telecommunications. Each of these applications will be explained as we proceed.

There are three reasons for learning how to use a computer. The first and most important is to develop problem-solving skills. This is done by learning how to analyze a problem carefully, develop a step-by-step solution, and then use the computer as a tool to produce a solution.

A second reason for learning about computers is to become acquainted with their capabilities and limitations. Because you are a part of a computerized society, learning to use a computer is probably the best way to become familiar with one.

Finally, using a computer can be fun. The intellectual challenge of controlling the operations of a computer is not only rewarding but also an invaluable skill. The techniques learned in this class can be applied to your personal and business life as well.

1.1 What is a Computer?

A computer is an electronic machine that accepts information (called *data*), processes it according to specific instructions, and provides the results as new information. The computer can store and manipulate large quantities of data at a very high speed and, even though it cannot think, it can make simple decisions and comparisons. For example, a computer can determine which of two numbers is larger or which of two names comes first alphabetically and then act upon that decision. Although the computer can help to solve a wide variety of problems, it is merely a machine and cannot solve problems on its own. It must be provided with instructions in the form of a computer *program*.

A program is a list of instructions written in a special language that the computer understands. It tells the computer which operations to perform and in what sequence to perform them. In this text we will use a computer program called ClarisWorks.

THE HISTORY OF COMPUTERS

Many of the advances made by science and technology are dependent upon the ability to perform complex mathematical calculations and to process large amounts of data. It is therefore not surprising that for thousands of years mathematicians, scientists, and business people have searched for "computing" machines that could perform calculations and analyze data quickly and accurately.

1.2 Ancient Counting Machines

As civilizations began to develop, they created both written languages and number systems. These number systems were not originally meant to be used in mathematical calculations, but rather were designed to record measurements like the number of sheep in a flock. Roman numerals are a good example of these early number systems. Few of us would want to carry out even the simplest arithmetic operations using Roman numerals. How then were calculations performed thousands of years ago?

Calculations were carried out with a device known as an *abacus* which was used in ancient Babylon, China, and throughout Europe until the late middle-ages. Many parts of the world, especially in the Orient, still make use of the abacus. The abacus works by sliding beads on a frame with the beads on the top of the frame representing fives and the beads on the bottom of the frame representing ones. After a calculation is made the result is written down.

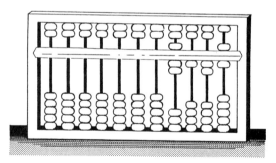

The abacus is a calculating device used throughout the Orient

1.3 Arabic Numerals

Toward the end of the middle ages, Roman numerals were replaced by a new number system borrowed from the Arabs, therefore called Arabic numerals. This system uses ten digits and is the system we still use today. Because the Arabic system made calculations with pencil and paper easier, the abacus and other such counting devices became less common. Although calculations were now easier to perform, operations such as multiplication and division were able to be done by only those few mathematicians who were well educated.

1.4 The Pascaline

One of the earliest mechanical devices for calculating was the Pascaline, invented by the French philosopher and mathematician Blaise Pascal in 1642. At that time Pascal was employed in the recording of taxes for the French government. The task was tedious and kept him up until the early hours of the morning day after day. Being a gifted thinker, Pascal thought that the task of adding numbers should be able to be done by a mechanism that operated similarly to the way that a clock keeps time.

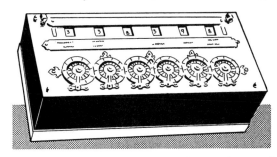

The Pascaline was a mechanical calculating device invented by Blaise Pascal in 1642

The *Pascaline* he invented was a complicated set of gears which could only be used to perform addition and not for multiplication or division. Unfortunately, due to manufacturing problems, Pascal never got the device to work properly.

1.5 The Stepped Reckoner

Later in the 17th century Gottfried Wilhelm von Leibniz, a famous mathematician credited with being one of the developers of the calculus, invented a device that was supposed to be able to add and subtract, as well as multiply, divide, and calculate square roots. His device, the *Stepped Reckoner*, included a cylindrical wheel called the Leibniz wheel and a moveable carriage that was used to enter the number of digits in the multiplicand.

Though both Pascal's and Leibniz's machines held great promise, they did not work well because the craftsmen of their time were unable to make machined parts that were accurate enough to carry out the inventor's design. Because of the mechanically unreliable parts, the devices tended to jam and malfunction.

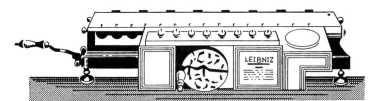

The Stepped Reckoner was another early attempt at creating a mechanical calculating device

1.6 The Punched Card

In 1810 Joseph Jacquard, a French weaver, made a revolutionary discovery. He realized that the weaving instructions for his looms could be stored on cards with holes punched in them. As the cards passed through the loom in sequence, needles passed through the holes and then picked up threads of the correct color or texture. By rearranging the cards, a weaver could change the pattern being woven without stopping the machine to change threads.

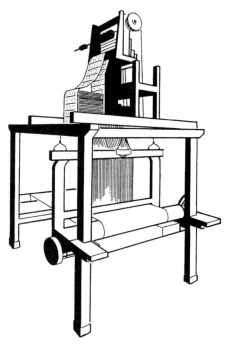

Jacquard's loom was the first device to make use of punched cards to store information

The weaving industry would seem to have little in common with the computer industry, but the idea that information could be stored by punching holes on a card was to be of great use in the later development of the computer.

1.7 Babbage's Difference and Analytical Engines

In 1822 Charles Babbage began work on the *Difference Engine*. His hope was that this device would calculate numbers to the 20th place and then print them at 44 digits per minute. The original purpose of this machine was to produce tables of numbers that would be used by ship's navigators. At the time navigation tables were often highly inaccurate due to calculation errors. In fact, several ships were known to have been lost at sea because of these errors. However, because of mechanical problems similar to those that plagued Pascal and Leibniz, the Difference Engine never worked properly.

Undaunted, Babbage later planned and began work on a considerably more advanced machine called the *Analytical Engine*. This machine was to perform a variety of calculations by following a set of instructions, or *program,* entered into it using punched cards similar to the ones used by Joseph Jacquard. During processing, the Analytical Engine was to store information in a memory unit that would allow it to make decisions and then carry out instructions based on those decisions. For example, in comparing two numbers it could be programmed to determine which was larger and then follow different sets of instructions. The Analytical Engine was no more successful than its predecessors, but its design was to serve as a model for the modern computer.

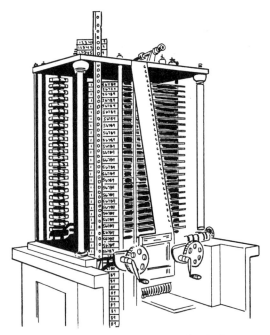

Babbage's Analytical Engine was a calculating machine that used punched cards to store information

Babbage's chief collaborator on the Analytical Engine was Ada, Countess of Lovelace, the daughter of Lord Byron. Interested in mathematics, Countess Lovelace was a sponsor of the Engine and one of the first people to realize its power and significance. She also tested the device and wrote of its achievements in order to gain support for it. Because of her involvement she is often called the first programmer.

Babbage had hoped that the Analytical Engine would be able to think. Countess Lovelace, however, said that the Engine could never "originate anything," meaning that she did not believe that a machine, no matter how powerful, could think. To this day her statement about computing machines remains true.

1.8 The Electronic Tabulating Machine

By the end of the 19th century, U.S. Census officials were concerned about the time it took to tabulate the count of the continuously increasing number of Americans. This counting was done every 10 years, as required by the Constitution. However, the Census of 1880 took 9 years to compile which made the figures highly inaccurate by the time they were published.

To solve the problem, Herman Hollerith invented a calculating machine that used electricity rather than mechanical gears. Holes representing information to be tabulated were punched in cards similar to those used in Jacquard's loom, with the location of each hole representing a specific piece of information (male, female, age, etc.). The cards were then inserted into the machine and metal pins used to open and close electrical circuits. If a circuit was closed, a counter was increased by one.

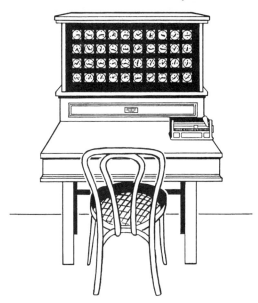

Herman Hollerith's tabulating machine, invented for the Census of 1880, used electricity instead of gears to perform calculations

Hollerith's machine was immensely successful. The general count of the population, then 63 million, took only six weeks to calculate, while full statistical analysis took seven years. This may not sound like much of an improvement over the nine years of the previous census, but Hollerith's machine enabled the Census Bureau to make a far more detailed and useful study of the population than had previously been possible. Based on the success of his invention, Hollerith and some friends formed a company that sold his invention all over the world. The company eventually became known as International Business Machines (IBM).

1.9 The Mark I

By the 1930s, key-operated mechanical adding machines had been developed which used a complicated assortment of gears and levers. Scientists, engineers, and business people, however, needed machines more powerful than adding machines; machines capable of making simple decisions such as determining which of two numbers was larger and then acting upon the decision. A machine with this capability is called a computer rather than a calculator. A calculator is not a true computer because, while it can perform calculations, it cannot make decisions.

The first computerlike machine is generally thought to be the *Mark I*, which was built by a team from IBM and Harvard University under the leadership of Howard Aiken. The Mark I used mechanical telephone relay switches to store information and accepted data on punched cards, processed it and then output the new data. Because it could not make

An Introduction to Computing Using ClarisWorks

decisions about the data it processed, the Mark I was not a real computer but was instead a highly sophisticated calculator. Nevertheless, it was impressive in size, measuring over 51 feet in length and weighing 5 tons! It also had over 750,000 parts, many of them moving mechanical parts which made the Mark I not only huge but unreliable.

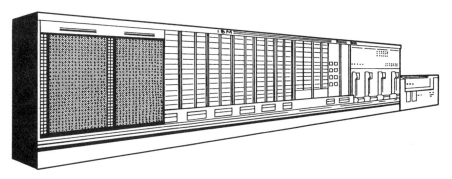

The Mark 1 weighed over 5 tons and was 51 feet long

1.10 ENIAC: The First Electronic Computer

In June 1943, John Mauchly and J. Presper Eckert began work on the Electronic Numerical Integration and Calculator, or *ENIAC*. It was originally a secret military project which began during World War II to calculate the trajectory of artillery shells. Built at the University of Pennsylvania, it was not finished until 1946, after the war had ended. But the great effort put into the ENIAC was not wasted. In one of its first demonstrations ENIAC was given a problem that would have taken a team of mathematicians three days to solve. It solved the problem in twenty seconds.

ENIAC was different from the Mark I in several important ways. First, it occupied 1500 square feet, which is the same area taken up by the average three bedroom house and it weighed 30 tons. Second, it used vacuum tubes instead of relay switches. It contained over 17,000 of these tubes, which were the same kind used in radios. Because the tubes consumed huge amounts of electricity the computer produced a tremendous amount of heat and required special fans to cool the room where it was installed. Most importantly, because it was able to make decisions, it was the first true computer.

Because it could make decisions, ENIAC was the first true computer

ENIAC had two major weaknesses. First, it was difficult to change its instructions to allow the computer to solve different problems. It had originally been designed only to compute artillery trajectory tables, but when it needed to work on another problem it could take up to three days of wire pulling, replugging, and switch-flipping to change instructions. Second, because the tubes it contained were constantly burning out, the ENIAC was unreliable.

Today, much of the credit for the original design of the electronic computer is given to John Atanasoff, a math and physics professor at Iowa State University. Between 1939 and 1942, Atanasoff, working with graduate student Clifford Berry, developed a working digital computer on the campus at Iowa State. Unfortunately, their patent application was not handled properly, and it was not until almost 50 years later that Atanasoff received full credit for his invention, the *Atanasoff Berry Computer* (ABC). In 1990, he was awarded the Presidential Medal of Technology for his pioneering work, and some of his early devices were exhibited at the Smithsonian.

1.11 The Stored Program Computer

In the late 1940s, John von Neumann considered the idea of storing computer instructions in a central processing unit, or *CPU*. This unit would control all the functions of the computer electronically so that it would not be necessary to flip switches or pull wires to change the instructions. Now it would be possible to solve many different problems by simply typing in new instructions at a keyboard. Together with Mauchly and Eckert, von Neumann designed and built the *EDVAC* (Electronic Discrete Variable Automatic Computer) and the *EDSAC* (Electronic Delay Storage Automatic Computer).

With the development of the concept of stored instructions or programs, the modern computer age was ready to begin. Since then, the development of new computers has progressed rapidly, but von Neumann's concept has remained, for the most part, unchanged.

The next computer to employ von Neumann's concepts was the UNIVersal Automatic Computer, or *UNIVAC*, built by Mauchly and Eckert. The first one was sold to the U.S. Census Bureau in 1951.

Computers continued to use many vacuum tubes which made them large and expensive. UNIVAC weighed 35 tons. These computers were so expensive to purchase and run that only the largest corporations and the U.S. government could afford them. Their ability to perform up to 1,000 calculations per second, however, made them popular.

1.12 The Transistor

It was the invention of the transistor that made smaller and less expensive computers possible, with increased calculating speeds of up to 10,000 calculations per second. Although the size of the computers shrank, they were still large and expensive. In the early 1960s, IBM, using ideas it had learned while working on projects for the military, introduced the first medium-sized computer named the model 650. It was still expensive, but it was capable of handling the flood of paper work produced by many government agencies and businesses. Such organizations provided a ready market for the 650, making it popular in spite of its cost.

One transistor replaced many tubes, making computers smaller, less expensive, and more reliable

These new computers also saw a change in the way data was stored. Punched cards were replaced by magnetic tape and high speed reel-to-reel tape machines. Using magnetic tape gave computers the ability to read (access) and write (store) data quickly and reliably.

Another important advance occurring at this time was the development of programming languages. Previously, computers had to be programmed by setting different switches to their On or Off positions. The first programming languages were consisted of strings of 1s and 0s representing the status of the switches (1 for On and 0 for Off). These were called low-level languages. Languages such as FORTRAN (FORmula TRANslator), which was one of the first popular high-level languages, allowed programmers to write in English-like instructions that had commands such as READ and WRITE. With high-level languages, it was possible to type instructions directly into the computer, eliminating the time-consuming task of rewiring.

One of the most widely used high-level programming languages has been COBOL. COBOL was first developed by the Department of Defense in 1959 to provide a common language for use on all computers. In fact, COBOL stands for COmmon Business Oriented Language. The designer of COBOL was Grace Murray Hopper, a Commodore in the Navy at the time. Commodore Hopper was the first person to apply the term *debug* to the computer. While working on the Mark I computer in the 1940s, a moth flew into the circuitry, causing an electrical short which halted the computer. While removing the dead moth, she said that the program would be running again after the computer had been "debugged." Today, the process of removing errors from programs is still called debugging.

A number of new high-level languages have been developed since that time. BASIC is a popular language used on microcomputers. C is a language designed by Bell Labs for programming large systems and is available on many computers today. Developed by the Swiss computer scientist Niklaus Wirth to teach the fundamentals of programming, Pascal is a language used by many schools and universities. The latest language developed by the Department of Defense is named Ada, after the first programmer, Ada the Countess of Lovelace.

1.13 Integrated Circuits

The next major technological advancement was the replacement of transistors by tiny integrated circuits or *chips*. Chips are blocks of silicon with logic circuits etched into their surfaces. They are smaller and cheaper than transistors and can contain thousands of circuits on a single chip. Integrated circuits also give computers tremendous speed allowing them to process information at a rate of millions of calculations per second.

A typical integrated circuit chip (approximately half an inch wide and 1.5 inches long)

One of the most important benefits of using integrated circuits is to decrease the cost and size of computers. The IBM System 360 was one of the first computers to use integrated circuits and was so popular with businesses that IBM had difficulty keeping up with the demand. Computers had come down in size and price to such a point that smaller organizations such as universities and hospitals could now afford them.

1.14 The Microprocessor

The most important advance to occur in the early 70s was the invention of the microprocessor, an entire CPU on a single chip. In 1970, Marcian Hoff, an engineer at Intel Corporation, designed the first of these chips. As a result, in 1975 the ALTAIR microcomputer was born. In 1977, working originally out of a garage, Stephen Wozniak and Steven Jobs designed and built the first Apple computer. Microcomputers were now inexpensive and therefore available to many people. Because of these advances almost anyone could own a machine that had more computing power and was faster and more reliable than either the ENIAC or UNIVAC. As a comparison, if the cost of a sports car had dropped as quickly as that of a computer, a new Porsche would now cost about one dollar.

1.15 Mainframe and Microcomputers

Today there are two main categories of computers—*mainframe* and *microcomputers*. The choice of which to use depends on what tasks are planned for it and how much data it must store.

Mainframe computers are large computer systems costing many hundreds of thousands, if not millions, of dollars. Mainframes can carry out many different tasks at the same time. They are used by large corporations, banks, government agencies, and universities. Mainframes can calculate a payroll, keep the records for a bank, handle the reservations for an airline, or store student information for a university—tasks requiring the storage and processing of huge amounts of information.

Mainframe computers are large, often requiring their own rooms

Microcomputers are small and usually inexpensive. Often called *personal computers* or *PCs*, they can cost as little as a few hundred dollars and fit on a desktop. Unlike mainframes, most microcomputers can carry out only a few tasks at one time. During the past few years the processing speed and ability of microcomputers to store large quantities of data has increased at such a rapid rate that some of them now rival older mainframe computers. The computer you will use is a microcomputer.

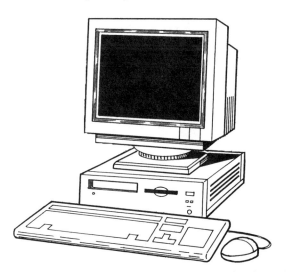

Today's modern microcomputer combines a keyboard, monitor, and CPU in a base unit in a desktop-sized package

Many of the microcomputers used in businesses and schools are *networked*. In a network, microcomputers are connected so that data can be transmitted between them. Because a network can include a large number of computers, it can perform many of the functions of a mainframe. The distinction between a mainframe computer and networked personal computers is rapidly becoming blurred.

1.16 How Computers Work

All computers process information, or *data*. This data may be in the form of numbers, letters, words, pictures, or symbols. In order to process data, a computer must carry out four specific activities:

1. Input data
2. Store data while it is being processed
3. Process data according to specific instructions
4. Output the results in the form of new data

As an example of computer processing, it is possible to input a list containing the names and addresses of one hundred thousand people and then ask the computer to search through this data and print only the names and addresses of those people who live in Florida. Another example would be to ask the computer to add all integers from 1 to 1000 and print their sum (i.e., 1 + 2 + 3 ... + 1000 = ?). In each of these examples, data must be input so that it may be processed by the computer. In the first case, the input is a list of names and addresses, while in the second, a list of numbers. In both cases the directions the computer would follow are given in a program.

1.17 The Components of a Computer

Computers contain four major components. Each component performs one of the following four tasks:

1. **Input Device:** a device from which the computer can accept data. Keyboards and disk drives are both examples of input devices.

2. **Memory:** chips inside the computer where data can be stored electronically.

3. **Central Processing Unit (CPU):** a chip inside the computer that processes data and controls the flow of data between the computer's other units. It is here that the computer makes decisions.

4. **Output Device:** a device that displays or stores processed data. Monitors and printers are the most common visual output devices while disk drives are the most common storage devices.

This diagram illustrates the direction in which data flows between the separate units:

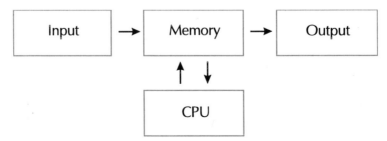

Notice that all information first flows through the CPU. Because one of the tasks of the CPU is to control the order in which tasks are completed, it is often referred to as the "brain" of the computer. This comparison with the human brain, however, has an important flaw. The CPU only executes tasks according to the instructions it has been given; it cannot think for itself.

1.18 Advantages of a Computer

Although computers cannot think, they do have some advantages over the human brain. For example, suppose you were given a list of ten numbers (input) and were asked to first, remember them (memory), second, calculate their average (process), and third, write down the average (output). In so doing, you would perform the same four tasks as a computer. Now suppose you were given 100 or 1,000 numbers and asked to calculate the average. Chances are you would get confused and tired performing all the calculations. The computer would have none of these problems. It would accurately remember all of the data and be able to quickly calculate the answers. The computer, therefore, has three important advantages over the human brain:

1. Reliable memory, with the ability to store and recall large amounts of data over long periods of time.
2. Speed, which enables it to process data quickly.
3. The ability to work 24 hours a day without rest.

Remember, however, that as reliable and fast as a computer is, it is only as "smart" as the instructions it is given by a program.

1.19 Hardware and Software

A computer requires both *hardware* and *software* to make it work. Hardware refers to the physical parts that make up a computer system and include keyboards, printers, memory units, CPUs, monitors, and disk drives. Software, on the other hand, describes the instructions or the program that is given to the computer. Some software is made a permanent part of most computers, so that the tasks a computer must always be ready to perform can be carried out easily. Other software is entered into the computer only when a specific task is required. In this text we will make use of applications software written to perform a number of different tasks.

1.20 Memory

Most computers have two types of memory contained on chips, *ROM* and *RAM*. Read Only Memory, or ROM, contains the most basic operating instructions for the computer. It is a permanent part of the computer and cannot be changed. The instructions in ROM enable the computer to complete simple jobs such as placing a character on the screen or checking the keyboard to see if any keys have been pressed.

Random Access Memory, or RAM, is temporary memory where data and instructions can be stored. Data stored here can be changed or erased. When the computer is first turned on, this part of memory is empty and, when turned off, any data it stores is lost. Because RAM storage is temporary, computers use disks as auxiliary memory storage. Before turning the computer off, the data stored in RAM can be saved as output on a disk so that it can be used again at a later time.

1.21 Central Processing Unit

The Central Processing Unit (CPU) directs all the activities of the computer. It can only follow instructions that it receives either from ROM or from a program in RAM. In following these instructions, the CPU guides the processing of information throughout the computer.

A CPU chip many times more powerful than the Mark I measures about 2 inches by 2 inches

The Arithmetic Logic Unit, or *ALU*, is the part of the CPU where the "intelligence" of the computer is located. It can perform only two operations. It can add numbers and compare numbers. Then the question is: How does the computer subtract, multiply, or divide numbers? The answer is by first turning problems like multiplication and division into addition problems. This would seem to be a very inefficient way of doing things, but it works because the ALU is so fast. For example, to solve the problem 5 × 2, the computer adds five twos, 2 + 2 + 2 + 2 + 2 to calculate the answer, 10. The time it takes the ALU to carry out a single addition of this type is measured in *nanoseconds* (billionths of a second). The other job of the ALU is to compare numbers and then determine whether a number is greater than, less than, or equal to another number. This ability is the basis of the computer's decision-making power.

1.22 How the Computer Follows Instructions

Memory storage, both RAM and ROM, and the CPU are made of tiny chips of silicon. These chips are so small that they must be housed in special plastic cases that have metal pins coming out of them. The pins allow the chips to be plugged into circuit boards that have their wiring printed on them.

Chips are covered by intricate circuits that have been etched into their surfaces and then coated with a metallic oxide that fills in the etched circuit patterns. This enables the chips to conduct electricity along the many paths of their circuits. Because there are as many as millions of circuits on a single chip, the chips are called integrated circuits.

An Introduction to Computing Using ClarisWorks

The electrical circuits on a chip have one of two states, OFF or ON. Therefore, a system was developed that uses only two numbers, 0 and 1: 0 representing OFF and 1 representing ON. A light switch is similar to a single computer circuit. If the light is off, it represents a 0, and if on, a 1. This number system, which uses only two digits, is called the *binary* (base 2) system.

Humans find a system with ten digits, 0 to 9, easier to use primarily because we have ten fingers. The computer uses binary digits to express not only numbers, but all information, including letters of the alphabet. Because of this a special code had to be established to translate numbers, letters and characters into binary digits. This code has been standardized for computers as the American Standard Code for Information Interchange, or *ASCII*. In this code, each letter of the alphabet, both uppercase and lowercase, and each symbol, digit, and special control function used by the computer is represented by a number. The name JIM, for example, is translated by the computer into the ASCII numbers 74, 73, 77. In turn, these numbers are then stored by the computer in binary:

Letter	ASCII	Binary code
J	74	01001010
I	73	01001001
M	77	01001101

1.23 Bits and Bytes

Each 0 or 1 in the binary code is called a *bit* (BInary digiT) and these bits are grouped by the computer into 8-bit units called *bytes*. Each ASCII code is one byte in length. Note how eight 0s and 1s are used to represent each letter in JIM in binary form.

The size of the memory, called RAM, in a computer is measured in bytes. For example, a computer might have 8MB of RAM. In computers and electronics *MB* stands for *megabytes* where mega represents 2^{20} or 1,048,576 bytes. Bytes are sometimes described as *kilobytes*, for example 256K. The K comes from the word *kilo* and represents 2^{10} or 1024. 64K of memory, therefore, is really 64×2^{10} which is 65,536 bytes.

It is possible to give a computer its instructions directly in binary code, typing in 0s and 1s using what is called *machine language*. This is extremely difficult to do, which is the reason that high-level programming languages have been developed. The English word instructions from these languages are translated by the computer into binary code. The software used in the applications chapters of this text has already been programmed.

1.24 Applications Software

One of the most useful ways in which a computer can be used is to run commercially produced *applications software*. This is software written by professional programmers to perform specific applications or tasks. In this text we will use an applications program named ClarisWorks which includes four common applications: word processing, database, and spreadsheet.

Word processors allow us to enter text from the keyboard into the computer and then manipulate it electronically. We will be able to insert and delete text, correct mistakes, move text and perform numerous other functions all on the computer screen. The text can then be printed.

Databases allow us to store and manipulate large quantities of data using the computer. For example, a database can store the names, addresses, grades and extracurricular activities for all of the students in a school. It will be possible to add or delete data and produce printed reports using the database.

Spreadsheets primarily store numeric data which can then be used in calculations. We will use a spreadsheet to store a teacher's grades and then calculate student averages. The primary advantage of a computerized spreadsheet is its ability to redo the calculations should the data it stores be changed.

One common factor shared by these four applications is their ability to store data on disk in a *file*. A file is simply a collection of data stored on a disk in a form the computer can read. Unlike the computer's RAM memory, data placed in a file is not erased when the computer's power is turned off. This way, the applications program can access the information again and again.

A major advantage of ClarisWorks is that it is an *integrated* program. This means that a single program performs all four applications, allowing data stored in a file by one application to be transferred to another. Later in this course you will produce a database file of names and addresses and then use this file in conjunction with a word processor file to produce personalized letters to everyone in the database file.

Besides integrated programs like ClarisWorks there are numerous other applications programs available. There are programs that can be used by musicians to produce musical scores and then play them on a synthesizer, programs that assist an architect in designing a building, programs that produce the special effects graphics that you see in the movies and on television, and much more. This book, for example, has been created and typeset using applications software.

As we progress in this text the usefulness of applications software will become increasingly obvious. With computers becoming more widely used, applications software is being written to assist people in almost every profession. Learning to use ClarisWorks will give you an idea of how the computer and applications software can be applied to help solve many types of problems.

Chapter Summary

Humans have searched for a machine to calculate and record data for thousands of years. The earliest of these devices were mechanical, requiring gears, wheels and levers, and were often unreliable. The advent of electricity brought about machines which used vacuum tubes, and were capable of performing thousands of calculations a minute. The unreliability of the vacuum tube lead to the development of the transistor and integrated circuit. Computers based on these devices were smaller, faster, more reliable and less expensive than before.

1

All computers have several parts in common: (1) an input device which allows data and commands to be entered into it, (2) some way of storing commands and data, (3) a Central Processing Unit which controls the processing, and (4) some way of returning the processed information in the form of output. In general, a computer is a machine which accepts information, processes it according to some specific instructions called a program, and then returns new information as output.

Today's microcomputer makes use of a CPU on a chip, the microprocessor, which controls the actions of the computer. Based on von Neumann's concept, the computer stores both data and instruction in its memory at the same time. Memory chips come in two forms, RAM, which can be erased and used over, and ROM, which is permanent. Keyboards and disk drives are used to input data. Monitors and printers are used to output data. Because the contents of RAM are lost when the computer's power is turned off, disks are used to store data. The CPU contains a special device called the Arithmetic Logic Unit (ALU) which performs any math or comparison operations.

Vocabulary

Abacus - Ancient counting device which used beads on a frame.

ALU - Arithmetic Logic Unit, the part of the CPU that handles math operations.

Applications software - Commercially produced programs written to perform specific tasks such as word processing.

ASCII - American Standard Code for Information Interchange, the code used for representing characters in the computer.

Bit - Binary Digit, a single 0 or 1 in a binary number.

Binary - Number system used by all computers. Uses only two digits (base 2).

Byte - A group of 8 bits.

CPU - Central Processing Unit, the device which electronically controls the functions of the computer.

Chips - Tiny integrated circuits etched into blocks of silicon.

Data - Information either entered into or produced by the computer.

Debug - To remove errors from a computer program.

File - Collection of data stored on a disk in a form the computer can read.

Hardware - Physical devices which make up the computer and its peripherals.

Input - Data used by the computer.

Integrated program - A single program that performs multiple applications.

K, kilobyte - Measurement of computer memory capacity. 1024 bytes.

Keyboard - Device resembling a typewriter used for inputting data into a computer.

Machine language - Computer program written in binary code, just 0s and 1s.

MB, megabyte - Measurement of computer memory capacity. 1,048,576 bytes.

Memory - Electronic storage used by the computer.

Microprocessor - CPU on a single chip.

Monitor - Television-like device used to display computer output.

Nanosecond - Billionths of a second.

Output - Data produced by a computer program.

Program - Series of instructions written in a special language directing the computer to perform certain tasks.

PC - Personal Computer, a small computer employing a microprocessor.
RAM - Random Access Memory. Memory which the computer can both read and write.
ROM - Read Only Memory. Memory from which the computer can only read.
Software - Computer programs.

1

1 Reviews

Sections 1.1 — 1.10

1. What is the primary difference between a computer and a calculator?

2. What is a computer program?

3. Why did early calculating devices not work well?

4. Was Pascal's Pascaline a computer? Why or why not?

5. If successful, could Babbage's Analytical Engine have been considered a computer? Why or why not?

6. a) What was the first calculating machine to make use of punched cards?
   b) What were the cards used for?

7. Why did scientists and business people want computers rather than calculators?

8. a) The Mark I was considered a calculator rather than a computer. Why?
   b) Why was the Mark I unreliable?
   c) What was the most important difference between the ENIAC and Mark I?

Sections 1.11 — 1.15

9. John von Neumann made one of the most important contributions to the development of modern computers. What was this contribution and why was it so important?

10. What made early computers so expensive?

11. What two innovations made the IBM Model 650 superior to earlier computers?

12. High-level programming languages such as FORTRAN and BASIC were developed in the 1960s. Why were they important?

13. a) What is an integrated circuit?
    b) In what ways is it superior to transistors?

14. What invention made the microcomputer possible?

15. Compare a microcomputer with ENIAC. What advantages does the microcomputer have?

16. List three jobs which could best be performed on each of the following computers:
    a) mainframe computer
    b) minicomputer
    c) microcomputer

Sections 1.16 — 1.24

17. Suppose you were to use a computer to store the names of all the students in your school and then print only those names beginning with the letter "P." Explain how each of the four activities needed to process data would be performed.

18. a) List three tasks for which a computer would be better than a human working without a computer. Tell why the computer is better.
    b) List three tasks for which a human would be better than a computer. Tell why the human is better.

19. a) What is computer hardware?
    b) What is software?

20. Which of the four major components of a computer would be used to perform each of the following tasks?
    a) display a column of grade averages
    b) calculate grade averages
    c) store electronically a set of grades
    d) type in a set of grades
    e) decide which of two grades was higher
    f) store a set of grades outside of the computer

21. What is the primary difference between the two types of memory contained in a computer?

22. How would the computer solve the problem 138×29?

23. Why does the computer use binary numbers?

24. How does the computer store a person's name in memory?

25. a) What is a bit?
    b) A byte?
    c) A K?

26. How many bytes of RAM are in a 4MB computer?

27. What is applications software?

Chapter 2
Introducing the Word Processor

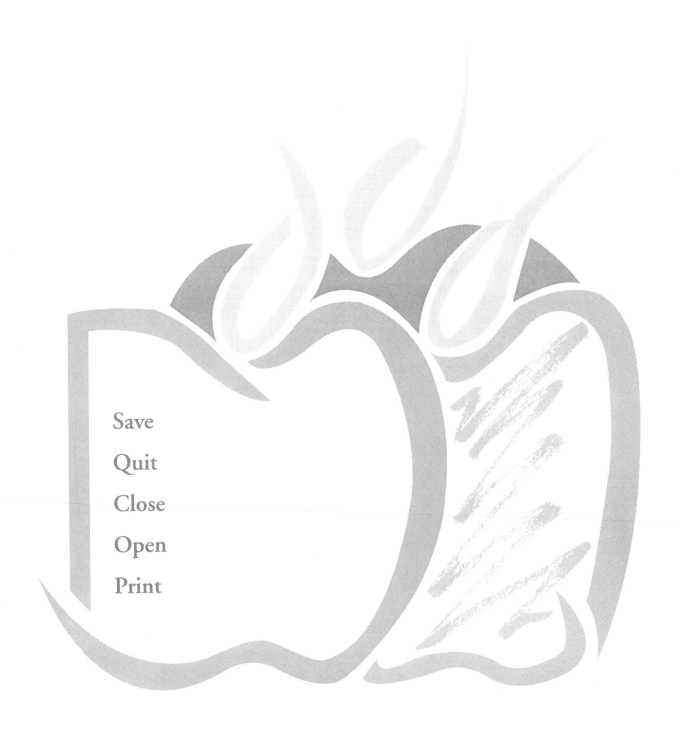

Save

Quit

Close

Open

Print

Objectives

After completing this chapter you will be able to:

1. Describe a word processor.

2. Explain why the word processor is ideal for producing a variety of different documents.

3. Start ClarisWorks and create a word processor file.

4. Use the word processor to enter and modify text.

5. Select menus from the Menu bar and choose different commands from them.

6. Save a file.

7. Close a file.

8. Open a previously saved file.

9. Use the Zoom controls to view a document.

10. Print a word processor file.

11. Exit ClarisWorks properly.

2

This chapter describes what a word processor is and why it is a powerful tool for preparing documents. Directions for using the ClarisWorks word processor to create, edit, print, and save documents are given.

2.1 What is a Word Processor?

A word processor is a computer application that is used to produce easy to read, professional-looking documents. It is a powerful tool that can be used to easily make changes (edit) in a document and to modify the look (format) of the document in a number of different ways.

When a word processor is used, a document can be edited electronically on the computer screen and printed later. To correct an error or make an editing change, only those words requiring changes need to be retyped. Words, phrases, and even whole paragraphs can be moved, copied, changed, or deleted. Editing options such as these can help improve the quality of your writing. Using a word processor allows the document to be continually refined until what has been written truly reflects what you wish to say.

Another useful feature of the word processor is the flexibility it provides when deciding how a document is to look. Does the document look better with a half-inch margin or an inch margin? Should text be double spaced or single spaced? With a word processor different formats can be viewed on the screen before printing.

When complete, a word processor document can be transferred to a disk. The saved document can then be recalled at any time, and changes made or another copy printed. It is also possible to combine pieces from one document with another so that lengthy paragraphs or several pages can be included in a new document without having to retype them.

2.2 How To Use This Text

Throughout this text new commands and procedures are introduced in a two step process. First, the command or procedure is discussed. You will be told what the command does and how to apply it, but will not use the computer at this time. The discussion is followed by a section titled *Practice*. Each Practice leads you through a step-by-step example of how to use the command. You will perform the steps given in a Practice on the computer using ClarisWorks. Practices also serve as reviews of the steps required to perform specific tasks.

Because the discussion sections explain the details of what is to be demonstrated, you should read them carefully before proceeding to the Practices. When performing a Practice, do each step in order as directed. Also, do not skip any Practices—because they are all related, skipping one may mean that you do not get the correct result at the end of the next.

2.3 Using Disks

Disks may be used to save the files you create. It is important to handle the disks carefully because they store large quantities of data in a magnetic format that is vulnerable to dirt and heat. Observing the following rules will help to ensure that your disks give you trouble-free service:

1. Keep disks away from electrical and magnetic devices such as computer monitors, television sets, stereos, and any type of magnet.

2. Make sure that your disks are not exposed to either extreme cold or heat. Because they are made of plastic they are sensitive to temperature.

3. Store disks away from dust, dirt, and moisture.

4. Never touch the disk's magnetic surface because this can damage it, destroying valuable data.

5. Do not bend, crush, or crimp the disk, and never use paper clips on it.

Computers are expensive electronic tools that should also be treated with care. A good rule to follow is never to eat or drink around computers.

2.4 Using the Mouse

The Macintosh comes equipped with a special input device called a *mouse* that is used to perform a variety of tasks:

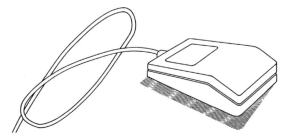

The mouse

When the mouse is in use, the *mouse pointer* is displayed on the screen. One common shape of the mouse pointer is an arrow:

The mouse pointer

Sliding the mouse along the top of the table causes the mouse pointer to move on the screen; slide the mouse to the left and the mouse pointer moves to the left, slide the mouse to the right and the mouse pointer moves to the right.

Pointing

By moving the mouse, it is possible to place the pointer on different objects on the computer screen. Placing the pointer on an object is called *pointing*. In this text, when we say to point to an object on the screen, we mean to place the pointer on it by moving the mouse.

Clicking

When the pointer is pointing to an object, it is possible to select that object by pressing the button on the mouse and releasing it quickly. This type of selection is called *clicking*. When we say to select or click on an item, we mean to move the pointer to it and then press and release the mouse button.

Double-Clicking

A special form of clicking is the *double-click*. As the name implies, double-clicking requires that the pointer be placed on an object and the button pressed twice in rapid succession.

Dragging

The last mouse technique is called *dragging*. An object is dragged by first placing the pointer on it. The mouse button is then held down while moving the mouse. In most cases this will move the selected object with the pointer. When we say to drag an object, we mean to place the mouse pointer on it, press and hold the mouse button, and move the mouse. When the object is in the desired location, release the mouse button.

2.5 Starting ClarisWorks

Before ClarisWorks can be started, the computer must have the disk operating system (simply called the *System*) loaded into the computer's memory. The System contains special programs that the computer needs to run. When the computer transfers the System from disk to computer memory it is called *booting*.

The System is a *graphical user interface*, or GUI (pronounced "gooey"). When a GUI is running it provides pictures called *icons* that are used to run programs and perform tasks. Once the system is started, the Claris-Works 4.0 *folder icon* is displayed. Your folder icon may have a slightly different name:

ClarisWorks 4.0

Double-clicking on the icon displays the contents of the ClarisWorks 4.0 folder. The contents of your folder may be slightly different:

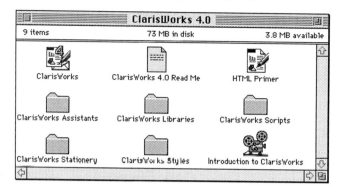

Double-clicking on the ClarisWorks icon starts the program.

Practice 1

In this Practice, you will turn on the computer and boot the System. The ClarisWorks program will then be run. The following instructions assume that you have a Macintosh with a hard drive that contains the System and the ClarisWorks program. If you are using ClarisWorks on a network your instructions will be slightly different.

1) BOOT THE SYSTEM

   a. Turn on the computer. A tone sounds. After a few seconds, the disk drive comes on and the computer automatically loads the System from disk.
   b. After the System has booted, the following is displayed on your screen (your screen may have different folders):

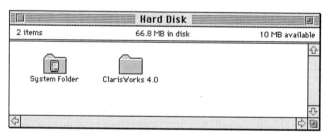

2) OPEN THE CLARISWORKS FOLDER

   a. Using the mouse, place the pointer on the ClarisWorks folder icon:

   b. Double-click on the ClarisWorks folder icon by pressing the mouse button twice in rapid succession.

An Introduction to Computing Using ClarisWorks

c. The ClarisWorks folder is opened, and its contents displayed on the screen. The contents of your folder may be slightly different:

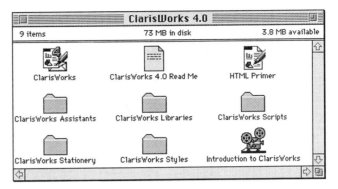

3) RUN THE CLARISWORKS PROGRAM

a. Using the mouse, place the pointer on the ClarisWorks icon:

b. Double-click on the ClarisWorks icon by pressing the mouse button twice in rapid succession.

c. The ClarisWorks program runs and displays a copyright screen:

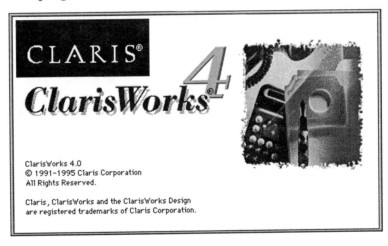

d. After a few seconds, the copyright screen is replaced by the New Document dialog box, described in the next section.

2.6 Creating a New Document

In ClarisWorks, each word processor document, database, and spreadsheet is stored on a computer disk (database and spreadsheet documents are explained later in this text). Each document stored on a computer disk is called a *file*. Before a stored file can be used, it must be opened by electronically transferring it from disk to the computer's memory to display it on the computer screen. If a new, empty file is desired, it must first be created by using the New Document dialog box.

The New Document dialog box is displayed after ClarisWorks is started:

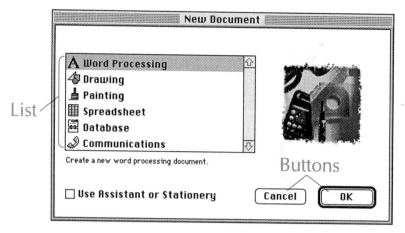

A new document is created in ClarisWorks using this dialog box

The **Word Processing** option is already selected in the New Document dialog box. Therefore, clicking on **OK** creates a new, empty word processor file.

2.7 Dialog Boxes

A *dialog box* offers a group of options from which you may choose. Its purpose is to supply the information ClarisWorks needs to execute a command. A dialog box can be removed without applying selected options by clicking on the **Cancel** button or by pressing the Escape key.

Buttons

A common dialog box element is the *button*. Clicking once on a button initiates an action. In the New Document dialog box, **OK** and **Cancel** are examples of buttons.

When a dialog box is displayed, there are options and buttons that have been preselected. These are called the *defaults*. The default options are usually the options that are chosen most often. In the New Document dialog box, **Word Processing** is a default option because it is already selected when the dialog box is displayed. A default button has a dark, heavy line around it such as the **OK** button in the New Document dialog box. The default button can be selected by clicking on it using the mouse or by simply pressing the Return key.

2.8 The Word Processor Screen

Word processor documents are displayed on the word processor screen. There are several features that will be important as you learn to use the word processor:

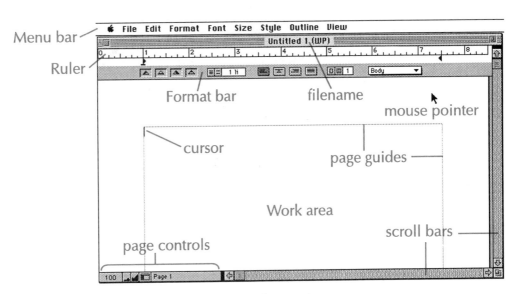

The ClarisWorks word processor screen

Along the top of the screen is the *Menu bar*. Each word in the Menu bar is the name of a pull-down *menu* which contains commands that will be discussed later. Below the Menu bar, ClarisWorks displays the name and type of file that is displayed. The filename `Untitled 1` shown on the screen above is used temporarily until a name is created for the file. The `(WP)` indicates that this is a word processor file. Below the filename is the *Ruler* which is used to judge horizontal spacing. The *Format bar* contains formatting options that will be explained later. On the far right and bottom of the screen are *scroll bars* that are used to display different parts of the document. In the lower-left corner of the screen are *page controls*, also discussed later.

The *Work area* is where text is entered and edited. Dotted lines called *page guides* indicate the boundaries of the Work area. Any text typed in the word processor appears within these boundaries. The *cursor* is a blinking vertical line that is always located within the Work area. In a new word processor document, the cursor is located in the upper-left corner of the Work area. It shows where characters typed will appear. Note the shape of the mouse pointer shown on the screen above. The arrow shape indicates the pointer is outside the Work area. The mouse is used to select menus from the Menu bar.

2.9 The Computer Keyboard and Word Processing

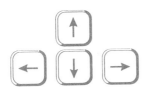

When the word processor screen is first displayed, the cursor is shown in the upper-left corner of the Work area. The cursor can be moved in a document, without erasing or entering text, by using the *cursor control keys*. Because these keys are marked with arrows (up, down, left, and right), they are also called *arrow keys*. The arrow keys can only be used to move the cursor where text has already been entered. To move the cursor down one line, press the key marked with a down arrow. Similarly, to move the cursor up, left, or right, use the key marked with the appropriate arrow. Each of the arrow keys is a *repeat key*, meaning that it will continue moving the cursor as long as it is held down.

To insert new text, the cursor control keys are used to place the cursor where the new material is to appear, and then the new material is typed. Any text following the insertion is moved to the right.

The Delete key is used to erase a character. Pressing Delete erases the character directly to the left of the cursor. When a character is deleted, any characters to its right are automatically moved over to fill the gap made by the deleted character. Do not confuse Delete with the left-arrow key. Both move the cursor to the left, but Delete erases characters and left-arrow does not.

The Escape key (marked esc) is used to cancel (escape from) the computer's current operation. The specific effect that pressing the Escape key will have depends on the operation being performed.

In the word processor, the Return key is used to end a paragraph or to terminate any line that does not reach the right side of the screen. When Return is pressed the cursor moves to the next line. Return may also be used to instruct ClarisWorks to accept a dialog box option.

A special key is the *Open-Apple* or *Command* key. The Command key (⌘) is used for many different purposes and is described in more detail in the next chapter.

....

Practice 2

In this Practice you will enter text into a new file and then edit it by using the arrow and Delete keys. ClarisWorks should be started and the New Document dialog box displayed from the last Practice.

1) CREATE A NEW WORD PROCESSOR FILE

    a. Because **Word Processing** is the default option, it should already be selected. If it is not selected, place the pointer on its name and click the mouse button once to select it.

    b. Place the pointer on the **OK** button and click the mouse. A new, empty word processor document named Untitled 1 is displayed on the word processor screen. Locate the Menu bar, Ruler, Format bar, page guides, cursor, mouse pointer, and scroll bars on your screen.

2) TYPE THE FOLLOWING LINE INTO THE FILE

Carefully type the following line. Hold down the Shift key to generate the capital letters and exclamation point (!):

```
Hello, World!
```

Do not press Return.

3) DELETE THE EXCLAMATION POINT

Press the Delete key once to erase the exclamation point. ClarisWorks automatically moves the cursor into the space formerly occupied by the erased character.

4) MOVE THE CURSOR WITHOUT ERASING ANY TEXT

Move the cursor to the right of the letter r by pressing the left-arrow key twice.

An Introduction to Computing Using ClarisWorks

5) DELETE THE LETTER "r"

Press the Delete key once. Note how the letters `ld` have moved over to fill the area where the letter `r` appeared. The document now contains the letters `Hello, Wold`.

6) INSERT A CHARACTER

Press the R key. An `r` is inserted at the current cursor position, and the text now reads `Hello, World`.

7) MOVE THE CURSOR TO THE END OF THE LINE

Press the right-arrow key until the cursor is to the right of the `d` in `World`. Press the right-arrow key again several times. ClarisWorks does not allow the cursor to be moved beyond the text.

8) DELETE ALL OF THE LETTERS IN THE LINE

Press the Delete key to erase the `d`. Continue to hold down Delete until all of the letters have been deleted.

9) ENTER THE FOLLOWING POEM

Type the following poem pressing the Return key at the end of each line. Use the Delete and arrow keys to correct any typing errors that you have made:

`Jack and Jill went up the hill`	*Return*
`to fetch a pail of water.`	*Return*
`Jack fell down and broke his crown,`	*Return*
`and Jill came tumbling after.`	

Return is pressed at the end of each line because the lines do not reach the right side of the screen. Your document should be similar to:

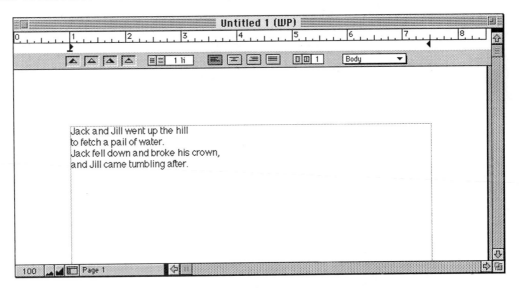

Insert new text and use the Delete and arrow keys as necessary to make the following changes to News Story:

- Insert BIG and a space before the word pail
- Change the word water to gold
- Change the word crown to arm
- Change came tumbling after to stood up and laughed

<u>Check</u> - The edited poem should appear as follows:

> Jack and Jill went up the hill
> to fetch a BIG pail of gold.
> Jack fell down and broke his arm,
> and Jill stood up and laughed.

2.10 Using Menus

At the top of the word processor screen is the Menu bar. Each word on the bar is the name of a pull-down menu from which different commands can be chosen. Placing the mouse pointer on a menu name and holding down the mouse button displays the available commands in that menu. For example, placing the pointer on the word "File" and holding down the mouse button displays the File menu:

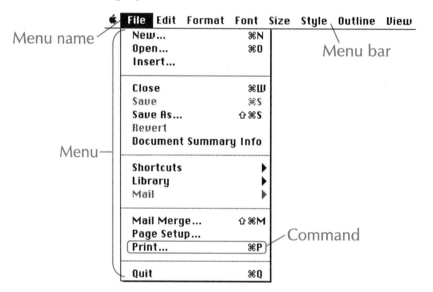

Menus are lists of commands

Commands in the displayed menu can be selected by dragging the pointer down the list. Highlighted commands are shown in reversed text (white letters on a black background). Releasing the mouse button executes the highlighted command. Releasing the button when no command is highlighted removes the menu from the screen.

On the menu, several commands have three dots (...) following the command name (New and Open are examples). This means that a dialog box asking for more information will appear when this command is executed. There are times when certain menu commands are displayed in dim text, meaning that these commands cannot be selected at this time. In the File menu shown, Save, Revert, and Mail cannot be selected.

2.11 Saving a Document

Because the computer's memory can only store data while the power is on, any data in memory is lost when the computer is turned off. However, if a copy of the document is saved on disk before the power is shut off, the document can later be retrieved from the disk and loaded into memory. Unfinished documents, as well as those that might need future editing or reprinting should always be saved on disk.

Another reason for saving a document is to prevent its accidental loss. A momentary power interruption can wipe everything out of the computer's memory. Even bumping the power cord may cause the memory to be erased. It is therefore a good practice to save the document repeatedly. It is also important to save before attempting to print because a problem involving the printer could cause the document to be lost.

When a document is saved, a copy of what is currently stored in the computer's memory is placed on the disk. The computer also retains the document in memory so that there are now two copies, one in memory that is displayed on the screen and one on disk. The copy in memory is erased when the computer is turned off, but the copy on disk can be recovered at any time.

Documents stored on disk are called *files* and must be given names to identify them. *Filenames* can be up to 31 characters long and can contain uppercase and lowercase letters, numbers, and spaces. Colons (:) may not be used. Special symbols such as question marks and periods are valid, but should generally be avoided. Examples of filenames are `Letter`, `CHAPTER 5`, and `2nd Memo`. It is important to give a file a name that describes what it contains. For example, a file containing a letter to Suzy Lee is better named `Suzy Letter` or `Letter to Suzy Lee` rather than just `Letter`. When a new file is first saved, ClarisWorks displays a dialog box so that you can supply a descriptive name. This name is then used each time the file is retrieved from disk.

Documents are saved by selecting the Save command from the File menu. The following dialog box is displayed the first time a file is saved:

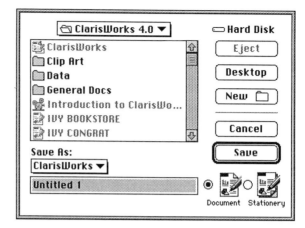

The Save command displays this dialog box

When this dialog box is displayed, type a descriptive name and then select **Save**. A copy of the document is then placed on the disk using the name you supplied.

It is important to realize that any editing changes made to a previously saved file are not stored on the disk unless the file is saved again. It is also important to realize that saving an edited document replaces the original copy on disk.

2.12 Quitting ClarisWorks

Whenever you want to stop using ClarisWorks, either to run another program or turn off the computer, the quit procedure should be performed. If ClarisWorks is not properly exited, files in memory can be damaged or lost. **Never turn the computer off before following the quit procedure.** The proper way to exit ClarisWorks is by selecting the Quit command from the File menu. After quitting you can again run the ClarisWorks program.

If you have created a new file or made editing changes to a previously created file, ClarisWorks informs you that any new information will be lost if the file is not saved before quitting:

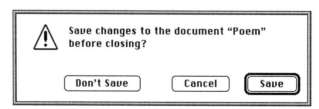

ClarisWorks displays a warning if you attempt to quit without saving a new or modified file

To save the changes, select the **Save** button. If you do not wish to save the new version, click on the **Don't Save** button and the previously saved version will remain on the disk unchanged. If the Quit command is selected by accident, click on **Cancel** in the dialog box to return to the word processor.

Practice 3

This Practice saves the file created in Practice 2 on disk using the name Poem. The file should still be displayed from the last Practice.

1) DISPLAY THE FILE MENU

    a. Using the mouse, point to the word File in the Menu bar.

    b. With the pointer on File, press and hold down the button to display the File menu.

2) SELECT THE SAVE COMMAND FROM THE FILE MENU

    a. Continuing to hold down the button, drag the mouse pointer down the menu until the Save command is highlighted.

    b. With Save highlighted, release the button to execute the Save command. ClarisWorks displays a dialog box prompting you to enter the name of the file.

3) ENTER THE NAME OF THE FILE TO BE SAVED

    a. The default filename Untitled 1 is highlighted. Type Poem to replace the default filename:

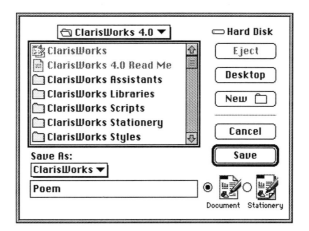

    b. Select the **Save** button. A copy of the file in memory is stored on disk using the name Poem. Note that the filename Poem (WP) is displayed at the top of the Work area.

4) PROPERLY QUIT CLARISWORKS

    a. Display the File menu by moving the mouse pointer to the word File in the Menu bar and then pressing and holding down the mouse button.

    b. Drag the mouse pointer to the bottom of the menu, highlighting the Quit command.

    c. With Quit highlighted, release the button.

The screen clears and the Macintosh System screen is again displayed, indicating that Claris-Works has been exited and that the computer is now ready to run a new program. Only at this point can the computer be safely turned off. If you wish to reload ClarisWorks, use the mouse to double-click on the ClarisWorks icon.

2.13 Word Wrap

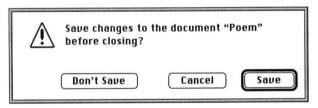

When a word processor is used, it is not necessary to determine if the next word will fit on the end of the current line or if it must go on the next line. ClarisWorks determines if there is sufficient room for a word at the end of a line. If not, the word is automatically moved to the beginning of the next line. This process is called *word wrap*.

The advantages of allowing ClarisWorks to determine the arrangement of words on a line can be seen when deleting or inserting text. When new text is added to a line, any words to their right are moved over. If there is not room on the current line, those words which do not fit are moved to the next line. There may be a "domino" effect as words move from one line to the next. Similarly, when text is deleted, words are moved up from previous lines.

Sometimes the typist needs to determine where the end of one line and the beginning of the next are located. For example, you can specify the end of a paragraph by pressing the Return key which moves the cursor to the beginning of the next line. Pressing Return again creates a blank paragraph containing one line. Therefore, to end a paragraph and insert a blank line before the next paragraph, press the Return key twice.

2.14 Closing Files

You will often need to work on more than one file after starting Claris-Works. When this is the case, the current file that you are working on should be saved and then *closed*. Closing a file means that it is removed from the screen and is no longer in the computer's memory. Selecting the Close command from the File menu closes the displayed file. If you attempt to close a file that has been edited but not saved, ClarisWorks warns you before proceeding:

ClarisWorks displays a warning before closing a modified file

If you wish to save the changes before closing, click on the **Save** button (or press Return to accept the default). If instead you wish to close the file without saving the edited version, click on the **Don't Save** button. **Cancel** terminates the Close command and returns the cursor to the Work area.

It is a good practice to close any open files when you are finished working with them. Closed files are no longer in the computer's memory and therefore cannot be accidentally changed.

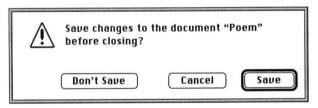

An Introduction to Computing Using ClarisWorks

2

Practice 4

This Practice demonstrates word wrap and shows how paragraphs are created. A new word processor file named News Story will be created.

1) BOOT THE MACINTOSH SYSTEM AND START CLARISWORKS

    a. If the computer is off, turn it on and boot the System as described in Practice 1.
    b. If the ClarisWorks folder is closed, double-click on it to open it.
    c. Start ClarisWorks by using the mouse to point to the ClarisWorks icon and then double-click on it.

2) CREATE A NEW WORD PROCESSOR FILE

When the New Document dialog box is displayed, the **Word Processing** option is already selected. Click on **OK** to create a new, empty word processor document.

3) ENTER THE FOLLOWING STORY

Type the story below, allowing ClarisWorks to determine the end of lines. Press Return only at the end of a paragraph or line which does not reach the right margin such as in the dinner menu. Use the Return key to create a blank line between each paragraph. Note that your lines will wrap at different positions than the text displayed below:

```
The annual Red Cross fund-raising dinner will be held in
the main ballroom of the Downtown Hilton at 7:30 p.m.
next Saturday night. Music for dancing will be provided
by the Thom Steves Trio. All community members are
invited.

The menu for the evening's event will be:

Fruit cup
Roast duck a l'Orange with wild rice stuffing
Garden salad
Mint parfait

After dinner, a reception will take place in the hotel's
Algonquin Room. Dancing will continue until 11:30 p.m.
```

Review the text and use the Delete and arrow keys to correct any typing errors.

4) SAVE THE FILE USING THE NAME NEWS STORY

    a. Using the mouse, point to the word File in the Menu bar. Press and hold down the button to display the File menu.
    b. Drag the pointer down the File menu to highlight the Save command. Release the button. A dialog box is displayed.
    c. Type News Story and select the **Save** button. A copy of the file is saved on disk using the name News Story.

5) EDIT THE STORY

Insert new text and use the Delete and arrow keys as necessary to make the following changes to News Story:

- Insert the name of your town and a space before the words `Red Cross`. Note how the rest of the paragraph is adjusted to make room.
- The dessert has been changed from a Mint parfait to Double chocolate chip ice cream.
- The event will end at 11:00 p.m., not 11:30.
- The location of the event was wrong. It will actually be held at the Eastside Sheraton, not the Downtown Hilton.

6) CREATE A NEW PARAGRAPH

a. Place the cursor just before the `A` that begins the sentence `All community members`....
b. Press Return twice to insert a blank line and create a new paragraph.
c. Add the following sentence to the end of the new paragraph:

`Tickets are $25.00 per person and are available from Mrs. Mitchell in the Red Cross office during regular business hours.`

7) ADD A HEADLINE TO THE STORY

a. Move the cursor to the very beginning of the document and type the following:

`FUND RAISER TO BE HELD AT THE EASTSIDE SHERATON`

Note how the rest of the text moves to the right to make room for the new text.
b. Press the Return key twice to terminate the headline and insert a blank line between it and the rest of the story.

8) SAVE THE FILE AGAIN TO RETAIN THE EDITING CHANGES

a. Display the File menu and drag the pointer down to the Save command, highlighting it.
b. With Save highlighted, release the button to save the edited News Story file on disk. The old file is now erased and cannot be recovered.

Check - The completed story should be similar to the following:

FUND RAISER TO BE HELD AT THE EASTSIDE SHERATON

The annual Lawrenceville Red Cross fund-raising dinner will be held in the main ballroom of the Eastside Sheraton at 7:30 p.m. next Saturday night. Music for dancing will be provided by the Thom Steves Trio.

All community members are invited. Tickets are $25.00 per person and are available from Mrs. Mitchell in the Red Cross office during regular business hours.

The menu for the evening's event will be:

Fruit cup
Roast duck a l'Orange with wild rice stuffing
Garden salad
Double chocolate chip ice cream

After dinner, a reception will take place in the hotel's Algonquin Room. Dancing will continue until 11:00 p.m.

9) CLOSE THE FILE

a. Display the File menu.

b. Drag the pointer down the menu and select the Close command to close the file. The file is removed from memory. The ClarisWorks Menu bar is displayed at the top of the screen.

2.15 Opening a File

Before a previously saved file can be edited it must first be transferred from the disk to the computer's memory. This is accomplished by selecting the Open command from the File menu to display a dialog box similar to the following:

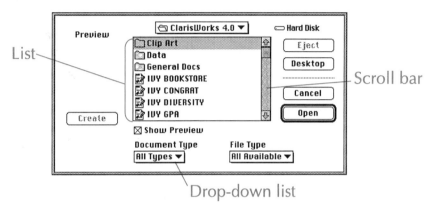

Filenames are displayed as a list

Highlight the desired file and select **Open** to transfer a copy of the file to the computer's memory and display it on the screen.

Lists

In the Open dialog box the names of the files saved on disk are displayed in a *list*. A list offers a group of items from which you may choose. To select an item from the list, place the pointer on the item and click once.

Lists may contain more information than can be displayed on the screen at one time. For this reason they can be *scrolled*. That is, it is possible to view different parts of a list by changing what part of the list is displayed. This is accomplished using the *scroll bar* at the right side of the list. Clicking the arrow at the bottom of the scroll bar displays items farther down in the list, and clicking the arrow at the top of the scroll bar displays items toward the beginning.

To select the file to be opened, click on the up and down arrows in the scroll bar until the desired filename is displayed. Once the file's name has been located, double-clicking on it transfers the file to the computer's memory.

A special type of list is the *drop-down list*. The **Document Type** option in the Open dialog box is displayed with a downward-pointing triangle (▼) indicating a drop-down list is available. Placing the mouse pointer on the triangle and then pressing and holding the mouse button displays a list of options:

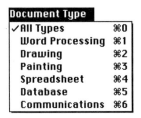

Pressing and holding the mouse button on the triangle
displays a drop-down list

In this case, a list of document types is displayed. All Types is currently selected as indicated by the check mark. Dragging down to Word Processing limits the filenames displayed to only word processor files.

Practice 5

In this Practice the News Story file will be transferred from disk into the computer's memory, edited, and then re-saved. ClarisWorks should be running. If not, start ClarisWorks by following the instructions given in Practice 1. After starting ClarisWorks, remove the New Document dialog box by clicking on the **Cancel** button.

1) SELECT THE FILE TO OPEN FROM THE FILES LIST

    a. From the File menu, select the Open command.

    b. Move the pointer to the list of filenames.

    c. If necessary, click on the up and down arrows in the scroll bar to move through the list until News Story is displayed.

    d. Place the pointer on News Story and double-click. A copy of News Story is transferred from the disk into the computer's memory and is displayed on screen.

2) EDIT THE FILE

Insert and delete text as necessary to make the following changes:

    • The event will start at 7:00 p.m.

    • The Schmenge Brothers Orchestra, not the Thom Steves Trio, will provide the evening's entertainment.

    • Guests will have the choice of Fruit cup or lime sherbet for an appetizer.

3) SAVE THE MODIFIED NEWS STORY

    a. Using the mouse, select File from the Menu bar.

    b. Drag the mouse down the File menu to select the Save command and release the button. The modified News Story is saved on disk, replacing the old version.

2

Check - When complete, the modified file should be similar to:

FUND RAISER TO BE HELD AT THE EASTSIDE SHERATON

The annual Lawrenceville Red Cross fund-raising dinner will be held in the main ballroom of the Eastside Sheraton at 7:00 p.m. next Saturday night. Music for dancing will be provided by the Schmenge Brothers Orchestra.

All community members are invited. Tickets are $25.00 per person and are available from Mrs. Mitchell in the Red Cross office during regular business hours.

The menu for the evening's event will be:

Fruit cup or lime sherbet
Roast duck a l'Orange with wild rice stuffing
Garden salad
Double chocolate chip ice cream

After dinner, a reception will take place in the hotel's Algonquin Room. Dancing will continue until 11:00 p.m.

2.16 Viewing a Document

ClarisWorks displays word processor documents in page view. This allows you to see the document on the screen as it will appear when printed. The page controls in the lower-left corner of the screen are used to change the *magnification* of the view:

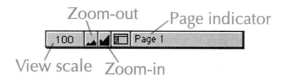

The page controls can be used to change the magnification of a document

Changing a document's magnification does not change the way it will be printed, only the amount of the document visible on the screen. The view scale indicates the magnification of the document. The default magnification is 100%, or actual size. However, at this scale only a portion of a document page is visible on the screen. Clicking on the Zoom-out control displays a smaller version of the document. This is useful for viewing an entire page on one screen. Zoom-in can be used to enlarge the current view. Since a document can be edited at any magnification, detail-oriented work is often easier if the document is first enlarged.

2.17 Printing a Document

Printing involves sending a copy of a document from the computer's memory to the printer. To do this, the computer must be connected to a printer. It is also important to make sure that the printer is turned on, is "online," and that paper is positioned correctly. Before printing a document it should be saved on disk because a problem involving the printer could cause the document to be lost.

To print a document, select the Print command from the File menu. The Print dialog box enables you to specify which pages and how many copies to print. Your print dialog may be different depending on the printer you have selected:

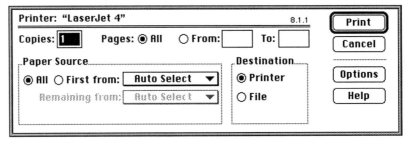

The Print command's dialog box. Note the Pages options.

Because the default values are most normally used, you will usually select only the **Print** button (or press Return) to begin printing. If more than one copy of the document is to be printed, type the number required in the **Copies** box.

Practice 6

This Practice demonstrates how a word processor document can be printed and should only be attempted if there is a printer connected to your computer. Attempting to print without a printer attached could cause the loss of your file. Start ClarisWorks and open the News Story file created in the previous Practices if you have not already done so.

1) USE THE ZOOM CONTROLS TO CHANGE THE VIEW SCALE

    a. Click once on the Zoom-out control (🔳). The view scale changes to display 66.7.
    b. Click on the Zoom-out control two more times. The view scale displays 33.3. Note how one entire page of the document is now visible on the screen.
    c. Click on the Zoom-in control (🔳)until the view scale indicates 100.

2) EXECUTE THE PRINT COMMAND

From the File menu, select the Print command. The Print dialog box is displayed.

3) PRINT THE DOCUMENT

Click on the **Print** button to accept the default of printing 1 copy. The document prints, and the computer returns to the word processor screen when printing is complete.

4) CLOSE THE FILE

From the File menu, select the Close command. The screen is cleared.

2.18 Screen Scroll

In ClarisWorks, about 25 lines of a word processor document can be displayed at a time depending on the size of the monitor. Most documents are too long to be displayed entirely on a single screen. Scroll bars on the right side and bottom of the window allow unseen parts of a document to be brought into view. Clicking on the arrows in the vertical and horizontal scroll bars will move the document accordingly. This is referred to as *screen scroll*. Any text scrolled off the screen is not lost, it is just not displayed at that time.

The scroll bars at the bottom and on the right of the word processor screen are used to move through a document:

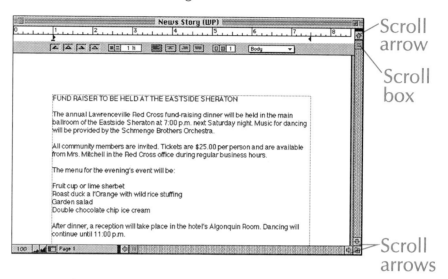

The scroll bars are used to move through a document

Clicking on the down arrow moves the document in the Work area down one line. Clicking on the up arrow moves the document up one line. When working with long documents it can be time consuming to move in such small increments. The document can be moved in larger increments by dragging the scroll box within the scroll bar. For example, dragging the box to the middle of the scroll bar displays the middle of the document. The scroll arrows can then be used to make fine adjustments. Clicking on the scroll bar above or below the scroll box scrolls one screen towards the top of bottom of the document.

Some Macintosh keyboards have keys that are labeled Page Up and Page Down. These keys scroll one screen towards the top or bottom of the document. The Home key displays the beginning of the document, and the End key displays the last page of the document.

Practice 7

This Practice demonstrates screen scroll and cursor movement. A previously created word processor file named SCROLL will be opened. Each line in SCROLL is numbered to help demonstrate screen scroll. Start ClarisWorks and remove the New Document dialog box by clicking on **Cancel** if you have not already done so.

1) OPEN THE FILE NAMED SCROLL

    a. Select the Open command from the File menu.

    b. Using the mouse, point to the triangle in the **Document Type** box. Press and hold the mouse button to display a drop-down list. Drag down to Word Processing and then release the mouse button to limit the files displayed to only word processor documents. Note the change in the files list.

c. If necessary, click on the up and down scroll arrows to move through the list until SCROLL is displayed.

d. Place the pointer on SCROLL and double-click to transfer a copy of the SCROLL file from disk into the computer's memory.

2) MOVE THE CURSOR TO THE BOTTOM OF THE SCREEN

Press the down-arrow key until the cursor is on the last line in the currently displayed screen.

3) MOVE THE CURSOR TO THE NEXT LINE

Press the down-arrow key again. Notice that several lines disappear off the top of the screen and more appear from the bottom.

4) SCROLL DOWN 5 LINES USING THE SCROLL ARROW

Click the pointer on the down arrow (▨) in the vertical scroll bar 5 times. Note that each time the down arrow is selected, a line scrolls off the top of the screen, and the next line in the document appears from the bottom.

5) JUMP TO THE LAST LINE IN THE DOCUMENT

a. Place the pointer on the scroll box in the vertical scroll bar.

b. Hold down the mouse button and drag the box to the bottom of the scroll bar.

c. Release the button. The screen moves immediately to the last line in the document, line number 80 in this file. The Page indicator reads "Page 2" indicating that page 2 is currently displayed.

6) SCROLL TO THE FIRST LINE IN THE DOCUMENT

a. Click on the up arrow in the vertical scroll bar and hold down the button. The screen will scroll as long as the button is held down. Note how the scroll box moves in the bar as the screen scrolls.

b. When line 1 is displayed, release the button. The Page indicator again displays "Page 1."

7) LOCATE THE PAGE BREAK

Drag the scroll box to the middle of the scroll bar. The middle of the document is displayed. After line 40 the end of the first page is displayed. Line 41 is displayed at the top of the next page. If the bottom of page 1 and the top of page 2 are not displayed on your screen click on the appropriate scroll arrow until they are:

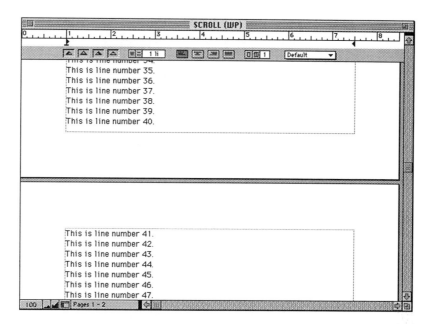

Because ClarisWorks represents pages as white areas on the screen, it is easy to see where one page ends and the next begins. The page indicator in the lower-left corner of the screen reads "Pages 1 - 2." In the example above, line 40 will be printed on page 1 and line 41 on page 2.

8) SCROLL UP TO THE BEGINNING OF THE DOCUMENT

Press and hold down the up-arrow key. The screen scrolls up until the key is released. When line 1 is displayed, release the key.

9) QUIT CLARISWORKS

From the File menu, select the Quit command to return to the System screen.

Chapter Summary

Documents ranging from research papers to business letters can be produced quickly and efficiently using a word processor. Word processing allows documents to be changed easily; text can be inserted, deleted, or modified without retyping the entire document. Formatting commands allow the appearance of text on the page to be changed. By saving the document in a file on disk, it can later be recalled, edited, and printed.

ClarisWorks uses a mouse as a special input device. An object is selected on the screen by pointing to the object and then pressing (clicking) the mouse button. Some objects are selected by double-clicking which is pressing the button twice in rapid succession. Dragging is the technique of holding down the mouse button while moving the mouse. The scroll bars below and on the right of the word processor screen are used to scroll through a document.

The computer needs the Macintosh operating system (System) to run. This is first loaded into the computer's memory from disk. Once the System is loaded, it is possible to run the ClarisWorks program by double-clicking on the ClarisWorks icon. Icons are small pictures that are selected by clicking once on them. After ClarisWorks loads, an opening copyright screen is displayed followed by the New Document dialog box. The New Document dialog box allows new files to be created.

Dialog boxes contain buttons and lists. Clicking once on a button initiates an action. An item in a list is selected by clicking once on it. When there are too many items in a list to be seen at one time, the list can be scrolled by clicking on the arrow buttons. Dialog boxes may also contain drop-down lists. When a dialog box is displayed, the most commonly chosen options and button are already selected. These selections are called defaults. The default button can be selected by pressing the Return key.

A new word processor file is created by selecting two options from the New Document dialog box. First, the **Word Processing** option is selected and then the **OK** button is selected.

The word processor screen is like a window that displays a limited number of lines of a document at a time. The document may be moved in the Work area to display different text using the scroll bars and arrows. Along the top of the word processor screen is the Menu bar. Each word in the Menu bar is the name of a pull-down menu. A menu is displayed by clicking on its name. Below the Menu bar ClarisWorks displays the filename. The Ruler is displayed below this and is used to judge horizontal spacing.

ClarisWorks determines if there is sufficient room for a word at the end of a line. If there is not, the word is automatically moved to the beginning of the next line in a process called word wrap. When new words are added to a line, any words to their right are automatically moved over. Deleting words causes words to be moved to the left to fill any empty space.

Cursor control keys, or arrow keys, are used to move the cursor through the document without changing any of the text. The Delete key is used to remove the character to the left of the cursor.

ClarisWorks uses menus to provide access to commands. Clicking on the menu name displays a list of commands, and dragging the pointer to the desired command executes that command. Many commands display a dialog box where information is entered before the command is executed.

Saving a document is accomplished by executing the Save command from the File menu. When a file is saved it is given a name of up to 31 characters which is then used to identify it. Each filename must be unique. To avoid possible data loss, each file must be saved before printing. Printing a document is accomplished by executing the Print command from the File menu.

To remove a file from the computer's memory it must be closed by using the Close command from the File menu. This frees computer memory and protects the file from an accident such as a power failure. Previously created files may then be opened by selecting the Open command. To quit ClarisWorks the Quit command from the File menu is executed.

2

This chapter discussed the commands and procedures necessary to produce a word processor document. The major steps in producing such a document are:

1. Boot the System and load the ClarisWorks program from disk into the computer's memory.
2. Display the word processor file on the screen—either by creating a new file or opening a previously created file.
3. Enter or edit the document.
4. Save the document on disk.
5. Print the document if desired.
6. Close the document.
7. Properly quit ClarisWorks.

Vocabulary

Arrow keys - Four keys that move the cursor up, down, right, and left on the screen without changing any text. Also called cursor control keys.

Boot - To turn on the computer and load the System from disk into the computer memory.

Button - An option in a dialog box used to initiate an action. Buttons are selected by clicking on them with the mouse.

Cancel button - Button available in most dialog boxes that removes the dialog box and returns to the ClarisWorks screen without making changes.

Character - Any letter, number, or symbol that can be displayed on the computer screen.

Clicking - Placing the mouse pointer on an object and pressing and releasing the mouse button once.

Closed file - A file that has been removed from the computer's memory.

Cursor - A blinking line on the screen which indicates where characters entered from the keyboard are placed.

Cursor control keys - Keys used to move the cursor without having any effect on the text. See also Arrow keys.

Default - An option that is preselected. It will be used if no other option is chosen.

Delete key - A key that erases the character directly to the left of the cursor.

Dialog box - Used to enter information and select options required by a command.

Document - Also called a file. See File.

Double-clicking - Placing the mouse pointer on an object and pressing the mouse button twice in rapid succession.

Dragging - Pressing the mouse button and holding it down while moving the mouse.

Drop-down list - A dialog box option that has a downward-pointing triangle. A drop-down list displays a list when the mouse pointer is pressed and held on the triangle.

Escape key - A key used to cancel (escape from) the ClarisWorks current operation.

File - A document that is stored on disk.

Filename - A name for a file stored on disk, up to 31 characters in length. Colons (:) may not be used in filenames.

Folder - A group of files or other folders.

Format - The arrangement of text on a page.

Format bar - Contains formatting options. Located at the top of the screen below the Ruler.

Graphical User Interface (GUI) - A program that allows the user to communicate with the computer using windows and small pictures called icons.

Icon - A small picture on the Macintosh screen used to run a program or perform other tasks.

Insert text - Add words or characters to a document.

List - Scrollable group of items from which you may choose.

Macintosh System - Special programs required to run the computer. Also called the System.

Magnification - The apparent size of a document on the ClarisWorks screen.

Menu - A list of commands that are available at a particular point in a program.

Menu bar - A horizontal bar at the very top of the screen showing names of available menus.

Mouse - An input device that is used to position the pointer on the screen.

Mouse pointer - A shape displayed on the screen when the mouse is in use.

New Document dialog box - Contains options for creating new files.

Page controls - Located at the bottom of the Work area.

Page guides - Dotted lines that indicate the boundaries of the Work area.

Page indicator - At the bottom of the Work area, displays the number of the page(s) visible in the Work area.

Pointing - Placing the mouse pointer on an object located on the screen.

Print - To send a copy of the document currently displayed on screen to the printer.

Quit - To end the ClarisWorks program, remove it from memory, and return to the Macintosh System.

Repeat key - A key that repeats its action when held down. The left-arrow key is one example of a repeat key.

Return key - Key used to indicate the end of an entry or to select the default option in a dialog box. In word processing Return is pressed at the end of each paragraph.

Ruler - Used to judge horizontal spacing. Located below the Title bar.

Save - Transfer data from the computer's memory to a file on disk.

Screen scroll - Bringing other parts of a document into view.

Scroll - To view different parts of a list by changing what part of the list is displayed.

Scroll bars - Used to display different parts of a document, they are located at the bottom and on the right of the screen.

Text - Any character or group of characters in a document.

Word processor - A computer application program that allows text to be entered, manipulated, printed, and saved.

Word wrap - When ClarisWorks decides whether to keep a word on the current line, or move it to the next based on the amount of space left on the line.

Work area - Area of the word processor screen where text is entered and edited.

Zoom controls - Located in the lower-left corner of the screen, the Zoom-in and Zoom-out controls are used to change the magnification of a document.

2 | Reviews

1. Name three useful features of a word processor.

2. How can using a word processor improve the quality of your writing?

3. Name three different organizations that could benefit from using word processors. Explain how each would benefit.

4. a) Why is it important to take good care of a disk?
   b) What should be avoided when handling or storing a disk?

5. What is pointing and how is it done?

6. a) What is clicking?
   b) What is double-clicking?

7. What steps are required to drag an object?

8. What is the Macintosh System and what is it used for?

9. What is meant by the term "booting" the computer?

10. How do you press a button in a dialog box?

11. How many radio buttons may be selected at one time when selecting options from a dialog box?

Sections 2.8 — 2.14

12. What two options must be selected from the New Document dialog box to create a new word processor file?

13. What is the Ruler used for? Where is it located?

14. What are page guides used for?

15. What is each of the following keys used for?
    a) Escape key
    b) Return key
    c) Delete key

16. How may the cursor be moved down 3 lines and then 10 places to the right without affecting text?

17. What does pressing the Return key do when typing text in the word processor?

18. What is the difference between pressing the Delete key four times and the left-arrow key four times when the cursor is located in the middle of a line of text?

19. Describe the operations necessary to change the word "men" to "people" in the sentence:

    ```
    Now is the time for all
    good men to come to the aid
    of the party.
    ```

20. a) How is a menu selected from the Menu bar?
    b) How can a menu be removed from the screen without executing a command?

21. a) What is a file?
    b) Why is a file given a name?
    c) What limitations are placed on the names which may be given to a file?

22. List three reasons why it is useful to save a word processor file on disk.

23. If you are working on a word processor document and the power goes off, how can you retrieve the document if it has not been previously saved on disk?

24. When a file is saved where does it go? Is it removed from the computer's memory?

25. a) If a previously saved file is edited will the changes be automatically made to the file on disk, or must the file be saved again?
    b) What happens to an original file if an edited version of the same file is saved?

26. a) Why is it important to exit ClarisWorks properly?
    b) List the steps required to exit ClarisWorks starting from the word processor screen so that the file currently being worked on is saved.

27. What is word wrap?

28. a) Why is it important to close a file when you are finished working with it?
    b) What happens to a file when it is closed? Is it automatically saved on disk?

29. What must be done to end a paragraph and start a new one?

Sections 2.15 — 2.17

30. What steps must be taken to load a previously saved file from disk into the computer's memory?

31. What is a dialog box and what is it used for?

32. If you display a dialog box by mistake how can you remove it from the screen?

33. a) What is a dialog box list?
    b) How is an item selected from a list?

34. How can the magnification of a document be changed?

35. a) Why is it important to save a document before printing it?
    b) What menu and command is used to print a document?

36. How can you interrupt the printing of a document?

37. a) What is screen scroll?
    b) Describe two ways to scroll through a document.

An Introduction to Computing Using ClarisWorks

2 | Exercises

1. Enter the following letter in a new word processor file:

> September 26, 1996
>
> Mrs. Joan Kugler
> 123 Main St.
> Reedsburg, WI 53959
>
> Dear Joan:
>
> I am writing to thank you for installing the CD-ROM drive on my computer. It's truly amazing to have so many reference books on a single disk.
>
> Yesterday my manager praised me for the speech I wrote for her. The facts I retrieved from the CD were all timely, accurate, and interesting. I didn't tell her how easy it was to do.
>
> Also, instead of calling the post office to get a zip code, I now look it up in seconds on the CD. Did you know that some staff members are asking management to add more CD-ROM drives to the Fall Budget Proposal?
>
> You have improved the productivity of our entire department. Thanks again for all your help.
>
> Sincerely,
>
>
> Brian Esser
> Administrative Assistant

a) Save the letter naming it Thank You.

b) Use the Zoom-out control to view the entire document at once. Print a copy of Thank You.

c) Edit the letter as follows:

- Delete the word `truly` in the last sentence of the first paragraph.
- Delete the sentence `I didn't tell her how easy it was to do.`
- Change `calling the post office` to `going to the mailroom`
- Change `some staff members` to `many of my co-workers`
- Replace `Brian Esser` with your name.
- Add the following sentences to the beginning of the third paragraph:

`Sometimes my manager asks me to quickly add new information to a memo or report. Having so many facts at my fingertips is great.`

d) Save the modified Thank You and print a copy.

2. Word processors can be used to create documents that store a variety of information. It is interesting to think about how famous people in the past might have used a word processor.

a) Enter each of the following sayings into a new word processor file. Press Return twice at the end of each line to insert a blank line between each paragraph:

> An apple a day keeps the doctor away.
>
> A penny for your thoughts.
>
> Every cloud has a silver lining.
>
> A penny saved is a penny earned.
>
> Early to bed, early to rise, makes a man healthy, wealthy and wise.

b) Save the file naming it Benjamin in honor of Benjamin Franklin who wrote many of the famous sayings that appear above.

c) Check the document on screen for any errors and make the necessary corrections. Save Benjamin again to retain any changes you made.

d) Print a copy of Benjamin.

e) Edit the sayings as follows:

> Saying 1: change `apple` to `orange`
> Saying 2: change `penny` to `dollar`
> Saying 3: change `silver` to `gold`
> Saying 4: change `penny` to `quarter` (twice)
> Saying 5: change `man` to `person`

f) Save the modified Benjamin and print a copy.

3. Your cousin is visiting you from out of town. The word processor can be used to create lists of directions that your cousin can follow to go from your house to various places.

a) In a new word processor file create lists of directions to the following places:

- Your school. Be sure to describe what time school gets out and where your cousin should meet you.
- A local fast food restaurant.
- The closest grocery store to your house. Include a list of items that your cousin should pick up for dinner.
- Your video rental club. Be sure to include your membership number in the directions so that your cousin can rent some videos.
- Your cousin is not the brightest person in the world. Leave complete instructions describing how to use your VCR to play a video.

b) Save the file naming it Directions and print a copy.

An Introduction to Computing Using ClarisWorks

2

4. A. Student is interested in attending Ivy University and needs a letter of application.

    a) In a new word processor file create the letter below that requests information and an application from IU.

September 26, 1997

Ivy University
Admissions Department
1 College Court
Newton, IA 63343

Dear Admissions Department:

I am interested in attending Ivy University. I will graduate in 1998 and plan to major in medical communications. I have been president of the Student Congress for 4 years and captain of the Debate Team for 2 years. I have varsity letters in three sports and was a member of the All-State gymnastics and swim teams. My current grade point average is 3.95.

Please send a course catalog and application to me at this address:

A. Student
223 Main Street
Anytown, USA 11111

Thank you very much.

Sincerely,

A. Student

    b) Check the document on screen for errors and make any necessary corrections.

    c) Save the letter naming it College Apply and print a copy.

    d) Modify the letter to contain your personal information as follows:

- Change the college name and address to a school you would like to attend. Be sure to also change the school name in the first sentence.
- Change the major in the second sentence to one of your choice.
- Change the activities listed in the letter to activities you have participated in.
- Change the GPA in the letter to your GPA.
- Change the name and address near the end of the letter to your name and address.

    e) Save the modified College Apply and print a copy.

5. Your local newspaper has an opening for an arts critic. In a new word processor file create a review of the last movie, concert, play, art show, or similar event that you attended. Save the file naming it Critic. Check your document on screen for errors and make any corrections. Save the modified Critic and print a copy.

6. A word processor can be used as a diary. Make a journal entry describing what you did last week in a new word processor file. Be sure to include your plans for the upcoming weekend. Check your document on screen for errors and make any corrections. Save the file naming it Diary and print a copy.

7. Your English teacher has asked you to write an original essay entitled "How I spent my summer vacation." In a new word processor file produce a 2 or 3 paragraph essay on this topic. Check your file on screen for errors and make any corrections. Save the file naming it Summer Essay and then print a copy.

8. In a new word processor file produce an advertisement for an upcoming dance or other special event. Be sure to include the date, time, location of the event, and cost (if any). Check your document on screen for errors and make any corrections. Save the file naming it Advertisement and print a copy.

9. Your science teacher has asked you to write a one page biography summarizing the life of the scientist you most admire. Include in the essay at least two references to outside sources. (Chapter Four will show you how to insert footnotes into a document.) In a new word processor file write the biography. Save the file naming it Science Bio. Check your document for errors and make any corrections. Save the modified Science Bio and print a copy.

10. You have opened a specialty retail store. Your store could be a jewelry store, clothing store, sporting goods store, or anything else you wish.

    a) In a new word processor file create a flyer that will be sent to prospective customers announcing your grand opening. Be sure to include the name, address, and phone number of your store, as well as a list of some of the special items you will be selling. Also include the date and time of the grand opening. Save the file naming it Grand Opening. Review the document and make any necessary corrections. Save the modified Grand Opening.

    b) Your promotions manager has suggested having a special sale at the grand opening. At the top of the flyer add the headline, 20% OFF AT THE GRAND OPENING, FANTASTIC ITEMS AT FANTASTIC PRICES! Save the modified Grand Opening and print a copy.

2

11. You are enrolled in an independent study of Shakespeare and your instructor wants a schedule listing topics and due dates for your research papers.

   a) In a new word processor file, create a schedule using the following memorandum as a guide, substituting your own name (use the same layout, or arrangement):

   > Memorandum
   >
   > To: Kevin Dumont, English Department
   > From: Daniel Booksmith, student
   > Date: January 3, 1996
   > Subject: Shakespeare topics and due dates
   >
   > The following schedule outlines the research paper topics and due dates for my independent study in Shakespeare:
   >
   > Paper Topic Due Date
   > Hamlet 1/15
   > Henry V 2/5
   > Macbeth 2/26
   > Julius Caesar 3/11
   > Romeo and Juliet 4/1
   >
   > One week before each due date I will submit an outline containing a specific topic and a list of sources for each paper.

   b) Save the file naming it Shakespeare Schedule.

   c) Check your memo for errors and make any corrections. Save the modified Shakespeare Schedule and print a copy.

12. Gibbons are apes that have a slender body with long arms and inhabit trees. Dr. Peter Helvetica and Dr. Lauren Williamson are studying the white-handed gibbons on Bashibashi Island. They have used the word processor to create a funding proposal for their gibbon research.

   a) Open RESEARCH and make the following changes:
   - In the second sentence of the first paragraph delete the phrase `of lesser and greater apes`.
   - In the same sentence insert the word `primate` before the word `studies`.
   - In the last sentence of the first paragraph change the words `partial funds` to `total funding`.
   - In the second sentence of the second paragraph insert the word `particular` between the words `unique to this` and `group`.
   - In the same paragraph insert the following sentence before the last sentence: `From a primate database, behavioral statistics are easily obtained and readily comparable.`

   b) Save the modified RESEARCH.

   c) Use the following steps to print only page 1:
   - Select the Print command from the File menu to display the dialog box.
   - Click the pointer in the **From:** box and type the number 1.
   - Click in the **To:** box and type a 1.
   - Select **Print** to print only the first page of this long document.

13. Businesses use word processors for everything from letters and memos to advertising material.

a) In a new word processor file, enter the following letter. Substitute your name for that of the president at the end of the letter, and your initials for JP:

```
1 Paradise Garden
Newtown, FL  33445


June 10, 1996


Mr. Philip Crando
Italian Tours, Ltd.
14 Dunkin Drive
Key West, FL  33040


Dear Mr. Crando:


Thank you for the info you gave me during our telephone conversation this morning.
As I explained, the head of our accounting department, Mr. Gordon Sharp, will leave
Fast Track Publishing at the end of November, and the company would like to give
him a trip to Italy as a retirement present.


We know that Mr. Sharp would like to spend the holiday season traveling, and I
understand you have three tours planned for that time of the year. I look forward to
receiving the price information and brochures you said were available.


Sincerely,



Janet Printmore
President



JP/jj
```

b) Check the file for errors and make any necessary corrections. Save the file naming it Crando.

c) A co-worker has read the draft of your letter and proposed the following corrections:

- Change the word `info` to `advice and suggestions` in the first paragraph.
- Add the sentence `Your company was recommended to us as a leader in tour packages of Italy.` at the end of the first paragraph.
- Add the words `and his wife` after `Mr. Sharp` in the second paragraph.
- Add a new paragraph before the closing which states `Please contact me at 555-9825 if you have any questions. Thank you.`

d) Save the modified Crando and print a copy.

14. You are responsible for a newsletter about recycling. In a new word processor file create the following article for the newsletter:

Autos, Autos, Everywhere

We all know that automobile exhaust pollutes the air, but did you know that vehicles are the source of many other forms of pollution? For instance, one pint of motor oil that seeps into the ground can create an oil slick over a whole acre of a stream, river, or ocean. Taking your used motor oil to a recycling center (or making sure your garage recycles it) can clean up our water.

Another big source of pollution is tires. Keeping them under-inflated makes them wear faster (and costs you money in poor gas mileage). As tires wear, small pieces break off, scattering along the roadways. Eventually, dumps fill up with the hundreds of millions of tires that are discarded each year, because only a small percentage are recycled. By buying your tires from a dealer who recycles the worn-out tires, you help the world to be a cleaner, safer place to live.

An added bonus for our efforts is that recycling produces new products at less cost and energy than it takes to produce the same items from raw materials. Everyone benefits from recycling!

Check your article for errors and make any corrections. Save the document naming it Recycle News and print a copy.

An Introduction to Computing Using ClarisWorks

Chapter 3

Manipulating Text with the Word Processor

Document

Insert Header

Insert Footer

Insert Page #

Insert Page Break

Undo

Select All

Paragraph

Shortcuts

Tab

Objectives

After completing this chapter you will be able to:

1. Manipulate a window.

2. Apply page formats, such as margins.

3. Create headers and footers in a document.

4. Apply paragraph formats, such as alignment and line spacing.

5. Apply character formats, such as different fonts and sizes.

6. Use the Shortcuts palette to quickly execute commonly performed actions.

7. Make special symbols visible, such as Return characters.

8. Create tables using tabs, and set tab stops.

3

Chapter Two introduced the commands necessary to create, edit, save, and print word processor documents. In this chapter, formatting options that improve the appearance and readability of such documents are covered. Included are features that:

- control the arrangement of text on the page, such as margins, headers and footers, and pagination.

- affect paragraphs, such as alignment, line spacing, tabs and tab stops.

- change the way text appears, such as bold, underline, italic, and different fonts and sizes.

3.1 Formatting Documents

A specific arrangement of text is called a *format*. A document's format includes the size of its margins, the alignment of text within those margins, and the spacing between lines and paragraphs. Formatting also includes the placement of text on the page, such as in tables composed of columns, and methods of emphasizing text such as underlined or boldface (darker) characters.

ClarisWorks allows you to format documents by selecting commands and options. Each formatting option is associated with a specific level: page, paragraph, or character. These levels describe how the format will affect a document. When a *page format* is applied, the changes affect the entire document. When a *paragraph format* is selected it applies to the entire paragraph that contains the cursor, and only to that paragraph. *Character formats* apply only to the currently highlighted text, which can be a single character, a word, or several sentences.

3.2 Using Windows

Each ClarisWorks document is displayed in its own *window*. All windows have similar features. For example, the vertical scroll bar you used in the last chapter is a common feature of a window. Other important window features are shown on the next page:

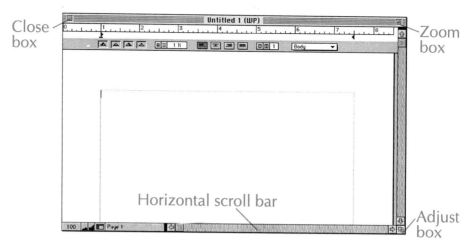

All windows in ClarisWorks have several common features

Close box

You can close a window by clicking the mouse pointer on its *Close box* in the upper-left corner. Closing a window closes the file in it and removes the window from the screen.

Adjust box

The size of the window can be changed with the *Adjust box* in the lower-right corner of the window. Dragging this box resizes the window: wider or narrower, taller or shorter.

Zoom box

The window expands to fill the screen when the *Zoom box* is clicked. The Zoom box is located in the upper-right corner of the window. When a window has been expanded, clicking again on the Zoom box restores the window to its original size.

Horizontal scroll bar

The Work area can be scrolled horizontally to display information that is currently off the screen to either side. To scroll horizontally, click on the right or left arrow, or use the mouse to drag the scroll box.

3.3 Page Formats - Margins

One way to affect the arrangement of text in a document is by changing its *margins*. Margins are shown on screen as the white region outside the page guides. ClarisWorks' default margin settings for an 8.5 inch by 11 inch page are 1 inch on the left, right, top, and bottom:

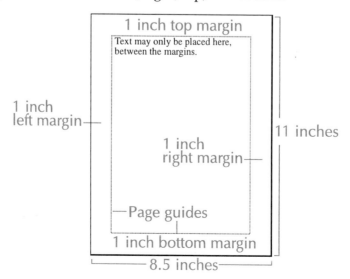

3

Margins can be widened or narrowed as desired. Changes to the margin settings have an inverse affect on the number of characters that fit on a line—widening a margin decreases the amount of text that a line can contain, while narrowing it increases the line's capacity. The length of a line that will fit across a page is determined by subtracting the size of the left and right margins from the width of the page. Using the default margins of 1 inch on an 8.5 inch page yields a line of text that is 6.5 inches long (8.5 − 1 − 1 = 6.5).

Selecting the Document command from the Format menu displays a dialog box that indicates the current margins:

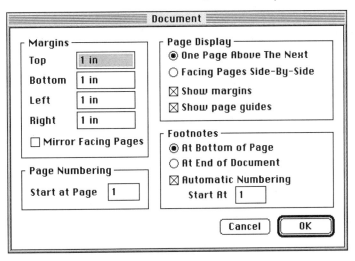

Margins can be set in the Document dialog box

Top, bottom, left, and right margins have their own entry box. To change a margin, simply type the desired measurement into the appropriate entry box and then select the **OK** button. For example, to change the bottom margin to 0.75 inches, double-click on the value in the **Bottom** box, type the new value, 0.75, and select **OK**.

....

Practice 1

To demonstrate the different formatting options, the Practices in this chapter use a promotional file for Ivy University named IVY PROMO.

1) BOOT THE SYSTEM AND START CLARISWORKS

    a. Following the directions given in Chapter Two, boot the System.
    b. Double-click on the ClarisWorks icon to start ClarisWorks. The New Document dialog box is displayed.
    c. Click **Cancel** to remove the dialog box.

2) OPEN IVY PROMO

    a. From the File menu, select the Open command. The Open dialog box is displayed.
    b. Press and hold the mouse on the triangle in the **Document Type** box to display a drop-down list. Drag down to Word Processing and then release the mouse button to limit the files listed to only word processor documents.
    c. Using the scroll arrows if necessary, locate IVY PROMO in the files list.
    d. Double-click on IVY PROMO to open it.

3) CHANGE THE VIEW SCALE

    a. Click on the Zoom-out control in the lower-left corner of the screen.

    b. Continue clicking on the Zoom-out control until the entire first page is visible on the screen without scrolling. Note the white space around all four sides of the text—the margins.

    c. Use the vertical scroll bar to scroll through the document. Note how the margins are the same on each page.

4) CHANGE THE MARGINS

    a. From the Format menu, select the Document command. The Document dialog box is shown.

    b. Double-click on the "1" in the **Left** margin box to highlight the measurement.

    c. Type 2.5 to replace the old value.

    d. Double-click on the "1" in the **Right** margin box. Type 2 to replace the old value.

    e. Select **OK** to close the Document dialog box and apply the changes. The document now has a left margin of 2.5 inches and a right margin of 2 inches. Note how much more room appears on the left and right of the page guides because the margins have been increased:

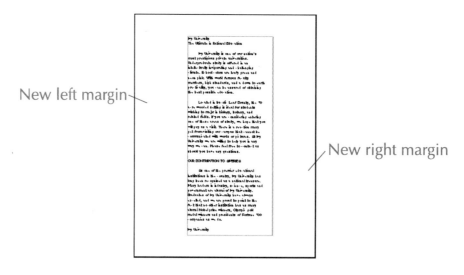

New left margin

New right margin

5) RESET THE MARGINS TO THE DEFAULT VALUES

    a. Scroll through the document to display the last page. Look at the Page indicator and note that there are now 5 pages in the document instead of 4. Increased margins mean less text per page, therefore more pages are required for the same amount of text.

    b. From the Format menu, select Document to display the Document dialog box.

    c. Change the **Left** and **Right** margins to 1 inch. Select **OK**.

    d. Display the last page of the document.

    e. Note how there are now only 4 pages in this document. Because the margins were decreased, ClarisWorks reformatted the document accordingly. Remember, decreasing the margins increases the amount of text that appears on a page.

    f. Click on the Zoom-in control to 100% magnification.

    g. From the File menu, select Save to save the modified IVY PROMO.

3.4 Using the Mouse to Move the Cursor

When the mouse pointer is moved within the page guides of the Work area, it changes from the arrow to a new shape called the text or *I-Beam pointer* (I). The I-Beam pointer allows the cursor to be placed using the mouse rather than the arrow keys. This technique is especially helpful when working with long documents. To move the cursor, the I-Beam pointer is first placed at the desired position in the document, scrolling as necessary. Then, clicking the mouse button once moves the cursor to the location of the pointer. Because this technique is often used before inserting text, it is sometimes referred to as creating an *insertion point*.

3.5 Page Formats - Headers and Footers

In ClarisWorks you may have text that appears at the top and bottom of each page in a document. Information that is automatically displayed at the top of each page is called a *header*. Similarly, information displayed at the bottom of each page is called a *footer*. Headers and footers are often used to indicate the current page number, the document or author's name, and similar information.

Selecting the Insert Header command from the Format menu displays a horizontal dotted line at the top of each page in the document to indicate the header area, and the cursor is automatically placed in the header so that text can be typed:

To move the cursor from the header, click the I-Beam pointer in the main body of the text. To change or edit an existing header, click in the header to place the cursor and then make changes as with any other text. The Insert Footer command works similarly:

It is important to understand that there can be only one header and one footer per document and that text entered in the header or footer on one page is displayed on every page of the document.

3.6 Using Page Numbers

A common use for headers and footers is to indicate the current page number. Executing the Insert Page # command from the Edit menu displays the following dialog box:

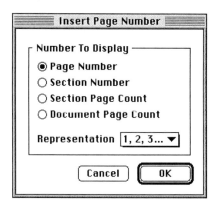

Selecting **OK** accepts the default options and inserts a code at the cursor position that displays the current page number. When the page number code is placed in a header or footer, the header or footer changes for each page in the document to display the appropriate page number.

Headers and footers displaying page numbers may be easier to understand if the page number code is placed after the word Page. A document with such a footer will show Page 1 at the bottom of page 1, Page 2 at the bottom of page 2, and so on.

3.7 The Command Key

The Command key, sometimes called the Open-Apple key, is located at the bottom of the keyboard, next to the spacebar. One application of this key is to execute menu commands without using the mouse. For example, in the File menu the Close command has the notation ⌘W next to it:

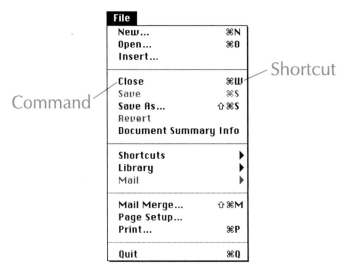

Command key shortcuts are listed next to the command names in the menu

An Introduction to Computing Using ClarisWorks

This means that holding down the Command key and pressing the W key at the same time (written in this text as ⌘W) executes the Close command without first displaying the menu. This shortcut can save time because you do not have to take your hands off the keyboard.

Some commands have the ⇧ notation beside the Command key notation. This is the Shift key symbol. For example, Save As has the notation ⇧⌘S beside it. This means that holding down the Shift and Command keys while pressing the S key executes the Save As command (written in this text as ⇧⌘S).

The Command key can also be used to select some dialog box options. When a dialog box is displayed, pressing and holding the Command key displays the dialog box with the available Command key shortcuts. For example, in the following warning dialog box each button displays a corresponding Command key shortcut when the Command is pressed and held:

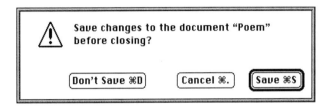

Unless specifically directed otherwise, you may use either the Command key shortcuts or the mouse in the Practices that follow.

Practice 2

In this Practice you will create a header and footer for the IVY PROMO document. Start ClarisWorks and open IVY PROMO if you have not already done so.

1) CREATE A HEADER

    a. From the Format menu, select the Insert Header command. The document is automatically scrolled to show the top of a page if one is not already visible. A horizontal line is displayed to indicate the header. Note the blinking cursor in the header.

    b. Type `Promotional Information`. These words will now appear at the top of each page in the document.

2) CREATE A FOOTER

    a. From the Format menu, select the Insert Footer command. The document is automatically scrolled to display the bottom of a page. A horizontal line has been inserted to indicate the footer.

    b. Type `Page` and press the spacebar.

    c. From the Edit menu, select the Insert Page # command. Select **OK** to select the **Page Number** option. The current page number is inserted at the cursor position.

3) SCROLL THROUGH THE DOCUMENT

    a. Use the mouse and the scroll bars to scroll through the document so that the footer of page 1 and the header of page 2 are visible on the screen. Your document should look similar to the following:

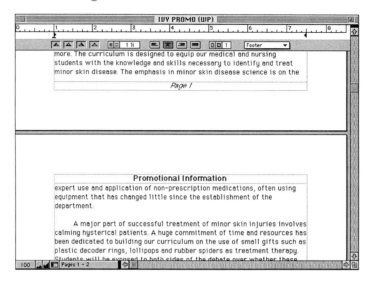

    b. Continue to scroll through the document until the footer of page 2 is displayed. Note how the correct page number has been inserted in the footer.

4) SAVE IVY PROMO USING A COMMAND KEY SHORTCUT

Hold down the ⌘ key and press the S key (⌘**S**) to execute the Save command and save IVY PROMO on disk. The header and footer are now stored in the document.

3.8 Page Formats - Pagination

Pagination is the division of a document into page-sized sections for printing. Using the specifications for page length and margins, ClarisWorks calculates the number of lines that fit on each printed page. Printed pages usually contain 40 to 50 lines of text, but the word processor screen can display only 15 to 25 lines of text. The page number ClarisWorks displays in the lower-left corner of the screen refers to printed pages.

A *page break* is the location where one printed page ends and another begins. Since ClarisWorks represents pages as the white area on the screen, it is easy to see where one page ends and another begins:

An Introduction to Computing Using ClarisWorks

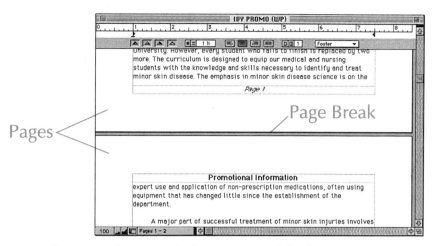

A page break marks the end of one page and the beginning of the next

After you make an edit, ClarisWorks automatically recalculates the page breaks and displays the updated document.

Some documents require starting a new page before filling the previous one. The beginning of a new chapter, a change in subject matter, or the presentation of a table or chart are all examples. You can force ClarisWorks to advance to the next page regardless of the number of lines left on the current page by inserting a *manual page break*. To do this, place the cursor where the new page is to start and select the Insert Page Break command from the Format menu. Text to the right of the cursor is moved to the next page. The keyboard shortcut ⇧⤧ may also be used to insert a manual page break. The ⤧ symbol represents the Enter key. Do not confuse the Enter key with the Return key.

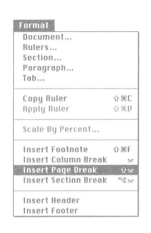

As discussed in Chapter Two, the Delete key is used to erase the character directly to the left of the cursor. Therefore, placing the cursor in the upper-left corner of a page and pressing Delete removes the manual page break and moves the text to the right of the cursor onto the previous page.

Practice 3

This Practice demonstrates automatic and manual page breaks. Start ClarisWorks and open IVY PROMO if you have not already done so.

1) LOCATE THE PAGE BREAKS

Scroll through the document, noting the location of page breaks. As pages scroll onto and off of the screen, the page number listed in the page indicator changes.

2) INSERT A MANUAL PAGE BREAK

   a. Scroll to the beginning of the document.
   b. Place the cursor just before the "L" in the second paragraph that starts "Located in bucolic Leaf County…."
   c. From the Format menu, select the Insert Page Break command. Text to the right of the cursor is moved to the next page.
   d. Scroll to the bottom of the document. Note how there are now 5 pages instead of the original 4.
   e. Scroll to the top of the document and note the empty space in the lower portion of page 1.

3) PREVIEW THE NEW PAGE

    a. Click on the Zoom-out control until the entire first page can be seen on the screen.

    b. Use the scroll bars to display page 2. Note the difference between page 1 and page 2—the manual page break causes much less information to be displayed on page 1.

    c. Return to 100% magnification using the Zoom-in control.

4) DELETE THE MANUAL PAGE BREAK

    a. Make sure the cursor is still to the left of the first word on page 2 of the document. The cursor should be just below the header created in Practice 2 and against the left page guide.

    b. Press the Delete key. Page 1 of the document is displayed. Text that was originally displayed on page 1 is again displayed on that page. The number of pages in the document is again 4.

    c. Save IVY PROMO.

3.9 The Undo Command

At times you will execute a command only to find that you have made a mistake. For this reason, the effects of the last command can be reversed by executing the Undo command from the Edit menu (⌘Z). Undo only works for the command just executed; it is not possible to reverse the effect of the second or third previous command. There are also some commands that cannot be reversed. Print is an obvious example—the document has already been printed. Changing margins is another example.

The Edit menu changes slightly depending upon the last command executed or action performed. For example, formatting text as Bold and then displaying the Edit menu shows the Undo Format command. Typing text and then displaying the Edit menu shows the Undo Typing command. Executing this command deletes all text entered since the last action performed. When menus change to reflect the current situation, like the Edit menu, they are called *smart menus*.

3.10 Selecting and Deleting Blocks of Text

When editing a document, it is sometimes necessary to remove large amounts of text. In the last chapter the Delete key was used to remove text one character at a time. To speed deleting, the text to be removed can first be selected. Selected text is shown *highlighted* on the screen. The highlight can contain any amount of text:

> Ivy University is one of our nation's most prestigious private universities. Undergraduate study is offered in an intellectually invigorating and challenging climate. School colors are leafy green and neon pink. With world famous faculty members, high standards, and a down to earth practicality, you can be assured of obtaining the best possible education.

The third sentence is highlighted in this example

When the Delete key is pressed, all of the highlighted text is removed.

3

The easiest way to highlight text is by dragging the I-Beam pointer over the desired text to form a *highlighted block*. This block can contain a single character to several pages of text. Be careful to include only the text to be deleted in the highlight when using this technique. Another reason to be careful is that pressing a key replaces a block with the typed character. If you delete a block by mistake, immediately execute Undo (⌘Z) to restore it. To remove the highlight, click the mouse once anywhere in the document. Pressing an arrow key also removes the highlight.

Here are several other methods for highlighting text:

- A single word can be highlighted by double-clicking on it. The highlight extends from the first character to the last and does not include the space after the word.

- A single line of text can be highlighted by clicking the mouse button three times in rapid succession (triple-clicking). Clicking four times in rapid succession highlights the entire paragraph.

- A highlight can be created from the current cursor position to the location of the mouse pointer by holding down the Shift key and clicking. This highlight can contain any number of paragraphs.

- The entire document can be highlighted by executing the Select All command from the Edit menu (⌘A).

Practice 4

This Practice demonstrates the selection and deletion of blocks. Start ClarisWorks and open IVY PROMO if you have not already done so. You will select and delete different blocks of text. Undo will be used to restore a deleted block.

1) SELECT TEXT BY DRAGGING

a. Place the pointer in the paragraph at the beginning of the document which begins "Ivy University is one…."

b. Hold down the mouse button and drag the mouse several words to the right. A highlight is created, and each character the pointer passes over is included in the block.

c. Release the button. The highlight remains.

2) REMOVE THE HIGHLIGHT

Click on any text. The highlight is removed.

3) SELECT BLOCKS OF TEXT

a. Place the pointer over a word and double-click the mouse button. The entire word is highlighted.

b. Place the pointer over a word and triple-click the mouse button. The entire line is highlighted.

c. Place the pointer over any text and click the mouse button four times in rapid succession. The entire paragraph is highlighted.

4) HIGHLIGHT THE ENTIRE DOCUMENT

    a. From the Edit menu, select the Select All command. The entire document is high-lighted.

    b. Click on any text to remove the highlight.

5) HIGHLIGHT A SENTENCE

    a. Place the pointer in the paragraph at the beginning of the document which begins "Ivy University is one…."

    b. Click on the "S" in "School colors are…." The cursor should be just to the left of the "S."

    c. Place the pointer **but do not click** after the space following the period at the end of the sentence. Make sure that the pointer is just to the left of "With."

    d. Hold down the Shift key and click. A highlight is created from the current cursor position to the pointer position. Be sure the space after the end of the sentence is included in the highlight.

6) DELETE THE HIGHLIGHTED BLOCK

Press Delete. All of the highlighted text, the entire sentence, is deleted and the highlight removed.

7) DELETE AND RESTORE THE NEXT PARAGRAPH

    a. Place the cursor in the next paragraph, which begins "Located in…."

    b. Click the mouse four times in rapid succession to highlight the entire paragraph.

    c. Press Delete to remove the paragraph.

    d. From the Edit menu, select the Undo Typing command. The paragraph is restored. Click on any text to remove the highlight.

8) SAVE IVY PROMO

From the File menu, select the Save command. IVY PROMO is saved on disk.

Any of these highlighting techniques may be used when directed to select blocks of text in future Practices.

3.11 Paragraph Formats - Alignment

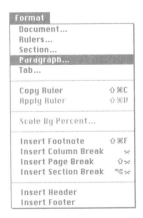

There are four ways to align text in a paragraph relative to the margins: left, centered, right, and justified. The **Align** option in the Paragraph dialog box or the alignment controls in the Format bar are used to change paragraph alignment:

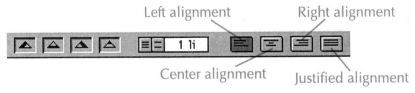

Left alignment   Right alignment

Center alignment   Justified alignment

The current paragraph can be formatted quickly by using the alignment controls

Left aligned, the default, means that each line of text begins at the left margin. The right edge of the paragraph is jagged. This is the format most often used in letters or research papers.

Centered is the alignment most often used for headings and titles. Each line of a centered paragraph is equidistant from the left and right margins.

Right aligned is the opposite of left aligned. Each line of a right-aligned paragraph is flush with the right margin while the left edge of the paragraph is jagged. This format is used infrequently, but can be found in some advertisements and catalogs.

Justified creates straight paragraph borders at both margins. When a paragraph is justified, ClarisWorks places extra space between words on each line of text so that it extends from the left margin to the right margin. Justified formats are common in newspapers and books—this textbook, for example.

Selecting an alignment option affects only the paragraph that the cursor is in. When applied, the paragraph is reformatted on the screen, showing the new alignment. Multiple paragraphs can be formatted by highlighting them first, and then applying the desired alignment. Paragraph alignments can also be used in headers and footers. Examples of each of the alignments are shown below:

Left

```
This text is left aligned, the default
alignment. Notice how the length of each line
is different. In a left aligned paragraph the
right margin appears jagged. This format is
often called "ragged-right" for this reason.
```

Centered

```
      This text is centered. Notice that each
line is centered between the margins. Centered
          text is often used for titles.
```

Right

```
         This text is right aligned. Each line is
     even with the right margin. The effect of a
        right aligned paragraph is that the left
                      margin appears jagged.
```

Justified

```
This text is justified. Each line is extended to
reach the right margin. The effect of justifying
a paragraph is that the borders on each margin
appear straight. Note that extra space is needed
between some words to extend the lines to the right
margin.
```

3.12 Paragraph Formats - Line Spacing

The amount of space between lines in a paragraph can be controlled. Single spacing places text on each line of the page and double spacing inserts a blank line between lines of text. Double spacing can make a document more readable, leaving room for notes to be written between lines. Examples of both formats are shown below:

Single spacing

> This paragraph is single spaced. There is little space between the lines for notes or comments, but more information can be placed on each page. Most printed text, including this book, is single spaced.

Double spacing

> This paragraph is double spaced. Note how space
>
> is left between each line for notes or comments.
>
> Double spacing is used mostly for academic papers
>
> and drafts.

Like alignment, spacing changes are applied only to the paragraph that currently contains the cursor, or to all of the paragraphs in a highlighted block. This allows one paragraph in a document to be single spaced and another double spaced. Single spacing is the default.

The **Line Spacing** option in the Paragraph dialog box or the Paragraph spacing controls in the Format bar are used to change line spacing:

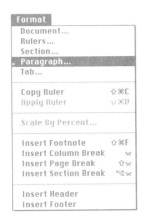

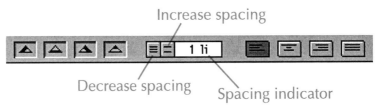

Increase spacing

Decrease spacing   Spacing indicator

Line spacing can be changed using the Format bar

Each time the Increase spacing control is clicked, the spacing of the current paragraph is increased by a half line. Therefore, clicking twice on the Increase spacing control double spaces the current paragraph. Clicking on the Decrease spacing control decreases the line spacing of the current paragraph by a half line. The Spacing indicator displays the line spacing of the current paragraph. Double-clicking on the Spacing indicator displays the Paragraph dialog box.

3

Practice 5

This Practice demonstrates the use of single spacing and double spacing, paragraph alignment options, block formatting, and the Undo command. Start ClarisWorks and open IVY PROMO if you have not already done so.

1) CENTER THE FIRST TWO LINES IN THE DOCUMENT

    a. Move the I-Beam pointer over the first line of the document, the title which reads "Ivy University," and click once to place the cursor.

    b. In the Format bar, click the Center alignment control (▦). The line is centered on the screen and the Center alignment control is highlighted in the Format bar.

    c. Place the cursor in the next line of the document (the subtitle).

    d. In the Format bar, click the Center alignment control. The paragraph that contains the subtitle is centered.

2) JUSTIFY THE FIRST PARAGRAPH

    a. Place the I-Beam pointer in the paragraph that begins "Ivy University is one of…" and click once to place the cursor.

    b. In the Format bar, click the Justified alignment control (▤). Note the increased space between some words.

3) DOUBLE SPACE THE SECOND PARAGRAPH

    a. Place the cursor in the second paragraph, which begins "Located in…."

    b. In the Format bar, click on the Increase spacing control (▤). There is increased space between the lines of the paragraph.

    c. Click on the Increase spacing control again. ClarisWorks double spaces the current paragraph and the Spacing indicator in the Format bar displays 2 li.

    d. Click on the Decrease spacing control twice (▤). The paragraph is again single spaced and the Spacing indicator displays 1 li.

    e. Click on the Increase spacing control twice to again double space the paragraph.

4) RIGHT ALIGN THE SECOND PARAGRAPH

    a. The cursor should be in the paragraph which begins "Located in…."

    b. In the Format bar, click the Right alignment control (▤). The paragraph is right aligned. This paragraph now has two formats: right alignment and double spacing.

    c. Note that the Right alignment control is still highlighted indicating that this is the format of the current paragraph. Click once in the first paragraph. The Justified alignment control is now highlighted indicating that this paragraph is justified. Your document should be similar to the following:

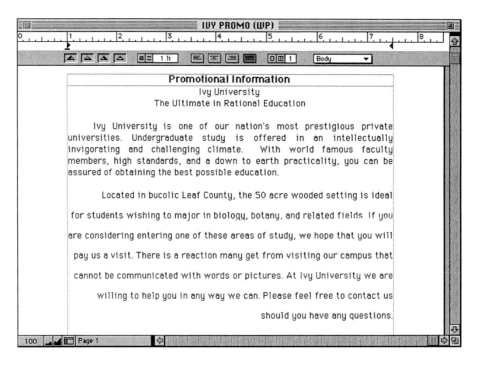

IVY PROMO (WP)

Promotional Information
Ivy University
The Ultimate in Rational Education

Ivy University is one of our nation's most prestigious private universities. Undergraduate study is offered in an intellectually invigorating and challenging climate. With world famous faculty members, high standards, and a down to earth practicality, you can be assured of obtaining the best possible education.

Located in bucolic Leaf County, the 50 acre wooded setting is ideal

for students wishing to major in biology, botany, and related fields If you

are considering entering one of these areas of study, we hope that you will

pay us a visit. There is a reaction many get from visiting our campus that

cannot be communicated with words or pictures. At Ivy University we are

willing to help you in any way we can. Please feel free to contact us

should you have any questions.

5) UNDO THE LAST COMMAND

From the Edit menu, select the Undo Format command. The effect of the previous command (right alignment) is undone, and the paragraph is returned to its original state.

6) PREVIEW THE MODIFIED FILE

a. Click on the Zoom-out control until page 1 can be seen entirely on the screen. Note how the paragraphs are aligned and spaced.
b. Use the Zoom-in control to display the document at 100 magnification.

7) JUSTIFY THE BODY OF THE DOCUMENT AS A BLOCK

a. Place the pointer in the paragraph which begins "Located in bucolic…." Click once to place the cursor in the paragraph.
b. Use the scroll bar to scroll to the last paragraph in the document.
c. Hold down the Shift key and click in the last paragraph that begins "We hope that…." A highlighted block is created that contains left-aligned text from every paragraph but the centered titles and the first paragraph of the body.
d. In the Format bar, click the Justified alignment button. The document is reformatted.
e. Click anywhere in the text to remove the highlight. Scroll through the document, noting the justified paragraphs.
f. From the File menu, select the Save command. When IVY PROMO is next used, all of the body paragraphs will be justified.

3.13 Character Formats - Style

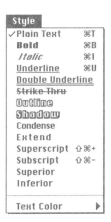

ClarisWorks' Style menu has a number of commands that change the way that individual characters appear. The most common character formats are Bold, Italic, and Underline and are used to emphasize different parts of the text in a document. The current style is indicated in the menu with a check mark. The default style is Plain Text, meaning no emphasis.

Two steps are required to create emphasized text:

1. Highlight the text to be emphasized. The block can be created using any of the methods discussed in Section 3.10.
2. Execute the desired formatting command. All highlighted characters are emphasized.

Bold text is printed darker so that words and phrases stand out on the page. It is most frequently used for titles and headings.

Italic text is slanted and is mostly used for emphasis. It is sometimes used for headings.

<u>Underlined text</u> is often used in footnotes and endnotes for referring to titles of publications.

Outline displays letters as hollow, while Shadow places a shaded shadow behind the letter. Both of these styles work best on laser printers.

Multiple formats can be applied to the same text. For example, a title can be bold and underlined at the same time. Remember, the text to be formatted must be highlighted before the format is applied.

A character format can be removed by highlighting the desired text and executing the Plain Text command from the Style menu. As shown in the menu, ClarisWorks also has Command key shortcuts for some character formats:

⌘T Plain Text
⌘B Bold
⌘I Italic
⌘U Underline

....

Practice 6

This Practice demonstrates the use of bold, italic, and underlined text. Start ClarisWorks and open IVY PROMO if you have not already done so.

1) HIGHLIGHT THE BLOCK TO BE BOLD

a. Move the pointer to the "Ivy University" title at the top of the document.
b. Triple-click the mouse button to highlight the entire title.
c. From the Style menu, select the Bold command. The highlighted text changes to bold on the screen.

2) ITALICIZE THE NEXT LINE USING THE KEYBOARD SHORTCUT

    a. Move the pointer to the next line, the subtitle which begins "The Ultimate…."

    b. Triple-click the mouse button to highlight the entire title.

    c. Press ⌘I to apply the Italic format using the keyboard shortcut. The text changes to italic on the screen.

3) UNDERLINE THE FIRST LINE IN THE NEXT PARAGRAPH

    a. Place the pointer to the left of the "I" in "Ivy University is one of…."

    b. Drag down one line and to the right to highlight the entire sentence. Do not include the space after the sentence in the highlight.

    c. From the Style menu, select the Underline command. The text is underlined.

4) REMOVE UNDERLINING FROM PART OF THE SENTENCE

    a. Place the cursor after the "y" in "University" in the first sentence.

    b. Highlight to the end of the sentence, including the period.

    c. Make this text plain by selecting the Plain Text command from the Style menu. Only "Ivy University" is now underlined.

    d. Click anywhere to remove the highlight.

Check - The title should be bold, the next line italicized, and the "Ivy University" in the first sentence underlined:

> **Promotional Information**
> **Ivy University**
> *The Ultimate in Rational Education*
>
> <u>Ivy University</u> is one of our nation's most prestigious private universities. Undergraduate study is offered in an intellectually

5) SAVE IVY PROMO

Save the modified IVY PROMO. The next time IVY PROMO is opened, the bold, italic, and underlined text will be present.

3.14 When to Apply Formats

Any new text inserted inside existing text will automatically be given the same format. That is, a character inserted between two bold characters is automatically made bold. This leads to a very common error. Suppose you are creating a new document and want to have a bold, centered headline. After typing the headline, you highlight the paragraph and apply the proper formatting commands to make it bold and centered. When you press Return and begin to type the next paragraph, it is also bold and centered. In fact, all of the paragraphs that you create from this point on will be bold and centered! This is probably not what you wanted.

This problem can be solved by highlighting everything but the original title and changing the text style to Plain Text and the alignment to left. However, the problem is best avoided by following this simple rule:

> Type all of the material for your document first and then go back and apply the desired formatting.

An Introduction to Computing Using ClarisWorks

3.15 Character Formats - Fonts

A *font* or *typeface* refers to the shape of the characters. The letters in this text line are shaped differently from the letters of the word "Fonts" in the heading above, and the letters in the footer at the bottom of the page. Each of these lines of text is printed in a different font.

ClarisWorks' Font menu has a number of different font choices which affect the way that individual characters appear, both on the screen and when printed. Font options are used to emphasize different parts of text in a document by changing the shape of a set of characters. The default ClarisWorks font is named Helvetica, but depending on your printer there are several others from which you may choose:

This is Helvetica. ABCDEF abcdef 1234567890

This is Chicago. ABCDEF abcdef 1234567890

This is Courier. ABCDEF abcdef 1234567890

✳✳✳▲ ✳❂▢ ✦■✳❂❂▼✎ ✛✝✦✛✦✦ ❂❂✳✳✳❂ ❏✔✕✖✗✚✎

Τηισ ισ Σψμβολ. ΑΒΧΔΕΦ αβχδεφ 1234567890

This is Times. ABCDEF abcdef 1234567890

To change the font of text, first highlight the desired text. In the Font menu, the current font is indicated by a check mark. Selecting a different font changes all the highlighted characters.

3.16 Character Formats - Size

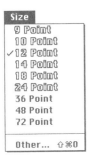

Characters can also be displayed in different sizes. Character size is measured in *points*, and there are 72 points to an inch. For example:

This is an example of 9 point Helvetica.
This is an example of 10 point Helvetica.
This is an example of 12 point Helvetica.
This is an example of 14 point Helvetica.
This is an example of 18 point Helvetica.

The default size is 12 point, but there are others from which you may choose in the Size menu. The current size is indicated with a check.

Executing the Other command from the Size menu (⇧⌘0) displays the Font size dialog box:

Font sizes can be changed using this dialog box

The desired point size can be entered and **OK** selected to change the high-lighted character's size.

Character Format Review

Type all the material for your document first. Next, highlight the text to be emphasized and then select the desired option from the Font, Size, or Style menu (or use a Command key shortcut). Multiple formatting options can be applied to a block of text. Once a block has been emphasized it stays that way until you change it. Any new text inserted inside an emphasized block will also be emphasized.

Practice 7

This Practice demonstrates the use of font and size character formats. Start ClarisWorks and open IVY PROMO.

1) CHANGE THE HEADER FONT

    a. Place the cursor in the first paragraph of the document.
    b. Move the mouse pointer to the Font menu in the Menu bar. Hold down the mouse button, but do not drag down the menu.
    c. Note the selected font. Geneva was used to format the entire document. Release the mouse button.
    d. Place the I-Beam pointer in the document's header. Triple-click the mouse button to highlight the header text.
    e. Move the mouse pointer to the Menu bar. Hold down the mouse button on the Font menu. Note the currently selected font is Helvetica—the default font.
    f. From the Font menu, select Geneva. The header text is reformatted in Geneva.

2) INCREASE THE SIZE OF THE TITLE

    a. Triple-click in the title at the top of the document, "Ivy University."
    b. From the Size menu, select 18 Point. The highlighted text is now bold and 18 points. Note how text is moved down to make room for the larger letters.

3) CHANGE THE FONT OF THE NEXT LINE

    a. Triple-click in the very next line which begins "The Ultimate in…." The entire line is highlighted.
    b. From the Font menu, select Monaco. The shape of the letters changes on the screen.
    c. Click anywhere to remove the highlight.

Check - The header should be Geneva, the title should be bold and 18 point text, and the next line italicized Monaco:

Promotional Information
Ivy University
The Ultimate in Rational Education

4) CHANGE THE FOOTER FONT

a. Scroll down until the document's footer is visible.
b. Place the I-Beam pointer in the document's footer. Triple-click to select the footer text.
c. From the Font menu, select Geneva. The footer text, including the page # code is reformatted in Geneva.

5) SAVE AND PRINT THE FIRST PAGE OF THE DOCUMENT

a. Save IVY PROMO. The next time IVY PROMO is opened the formatted text will be present.
b. Press ⌘**P** to display the Print dialog box.
c. Click on the radio button beside the **From** option. Note the blinking cursor in the **From** box. Type 1 in this box. Move the pointer to the **To** box and click the mouse. Type 1 in this box.
d. Select **Print** to print the file. Only the first page of the document will be printed. Note how the text in the printout resembles that shown on the screen.

3.17 Character Formats - Superscripts and Subscripts

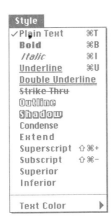

A *superscript* is a section of text which is raised slightly above the current line while a *subscript* is printed slightly below the current line. For example:

> In her 9th Street laboratory, Dr. Sulfuric proved that the formula for water is H_2O.

The "th" after the 9 is a superscript, and the "2" in H_2O is a subscript.

To create superscripts and subscripts, highlighted the desired text and then select the appropriate command from the Style menu. Command key shortcuts may also be used to create either superscripted (⇧⌘+) or subscripted (⇧⌘–) text.

Footnotes and endnotes are usually marked with superscripted text. A special method for creating these marks is described in Chapter Four.

Practice 8

In this Practice you will create superscripts and subscripts. Start ClarisWorks and open IVY PROMO if you have not already done so.

1) LOCATE THE FACULTY LIST

Scroll through IVY PROMO until the Faculty Members list is on the screen (near the middle of page 3). We will create the superscripts and subscripts for the formula in Dr. Scalp's description—$C_2H_5OH^3$.

2) CREATE THE FORMULA SUBSCRIPTS

a. Place the cursor before the "2" and drag one character to the right, highlighting only the "2."
b. From the Style menu, select the Subscript command. Note how the highlighted text is placed slightly below the line.

c. Highlight the "5" in the formula.

d. Press and hold the Shift and Command keys. Press the Minus (–) key. The 5 is now subscripted.

3) CREATE THE FORMULA SUPERSCRIPTS

a. Drag the mouse over the "3," highlighting it.

b. From the Style menu, select the Superscript command or press ⇧⌘+ to create a superscript.

4) SAVE IVY PROMO

<u>Check</u> - Your document should be similar to:

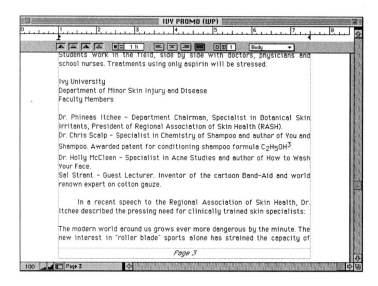

3.18 Submenus and the Shortcuts Palette

The Shortcuts command from the File menu has a triangle (▶) to its right. Highlighting a command with a triangle displays a *submenu* where other commands appear:

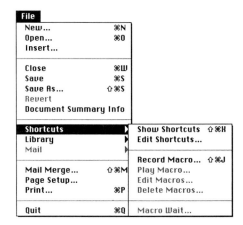

Dragging down to the Shortcuts command displays the Shortcuts submenu

To execute a submenu command, drag the highlight into the submenu, highlight the desired command, and release the mouse button.

Executing the Show Shortcuts command from the submenu (⇧⌘**H**) displays the Shortcuts palette. Many commonly performed actions such as changing the text style in a document, opening a file, and printing a document can be performed using the *Shortcuts palette*:

Buttons on the Shortcuts palette can be used to execute commonly performed actions

Listed below are some of the Shortcuts palette buttons and their function:

	Open command in the File menu
	Save command in the File menu
	Print command in the File menu
	Undo command in the Edit menu
B	Bold command in the Style menu
I	Italic command in the Style menu
U	Underline command in the Style menu
	Left alignment control in the Format bar
	Center alignment control in the Format bar
	Right alignment control in the Format bar
	Justified alignment control in the Format bar

The Shortcuts palette changes depending upon the application. For example, if there are currently no open documents the Shortcuts palette changes to the following:

Word Processing  Open

These buttons are displayed on the Shortcuts palette when there are no open files

A new word processing document can be opened by clicking on the Word Processing button. To display the Open dialog box, the Open button is clicked. The Shortcuts palette can be removed by clicking on its Close box or by executing the Hide Shortcuts command from the Shortcuts submenu (⇧⌘**H**).

3.19 More About Palettes

A *palette* is a small window that allows you to easily select different options. Once displayed, a palette remains on the screen until it is closed. Clicking on the Close box in the upper-left corner of a palette closes it. Palettes also contain a *Roll-up box* located in the upper-right corner. Clicking on it displays only the title bar of the palette. For example, clicking on the Roll-up box of the Shortcuts palette causes its buttons to disappear or "roll-up" into the title bar:

 Roll-up box

When the Shortcuts palette is rolled-up, it uses less room on the screen

To redisplay a palette, click on the Roll-up box again. A palette can be repositioned on the screen by placing the pointer on its Title bar (to the right of its Close box) and dragging.

3.20 The Show Invisibles Button

Some characters, such as spaces and tabs, are shown as *white space* in a document. Because of this, an editing change that leaves two spaces between a word instead of one may not be readily apparent on the screen. For this reason, ClarisWorks includes the Show Invisibles button on the Shortcuts palette ().

Clicking on the Show Invisibles button displays special symbols for some characters:

· (raised dot)	Space character
↵	Return character
⊞	Manual page break character
➡	Tab character (described later)

These symbols are shown on the screen as an aid in formatting and do not appear when the document is printed. To remove the symbols, click on the Show Invisibles button again. The characters are replaced by the appropriate white space and the symbols are no longer displayed on the screen. It is always a good practice to use the Show Invisibles mode, especially when formatting and editing text.

3.21 Entering Special Characters

There are characters available for your use that do not appear on a specific key. One example is the Copyright symbol, ©.

Special characters are entered using the Option key. Option works like the Command or Shift key—it must be held down while another key (or keys) is pressed. On the next page is a table of several useful Option key combinations:

• (bullet)	Option+8	π (Pi)	Option+P
© (copyright)	Option+G	√ (square root)	Option+V
® (registered)	Option+R	£ (Pound)	Option+3
™ (trademark)	Option+2	¢ (cent)	Option+4
Σ (Sigma)	Option+W	¥ (Yen)	Option+Y

Practice 9

In this Practice you will use the Shortcuts palette to show invisible characters and change the style and alignment of selected text. The Option key will be used to enter a special character. If you have not already done so, start ClarisWorks and open IVY PROMO.

1) WORK WITH THE SHORTCUTS PALETTE

a. From the File menu, drag down to the Shortcuts command. From the submenu shown, select the Show Shortcuts command.
b. Place the pointer on the Shortcuts palette's title bar (not on the Close box).
c. Drag the Shortcuts palette to a new location on the screen and release the mouse.
d. Roll up the Shortcuts palette by clicking on its Roll-up box. The buttons disappear and only a title bar is displayed in the upper-right corner of the screen near the Ruler.
e. Click on the Shortcuts palette Roll-up box again. Note that the palette is restored to its last location and its buttons are visible.
f. Drag the palette to the upper-right corner of the window so that it obscures as little text as possible.

2) SHOW INVISIBLE CHARACTERS

Click on the Show Invisibles button on the Shortcuts palette (⬚). Note the special symbols displayed on the screen.

3) INSERT A SPECIAL CHARACTER

a. Place the cursor at the end of the subtitle at the top of the document, the line which begins "The Ultimate in…." The blinking cursor should be displayed just before the Return character at the end of the line.
b. Hold down the Option key and press the R key. A registered mark appears. The mark is italic because this entire line was formatted as italic in a previous Practice. The modified portion of your document should be similar to:

Promotional·Information

Ivy·University↵
The·Ultimate·in·Rational·Education®↵

↵
• ⎯ Ivy·University·is·one·of·our·nation's·most·prestigious·private universities.··Undergraduate·study·is·offered·in·an·intellectually invigorating·and·challenging·climate.·With·world·famous·faculty·members, high·standards,·and·a·down·to·earth·practicality,·you·can·be·assured·of obtaining·the·best·possible·education.↵
↵

4) CHANGE THE STYLE OF TEXT

a. Scroll through IVY PROMO until the Faculty Members list is on the screen (near the middle of page 3).

b. Highlight the title of Dr. Scalp's book `You and Shampoo`. Do not include in the highlight the space before the title or the period after the title.

c. On the Shortcuts palette, click on the Underline button ([U]). The book title is underlined.

d. Underline the title of Dr. McCleen's book, `How to Wash Your Face`.

5) LEFT ALIGN THE HEADER TEXT

a. Move the I-Beam pointer so that it is in the header area of the document and click the mouse. Note the insertion point in the header.

b. Click on the Align Left button on the Shortcuts palette ([≡]). The header is now left aligned and should be similar to:

```
Promotional Information
```

6) SAVE IVY PROMO

Click on the Save button on the Shortcuts palette ([▣]). IVY PROMO is saved.

7) CLOSE IVY PROMO

Click on the Close box in the upper-left corner of the IVY PROMO window. The file is removed from memory and the screen clears. The Shortcuts palette now displays a different set of buttons.

3.22 Tabs and Tab Stops

Tabs are used to position text within a line or to create tables of data. Pressing the Tab key moves the cursor to the next tab stop to the right. ClarisWorks has default tab stops at every half inch. Do not confuse tab stops with tabs themselves. *Tabs* are actual characters that are placed in a document by using the Tab key. *Tab stops* are only locations specifying the position of the tab character (how far it moves the cursor).

Default tab stops, which exist at every half inch, are generally used for indenting text from the margin. When beginning a new paragraph, pressing Tab once indents the first line half an inch. Each paragraph in the body of IVY PROMO has been formatted this way. Tabs are also used to create tables consisting of columns of data. Rather than using the default tab stops, new tab stops are usually created at the desired intervals for the table.

Tabs are generated by a single keystroke and may be inserted or deleted the same as any other character. Pressing the Tab key does not insert spaces to move the cursor to the next tab stop. Instead, a code is placed in the text which tells ClarisWorks to move the cursor to the next tab stop. Deleting a tab requires only that the code be deleted. The text is then automatically moved to the left to fill the space created.

It is possible to insert a tab into a previously entered line of text by positioning the cursor in the line and pressing the Tab key. This places a tab character at that point and moves the characters to the right to the next tab stop.

3.23 The Ruler

Above the Format bar is a Ruler that is used to gauge the placement of horizontal formatting features including tab stops, margins, and indents. (Indents are discussed in Chapter Four.) User-defined tab stops are also shown on this line. The Ruler measures from the edge of the page, with each vertical line representing one eighth of an inch, and full inches indicated by a number.

Practice 10

This Practice demonstrates tabs. If you have not already done so, start ClarisWorks display the Shortcuts palette.

1) OPEN A WORD PROCESSOR FILE

    a. Click on the Open button on the Shortcuts palette ( ). The Open dialog box is displayed.

    b. Scroll through the files list until News Story is displayed. News Story was created in the Practices in Chapter Two.

    c. Place the pointer on News Story and double-click to open a copy of the News Story document.

2) USE THE SHORTCUTS PALETTE TO ALIGN THE TITLE

    a. Click on the Show Invisibles button on the Shortcuts palette. Note the special symbols that are displayed.

    b. Place the pointer anywhere on the title in the first line of the document. Click the mouse to place the cursor.

    c. On the Shortcuts palette, click on the Align Center button. The title is now centered.

3) INDENT THREE PARAGRAPHS WITH TABS

    a. Move the cursor to the beginning of the paragraph that starts "The annual…."

    b. Press the Tab key. A tab character is inserted and its symbol (➡) displayed on the screen. The paragraph is now indented to the first tab stop at 0.5 inches.

    c. Move the cursor to the beginning of the next paragraph and indent it like the first.

    d. Use the Tab key to indent the line that begins "The menu…."

4) INDENT THE MENU

    a. Move the cursor to the beginning of the first menu item, Fruit cup or lime sherbet.

    b. Press the Tab key twice. The line is indented 1 inch. Note the position of the first character in the line in relation to the Ruler.

    c. Follow parts (a) and (b) to indent the remaining menu items.

    d. Indent the last paragraph of News Story with one tab.

Check: When complete, News Story should appear similar to the following:

FUND·RAISER·TO·BE·HELD·AT·EASTSIDE·SHERATON↵

↵

◆ The·annual·Lawrenceville·Red·Cross·fund-raising·dinner·will·be·held·in·the·main·ballroom·of·the·Eastside·Sheraton·at·7:00·p.m.·next·Saturday·night.·Music·for·dancing·will·be·provided·by·the·Schmenge·Brothers·Orchestra.·↵

↵

◆ All·community·members·are·invited.··Tickets·are·$25.00·per·person·and·are·available·from·Mrs.·Mitchell·in·the·Red·Cross·office·during·regular·business·hours.↵

↵

◆ The·menu·for·the·evening's·event·will·be:↵

↵

◆ ◆ Fruit·cup·or·lime·sherbet↵

◆ ◆ Roast·duck·a·l'Orange·with·wild·rice·stuffing↵

◆ ◆ Garden·salad↵

◆ ◆ Double·chocolate·chip·ice·cream↵

↵

◆ After·dinner,·a·reception·will·take·place·in·the·hotel's·Algonquin·Room.··Dancing·will·continue·until·11:00·p.m.

5) SAVE, PRINT, AND THEN CLOSE NEWS STORY

a. On the Shortcuts palette, click on the Save button (▣) to save the modified News Story.

b. On the Shortcuts palette, click on the Print button (▣) to print the file.

c. Click on the Close box to remove the file from the screen.

3.24 Setting Individual Tab Stops

A tab stop can be set at any position on the Ruler. When a tab stop is set ClarisWorks automatically removes the default stops to the left. That is, setting a tab stop at 1.4 inches automatically removes the default stops at 0.5 and 1.0 inches. The default stop at 1.5 inches is not affected.

When the Tab key is pressed, a tab is inserted in the text and text to the right of the tab is aligned at the next tab stop. A left-aligned tab stop aligns the beginning of the text at the stop, and is marked with a ◭ below the Ruler. Right-aligned (◮), center-aligned (◮), and decimal-aligned (◮) tab stops can also be created. A right-aligned tab stop aligns the end of the text at the stop, and a center-aligned tab stop centers the text equidistant over the stop. Decimal tabs, sometimes called *align on* tabs, are used with numbers and align the decimal point at the stop. Examples of each stop are shown below with the corresponding Ruler:

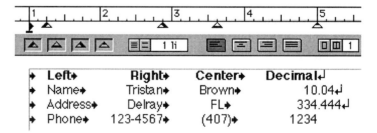

◆	**Left**◆	**Right**◆	**Center**◆	**Decimal**↵
◆	Name◆	Tristan◆	Brown◆	10.04↵
◆	Address◆	Delray◆	FL◆	334.444↵
◆	Phone◆	123-4567◆	(407)◆	1234

Tab stops are indicated by markers directly below the Ruler

Individual tab stops are set by using the tab markers in the Format bar:

Tab markers in the Format bar are used to create tab stops

For example, dragging the Right tab stop marker into the Ruler creates a right-aligned tab stop at that position.

To remove a specific stop, its marker is dragged from the Ruler into the Work area and the mouse button released. Any text which was aligned at that stop is automatically reformatted. Changes made to a document by setting or clearing tab stops are retained when it is saved on disk.

Tab stops can also be inserted by selecting the Tab command from the Format menu which displays the following dialog box:

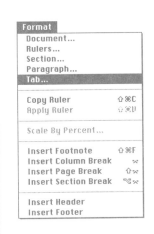

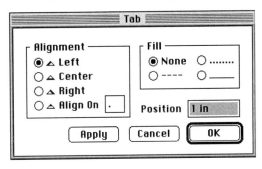

Multiple tab stops can be set at the same time using this dialog box

After clicking on the appropriate **Alignment** option, a value is typed in the **Position** box. The value in the **Position** box corresponds to the distance from the left margin. Clicking on **Apply** creates a tab stop at that position. This procedure may be repeated to enter multiple tab stops. When complete, **OK** is selected to remove the dialog box.

It is important to realize that tab stops are a paragraph format like paragraph alignment or line spacing. That is, when tab stops are created, they are set for the current paragraph only. Any paragraphs before or after are not affected. This makes it possible for different paragraphs to have different sets of tab stops. As the cursor is moved through the text, the Ruler changes to show the tab stops set for the current paragraph. Like all formatting commands, the same set of tab stops can be applied to a number of paragraphs by highlighting first and then setting the stops.

Practice 11

In this Practice you will set and delete tab stops, creating a formatted table. Start ClarisWorks and open IVY PROMO. Display the Shortcuts palette and use the Show Invisibles button to display special symbols if they are not already displayed.

1) LOCATE THE STUDENT DIVERSITY TABLE

Scroll to the Student Diversity section, located near the end of the document. This table has been entered using the Tab key and default tab stops. There is a single tab between each column—one tab between "Area" and "Students," another between "Students" and "Percentage," and so on for the entire table. However, because tab stops have not yet been set, this table is not easy to read.

2) ADD A LINE TO THE UNFORMATTED TABLE

a. You will add a line to the table. Place the cursor at the end of the South America line, after 10.47%, but before the Return character.

b. Press Return. A new line is added to the table.

c. Press the Tab key once to indent the line. Type `Other` as the area.

d. Press Tab again and type `49` as the number of students.

e. Press Tab and type `0.90%` as the percent. Each line in this table was entered similarly. The table should be similar to:

```
   ◆   Area◆Students◆ Percentage↵
   ↵
   ◆   Africa◆   213◆ 3.87%↵
   ◆   Asia◆471◆ 8.56%↵
   ◆   Europe◆   689◆ 12.52%↵
   ◆   North·America◆ 3,503◆    63.68%↵
   ◆   South·America◆ 576◆ 10.47%↵
   ◆   Other◆49◆ 0.90%↵
   ◆   ◆   5,501◆    100.00%↵
```

3) HIGHLIGHT THE TABLE

a. We want to set three tab stops that are the same for the entire table. So that we only have to enter the tab stops once, we will highlight the table first. Any tab stops created then affect the entire highlighted block. Place the cursor anywhere in the title of the table, "Area Students Percentage."

b. Drag the mouse slowly down the table. When the highlight is in the last line of the table (5,501), release the button. Any tab stops now set will affect each highlighted line in the table.

4) SET THE FIRST TAB STOP FOR THE TABLE

a. The first column of the table should be left aligned at 1¾ (1.75) inches. Drag the Left tab stop marker (▲) from the Format bar into the line below the Ruler. Release the mouse. A left aligned tab stop is set at the current location. Note how the table is reformatted.

b. Drag the inserted tab marker towards the 1¾ inch marker. When the marker is at 1¾ inches, release the mouse. The table is reformatted with each line starting at 1¾ inches.

5) SET THE SECOND AND THIRD TAB STOPS

a. The second column of the table should be right aligned at 4 inches. Drag the Right tab stop marker (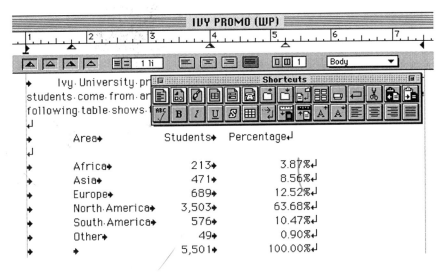) into the space below the Ruler.

b. Drag the right tab stop marker to the 4 inch mark.

c. The last column is decimal aligned at 5¼ inches. Drag the Decimal tab stop marker ( ) down to the 5¼ inch mark. The table is now complete, and easy to read. Click anywhere to remove the highlight. Note the alignment of "Percentage" in the title. Since the text does not contain a decimal it is right aligned to the decimal-aligned tab stop.

Check - Your table and Ruler should be similar to:

6) SAVE AND PRINT IVY PROMO

a. Save IVY PROMO. The next time it is opened, IVY PROMO will have tab stops set.

b. From the File menu, select the Print command and print the entire document. Note on the printed copy all of the formatting options created in this chapter: headers, footers, paragraph formats, text formats, fonts and styles, tab stops, etc.

c. Close IVY PROMO.

d. From the File menu, select Quit to leave ClarisWorks and return to the System screen.

Chapter Summary

This chapter explained how a word processor document can be formatted to improve its appearance and readability. ClarisWorks displays each open file in a window which can be closed, adjusted, expanded, and scrolled.

A specific arrangement of text is called a format. There are three levels of formats in ClarisWorks: page, paragraph, and character. Each level describes how the format will affect a document.

Margins are the blank spaces between the edges of the paper and text. ClarisWorks' default margin settings can be changed using the Document command from the Format menu. When a margin is changed it affects the whole document.

When the pointer is placed within a document's page boundaries, its shape changes from an arrow to an I-Beam. An insertion point is created by clicking the I-Beam pointer in the text.

A header is text displayed at the top of each page and a footer is text displayed at the bottom of each page. Page numbers and information such as a title or name can be printed in either. To create a header or footer the Insert Header or the Insert Footer command is selected from the Format menu.

The Command key can be used to execute menu commands without the mouse. For example, holding down the Command key and typing P (⌘P) executes the Print command. The Shift key can be used with the Command key to perform some commands. Pressing ⇧⌘H displays the Shortcuts palette.

Pagination is the division of a document into page-sized sections for printing. ClarisWorks automatically displays pages as white areas on the screen, similar to the pages of a printed document. After an editing change, the positions of the page breaks are recalculated. When it is necessary to end the current page, a manual page break can be inserted using the Insert Page Break command from the Format menu. Pressing the Delete key removes a page break.

To reverse the effects of the last command, the Undo command from the Edit menu (⌘Z) is used.

Blocks are highlighted sections of text created by dragging the mouse. When executing a formatting command, the format is applied to the highlighted block. Blocks can be deleted by pressing the Delete key.

The alignment controls in the Format bar are used to set the alignment of a paragraph. Left alignment creates a straight left border and a jagged right border. Right alignment is the opposite, creating a straight right border and a jagged left border. Centering positions a line equidistant from the left and right margins. Justified alignment creates straight borders at both margins. When alignment is set, it affects all lines in the current paragraph or all paragraphs in the selected block.

Single and double spacing are controlled by the Paragraph command from the Format menu or the Spacing controls in the Format bar. When line spacing is set, it affects all lines in the current paragraph or all paragraphs in the selected block.

The Style menu contains commands that affect the way that characters appear on the screen and on the printed page. Text to be formatted is first highlighted and then the appropriate command executed. Bold (⌘B), Italic (⌘I), and Underline (⌘U) styles can be selected to format text. Text can also be made to appear superscripted or subscripted using commands from this menu.

The Font menu contains a number of different font choices which affect the way characters appear. To change the font, text is highlighted and the desired font selected. Characters can be displayed in different sizes by highlighting them and selecting a size from the Size menu.

3

The Shortcuts palette contains buttons that are used to execute many commonly performed actions and commands. The Shortcuts palette can be opened using the Show Shortcuts command from the Shortcuts submenu and then placed anywhere on the screen by dragging. It is closed using the Hide Shortcuts command also from the Shortcuts submenu.

The Show Invisibles button on the Shortcuts palette can be used to display normally invisible characters using symbols. This can be especially useful when editing a document.

Special characters such as bullets (•) and copyrights (©) can be added to a document using the Option key with other keys.

Tabs are characters used to position text within a line. Tab stops are locations specifying the position of the tab character. There are several types of tab stops—left, right, center, or decimal aligned. Individual tab stops are set using the mouse and Ruler. The Tab command from the Format menu can also be used to set tab stops.

Vocabulary

Adjust box - Box in the lower-right corner of a window. Dragging it changes the size of a window.

Align on tab - Also called the decimal tab stop. Used to align a decimal point in the text at the stop.

Block - A highlighted section of text that may contain anything from a single character to an entire document. A block can be created by dragging the mouse over the desired text. Any applied formatting affects the currently highlighted text.

Bold text - Character format that makes text appear darker. Used for making words or phrases stand out on a page.

Centered alignment - Alignment format that positions text evenly between the left and right margins.

Character - Any letter, number, or symbol that can be displayed on the computer screen.

Character format - Formatting option that affects the currently highlighted characters. Character formats include font (e.g., Helvetica), size (e.g., 12 point), and style (e.g., bold).

Close box - Hollow square in the upper-left corner of a window. Clicking it closes the current window and file. Also used to close palettes.

Command key - Key used with one or more other keys to execute menu commands without using the mouse to select commands from menus.

Delete text - A highlighted block that is removed from a document.

Double space - Formatting a paragraph so that there is a blank line between each line of text.

Font - Shape of a set of characters. For example, Geneva or Helvetica.

Footer - Information that is printed at the bottom of each page.

Format - The way that text appears on a page, including options such as margins, fonts, emphasized text, and headers and footers.

Format bar - Line of buttons below the Ruler used to set formatting options such as alignment and spacing.

Header - Information that is printed at the top of each page.

Highlighted text - Text that has been selected as a block. Highlighting is usually done by dragging or clicking the mouse.

I-Beam pointer - Shape the mouse pointer becomes when moved onto the text of a document. Clicking the mouse places the cursor at the current location of the I-Beam pointer.

Insertion point - Another name for the cursor. The point at which text will be entered when typed from the keyboard.

Italic text - Character format that makes text appear slanted. Sometimes used for headings.

Justified alignment - Paragraph format in which each line of text is made to extend from the left margin to the right by adding extra space between words.

Left alignment - Default paragraph format where text is even with the left margin, while the right side is ragged.

Manual page break - A page break that is inserted to force text onto the next printed page.

Margin - Blank spaces between the edge of the paper and the text.

Option key - Used with one or more other keys to enter special symbols not displayed on the keyboard.

Page break - The location where one printed page ends and another begins.

Page format - Formatting option that affects the entire document, such as margins.

Pagination - The division of a document into page-sized sections for printing.

Palette - A small window that allows you to easily choose different options.

Paragraph alignment - How text is printed in relation to the margins: left (default), right, centered, or justified.

Paragraph format - Formatting option that affects the current paragraph including alignment, spacing, and tab stops.

Point - The unit used to measure character size. There are 72 points per inch.

Right alignment - Paragraph format where text is set even with the right margin while the left side is ragged.

Roll-up box - Used to display only the title bar of a palette.

Ruler - An area above the Format bar showing placement of tab stops and indents.

Shortcuts palette - Contains buttons that are used to execute commonly performed commands and actions.

Single space - The default paragraph format where each line of text is placed so that there is no space in between.

Smart menu - A menu that changes to reflect the current situation.

Submenu - Additional commands that appear when a menu command that has a triangle is highlighted.

Subscript - Text printed slightly below the normal line.

Superscript - Text printed slightly above the normal line.

Tabs - Characters used to position text within a line. Used to create tables or to indent the first line of a paragraph.

Tab stop - A location specifying the position of the tab character.

Typeface - Also commonly referred to as font. See font.

Underlined text - Character format that puts a line under text. Used to emphasize text.

Undo command - Reverses the effect of the last command issued.

White space - The way characters such as spaces and tabs are displayed in a document.

Window - Area of the screen where a file is displayed.

Zoom box - Box in the upper-right corner of a window. Clicking on the Zoom box expands the window so that it fills the screen. Clicking on the Zoom box of an expanded window restores the window to its previous size.

3 Reviews

Sections 3.1 — 3.7
1. What does a document's format include?

2. a) What is meant by formatting text?
   b) List three publications in which you have seen formatted text and describe the formats used (in terms of margins, headers and footers, pagination, and paragraph alignment).

3. a) What is a window?
   b) What steps are required to make a window smaller? To make a window fill the screen?

4. a) What are margins?
   b) What are the default (standard) ClarisWorks margins?

5. a) List the steps required to change the margins of a document so that the left margin is 2 inches and the right margin 3 inches.
   b) How long is a line of text after these margins have been set? (Assume an 8.5 x 11 inch sheet of paper.)

6. Explain how the mouse can be used to move the cursor to the middle of the third paragraph in the second page of a document.

7. a) What is a header?
   b) What is a footer?
   c) What type of information is typically included in a header or footer?

8. Explain the steps required to have ClarisWorks print the header "My Summer Vacation" and a footer containing the page number on each page of a document.

9. What is the Command key used for? Give an example.

Sections 3.8 — 3.12
10. a) What is pagination?
    b) How is pagination indicated on the word processor screen?

11. a) Explain two situations when you might want to control the pagination in a document.
    b) How can you create a page break in the middle of a page?
    c) How can you remove the page break set in part (b)?

12. If you make a mistake when formatting a paragraph and realize it before performing a second command, what is usually the fastest method of correcting the error?

13. a) What is meant by a "block" of text?
    b) How can you tell which text is included in a block?

14. List two ways that a single word could be highlighted as a block.

15. List the steps required to delete the second paragraph in a five paragraph document.

16. a) What is meant by justified text?
    b) Explain how to justify a paragraph.

17. a) What is meant by centered text?
    b) What type of text is usually centered?

18. a) What is meant by text that is left aligned?
    b) What types of documents are usually formatted using left alignment?

19. What is the easiest way to justify all of the paragraphs in a document?

20. a) What is double spacing?
    b) Why might you want text to be double spaced?

21. a) List the steps required to double space only the second paragraph in a document that contains five paragraphs.
    b) Will the second paragraph appear double spaced on the screen?
    c) How can a double-spaced paragraph be returned to single spacing?

22. List the steps required to bold the first line of text and underline the second line in a word processor document.

23. a) What happens if you bold a paragraph and then continue typing?
    b) How can you best avoid this problem?

24. a) What is a font?
    b) List three fonts available on your Macintosh.

25. a) What is a point?
    b) How many points are there in an inch?

26. List the steps required to format the title of a document to bold, 24 point Chicago type.

27. Explain how to superscript the word "likes" and subscript the word "juice" in the sentence:

        Mary likes orange juice.

28. a) What is the Shortcuts palette used for?
    b) What formatting options can be selected on the Shortcuts palette?

29. a) How can normally invisible characters be displayed?
    b) Name two characters that are normally invisible.

30. What key is used to enter special characters such as bullets?

31. a) What are tabs used for?
    b) What is a default tab stop? How are they set?

32. a) What is the Ruler and what is it used for?
    b) What do the triangles below the Ruler indicate?

33. Explain what each of the following tab stops does:
    a) left aligned
    b) right aligned
    c) center aligned
    d) decimal aligned

34. a) Explain the steps required to set a center aligned tab stop at 2¼ inches.
    b) How can the tab stop described in part (a) be removed?
    c) How can you tell where tab stops have been set?

3

3 | Exercises

1. The file named COMPUTER ED contains information about computers in education.

    a) Open COMPUTER ED and make the changes noted below:

Justify all paragraphs

Computers in Education *Center and bold title in 18 point Geneva*

Over the past ten years it has become obvious that computers will play an increasingly important role in education. The invention of the microcomputer has made it possible for schools to purchase large numbers of computers at affordable prices. Now that computers are available for student use, educators have been discussing how they should be used. Below are a few examples of how schools are using their computers.

Computer Aided Instruction *Bold subtitle in 14 point Chicago*

Underline 2nd sentence

Computer programs have become available which instruct students in different academic disciplines. These programs have been especially effective in instructing students in languages and mathematics. When used with elementary school students, computer aided instruction (CAI) has been found to keep students interested in a subject while entertaining them at the same time. This is especially true of programs that employ multimedia -- integrating the computer with devices such as CD players and video disks. Mrs. Groves, a teacher at West Lawrence Elementary School, said, "When used as part of a complete learning system, computers help reinforce skills learned in the classroom."

Applications Programs *Bold subtitle in 14 point Chicago*

Many students are now taking courses which introduce them to applications software. They are taught how to use word processing, database, and spreadsheet software. Most students find that knowing how to use such software can help them in their other courses. Mr. Ronald Johnson of Ivy University said, "Our students are especially interested in learning how to use integrated software like ClarisWorks and Microsoft Works."

Writing Programs *Bold subtitle in 14 point Chicago*

Italicize "BASIC" and "C++"

Students who would like to pursue careers in computing often elect to take courses that teach them how to write computer programs. The languages most often learned are BASIC and C++. Besides teaching programming, these courses teach valuable problem-solving skills.

Lawrence Township Computer Usage *Bold subtitle in 14 point Chicago*

The following table shows the number of computers in Lawrence Township schools and percentage by manufacturer:

Manufacturer	Number	Percent
Apple II	35	7.9%
IBM and clones	187	42.3%
Macintosh	212	48.0%
Other	8	1.8%

b) Create a footer that prints the page number. Right align the footer text.

c) Format the table at the bottom of the document with the following tab stops:

- 3 inch right aligned tab stop (for the number of computers)
- 4¼ inch decimal aligned tab stop (for the percentage of computers)

d) Bold the table titles.

e) Save the modified COMPUTER ED and print a copy.

2. The file named OPENINGS contains several lines that could be used to start a short story. Open OPENINGS.

a) Choose one of the lines, delete the rest, then write a short paragraph using the remaining line as the opening line.

b) Justify and double space the paragraph.

c) Create a title, then format it as 18 point and bold.

d) Create a centered header with your name.

e) Save the modified OPENINGS and print a copy.

3. The SuperSub sandwich shop has just opened a new store in this area. They are creating a flyer and need your help to improve its appearance. Open SUPERSUB.

a) Center and bold the flyer's heading.

b) Change the font for the heading and increase its size to 18 points.

c) Format all occurrences of the word "SUPER" in SUPERSUB as superscript. Format all occurrences of the word "SUB" in SUPERSUB as subscript.

d) Bold each occurrence of the word SUPERSUB.

e) Justify the entire body of the advertisement (do not justify the title).

f) Change the font of all the occurrences of the word "FREE" so it stands out.

g) Insert a superscripted asterisk (*) after the word "FREE!" in the first paragraph. Create a new paragraph at the very bottom of the flyer in a different font and size:

```
*Availability and number of customers may make the offer
null and void. No refunds, rainchecks, or apologies.
```

h) Save the modified SUPERSUB and print a copy.

4. In Chapter Two, Exercise 5 you wrote a review of a movie or concert and saved it in a file named Critic.

   a) Open Critic and make a bold, centered headline that has the name of the event you reviewed.

   b) Italicize any titles in the review, such as the title of a movie, an album or song title, etc.

   c) The paper's editors like all submissions to be doubled spaced. Format the body of your review to conform with their wishes.

   d) Add the centered header CRITIC'S CHOICE.

   e) Justify the body of the review so that it looks more like a newspaper article.

   f) Save the modified Critic and print a copy.

5. Tables make information easier to read and understand. It is a simple process to use tabs to create tables in documents.

   a) In a new word processor file, enter the following data. Precede the first column and separate the opponent column from the record column with a single tab character. After entering the data, set a left aligned tab stop at 2 inches and a right aligned tab stop at 4 inches so that the table appears similar to the following:

Opponent	Record
Audubon	7-4
Cherry Hill East	7-4
Cherry Hill West	4-7
Collingswood	2-8
Gulf Stream	6-5
Haddon Heights	10-1
Pine Crest	8-1

   Note: Your table will not look like the one above until tab stops have been set.

   b) Save the document naming it Table.

   c) Bold the column titles.

   d) Add a third column as shown below. Separate it from the second using a single tab character. After entering the new data, set a centered tab stop at 4¾ inches for the entire table:

Opponent	**Record**	**Division**
Audubon	7-4	I
Cherry Hill East	7-4	IV
Cherry Hill West	4-7	IA
Collingswood	2-8	III
Gulf Stream	6-5	IV
Haddon Heights	10-1	V
Pine Crest	8-1	I

   e) Save the modified Table and print a copy.

6. In Chapter Two, Exercise 4 you created a file named College Apply that contains an application letter for a college. Open College Apply and follow the directions below to create a table in the application letter:

a) Insert two blank lines at the end of the body of the letter, just before the closing.

b) Using single tab characters to precede the first column and separate the remaining columns, enter the table below:

Year	Semester	GPA	Special Activities
1995	Fall	3.6	president of Student Congress
1996	Spring	3.9	captain of Debate Team
1996	Fall	4.0	All-State swim team
1997	Spring	3.95	All-State gymnastics team

Note: Your table will not look like the one above until tab stops have been set.

c) After entering the data, set the following tab stops for the entire table:
   - At 1½" create a left aligned tab stop (for the Year)
   - At 2½" create a centered tab stop (for the Semester)
   - At 3½" create a decimal aligned tab stop (for the GPA)
   - At 4¼" create a left aligned tab stop (for the Special Activities)

d) Save the modified College Apply.

e) Bold the column titles.

f) Double space the first paragraph of the letter.

g) Save the modified College Apply and print a copy.

7. Red Barn petting zoo needs a listing of their farm animals. In a new word processor file, enter the following table, preceding the first column and separating the remaining columns with a single tab character:

Name	Color	Gender	Type
Betsey	Black/White	F	Guernsey cow
Bluebell	Brown	F	Ayrshire cow
Lucy	Brown	F	Morgan horse
Sandy	Tan/White	F	Mustang horse
Toby	White	F	Shetland pony
Harriot	Red	F	Shetland pony
SusieQ	Red	F	Jersey Red hen
Harry	Red	M	Maine Red rooster
Marylou	White	F	Long Island duck
Larry	White	M	Long Island duck

Note: Your table will not look like the one above until tab stops have been set.

a) After entering the data, Set the following tab stops for the entire table:
   - At 1½" create a left aligned tab stop (for the Name)
   - At 2½" create a left aligned tab stop (for the Color)
   - At 3¾" create a center aligned tab stop (for the Gender)
   - At 4¼" create a left aligned tab stop (for the Type)

b) Save the file naming it Red Barn.

c) Create a title above the table which reads: `Red Barn Farm Animal Inventory`

d) Bold and center the title, then bold the column headings.

e) Change the top and bottom margins to 0.75".

f) Add the Location column shown below. Separate it from the fourth column using a single tab character. After entering the new data, set a centered tab stop at 6¾" for the entire table:

Red Barn Farm Animal Inventory				
Name	**Color**	**Gender**	**Type**	**Location**
Betsey	Black/White	F	Guernsey cow	Farm Stall A1
Bluebell	Brown	F	Ayrshire cow	Farm Stall A2
Lucy	Brown	F	Morgan horse	Farm Stall A3
Sandy	Tan/White	F	Mustang horse	Farm Stall B1
Toby	White	F	Shetland pony	Farm Stall B2
Harriot	Red	F	Shetland pony	Farm Stall B3
SusieQ	Red	F	Jersey Red hen	Barn Yard
Harry	Red	M	Maine Red rooster	Barn Yard
Marylou	White	F	Long Island duck	Farm Pond
Larry	White	M	Long Island duck	Farm Pond

g) Save the modified Red Barn and print a copy.

8. The Ivy University literary magazine would like to print the essay you wrote for Chapter Two, Exercise 7. Open Summer Essay and make the following changes:

a) Create a title that describes your essay. Bold and center align the title, then change the point size and font of the title.

b) Double space the body of the essay.

c) Create a header showing your name. Left align the header.

d) Create a footer that prints the page number. Center the page number.

e) Change the top and bottom margins of the paper to 0.75 inches.

f) Save the modified Summer Essay and print a copy.

9. The memo you wrote in Chapter Two, Exercise 11 needs to be formatted. Open Shakespeare Schedule and make the following changes:

a) Create a header showing the course title: `Independent Study of Shakespeare`. Center the header.

b) Format the word "Memorandum" as bold and italic.

c) Underline the words "To," "From," "Date," and "Subject."

d) Italicize the "Paper Topic" and "Due Date" titles.

e) Edit the listing of research papers so that there is a single tab before each paper topic and each due date. Delete any spaces that were previously used to separate the columns.

f) Set the following tab stops for the entire table:
- Centered at 2 inches (for the paper topic)
- Right aligned at 4 inches (for the due date)

The tabs stops could be improved, so they will be changed in the next step.

g) Modify the previous tab stops for the entire table to:
- Right aligned at 2 inches
- Left aligned at 4 inches

h) Delete the tab stops and create new ones for the entire table:
- Left aligned at 1½ inch
- Right aligned at 3¾ inches

i) Insert a blank line between the column titles and the column information.

j) Save the modified Shakespeare Schedule and print a copy.

10. Open Science Bio, which contains the biography you wrote in Chapter Two, Exercise 9 and make the following changes:

a) Create a header showing your name. Center your name.

b) Create a footer showing the page number. Right align the page number.

c) Change the top and bottom margins to 0.75 inches.

d) Center, bold, and underline the title of your paper.

e) Double space the body of the biography.

f) Save the modified Science Bio and print a copy.

11. In Chapter Two, Exercise 8 you created an advertisement for an upcoming event in a file named Advertisement.

a) Open Advertisement and use at least four different formatting options such as tabs, centering, fonts, sizes, and styles to make the advertisement more attractive.

b) Save the modified Advertisement and print a copy.

12. The Gibbon Research Proposal you corrected in Chapter Two, Exercise 12 needs further refinement before it is finished. Open RESEARCH and make the following changes:

a) Center the paragraphs from "A PROPOSAL FOR RESEARCH" up through and including the "University of Eastern Florida" paragraph.

b) Bold the first three paragraphs of the proposal (the first three titles).

c) Change the top and bottom margins to 0.75 inches.

d) Create a footer that prints the word Page followed by the page number. Left align the page number information.

e) Underline the headings: "Summary," "Purpose and Description," "White-handed Gibbons," and "Computerized Guide."

f) Place the cursor in the space above the title "BUDGET" on page 2 and insert a page break.

g) Center the "BUDGET" title and make it bold and a larger point size.

h) Set the following tab stops for the lines containing dollar values:
   • Left aligned at 2 inches
   • Decimal aligned at 6 inches

i) In the Notes section on page 3 insert a tab before each of the funding/support items.

j) Save the modified RESEARCH and print a copy.

13. The store opening you announced in Chapter Two, Exercise 10 needs to be formatted. Open Grand Opening and make the following changes:

a) Bold all occurrences of the store name.

b) Use appropriate paragraph alignment throughout the flyer.

c) Use appropriate tabs throughout the flyer.

d) Since this is a flyer, increase the font size of all the text so that the information fills the page.

e) Save the modified Grand Opening and print a copy.

14. City Zoo keeps a list of their animals in the word processor. Open the CITY ZOO file and make the following changes:

a) Set the following tab stops for the entire table (including column titles):
   • create a 3.5" center aligned tab stop (for the Number/Gender)
   • create a 4.5" left aligned tab stop (for the Type)
   • create a 5" left aligned tab stop (for the Location)
   • create a 7.25" right aligned tab stop (for the Staff)

b) Bold all the column titles in the table.

c) Center the title "City Zoo Catalog" and make it a different font and larger point size.

d) Create a footer that prints Dr. Deborah Lynn - President of City Zoo. Center the footer.

e) Below the listing add the following legend:

   Animal Type
   M - Mammal
   R - Reptile
   B - Bird
   I - Insect
   F - Fish

f) Save the modified CITY ZOO and print a copy.

15. You are to produce a questionnaire that could be used to survey students in your school.

    a) Create a new word processor file and enter a list of at least six survey questions. Each question should be on a separate line to leave room for responses. Include questions concerning personal statistics, favorite course in school, favorite movie or band, and anything else you would like to know.

    b) Save the questionnaire naming it Survey Form.

    c) At the top of the questionnaire, create the title `Student Survey` and make it bold, centered, and in a larger font size.

    d) Change the font of the entire questionnaire. Double space the survey questions.

    e) Create a header that includes your name and the name of the file.

    f) Save the modified Survey Form and print a copy.

16. Open the file Recycle News which you created in Chapter Two, Exercise 14. Improve your article's appearance as follows.

    a) Bold the headline and increase its size to 14 points.

    b) Add your byline (by *your name*) under the headline. Format the byline as italics.

    c) Justify the body of the article.

    d) Add a header with the words `Recycle News` centered and bolded.

    e) Add a footer with the word `Page` and a code for the page number centered.

    f) Save the modified Recycle News and print a copy.

Chapter 4
Advanced Word Processor Techniques

Copy

Paste

Cut

Show Clipboard

Find/Change

Find Again

Check Document Spelling

Check Selection Spelling

Thesaurus

Insert Footnote

Insert Endnote

Insert Date

Insert Time

Word Count

Library

Objectives

After completing this chapter you will be able to:

1. Move and copy highlighted blocks of text.

2. Find and replace text using the Find/Change command.

3. Use the spelling checker to check the spelling of a document.

4. Use the thesaurus to suggest synonyms for words.

5. Indent paragraphs and create hanging indents for bulleted lists.

6. Create and edit footnotes.

7. Time stamp documents.

8. Add graphics to a document and change the graphic's size.

9. Create a multi-column document.

4

This chapter discusses some of the advanced capabilities of the word processor. Editing commands such as Cut, Copy, and Paste are introduced. Specialty features, such as the spelling checker, are also covered.

4.1 Copying and Pasting Blocks of Text

There are times when text needs to be repeated in a publication. Rather than typing the text multiple times, it can be duplicated by using the Copy and Paste commands from the Edit menu. The duplicated text can be as small as a single character or word or as large as several pages.

When the Copy command is executed, highlighted text is copied to a special area of memory called the *Clipboard*. Next, executing the Paste command places a copy of the Clipboard contents at the current cursor position. If the cursor is positioned within existing text, any text after the cursor is automatically moved down to make room for the new block.

Duplicating text is a four step process:

1. Highlight the text to be copied.
2. Execute the Copy command from the Edit menu (⌘**C**).
3. Place the cursor where the copied block is to be inserted.
4. Execute the Paste command from the Edit menu (⌘**U**). A copy of the block is placed at the cursor position.

4.2 Moving Text and Viewing the Clipboard

The Cut command is a powerful editing tool that is used to move highlighted text from one area of a document to another. For example, a sentence can be moved from one paragraph and placed on the next page. Text that is cut is removed from the document and placed on the Clipboard. The space in the document where the cut text was is automatically closed.

Moving a block of text is a four step process very similar to that of duplicating text:

1. Highlight the text to be moved.
2. Execute the Cut command from the Edit menu (⌘**H**). The highlighted text is removed from the screen.
3. Place the cursor where the moved block is to be inserted.
4. Execute the Paste command from the Edit menu (⌘**U**). The previously cut text is inserted into the document at the cursor position.

When text is Cut or Copied, it is moved to a special area in memory called the Clipboard. The Clipboard can only store one block of text at a time, so the next Copy or Cut replaces the contents of the Clipboard with new text. When the Paste command is executed, ClarisWorks copies the information on the Clipboard to the current cursor position. It is possible to view the contents of the Clipboard by selecting the Show Clipboard command from the Edit menu:

4

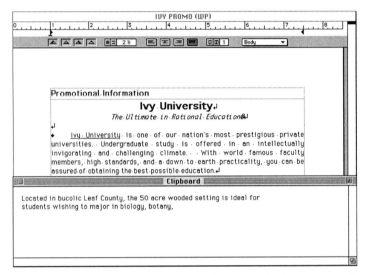

Cut or Copied text can be viewed in the Clipboard window

The Clipboard window can be removed from the screen by clicking on its Close box. Text on the Clipboard cannot be edited, only pasted.

Buttons on the Shortcuts palette can also be used for editing:

Cut

Copy

Paste

Practice 1

In this Practice you will use the Cut, Copy, and Paste commands and the Clipboard. A block consisting of a sentence will be moved, and a paragraph copied. The Clipboard window will be displayed and then closed.

1) START CLARISWORKS AND OPEN IVY PROMO

a. Following the directions given in Chapter Two, boot the System.
b. If necessary, double-click on the ClarisWorks folder to open it.
c. Double-click on the ClarisWorks icon to start ClarisWorks. The New Document dialog box is displayed.
d. Select **Cancel** to remove the dialog box.
e. From the File menu, select Open. In the Open dialog box, double-click on IVY PROMO to open it.
f. From the File menu, drag down to Shortcuts. From the submenu shown, select Show Shortcuts. The Shortcuts palette is displayed.
g. On the Shortcuts palette, click on the Show Invisibles button ([🔊]) to display special symbols if they are not already shown.

An Introduction to Computing Using ClarisWorks

2) HIGHLIGHT THE BLOCK TO BE MOVED

  a. Place the cursor at the beginning of the sentence which begins "There is a reaction…" in the second paragraph. Do not include the space before the "T."

  b. Drag the mouse down and to the right to highlight the sentence, making sure to include in the block the period at the end of the sentence and the space after the period.

3) MOVE THE HIGHLIGHTED BLOCK

  a. From the Edit menu, select the Cut command. The text is removed from the screen and placed on the Clipboard.

  b. Place the cursor before the "W" that begins the sentence "With world famous…" in the first paragraph.

  c. From the Edit menu, select the Paste command. The sentence is inserted in the paragraph at the cursor position.

4) HIGHLIGHT THE BLOCK TO BE COPIED

You will produce a copy of the first paragraph at the end of the document. Place the cursor in the first paragraph and click the mouse button four times in rapid succession to highlight the entire paragraph.

5) COPY THE HIGHLIGHTED BLOCK

  a. Execute the Copy command using the keyboard shortcut ⌘**C**.

  b. Use the scroll bars and mouse to place the cursor after the period in the last sentence in the document.

  c. Press the Return key twice to insert a blank line and create a new paragraph.

  d. Paste the block using the shortcut ⌘**U**. The paragraph is inserted at the bottom of the document:

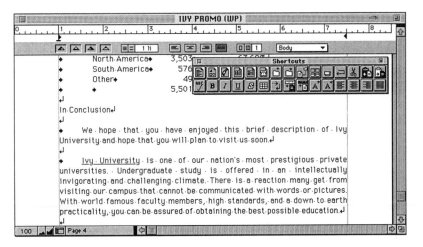

  e. Scroll to the top of the document and verify that the original paragraph is still there.

6) VIEW THE CONTENTS OF THE CLIPBOARD

  a. From the Edit menu, select the Show Clipboard command. The Clipboard window is displayed on the screen. The text on the Clipboard was placed there by the last Copy command.

  b. Remove the Clipboard window by clicking on its Close box.

7) SAVE IVY PROMO

The Find/Change command is used to scan a document for *search text*. This text may be a single character, word, or phrase. Selecting the Find/Change command from the Find/Change submenu in the Edit menu (⌘**F**) displays a dialog box where search text is typed:

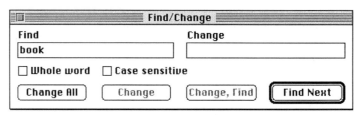

Search text is typed in the Find box

In this case, the word "book" has been entered as the search text. When **Find Next** is selected, ClarisWorks starts searching from the current cursor position and continues through the document looking for the search text. If a match is found, ClarisWorks stops scanning and highlights the text. To continue searching the document, the **Find Next** button is selected again. If the search text is not found, a message similar to the following is displayed:

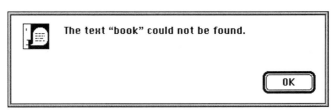

ClarisWorks could not find the search text "book"

The **Whole word** option in the Find/Change dialog box is used when occurrences of the search text that are not part of another word are to be found. For example, specifying a search text of `the` will not only find "the" but also words which contain a "the" such as `they`, `theory`, `another`, etc. unless **Whole word** is selected.

The **Case sensitive** option is used when text with the same capitalization as the search text is to be found. For example, a **Case sensitive** search for `CAT` will not find `Cat` or `cat`. The **Case sensitive** and **Whole word** options can be used together to perform a very precise find.

On some occasions, the search text may be displayed behind the Find/Change dialog box. When this occurs, it is possible to move the dialog box by dragging on its Title bar. Clicking on the Close box of the dialog box terminates the search and the last search text found is left highlighted.

Selecting the Find Again command, also in the Find/Change submenu (⌘**E**), searches a document using the same search text and options last used in the Find/Change dialog box.

Search text can also be defined by highlighting. For example, double-clicking on the word `Ivy` in the IVY PROMO file used in the practices highlights the word. The Find Selection command from the Find/Change submenu (⇧⌘**E**) can then be used to find the next occurrence of `Ivy`.

4.4 Finding Special Characters

Special characters such as tab and paragraph characters can also be found using the Find/Change command. For example, suppose you wish to locate only occurrences of the word Because if it is at the beginning of a paragraph. If all paragraphs in the current document are indented with a single tab, a more precise search would include the tab character before the word because:

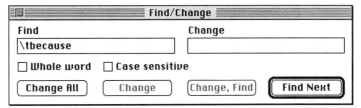

Find Next highlights the next "because" preceded by a tab

As shown in the dialog box above, a tab character is represented by typing \t. Entering \p as the search text finds the paragraph marker (return character).

4.5 Going to a Specific Page

Double-clicking on the page indicator in the lower-left corner of the screen displays the Go to page dialog box:

Go to page may be used to move quickly to a specific page

Typing a page number and then selecting **OK** displays that page. This can be much quicker than using the arrow keys or scroll bars, especially when the document is long. Once the desired page is displayed, the mouse can be used to place the cursor on that page.

A benefit of this command is that it can be used to limit the amount of text that is checked by the Find/Change command. For example, if you wish to locate the occurrence of text, such as a name, which is on page 15 or later, you can use the Go to page dialog box to display page 15 and then click the mouse at the top of the page to place the cursor. Executing the Find/Change command begins a search from the current cursor position.

Practice 2

This Practice demonstrates the Find/Change command. The Go to page dialog box will also be used to display a page. You will begin by searching for each occurrence of the word "bandage" in the Ivy University promotional file. Start ClarisWorks if you have not already done so and open IVY PROMO.

1) EXECUTE THE FIND/CHANGE COMMAND

a. Make sure that the cursor is at the top of the IVY PROMO document.
b. From the Edit menu, select the Find/Change command from the Find/Change submenu. The Find/Change dialog box is displayed.

2) ENTER THE SEARCH TEXT

a. Type the word Bandage (with a capital "B") in the **Find** box and select the **Find Next** button. There is a slight pause as ClarisWorks searches the document. The first "bandage" found is in the course description for class 101.
b. If the search text found is not visible, it may be covered by the Find/Change dialog box. Drag on the Title bar of the dialog box to move it to a new position. Note that "Bandage" is highlighted in the text.

3) REPEAT THE FIND USING THE SAME SEARCH TEXT

a. To repeat the command using the same search text, simply select the **Find Next** button in the Find/Change dialog box. The cursor moves to the next occurrence of "bandage." Move the dialog box if necessary to view the search text.
b. Select **Find Next** again. Note that the highlighted word is "bandage" with a lowercase "b" even though the search text is "Bandage."
c. Continue to select **Find Next** until the first occurrence of the word "bandage" is again found (the course description for class 101). Move the dialog box as necessary to view the highlighted text. How many did you find?
d. Remove the Find/Change dialog box by clicking on its Close box. Note how the last occurrence found remains highlighted in the text.

4) GO DIRECTLY TO THE TOP OF PAGE 1

a. Double-click on the page indicator in the lower-left corner of the screen. The Go to page dialog box is displayed.
b. Select **OK** to go to page 1, the default page. The top of page 1 is displayed. Move the I-Beam pointer so that it is at the beginning of the document (before the Ivy University title). Click the mouse to place the insertion point.

5) MODIFY THE SEARCH TEXT

a. Press ⌘**F** to execute the Find/Change command. The previously entered text is displayed in the **Find** box.
b. Click on the **Case sensitive** option so that only "Bandage" with a capital "B" will be found.
c. Select the **Find Next** button. Note how the highlighted search text has an uppercase "B."
d. Continue to select **Find Next** until all occurrences of "Bandage" have been found. How many did you find? Note how a more specific search has been created by using the available options.
e. Close the Find/Change dialog box.

6) SEARCH FOR A SPECIAL CHARACTER

a. Use the Show Invisibles button on the Shortcuts palette to display symbols for normally invisible characters if they are not already displayed.

b. We want to locate all occurrences of the word "Ivy" which begin a paragraph. We can do this by searching for a tab, and then the word. Move the cursor to the top of the document.

c. Display the Find/Change dialog box and type `\t` to start the search text with a tab. Type the word `ivy`.

d. Click on the **Case sensitive** option to deselect it. Your dialog box should look like the following:

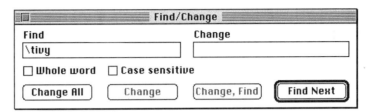

e. Select **Find Next** to start the search. The first "ivy" located is in the first sentence of the first paragraph. Note how the tab symbol is also highlighted.

f. Continue to select **Find Next** until all occurrences of the search text have been found. How many did you find?

g. Remove the Find/Change dialog box by clicking on its Close box.

4.6 Replacing Text

The Find/Change command can also be used to locate text and then replace it with another piece of text you supply called the *replace text*. This makes it easy to create different versions of the same document. For example, ClarisWorks could be used to create a letter requesting an admissions interview with Ivy University. After printing the letter, the Find/Change command could then be used to change each occurrence of "Ivy University" to "Trenton State" and the new letter printed. Then "Trenton State" could be changed to "New Brunswick College" and so on. Thus, all the letters could be easily created without having to type each one separately; the master letter is typed once and the name of the school changed using Find/Change:

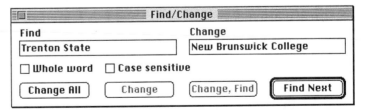

ClarisWorks will search for "Trenton State" and replace it with "New Brunswick College"

The Find/Change command starts from the current cursor position. Tab and paragraph characters may be used in either the search or replace text.

The **Whole word** option is used when occurrences of the search text that are not part of another word are to be replaced. The **Case sensitive** option is used when text that has the same capitalization as the search text is to be replaced.

Find Next must be selected to find the first occurrence of the search text. After the first occurrence has been found, the **Change, Find** button and the **Change** button are no longer dimmed. Selecting **Change, Find** replaces the currently highlighted text with the replace text and then finds the next occurrence of the search text. Clicking the **Change** button simply changes the search text with the replace text. These buttons allow each replacement to be verified before it is made. The Find/Change dialog box also has the option of replacing all occurrences with the new text automatically using the **Change All** button. It is usually not advisable to use this button because it may make unwanted changes, and it is not possible to Undo this action.

Practice 3

Ivy University is considering updating its image by changing its name. This Practice will use the Find/Change command to change each occurrence of "Ivy University" to "Modern College" in IVY PROMO. This will allow the administration to see how the document looks with the new name. If you have not already done so, start ClarisWorks and open IVY PROMO.

1) EXECUTE THE FIND/CHANGE COMMAND

    a. Make sure the cursor is at the beginning of IVY PROMO and page one displayed.
    b. From the Edit menu, select the Find/Change command from the Find/Change submenu. In the dialog box note that some search text and options may be displayed from the previous Practice.
    c. Type Ivy University for the **Find** text, replacing any old search text.
    d. Press the Tab key once to move the cursor to the **Change** box and type Modern College.
    e. Select the **Find Next** button to highlight the first occurrence of Ivy University.

2) REPLACE EACH OCCURRENCE

    a. ClarisWorks moves the cursor to the first occurrence of Ivy University and highlights it. Move the dialog box, if necessary, so that the highlighted text is visible.
    b. Click on the **Change** button to replace the highlighted text with Modern College. The change is made on screen. Note how any formatting options (font, size, etc.) are retained.
    c. Select the **Find Next** button to highlight the next occurrence of Ivy University.
    d. Click on the **Change, Find** button. ClarisWorks changes the highlighted occurrence and then highlights the next occurrence of the find text.
    e. For each Ivy University found, click on the **Change, Find** button to make the replacement and then locate the next occurrence. When all occurrences of Ivy University have been replaced, the following message is displayed:

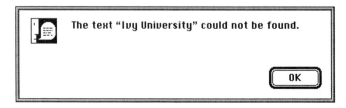

An Introduction to Computing Using ClarisWorks

Select **OK**. All occurrences of Ivy University have been changed to Modern College.

f. Remove the Find/Change dialog box by clicking on its Close box. Scroll through the document to verify the changes.

3) REPLACE ALL OCCURRENCES OF MODERN COLLEGE

a. University officials have decided against the name change. From the Edit menu, execute the Find/Change command.

b. Type `Modern College` in the **Find** box and `Ivy University` in the **Change** box.

c. Select the **Change All** button. Because this feature can make unwanted changes that cannot be reversed, a warning dialog box is displayed:

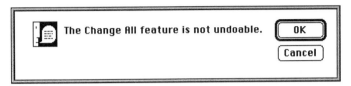

Select **OK** to replace all of the occurrences of the search text with the find text.

d. ClarisWorks displays a dialog box indicating the number of occurrences replaced. Select **OK** to remove the dialog box.

e. Click on the Close box in the Find/Change dialog box. Scroll through the document to verify that all occurrences of Modern College have been replaced by Ivy University.

4) SAVE IVY PROMO

4.7 Using the Spelling Checker

One of the most useful features of a word processor is its ability to check the spelling of the words in a document. In ClarisWorks, this is accomplished using the Check Document Spelling command from the Writing Tools submenu (⌘=) in the Edit menu. The Check Spelling button on the Shortcuts palette (▧) can also be used. When spelling is checked, each word in a document is compared to words in a dictionary file. If a word is not found in the dictionary it is displayed in a dialog box:

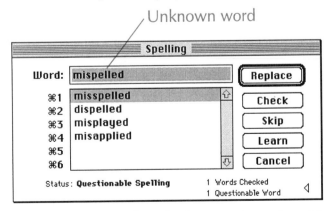

Check Document Spelling displays words not found in the ClarisWorks dictionary in this dialog box

From the Spelling dialog box you can type a correction in the **Word** box or select a correctly spelled word from a list of suggestions, and then select **Replace** to make the correction in the document.

Because the dictionary file does not contain every word in the English language, it is possible that the spelling command will not find a correctly spelled word, such as a proper name or abbreviation. When this happens, **Skip** can be selected to ignore the word. If the word is one that you will use often, such as your name, you can have ClarisWorks add it to a dictionary file by selecting **Learn**.

After ClarisWorks has checked the entire document, including any header, footer, and footnotes, a **Done** button appears in place of the **Replace** button. Selecting **Done** removes the Spelling dialog box. After using the spelling command to correct words, you must save the file in order to make the corrections permanent.

The Spelling dialog box may obscure the word currently in question. However, the Spelling dialog box can be expanded to show the questionable word as it appears in the document:

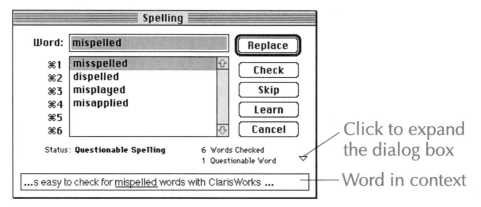

*It is easier to determine the correct spelling of a word
when it is viewed in context*

Clicking again on the triangle reduces the dialog box to its original size.

It is possible to limit the number of words checked by first highlighting a section of text. Executing the Check Selection Spelling command from the Writing Tools submenu (⇧⌘Y) tells ClarisWorks to check only the highlighted words. When the spelling check is complete, select **Done** to remove the dialog box.

Practice 4

Ivy University is about to have 50,000 copies of its promotional file printed. This Practice uses the Check Document Spelling command to verify the spelling in that document before sending it to the print shop. Start ClarisWorks if you have not already done so and open IVY PROMO.

1) EXECUTE THE SPELLING COMMAND

a. From the Edit menu, select the Check Document Spelling command from the Writing Tools submenu to start the spelling check. There is a slight pause as ClarisWorks checks the spelling. ClarisWorks finds a word that may be misspelled and displays it in the Spelling dialog box.

b. Click on the triangle in the Spelling dialog box to see the questionable word in context:

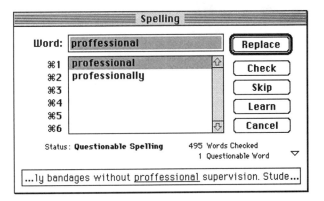

2) CORRECT THE MISSPELLED WORD

ClarisWorks finds the word "proffessional", checks its dictionary file, and highlights the most probable spelling "professional." Because "professional" is the word we want, click on the **Replace** button to accept the suggested spelling and have it replace the misspelled word in the file. ClarisWorks makes the correction and continues to check the spelling.

3) CORRECT THE NEXT MISSPELLED WORD

a. ClarisWorks finds the word "Decy" and suggests the spelling "Dewy."
b. Because the suggestion is not the one we want, click on the down scroll arrow to scroll through the list and locate the correct spelling, "Decay."
c. Double-click on "Decay" to replace the misspelled word with it.

4) SKIP THE NUMBER AND PROPER NAMES

a. The next word in question is "20th". Click on **Skip** to ignore this text.
b. Click on the **Skip** button to ignore the correct spelling of the name "Phineas."
c. Continue to **Skip** any proper names.
d. **Skip** the chemical formula $C_2H_5OH^3$.
e. Continue to **Skip** any proper names.
f. When the spelling check is finished the **Done** button is displayed and the other buttons are dim. Click on **Done** to remove the dialog box.

5) SAVE IVY PROMO

4.8 Using the Thesaurus

Using a *thesaurus* can help make your writing more interesting. A thesaurus is a collection of *synonyms*, which are words that have similar meanings. For example, chilly is a synonym for cool. ClarisWorks contains a built-in thesaurus that supplies synonyms for many words and phrases. To display a list of synonyms for a word, highlight the word and then select the Thesaurus command from the Writing Tools submenu (⇧⌘Z):

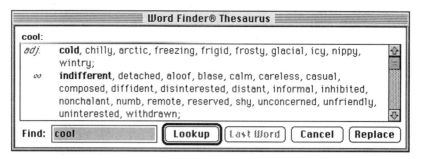

The Thesaurus command displays synonyms for a selected word

Because words can have different definitions, ClarisWorks provides a list of synonyms identified by their parts of speech (adjective, noun, verb, etc.). In the dialog box above, adjectives are displayed in the list of synonyms. The ∞ indicates a slightly different variation of the word but of the same part of speech. A word in the list can be highlighted by clicking on it. Selecting **Replace** replaces the word in the document with the highlighted meaning or synonym. Selecting **Cancel** removes the dialog box, leaving the word unchanged.

ClarisWorks displays additional synonyms for any of the suggested synonyms by highlighting the word in the list and selecting **Lookup**. This procedure may be continued for as many words as desired. In order to return to a previous list of synonyms, click the **Last Word** button to display the LAST WORDS dialog box:

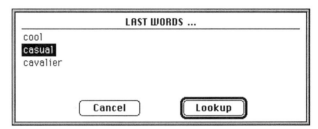

*The LAST WORDS dialog box displays a list of words that
have been previously looked up*

Clicking on a word in the dialog box and then selecting **Lookup** displays the list of synonyms for that word.

Like the dictionary, ClarisWorks uses a file for its thesaurus which does not contain every possible word. If the selected word cannot be found, a dialog box similar to the following is displayed:

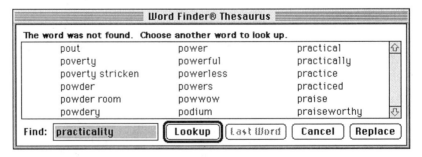

*When a selected word is not found, an alphabetical list
of words that are close in spelling is displayed*

This is especially useful if you have misspelled the original word. For example, if you highlight "bucholic" and execute the Thesaurus command, ClarisWorks shows "bucolic" in a list. Clicking on bucolic and then selecting **Lookup** provides a list of synonyms. However, this ability is limited and will not find a severely misspelled word. It is a good practice to check the spelling of a document before using the thesaurus.

It is important to realize that the thesaurus will only replace the highlighted word or phrase. For example, the word "bucolic" might appear five times in a document. However, only the highlighted one will be replaced with the selected synonym. Multiple occurrences can be replaced using the Find/Change command. After using the thesaurus to change words, you must save the file to make the changes permanent.

Practice 5

In this Practice you will use the thesaurus to suggest synonyms for two words. Start ClarisWorks and open IVY PROMO if you have not already done so.

1) LOCATE THE WORD TO BE CHANGED

Double-click on the word "major" in the sentence which begins "A major part of successful treatment..." near the top of page two.

2) EXECUTE THE THESAURUS COMMAND

From the Edit menu, drag down to the Writing Tools command. From the sub-menu, select the Thesaurus command. The dialog box is displayed:

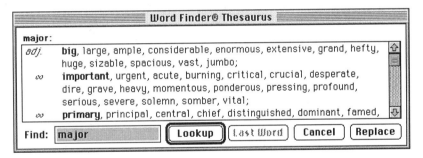

3) SELECT THE DESIRED SYNONYM AND REPLACE THE WORD

a. The definition of "major" that is being used in the sentence is most similar to "important." From this group of synonyms, click on "vital" to select it.
b. Click on the **Replace** button. The word "major" is replaced with "vital" and the box removed.

4) CHANGE THE WORD "COMMON"

a. Double-click on the word "common" in the description for course 101 to select it.
b. Execute the Thesaurus command by pressing ⇧⌘Z. "Common" has many meanings.
c. Scroll through the list to view the different synonyms.
d. Click on the meaning "typical" near the end of the list and then select **Lookup** to get another list of synonyms.
e. Select "prevalent" from the list of synonyms and click on **Replace**. The word "Common" is changed to "prevalent" in the document.

5) SAVE IVY PROMO

Margin settings apply to the entire document and cannot change from paragraph to paragraph. However, it is possible to decrease the width of the text lines in a specific paragraph by using *indents*. Indents are often used to set off a paragraph, such as a quotation.

The default indents are 0 inches, meaning that lines extend from the left margin to the right margin. Specifying left and right indents causes a paragraph to have a shorter line length:

```
This is a normal paragraph. Each full line extends
from  the  left  margin  to  the  right  margin.

        This paragraph is indented. The
        lines of text extend from the left
        to the right indent, making a shorter
        line length.
```

Indents may be set using the markers below the Ruler:

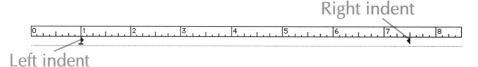

The indent markers appear below the Ruler

Dragging an indent marker to a new position sets an indent for the paragraph which currently contains the cursor or for the highlighted block of paragraphs. When the cursor is moved through the text, the markers below the Ruler change to show the indents for the current paragraph.

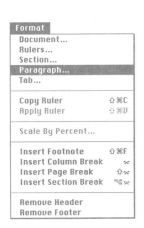

The Paragraph command from the Format menu can also be used to set indents. For example, 1 inch left and right indents would be created by typing 1 in the **Left Indent** box and 1 in the **Right Indent** box:

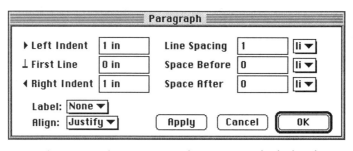

Indents may be set using the Paragraph dialog box

Clicking on **Apply** changes the indents in the document without removing the dialog box. The **OK** button is selected to apply the changes and remove the dialog box.

Practice 6

In this Practice you will set and change paragraph indents. Start ClarisWorks and open IVY PROMO if you have not already done so.

1) CREATE PARAGRAPH INDENTS

   a. Place the cursor in the paragraph which begins "The modern world around us...," the quote below the faculty listing at the bottom of page 3.

   b. Place the mouse pointer on the left indent marker (▶) below the Ruler. Drag the marker to the 2 inch point on the Ruler. Release the mouse button and the current paragraph is reformatted with a 1 inch left indent.

   c. Drag the right indent marker to the 7 inch point. The paragraph now has a right indent of 0.5 inches.

   d. Move the cursor out of the quote paragraph. Note how the positions of the indent markers change.

2) CHANGE THE LEFT INDENT

   a. Move the cursor back into the quote paragraph.

   b. From the Format menu, select the Paragraph command. The Paragraph dialog box is displayed.

   c. Type 0.5 in the **Left Indent** box. Select **Apply**. Note how the paragraph is reformatted on the screen.

   d. Change the **Left Indent** to 0.75. Select **OK**. Note the position of the indent marker on the Ruler.

3) SAVE IVY PROMO

<u>Check</u> - Your screen should be similar to:

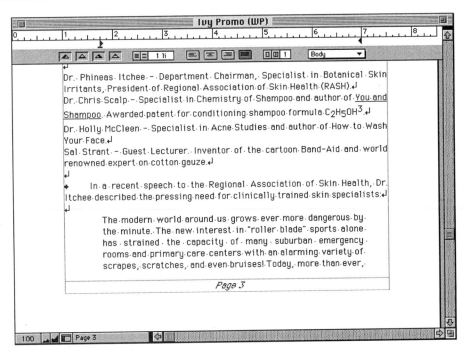

4.10 Hanging Indents and Bulleted Lists

A special type of indent is the *hanging indent*. As the name implies, the first line of this indent hangs out to the left over the lines below it. Hanging indents are useful when preparing lists, creating outlines, or including a standard bibliography in a research paper. Below is a bibliography entry using a hanging indent:

Canine, Butch S. <u>My Life as a Dog: A True-Life Story</u>.
New York: Sirius Press, 1993.

The first line, which contains the author's name, sticks out from the rest of the bibliography entry.

Below the Ruler, the left indent marker is split into two pieces. An inverted T represents the first line indent and the triangle (▶) represents the left indent for the rest of the paragraph:

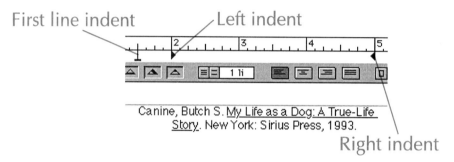

A negative first line indent creates the hanging effect

The first line marker can be dragged freely to either the left or the right of the left indent marker, within the document's margins. Moving the left indent marker (▶) also moves the first line marker, even when the two are separated.

A first line indent can also be set using the Paragraph command. To create a hanging indent, a negative first line indent is entered in the Paragraph dialog box:

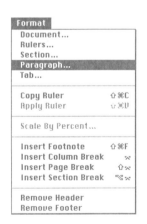

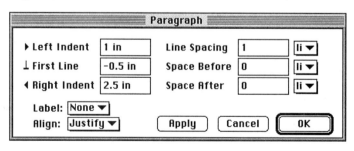

These measurements will produce a hanging indent with the first line ½ inch to the left of the remaining lines of the paragraph

4

A special use for the hanging indent is in the creation of *bulleted lists*. A bulleted list is a unique way to vertically list separate items, sentences, or paragraphs using a special symbol or character to introduce each line. The following is an example of a bulleted list:

Today's Lunch Specials

- *Pizza Bianca* - A delicate blend of four imported cheeses with fresh Italian herbs on a thin, crispy crust.
- *Insalata di Pollo* - Oak grilled chicken breast served with fresh salad greens, mozzarella, roasted peppers, and olives in a light vinaigrette.
- *Veal Chop* - Mesquite grilled with mushrooms.

In a bulleted list each item is a separate paragraph formatted with a hanging indent. After creating the hanging indent, a bullet character such as an asterisk or the `Option+8` character is added to draw attention to each item of the list. A tab is used after the bullet to align the first line with the rest of the paragraph:

Tab

•➡ *Pizza Bianca* - A delicate blend of four imported cheeses with fresh Italian herbs on a thin, crispy crust.↵ —— Return
•➡ *Insalata di Pollo* - Oak grilled chicken breast served with fresh salad greens, mozzarella, roasted peppers, and olives in a light vinaigrette.↵
•➡ *Veal Chop* - Mesquite grilled with mushrooms.↵

Bulleted lists do not show order of importance within the list; each item is equally important. *Numbered lists* show a priority of importance and should be used, for example, when listing steps in a recipe. Tabs and hanging indents are also used to create numbered lists. The following recipe is an example of a numbered list created with a hanging indent:

1. Pour chicken broth into saucepan and bring to a boil.
2. Add noodles and cook for 5-7 minutes, stirring occasionally.
3. Reduce heat and add chicken chunks. Let simmer for 3-4 minutes.
4. Serve immediately with crackers.

Numbers are used as the "bullets" for this recipe because each step logically follows the previous one.

Practice 7

In this Practice you will create a bulleted list in the course description of IVY PROMO using hanging indents. Start ClarisWorks and open IVY PROMO if you have not already done so. Use the Show Invisibles button on the Shortcuts palette to display special symbols if they are not already displayed.

1) SCROLL TO THE COURSE DESCRIPTIONS

Scroll to the course descriptions and place the cursor in the paragraph describing course 101, which begins "A comprehensive survey...."

2) SET LEFT AND RIGHT INDENTS

a. Using the Ruler as a guide, drag the left indent marker to the 1¾ inch mark.

b. Drag the right indent marker to the 7¼ inch mark. The paragraph is now indented 0.75 inches on the left and 0.25 inches on the right.

3) CREATE THE HANGING INDENT

a. Make sure that the cursor is still in the course 101 description paragraph.

b. Drag the first line indent marker (the line below the left indent marker) towards the left, to the 1½ inch mark, creating a hanging indent:

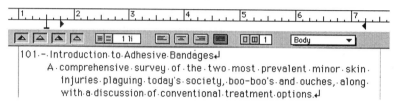

Note the shape of the first line indent marker. It is actually an inverted T. This is not apparent when the first line and left indents are the same.

4) ADD THE BULLET

a. Move the cursor to the left of the first character in the current paragraph, the "A" in "A comprehensive survey...."

b. Hold down the Option key and press the 8 key to create a bullet.

c. The bullet must be separated from the first word in the paragraph. Press the Tab key to insert a tab between the bullet and the "A." This aligns the text in the first line with the rest of the indented paragraph. The course description paragraph is now a bulleted list:

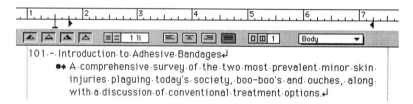

5) BULLET THE NEXT COURSE DESCRIPTION

a. Place the cursor in the paragraph describing course 102, which begins "A complete and systematic...."

b. From the Format menu, select the Paragraph command. Indents will be set using the Paragraph dialog box.

c. In the **Left Indent** box, type 0.75. Type -0.25 for the **First Line**, and 0.25 for the **Right Indent**. Select **OK** to remove the dialog box.

d. At the beginning of the paragraph, type a bullet and then press Tab to align the text. The course description for 102 now has the same format as course 101.

6) FORMAT THE REMAINING COURSES

Follow the instructions in step 5 to format the seven remaining course descriptions.

7) SAVE IVY PROMO

An Introduction to Computing Using ClarisWorks

4.11 Creating Footnotes and Endnotes

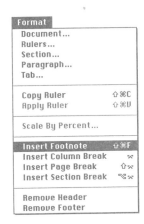

Research papers and reports often include *footnotes* to document sources. Selecting the Insert Footnote command from the Format menu (⇧⌘F) adds a number at the current cursor position and then adds the same number at the bottom of the page. The cursor is automatically placed to the right of the footnote number at the bottom of the page so that the footnote can be entered:

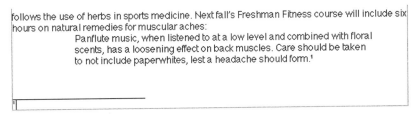

A short horizontal line separates footnotes from the rest of the text

Footnote text can be edited and formatted like any other text. To return the cursor to the document, simply click the I-Beam pointer in the text. To place the cursor back in the footnote, click the I-Beam pointer in the footnote text.

ClarisWorks sequentially numbers footnotes. A document's footnotes are automatically renumbered when one of its footnotes is moved, copied, or deleted. Deleting a footnote number in the text also removes the reference from the bottom of the page.

Endnotes appear separately on the last page of a document, and can be used instead of footnotes. To document sources in endnotes, select the **At End of Document** option from the Document dialog box:

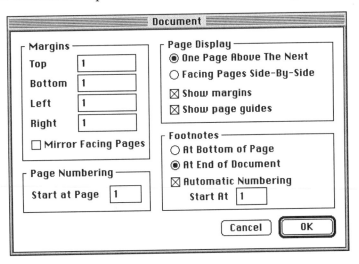

Footnote options are available in the Document dialog box

When this option is selected, the Format menu contains an Insert Endnote command that works similarly to the Insert Footnote command. Existing footnotes are converted to endnotes when the **At End of Document** option is selected.

Practice 8

In this Practice you will create a footnote. Start ClarisWorks and open IVY PROMO if you have not already done so. Use the Show Invisibles button on the Shortcuts palette to display special symbols if they are not already displayed.

1) LOCATE THE TEXT TO FOOTNOTE

At the top of page 4, the quote by Dr. Itchee that starts "The modern world…" needs to be properly referenced. Place the cursor at the end of the quote, just after the period ending "…skin care specialists."

2) EXECUTE THE INSERT FOOTNOTE COMMAND

From the Format menu, select the Insert Footnote command. ClarisWorks inserts a superscripted "1" in the text and moves the cursor to the bottom of the page where the footnote text may be entered. Note the horizontal line separating the reference from the rest of the text.

3) ENTER THE FOOTNOTE TEXT

Type the following text:

```
Dr. Phineas Itchee, "Keynote Address," 15th Annual RASH
Conference, Crane Hotel, Cincinnati, 15 Oct. 1996.
```

4) FORMAT THE FOOTNOTE TEXT

a. Highlight all the footnote text.
b. Change the font to Geneva to match the rest of the text in the document.

5) SCROLL THE DOCUMENT

a. Move the I-Beam pointer so that it is in the paragraph above the footnote.
b. Click the mouse to place the cursor.
c. If it is not currently visible, scroll to the end of Dr. Itchee's quote. Note the superscript "1" that ClarisWorks has placed at the end of the quote.

6) EDIT THE FOOTNOTE

a. Scroll down until the footnote is visible.
b. Move the I-Beam pointer into the footnote and then click the mouse. The cursor is now in the footnote.
c. Highlight the "th" in "15th."
d. From the Style menu, select the Superscript command.
e. Create a first line indent of ½ inch for the footnote.

Check - The footnote should look similar to the following:

> ¹·Dr.·Phineas·Itchee,·"Keynote·Address,"·15th·Annual·RASH·Conference,·Crane·Hotel,·
> Cincinnati,·15·Oct.·1996.
>
> *Page 4*

7) SAVE AND PRINT IVY PROMO

Save IVY PROMO and then print a copy of the entire document.

4.12 Time Stamping Files

It is easier to keep track of printed documents when they have a time stamp. A *time stamp* can include the current date as well as the current time.

ClarisWorks provides an easy way to time stamp a document using two commands from the Edit menu. The Insert Date command places the current date at the cursor position, and the Insert Time command places the current time. A time stamp may resemble the following:

```
6/27/96   8:35 PM
```

These dates and times are not composed of separate characters, but are instead codes. When the file is opened or printed, the date and time codes are automatically updated.

Placing a time stamp in the header or footer of a document is even better because the information appears on each page.

4.13 Counting Words

It can be useful to know the number of words, lines, and paragraphs contained in a document. For example, journalists often *write for space*, which means writing to fill a precise amount of newspaper or publication space. Some student assignments also require a certain number of words. Dragging down to the Writing Tools command in the Edit menu and then selecting the Word Count command from the submenu displays document statistics in a dialog box:

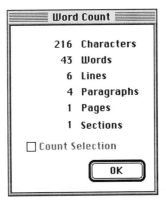

Document statistics are displayed in the Word Count dialog box

To display statistics for a portion of a document, simply highlight the desired text, execute the Word Count command, and then select the **Count Selection** option in the Word Count dialog box.

A word processor document that includes graphics is usually more interesting and informative. Because of this, ClarisWorks provides libraries of graphics. Dragging down to the Library command in the File menu displays the names of available libraries:

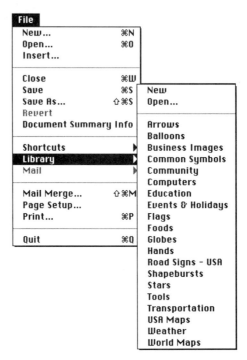

The Library submenu displays the names of available libraries

A *library* is a group of related items displayed on a palette. For example, selecting the Business Images command displays the following library palette:

The items on the Business Images library palette are related to offices and businesses

A preview of the highlighted graphic is displayed at the top of the palette. Clicking **Use** places the selected object at the current cursor position. Graphics can be inserted anywhere in a word processor document, including the header and footer. Once inserted, a graphic can be resized by clicking once on it and then dragging its size box:

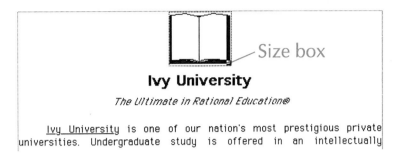

Graphics can be added and resized in a word processor document

Formatting features such as paragraph alignment and tab stops can be used to change the placement of a graphic.

Practice 9

In this Practice you will insert a picture and add a time stamp to the document's header. Start ClarisWorks if you have not already done so and open IVY PROMO.

1) INSERT A PICTURE

   a. Move the pointer so that it is just to the left of "Ivy" in the first line (the title) of the document. Click the mouse to create an insertion point.

   b. From the File menu, drag down to the Library command. From the submenu, select the Education command. The Education palette is displayed.

   c. On the Education palette list, click on Graduation Cap. A preview of the Graduation Cap graphic is displayed.

   d. On the Education palette, click on the **Use** button. The Graduation Cap graphic is inserted to the left of the title.

   e. Close the Education palette by clicking on its Close box.

   f. Press the Return key to move the title to the next line. Note how the graphic is centered because the paragraph is formatted for center alignment.

2) CHANGE THE SIZE OF THE GRAPHIC

   a. Move the I-Beam pointer so that it is on top of the graphic.

   b. Click the mouse button. The dotted lines around the graphic indicate that it is selected.

   c. Place the pointer on the black box in the lower-right corner of the graphic. The I-Beam pointer changes to an arrow shape.

   d. With the arrow-shaped pointer on the size box, drag the size box. Note how the dotted lines move with the mouse to indicate the size of the graphic. When the graphic is slightly larger, release the mouse button.

Check - The first page of your document should look similar to the following:

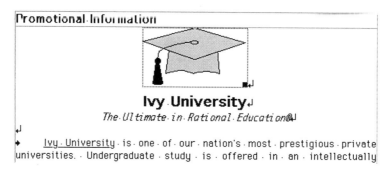

3) INSERT THE DATE AND TIME IN THE HEADER

    a. Scroll to display the header in page 1 of the document if it is not already shown.

    b. Place the I-Beam pointer just to the right of "Information" and click the mouse to create an insertion point. Press the spacebar to enter a space.

    c. From the Edit menu, select the Insert Date command. The current date is inserted at the current cursor position.

    d. Type a space to separate the date and time.

    e. From the Edit menu, select the Insert Time command. The time is inserted at the cursor.

    f. Drag the pointer over the date and attempt to highlight just the day. Because the displayed date and time are codes for the actual date and time, it is impossible to highlight just a character—either the entire date or entire time is highlighted or nothing is.

4) DISPLAY DOCUMENT STATISTICS

    a. Click the I-Beam pointer in the main body of the text to place the cursor.

    b. From the Edit menu, drag down to the Writing Tools submenu. From the submenu, select the Word Count command. A dialog box is displayed. How many words and paragraphs does IVY PROMO contain?

    c. Select **OK** to remove the dialog box.

5) DEMONSTRATE HOW THE TIME STAMP IS UPDATED

    a. Save IVY PROMO.

    b. The time stamp will be updated each time the document is opened or printed. Carefully note the current time, especially the minutes.

    c. From the File menu, select Print. Change the **Pages** options so that only the first page of the document is printed by typing a 1 in the **From** and **To** boxes. Select **Print** to print the first page. Note the time in the header printed at the top of the page. Also note that the document has been updated on the screen.

6) CLOSE IVY PROMO

4.15 Columns

Columns are commonly used in newspapers, newsletters, magazines, and similar publications to make text easier to read. The column controls in the Format bar are used to format a document for multiple columns. Clicking on the Increase columns control (▥) adds one column to the document. For example, a two column document is created by clicking once on the Increase columns control. A three column document is creating by clicking twice on the Increase columns control. All previously learned formatting features may be applied to columns of text—character formats, paragraph formats, footnotes, etc. The Decrease columns control (▣) removes one column from the document each time it is clicked.

The white space between columns is referred to as the *gutter*. The space not allocated to gutters is divided between the columns. The width of two adjacent columns can be changed by moving the gutter. To move a gutter, place the mouse pointer in the gutter, then press and hold the Option key while dragging the mouse:

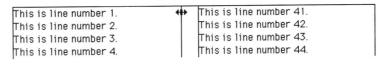

This is line number 1.	This is line number 41.
This is line number 2.	This is line number 42.
This is line number 3.	This is line number 43.
This is line number 4.	This is line number 44.
This is line number 5.	This is line number 45.

Dragging the gutter changes the width of two columns

Moving a column guide decreases or increases the width of the gutter. To move a column guide, place the mouse pointer on the desired guide-line and press and hold the Option key while dragging the mouse:

This is line number 1.	This is line number 41.
This is line number 2.	This is line number 42.
This is line number 3.	This is line number 43.
This is line number 4.	This is line number 44.

Dragging the column guide changes the width of the gutter

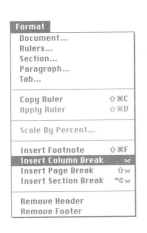

Format

Document...
Rulers...
Section...
Paragraph...
Tab...

Copy Ruler   ⇧⌘C
Apply Ruler   ⇧⌘U

Scale By Percent...

Insert Footnote   ⇧⌘F
Insert Column Break   ✕
Insert Page Break   ⇧✕
Insert Section Break   ⌥✕

Remove Header
Remove Footer

You can force text to the next column regardless of the amount of space left in the current column by inserting a *manual column break*. To do this, place the cursor at the desired position and select the Insert Column Break command from the Format menu (✕). Text to the right of the cursor is moved to the next column. To remove the manual column break, place the cursor to the left of the text forced to the next column and press the Delete key. More advanced uses of columns is covered in Chapter Twelve.

Practice 10

In this Practice you will format a document for multiple columns. Start ClarisWorks if you have not already done so.

1) OPEN A WORD PROCESSING FILE

    a. From the File menu, execute the Open command.
    b. In the Open dialog box, highlight the COURSE OFFERINGS filename.
    c. Select **Open**. COURSE OFFERINGS contains the course descriptions for the Department of Minor Skin Injury and Disease at Ivy University.
    d. Display the Shortcuts palette and click on the Show Invisibles button to display special symbols.

2) CREATE A HEADER

    a. From the Format menu, select the Insert Header command. Note the horizontal line indicating the header.

b. Enter the following text for the header:

```
Ivy University                                      Return
Department of Minor Skin Injury and Disease         Return
Course Descriptions
```

c. Change the font of all the header text to Geneva.

3) FORMAT THE DOCUMENT FOR TWO COLUMNS

a. Move the I-Beam cursor to the main body of text. Click the mouse button to place the cursor.
b. In the Format bar, click once on the Increase columns button (▥). The text in the document is reformatted for two columns. Note how the header remains formatted as one column. Changing the number of columns in a document does not affect headers and footers. Also note the additional page guides which indicate the number of columns.

4) MODIFY THE WIDTH BETWEEN THE COLUMNS

The spacing between the columns makes it difficult to read the course descriptions.

a. Hold down the Option key while placing the pointer on one of the column guides. The cursor changes to a double-headed arrow with two lines between.
b. Continue to hold down the Option key and then drag the column guide until the gutter is approximately ½" wide.

5) MOVE THE COLUMN GUTTER

a. Hold down the Option key while placing the pointer in the gutter. The cursor changes to a double-headed arrow with a box between.
b. Continue to hold down the Option key and then drag the gutter to the left until it is centered on the page.

6) INSERT A BREAK

a. Scroll so that the description for course 177 near the bottom of the first column of text is visible. Place the cursor so that it is just before the Return character symbol above the course description.
b. From the Format menu, select Insert Column Break. Note the text below the cursor is moved to the next column, not the next page.

Check - Your document should look similar to the following:

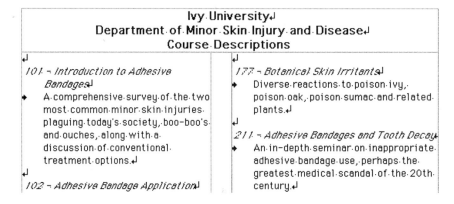

7) SAVE AND THEN PRINT COURSE OFFERINGS

    a. Save the modified COURSE OFFERINGS and print a copy.

    b. Close COURSE OFFERINGS and quit ClarisWorks.

4.16 Where can you go from here?

The last three chapters have introduced you to the concepts of word processing. You can now create, edit, format, and print word processor documents using ClarisWorks. Later in this text you will learn how to integrate charts and graphics into a word processor document and create personalized form letters. ClarisWorks has several other word processor options that you may wish to learn about. The best place to begin is by reading the word processor sections in the manual supplied by Claris.

For many people, the ability to word process justifies the expense of purchasing a personal computer. There are many different word processor programs available, some of which have options and features not included in ClarisWorks. Some of the more popular packages are Microsoft Word and WordPerfect. Because you have learned how to use the ClarisWorks word processor, you will easily be able to learn and use other programs such as those listed above.

Chapter Summary

Blocks are highlighted sections of text created by dragging or clicking the mouse. Blocks may be moved or copied using commands from the Edit menu. To move a block of text from one location to another within a document, the Cut command is executed, the cursor moved to the new location, and the Paste command selected. To copy a block of text so that it appears both at its original location and at a new location, the above procedure is used except the Copy command is selected rather than Cut. When text is Cut or Copied it is moved to the Clipboard where it may be viewed by executing the Show Clipboard command, also from the Edit menu.

The Find/Change command searches a document for a particular combination of characters called the search text. Including replace text in the Find/Change dialog box replaces the search text with the replace text. Searches start from the current cursor position. The Go to page command can be used to display a designated page.

Two of the most powerful features of the ClarisWorks word processor are the spelling checker and thesaurus. The Check Document Spelling command compares the words in a document to a dictionary file. A word that is not in the dictionary file is displayed in a dialog box where a correctly spelled word can be selected or the word in question edited. The Thesaurus command lists synonyms for a highlighted word and then allows the word to be replaced with one of the synonyms.

Indents are used to decrease the width of the text lines in a paragraph. A hanging indent has a first line indent that hangs out to the left over the lines below it. Bulleted and numbered lists are produced in this way.

Footnotes are created using the Insert Footnote command from the Edit menu. The text for a footnote is entered at the bottom of the page on which the footnote occurs. ClarisWorks automatically numbers and renumbers footnotes. When a footnote number is deleted from the text, its corresponding footnote is removed from the bottom of the page and any remaining footnotes are renumbered. Endnotes appear on the last page of a document, and may be used in place of footnotes in a document.

To keep track of document revisions, the current date and time can be included using the Insert Date and Insert Time commands from the Edit menu. It is often useful to include these codes in headers or footers.

The Word Count command from the Writing Tools submenu in the Edit menu is used to display document statistics.

ClarisWorks includes libraries of graphics. A library is a group of related items displayed on a palette. Graphics may be inserted into a document using the Library command from the File menu. Graphics can be placed anywhere including the header and footer. A selected graphic is resized by dragging on its size box.

Columns can make a document easier to read. The column controls in the Format bar are used to increase and decrease the number of columns in a document. The white space between columns is called the gutter, and may be moved and resized.

Vocabulary

Bulleted list - List created with a hanging indent and a tab character where each item is set off by a special character.

Check Document Spelling - Edit menu command that checks the spelling of a document and allows words not found in the ClarisWorks dictionary to be changed. See also Writing Tools.

Check Selection Spelling - Edit menu command that checks the spelling of highlighted text and allows words not found in the ClarisWorks dictionary to be changed. See also Writing Tools.

Clipboard - Area in memory where Cut or Copied text is stored. The Clipboard contents are displayed by using the Show Clipboard command in the Edit menu.

Copy command - Copies a highlighted block to the Clipboard without removing the text from its original location.

Cut command - Removes a highlighted block and places it on the Clipboard.

Endnote - Used to document a source. Appears on the last page of a document.

Find/Change command - Searches a document for specified text. May be used to replace specified text with other text.

Footnote - Used to document a source. Appears at the bottom of the page containing the footnoted material.

Go to page command - Used to display the top of a specified page.

Gutter - The white space between columns.

Hanging indent - First line of a paragraph that hangs out to the left over the lines below it. Created with a negative first line indent.

Indent - Paragraph formatting option that decreases the width of text lines.

Library - Group of related items displayed on a palette.

Manual column break - To force text to the next column regardless of the amount of space left in the current column.

Numbered list - List created with a hanging indent and a tab character where each item is set off by a number that indicates each item's order in the list.

Paste command - Copies text from the Clipboard to the document at the cursor location.

Replace text - Text entered by the user that is to take the place of search text.

Search text - Text to be found that is entered by the user.

Show Clipboard command - Displays a window that contains the contents of the Clipboard.

Synonym - A word that has the same or similar meaning as another word.

Thesaurus - A collection of synonyms.

Thesaurus command - Lists words with meanings similar (synonyms) to a highlighted word.

Time stamp - A placeholder in a document that automatically displays the current date or time when a file is opened or printed.

Writing for space - Writing to fill a precise amount of newspaper or publication space.

Writing Tools command - Contains a submenu with commands used to check the spelling of a document, offer synonyms for selected words, and display document statistics.

Reviews

Sections 4.1 — 4.6

1. a) What is meant by duplicating a block of text?
    b) List the steps required to copy the second paragraph in a document to a point directly after the fourth paragraph.

2. a) What is meant by "moving" a block of text?
    b) What is the difference between moving and duplicating a block of text?

3. a) Explain what the Clipboard is used for.
    b) How can the Clipboard be displayed?

4. a) What is meant by looking for search text?
    b) Give three examples of where you might use the Find/Change command.

5. List the steps required to find each occurrence of "Jan Habersham" in a document.

6. In a search for the word `hat` how can you avoid finding the word `that`?

7. Explain how to precisely search for the word `The` at the beginning of each paragraph if the paragraphs begin with a tab.

8. What is the fastest way to display the top of page 12 in a 15-page document?

9. What is meant by "replace text"?

10. Why is it usually inadvisable to use the **Change All** button in the Find/Change dialog box?

Sections 4.7 — 4.10

11. a) Explain what steps must be taken to have ClarisWorks check the spelling of a document starting from the beginning of the document.
    b) What does ClarisWorks do when it finds what it considers a spelling error?
    c) Is it possible that ClarisWorks might indicate an error when a word is spelled correctly? What should be done if this occurs?

12. a) What is a thesaurus?
    b) Explain what steps must be taken to have ClarisWorks list the synonyms for the word "house" in a word processor document.

13. What is an indent and when might one be used?

14. How can a half-inch left and right indent be produced for a paragraph?

15. Explain how a hanging indent of –0.25 inches can be created for the indented paragraph in Review question 14.

16. Explain how indents are used to create a numbered list.

Sections 4.11 — 4.15

17. a) What is a footnote used for?
    b) List the steps required to create a footnote.
    c) How can footnotes be converted to endnotes?

18. a) Where in the document are footnotes displayed?
    b) How can a footnote be edited?

19. a) What is a time stamp and when is it used?
    b) How can a time stamp be created in a ClarisWorks document?

20. a) What command is used to determine the number of words in a document?
    b) What other document statistics can be displayed by ClarisWorks?

21. List the steps needed to add a graphic to a document.

22. a) How can a three column document be produced?
    b) How can a three column document be converted to a two column document?

4 Exercises

1. The file named PARTY gives directions to a party, but the steps are listed out of order. Open PARTY and use the Cut and Paste commands to place the directions in proper order. Be sure there is a blank line between each step. Save the modified PARTY and print a copy.

2. The Copy command is useful when text must be repeated in a document.

   a) Use the Copy and Paste commands to create a file that contains your name 40 times, each on a separate line. Hint: Consider using a block with more than 1 line.

   b) At the end of the file have ClarisWorks print the current date and time.

   c) Save the file naming it My Name and print a copy.

3. This summer you are going on a vacation to Phoenix, Arizona for a whole month. You need to start planning now so that you will be ready. Bulleted lists can be very useful for planning.

   a) In a new word processor file, type the following:

   `List of clothing to pack for Phoenix vacation:`

   b) Save the file naming it Phoenix.

   c) Below the "List of clothing…" sentence, make a bulleted list of clothing items that you need to pack for your vacation. Be specific by including the color, fabric, size, etc. For example "long sleeve blue cotton Ivy University sweatshirt." Be sure to make hanging indents for the bulleted list.

   d) Change the indents of your list to ½ inch for the left indent and –¼ inch for the first line indent.

   e) Make the list very narrow by changing the left margin to 3" and the right margin to 3.5".

   f) Use the spelling checker to check the spelling and make any corrections.

   g) Use the thesaurus to find a synonym for `vacation` and replace it.

   h) Save the modified Phoenix and print a copy.

4. The research proposal last modified in Chapter Three, Exercise 12 needs further refinement. Open RESEARCH and make the following changes:

   a) On page two of the proposal is a numbered list (1-3) that outlines the phases of the development of a computerized guide to be used by the study. Create hanging indents for these phases using the following indents:

   - ¾ inch left indent
   - –½ inch first line indent
   - ½ inch right indent

   Insert a tab between the number and the text for each indented paragraph.

b) Use ClarisWorks to check the spelling and make any necessary corrections.

c) Use the Find/Change command to find the word `incalculable`. Use the thesaurus to replace it with a synonym.

d) Replace all occurrences of `Archaeological` with `Anthropological` and all occurrences of `Archaeology` with `Anthropology`.

e) Locate the sentence that begins "Years two through..." Move the entire sentence to its new location below phase 3. Separate the two paragraphs with a blank line.

f) Save the modified RESEARCH and print a copy.

5. The scientist's biography last modified in Chapter Three, Exercise 10 needs to be refined. Open Science Bio and make the following changes:

a) Modify the biography, if necessary, to include information from two outside sources. Create proper footnotes for these references using the Insert Footnote command.

b) Use the spelling checker to check the spelling and make any necessary corrections.

c) Use the thesaurus to change three words you believe could be improved. Italicize the new words.

d) Save the modified Science Bio and print a copy.

6. The review last modified in Chapter Three, Exercise 4 needs to be refined. Open Critic and make the following changes:

a) The school newspaper needs to know that they are getting the most recent copy of your review. Have ClarisWorks print the current date and time in a footer.

b) Create left and right indents of 0.5 inches for the first paragraph of your review.

c) Use the spelling checker to check the spelling and make any necessary corrections.

d) Make the document two columns. Increase the gutter slightly to allow for easier reading.

e) Save the modified Critic and print a copy.

7. You created a document containing directions to a number of different places in Chapter Two, Exercise 3. Unfortunately, your cousin is having a hard time reading and following these directions. Open Directions and make the following changes:

   a) Use the spelling checker to check the spelling and make any necessary corrections.

   b) Separate the directions into individual lettered steps and use hanging indents to make them easier to read. Create a left indent of 0.75 inches, a 0.5 inch right indent, and a first line indent of –0.25 inches. Use the following example as a guide:

   Directions to Gargantuan Gulch:

       a. Go South on Sibley Avenue until you come to a stop sign. Turn right.

       b. After about one mile you will cross a bridge. Gargantuan Gulch will be on your left.

   c) Use the Edit menu to insert the current date and time in a header.

   d) Save the modified Directions and print a copy.

8. You last modified a college application letter in Chapter Three, Exercise 6. Open College Apply and make the following changes:

   a) Replace all occurrences of the school's name with New Brunswick College.

   b) Use the spelling checker to check the spelling and make any necessary corrections.

   c) Save the modified College Apply and print a copy.

9. The file named COMPUTER ED contains information about computers in education, and was last modified in Chapter Three, Exercise 1. Open COMPUTER ED and make the following changes:

   a) This document contains information to be presented at the Conference of American Education. Create a header with the conference name.

   b) Create 0.5 inch right and left indents for the paragraph that begins "Computer programs have become...."

   c) Move the entire last section concerning Computer Usage (including the subtitle and table) to its new location after the indented paragraph. The section titled Lawrence Township Computer Usage should now be the third section of the document. Be sure each section is separated by a blank line.

   d) Save the modified COMPUTER ED and print a copy.

10. Open Grand Opening last modified in Chapter Three, Exercise 13 and make the following changes to create a more effective selling tool:

    a) Use ClarisWorks to check the spelling and make any necessary corrections.

    b) To make the flyer look more exciting, create right and left indents of 0.75 inches for each paragraph in the body of the flyer.

    c) Save the modified Grand Opening and print a copy.

11. Ivy University is launching a new campaign to attract students. Open IVY PROMO which contains a promotional advertisement for IU and make the following changes:

    a) Ivy's English department has pointed out that the term "A huge" is too informal to be used in this important document. Search for "huge" and then replace it with a more appropriate word using the thesaurus.

    b) Create hanging indents for the list of faculty members of the Department of Minor Skin Injury and Disease. Make the left and right indents 0.5 inches. Create a first line indent of –0.25 inches.

    c) Aside from Dr. Itchee, two other faculty members have published works, Dr. McCleen and Dr. Scalp. Find their names in the faculty list and create the following footnotes for their works:

> [1]Dr. Chris Scalp, <u>You and Shampoo</u> (Pennington: Lawrenceville Press, 1989).
> [2]Dr. Holly McCleen, <u>How to Wash Your Face</u> (New York: Maple, Snow & Daughters, 1991).

    In the footnotes and in the text, underline the titles of the works. Change the font of the footnotes to Geneva to match that of the rest of the document.

    d) Create a 0.5 inch first line indent for the new footnote references.

    e) Save the modified IVY PROMO and print a copy.

12. In Chapter Three, Exercise 3 you assisted in the design of a flyer for the SuperSub store opening. Open SUPERSUB and make the following changes:

    a) Replace all occurrences of `best` with `greatest`.

    b) Insert the following sentences below the paragraph which begins: "Lemonade isn't the only thing...." Be sure to press Return after each dessert.

> Here are some of Nanny's favorites:
> Pure Chocolate Dream Cream Pie with chocolate crust and fudge frosting.
> New York Cheesecake with bits of cream cheese, raspberries in syrup, and chocolate shavings.
> Fresh Strawberry Pie on a graham cracker crust topped with whole strawberries and homemade vanilla ice cream.

    c) Create a bulleted list of the desserts. Use left and right indents of 0.75 inches and a first line indent of –0.25 inches.

    d) Italicize the dessert names in the list.

    e) Use the spelling checker to check the spelling of the entire document.

    f) Save the modified SUPERSUB and print a copy.

13. City Zoo needs more work done on the animal inventory you created for them in Chapter Three, Exercise 14. Open CITY ZOO and make the following changes:

   a) The Staff column should include the caretaker's name for each animal. Copy each staff member's name into the proper location for the remainder of the list.

   b) The heading "Location" is not very descriptive. Replace it with a more descriptive name from the thesaurus.

   c) Scroll down to the bottom of the catalog and insert two blank lines. Then copy the title of the catalog and insert it at the bottom of the page. Under the title, enter the address and phone number of the zoo, and then center the four lines:

   City Zoo Catalog
   2323 Big Cat Bend
   Long Boat Key, FL 33548
   (555) CITY ZOO or 248-9066

   d) Save the modified CITY ZOO and print a copy.

14. Fax machines are used daily by many businesses. A fax cover sheet is used to tell the receiver where the fax came from. In a new word processor file, create a fax cover sheet for an imaginary company that includes at least the following:

   • The name, address, telephone number, and fax number of your company.
   • Date and time stamps.
   • A message area for the sender.

   Save the file naming it Faxcover and print a copy.

15. In Chapter Three, Exercise 16 you modified an article for a recycling newsletter. The editor has read your article and suggested ways to make it more effective. Open Recycle News and make the following changes:

   a) Under the headline "Autos, Autos, Everywhere" insert the graphic of a car which can be found on the Transportation library palette.

   b) Insert a blank line after the second paragraph which ends "safer place to live", then add the information below. Format the items as a bulleted list. Use a 0.5" left indent, a 0.25" right indent, and a first line indent of –0.25 inches. The new information should look similar to:

   Here are three easy things you can do:
   • Don't throw away your used motor oil. Leave it at a garage that recycles or take it to a recycling center.
   • Keep your tires properly inflated so that they will last longer.
   • Buy your new tires from a dealer who recycles the worn-out tires.

   c) Use the spelling checker to check the spelling and make any necessary corrections.

   d) To make this look more like a newsletter, format the document as two columns.

   e) Save the modified Recycle News and print a copy.

16. You are to create a two-page newsletter on any topic that you wish. In a new word processor file, create a newsletter that contains the following features:

- At least four different stories.
- At least one table of information.
- A header with the title of the newsletter.
- A footer with a centered page number.
- Two advertisements.
- Justified paragraphs.
- Correct spelling.
- At least one footnote.
- Multiple columns per page (like a newspaper).

An example newsletter design is shown below:

Ivy University
CAMPUS NEWS
Weekly news from around campus and beyond...
11/3/97

Gill Hall renovations to commence early next week

The renovations to Gill Hall will start at 8 a.m. next Monday. residents are advised that the water will be turned off promptly at 8 a.m. and should make concessions to not be using bathroom facilities at that time.

The bathrooms will be renovated first, followed by all hallway walls and floors, and finally the dorm lounge. An added attraction in the new lounge will be three computer terminals.

All renovations are the result of the Hazel B. Gladoff memorial fund. Gladoff lived in Gill Hall for her four years at Ivy in the early 1950s, and recently passed away in her Manhattan townhome. She is survived by her husband, Barry, and her prized poodle Mootsie.

IT'S TIME TO SIGN UP FOR INTRAMURALS

Sign up for next semester's teams NOW. Lists are posted by the Information Desk.

Photography workshop offered

The Studio Arts department is offering a two day workshop next weekend on black and white photography.

The first in a series, the workshop will focus on photographing nature. The next workshop will focus on developing black and white film. The workshops are for students, faculty, and staff who have not taken Photography 101 or later.

"This is a good chance for students to try out photography, and see if they're truly interested before they take the intense, one semester course," Nina Johnson said. Johnson is the photography coordinator for Ivy U. She oversees the labs, curriculum, and senior projects.

The workshop will be next Saturday and Sunday from 11 a.m. to 3 p.m. and is free to students, faculty and staff. A camera and film is required.

Editorial - Dana Warheit

It comes as no surprise to those who have followed this year's Student Congress Election that Thom Steves was not re-elected. What is surprising is the actual number of people who realized that for the last three and a half years this guy has been sandbagging it. If ever there was a case for impeachment, this was it. The well-oiled political machine that passed as Steve's campaign staff was a joke. It's time we realized that the Student Congress can actually make a difference, and we must vote someone in who will try.

This Week at IVY U

Tuesday
V. Football at Newbury	3:00 p.m.
Open Mike Night, Ivy Cafe	6:30 p.m.
Tuesday's Movie, auditorium, TBA	8:00 p.m.

Wednesday
2-4-1 Pizza, Ivy Cafe	all day
Poetry Reading, Wilbur Hall	7:00 p.m.

Thursday
V. Men's Soccer at Milltown	3:30 p.m.
Ultimate Frisbee Tryouts, Bug Field	4:00 p.m.
Comedy Night, Ivy Cafe	6:00 p.m.

Friday
V. Women's Field Hockey at Iona	4:00 p.m.
Live Music by Twist, Ivy Cafe	9:00 p.m.
Friday's Movie, auditorium, TBA	8:00 p.m.

Saturday
2-4-1 Pizza, Ivy Cafe	all day
Photo Workshop	11:00 a.m.
V. Men's Soccer at Newbury	1:00 p.m.
V. Football at Milltown	2:30 p.m.
Live Music by Treet, Ivy Cafe	9:00 p.m.

Sunday
Photo Workshop	11:00 a.m.
Choral Concert, auditorium	8:00 p.m.

Varsity Men's Soccer 6-0

Ivy's varsity men's soccer team, the Oak Leaves, have a winning season so far. This is the best record ever, according to Coach Zoran.

"We trained an extra three weeks this summer and it paid off," Zoran said. *(continued next page)*

Page 1

a) Make the titles of each article bold and in a larger point size than the article's text.

b) Italicize any titles of books, magazines, songs, team names, etc. that appear in any of your articles.

c) Be sure to use tabs and tab stops to align the information in the tables.

d) Use the spelling checker to check the spelling of the document.

e) Save the file naming it Newsletter and print a copy.

An Introduction to Computing Using ClarisWorks

Save

Layout

Browse

New Record

Print

Page View

Find

Show All Records

Objectives

After completing this chapter you will be able to:

1. Describe a database.

2. Define records, fields, and entries.

3. Plan and design a database.

4. Create a database and modify its record layout.

5. Print a database.

6. Enter data into a new database, record by record.

7. Print a database.

8. Use Find to display specific records.

5

This chapter provides an introduction to databases and describes how they can be used to organize and store information. Attention is given not only to understanding what a database is, but also to the planning and design considerations that make them efficient and easy to use. This chapter also explains the step-by-step process of creating and modifying a ClarisWorks database, from paper and pencil sketches to computerized printouts.

5.1 What is a Database?

As you discovered using the word processor, the computer is a powerful tool for storing and manipulating information. Its speed and storage capabilities make the computer an ideal tool for managing large amounts of information in the form of databases.

A *database* is simply a group of related pieces of information. Almost all businesses and organizations use databases in some way. A bank uses a database to store the account information of its depositors and a school to store student records. Department and grocery stores use databases to keep track of the different items they have for sale, their prices, and how many of each are in stock. A major advantage of using a computer is its ability to rapidly search a large database for a specific piece of information.

Databases can be used to organize any information: addresses, inventories, payrolls, research data, and more. Any information that can be stored in a list or on individual forms can be put into a database. Many historians refer to our present time as the "Information Age" primarily because of the ability databases have given us to store and manipulate huge amounts of information.

5.2 Database Structure

All databases have the same structure and the same words are used to describe that structure. A *record* is information about a single item in a database. For example, Ivy University uses a database to organize student information. In their database, a record is the information about a single student. Information within a record is divided into *fields*. Each field has a *field name* that describes its contents, and the data stored in an individual field in a single record is called an *entry*. For example, First Name, Last Name, and GPA are the names of three separate fields in an Ivy U database record. The entries for the fields in the database vary from record to record. For example, the GPA entry for student Sam Adams is 1.5; the same field in the record for student Roberta Poisson contains an entry of 4.0. The order and placement of fields in a record is referred to as its *layout*. It is important to note that each record in a database has the same layout, but that the entries vary from record to record. The following illustrates the structure of a database:

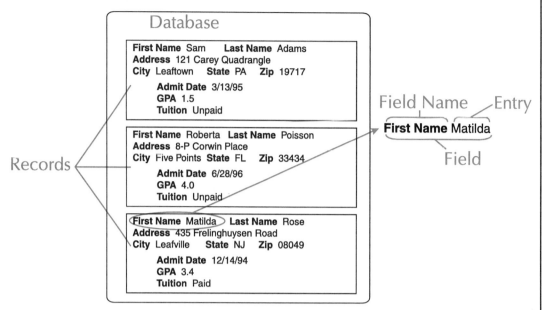

The size of a record depends on the number of fields it contains. A record may have as few as one or two fields, such as a name and phone number, or there may be hundreds of fields in each record.

5.3 Field Names and Types

Each field in a record is identified by its field name. In ClarisWorks, field names may be up to 63 characters long and can contain spaces. For example, in the Ivy U database First Name is a field name which contains a space and is less than 63 characters long.

Fields are classified by the *type* of data they store. Fields that store characters (letters, symbols, words, a combination of letters and numbers, etc.) are called *text fields*. In the Ivy U student database, the name and address for each student are stored in text fields. Another common field type is the *number field* that stores only numeric values. Ivy U's student database stores grade point averages (GPA) in a number field. The last two of the basic field types are *date fields* and *time fields*. At Ivy U, the student's admission date is stored in a date field.

5.4 Planning a Database

A great deal of time and thought should go into the planning of a database before it is created. Careful planning saves time and eliminates frustration later. There are four steps for planning a database:

1. Determine what data should be stored in each record. This is best accomplished by examining the needs of the different users of the database. Start by creating a list on paper of the data available. Eliminate any information that is not directly related to the overall purpose of the database.

2. Examine the specific uses of the database. Do these uses require any information that is missing from the current list? Is there a need for a complete mailing address or will a street address be enough? Will there be a need to separate the first name from the last? Is a phone or fax number required? Make any changes required to the list produced in step 1.

3. Create a list of appropriate field names using the data from step 2. Determine the type (text, numeric, date, etc.) of each field.

4. Sketch the layout of a sample record on paper. This helps to show where potential problems may occur.

Careful planning requires information about both the user of the database and how the database will be used. Database designers often spend a great deal of time talking to the prospective user(s) and analyzing their needs before making any decisions about fields and types. It is also important to realize that most databases are accessed by more than one user, and each user has different requirements. For example, the dean's office needs access to student names and GPAs, and the admission's office needs access to student names and addresses. Therefore, the database must contain at least fields for all of this information.

The time spent planning a database makes it easier for each user to get the fullest use from the stored information and avoids having to later make major modifications to the database.

In the sections that follow, we will use the four steps for planning a database to create the Ivy U student database in ClarisWorks.

5.5 Planning Records and Fields

The first two steps in planning a database are completed by answering "What information should be stored?" and "What operations will be performed with that information?" These are the two most important questions when designing a database.

Deciding what information to store depends on what the database will be used for. A student database would not contain information about faculty salaries or how many desks are in certain classrooms, only information that is directly related to the students. Therefore the Ivy U student database should include the following information:

> Student Name
> Address
> Date student was admitted
> Current GPA
> Has tuition been paid?

The database will contain one record for each student which stores information for only that student.

Next, the operations performed on the database should be considered. Ivy University keeps its student records in order by last name. Therefore, the Student Name category needs to be expanded to First Name and Last Name:

> First Name
> Last Name
> Address
> Date student was admitted
> Current GPA
> Has tuition been paid?

Finally, the administration would like to be able to mail warning letters to each student who has a low GPA. In order to use the database to produce complete mailing labels, the Address category must be expanded to Street address, City, State (or province), and Zip code (or postal code):

> First Name
> Last Name
> Street address
> City
> State
> Zip code
> Date student was admitted
> Current GPA
> Has tuition been paid?

Several problems have been avoided by carefully considering the uses for this database before it is created. For example, the ability to produce mailing labels is valuable. Had this not been planned for, a great deal of work would have to be done to later modify the database.

5.6 Choosing Field Names and Types

The third step in planning a database is creating a list of field names. Each field must have a distinct name to distinguish it from the other fields in a record. A well-chosen field name describes the data stored in that field. Below are good examples of field names for the student database using the list of categories created in Section 5.5:

Data	Field name
Student first name	First Name
Student last name	Last Name
Street address	Address
City	City
State	State
Zip code	Zip
Date student was admitted	Admit Date
Current GPA	GPA
Has tuition been paid?	Tuition

Choosing the shortest possible name that accurately describes the contents of the field is important. This is why the name Address rather than Street Address was chosen to represent the street address field. It is a good idea to use complete words instead of numbers or abbreviations as field names. First Name, for example, is better than 1st Name, F. Name, and No. 1 Name.

After creating the list of field names, the type of data each field will contain needs to be defined. For example, First Name will contain text. The GPA field will store only numbers and is therefore a number field. The Zip field is text because many countries use letters as well as numbers in their codes. The field names for the student record database and their types are as follows:

Field names and their type
First Name (text)
Last Name (text)
Address (text)
City (text)
State (text)
Zip (text)
Admit Date (date)
GPA (number)
Tuition (text)

Practice 1

Mega Music, a national retail store that specializes in compact discs, cassette tapes, music videos, and other accessories has hired you to computerize their customer mailing list. The list of categories below is a result of the first two steps for planning a database. You are to complete the third step of planning a database.

On a piece of paper, write down appropriate field names and indicate the type (text, number, date, or time) for each field based on the categories below:

Customer's name
Customer's mailing address
Is the customer male or female?
What type of music do they like?
Why did they make the purchase (gift, personal, work, etc.)?
When was the sale made?
Customer's account number
How many items did they purchase?
How did they pay for the purchase?

5.7 Creating a New Database

To create a new database, the **Database** option is selected in the New Document dialog box and then **OK** selected. When a new database is created, the Define Database Fields dialog box is automatically displayed:

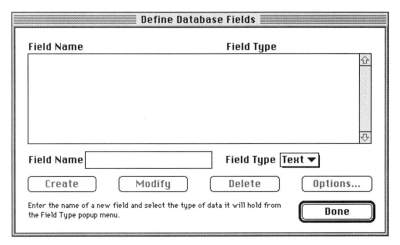

The Define Database Fields dialog box is displayed
when a database is created

Fields are defined by typing a field name, selecting the appropriate type, and then selecting the **Create** button. For example, consider the Ivy U student database discussed previously. To create the First Name field, `First Name` is typed in the **Field Name** box and then the **Create** button selected. ClarisWorks adds the field to the field list with **Text** as its type because this is the default. The GPA field is created by typing GPA for the **Field Name**, selecting Number from the **Field Type** drop-down list, and then selecting **Create** to add it to the list:

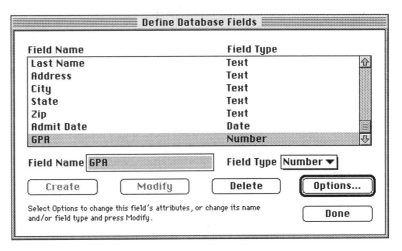

Fields are created in the Define Database Fields dialog box

When all fields have been created, selecting the **Done** button removes the Define Database Fields dialog box and ClarisWorks displays an empty record ready to receive data. The default layout of a record in a new database is all the fields placed in a column in the order in which they were entered:

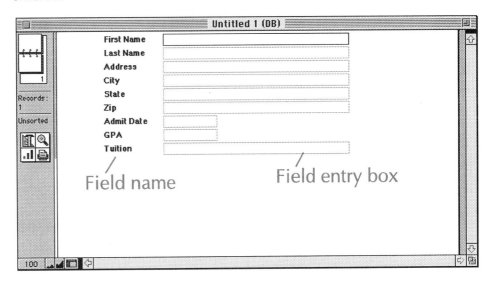

An empty record in a new database appears similar to this

To the right of each field name is an *entry box* where data for that field is entered. Later in this chapter, we will discuss how the order of the fields can be changed and how the width of entry boxes can be adjusted to accommodate data.

5.8 Saving a Database

Executing the Save command from the File menu (⌘S) or clicking on the Save button on the Shortcuts palette (📄) saves the database. When a database is saved, a copy of each of the records currently in the computer's memory is made on disk. Once a file has been saved, it may be opened later and the data stored in it displayed, printed, or changed. After it has been saved, the file should be closed if it is no longer needed by selecting the Close command from the File menu (⌘W).

Practice 2

In this Practice you will create the student database described in Section 5.7.

1) START CLARISWORKS

    a. Following the directions given in Chapter Two, boot the System.

    b. Double-click on the ClarisWorks application icon to start ClarisWorks and display the New Document dialog box.

2) CREATE A NEW DATABASE

Select **Database** from the New Document dialog box and then select **OK**. The Define Database Fields dialog box is displayed.

3) DEFINE THE FIRST NAME FIELD

    a. Type First Name in the **Field Name** box.

    b. Because Text is already chosen in the **Field Type** list, select the **Create** button to define the First Name field and display it in the field list:

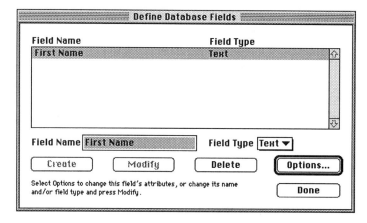

4) DEFINE THE LAST NAME FIELD

    a. Type Last Name in the **Field Name** box.

    b. Select **Create** to add the Last Name field to the list. Your screen should now show the First Name and Last Name text fields in the Define Database Fields dialog box.

5) DEFINE THE REST OF THE FIELDS

Use the steps described above to define the remaining fields listed below. To select the appropriate field type for each field, press and hold the mouse button on the **Field Type** drop-down list and then drag down to the appropriate option:

Field Name	Field Type
Address	Text
City	Text
State	Text
Zip	Text
Admit Date	Date
GPA	Number
Tuition	Text

When all fields are defined, click on the **Done** button to remove the Define Database Fields dialog box and display an empty record.

6) SAVE AND THEN CLOSE THE NEW DATABASE

a. From the File menu, select the Save command to display the dialog box.
b. Type the file name Student and select the **Save** button. The empty (no records) database is saved on disk. Note that the entry boxes have temporarily disappeared.
c. From the File menu, select the Close command.

5.9 Layout Design

The fourth step in planning a database is producing a sample record layout using paper and pencil. On paper you can decide the order and positioning of the fields. A good layout has related fields grouped together (like parts of an address) and more important and frequently used fields placed first. A sketch of the Student database layout could look similar to the following:

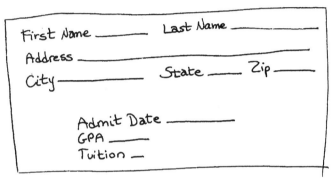

A sketch of the Student database layout—note how the address and university information are grouped separately

Layout design also includes determining the width of the field entry boxes displayed on the screen. For example, to fully display a Last Name field entry, the Last Name field will normally require more space than the First Name field. Later in the book, you will learn how you can include lines, boxes, and labels to give the record layout a more professional look.

Remember, careful planning of a database can save you time and aggravation later. Adding and deleting fields at random can make the records a hodgepodge of data, limiting the usefulness of the database, so take special care when planning the layout.

Practice 3

In this Practice you will sketch three layouts for two different databases, Ivy University's student enrollment and Mega Music's customer list. Refer to the sketch in Section 5.9 as an example of a layout sketch.

a. Ivy University wants to see examples of different layouts for their student database. Sketch three different layouts using the fields supplied in Section 5.6.

b. Mega Music liked your preliminary ideas on the contents of their customer database and now wants to see some ideas on layout. Using the field names you created in Practice 1, sketch three different layouts on the same piece of paper, experimenting with field grouping and order.

5.10 Browse and Layout View

A newly created database is shown in *Browse* view. In this view, data can be entered, updated, and deleted. However, a record's layout in Browse view can only be changed when the database is in Layout view.

In *Layout* view, field widths can be changed and fields repositioned to modify the record layout. Executing the Layout command from the Layout menu (⇧⌘**L**) changes the database view:

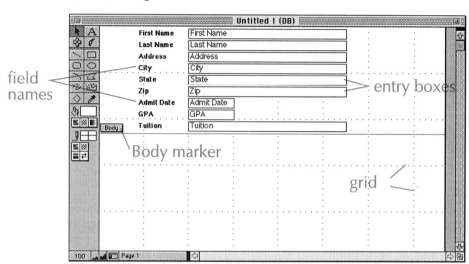

field names — entry boxes

Body marker

grid

The record layout can be changed only in Layout view

Field names, entry boxes, and the record *Body* are displayed in Layout view. The Body marker defines the record area and can be dragged up or down. Field names and entry boxes moved below the Body no longer appear in the layout when in Browse view or when the database is printed. The grid is used to help align fields in the layout. To return to Browse view select the Browse command from the Layout menu (⇧⌘**B**).

5.11 Changing Entry Box Widths

In Layout view, field names and entry boxes can be resized. Normally, a field's entry box will be changed from its default to accommodate the data to be entered for that field. When the mouse pointer is placed on an entry box and clicked once, square *handles* appear:

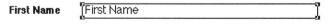

First Name   First Name

A selected entry box displays handles

These handles indicate that the entry box is *selected*. The vertical or horizontal width of a selected entry box can then be changed by dragging a handle. Both field name and entry box widths can be changed, but field names can only be horizontally widened or narrowed. Shown below are examples of different entry box widths:

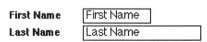

First Name   First Name
Last Name   Last Name

Field widths can vary from field to field

A field should be wide enough to entirely display the data it stores. For example, consider a field storing a person's first name. A field that can display only 5 characters is too short, while 30 characters is probably too long. Somewhere between 10 and 20 characters is probably best. It is important to realize that a field's width only determines the number of characters displayed on the screen, not the number of characters actually stored in that field. For example, a field storing the name Shakespeare will display `Shake` if the field is sized to display only 5 characters and `Shakespe` if it sized to display 8.

5.12 Moving Fields in a Layout

In Layout view, one way to move a field name or entry box is by dragging it. A second way is to select the field name or entry box and then use the arrow keys to move it. For example, it is sometimes useful to reduce the empty space between a field's name and its entry box. To close this gap and move the field closer to its entry box, simply click once on the field to select it and then move it to the left by pressing the left-arrow key:

GPA ⟵ ⟵ [GPA]

GPA [GPA]

Moving the GPA entry box to the left makes it easier to see that the entry is stored in the GPA field

To move both the field's name and its entry box at the same time, press and hold down the Shift key while clicking on each. They are now both selected and can be dragged to a new location together:

First Name [First Name]

Many objects can be selected at the same time

Selecting while holding the Shift key is a quick way to select many field names and entry boxes (more than two can be selected) simultaneously so that they can be moved while maintaining their original spacing. To deselect an object, hold down the Shift key and click on it. Clicking the mouse in an empty space in the layout deselects all previously selected objects.

Practice 4

In Practice 2 you created a database. In this Practice you will modify that database layout by changing the widths of field names and entry boxes and moving them to new locations in the layout. Start ClarisWorks if you have not already done so and open the Student database.

1) CHANGE THE WIDTH OF THE FIRST NAME ENTRY BOX

   a. From the Layout menu, select the Layout command. Entry boxes are shown with solid borders and field names displayed inside.

   b. Place the pointer on the Last Name entry box and click once. Handles appear on the box indicating that it is selected. Click on other entry boxes and notice the handles for each.

   c. Click on the First Name entry box to display the handles.

d. Place the pointer on one of the far right handles and drag the handle approximately two-thirds of the distance to the left, narrowing the entry box. Be sure you do not increase or decrease the height of the box. Your field should be similar to:

Note - If you accidentally moved the entire entry box, select Undo from the Edit menu or place the pointer on the First Name entry box and drag so that the entry box is positioned evenly with the First Name field name.

2) CHANGE THE WIDTH OF THE FIELD NAME

a. Click on the First Name field <u>name</u> to select it, displaying the handles.
b. Place the pointer on one of the far right handles and drag it to the left. Release the mouse just before reaching the "e" in "Name." If "Name" accidentally moves to the next line, drag one of the right handles to the right until both words are on the same line. The First Name field name is now reduced and should be similar to:

Note - If you accidentally moved the entire field name, select Undo from the Edit menu or manually reposition it.

3) CHANGE THE WIDTH OF THE OTHER FIELDS

Using the procedure described in steps 1 and 2 above, change the widths of the remaining fields until they are similar to:

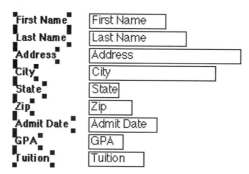

Note - All the field names above are selected for illustration purposes only. Yours should not be selected.

4) MOVE THE ENTRY BOXES CLOSER TO THEIR FIELD NAMES

a. Place the pointer on the First Name entry box and click once to select it.
b. Press the left-arrow key to move the First Name entry box to the left. Continue pressing the left-arrow key until the space between the entry box and field name is reduced. Your field should be similar to:

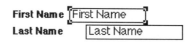

5) REDUCE THE SPACE BETWEEN THE REMAINING FIELDS

Using the procedure described in step 4 above, reduce the space between the remaining field names and their entry boxes.

An Introduction to Computing Using ClarisWorks

6) CHANGE THE POSITION OF THE LAST NAME FIELD

a. Place the pointer anywhere within the Last Name field name and drag it toward the upper right. Place it next to (but not on top of) the First Name entry box and release the mouse button.

b. Place the pointer anywhere within the Last Name entry box and drag it toward the upper right. Place it next to (but not on top of) the Last Name field name that you just moved and release the button. The field placements should be similar to:

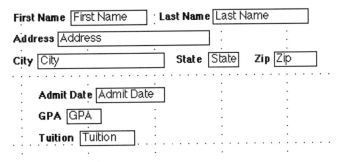

c. Adjust both objects until they are even with the First Name field.

7) MOVE THE ADDRESS FIELD BY SELECTING BOTH OBJECTS

a. Place the pointer on the Address field name and click to select it. Handles appear.

b. Place the pointer over the Address entry box and while holding the Shift key, click the mouse button. Both the Address field name and entry box are now selected.

c. Place the pointer anywhere within the Address field and drag it up so that it is closer to the First Name field. Because both objects are selected, they move together and maintain their original spacing.

8) MOVE THE OTHER FIELDS

Using the procedure described in step 7 above, position the remaining fields until they are similar to the following layout:

9) SWITCH TO BROWSE VIEW

From the Layout menu, select the Browse command. The modified layout is displayed. Note that entry boxes are temporarily not displayed.

10) SAVE THE MODIFIED STUDENT DATABASE

5.13 Entering Records

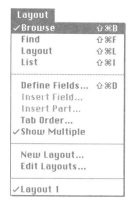

In Browse view, pressing the Tab key displays the field entry boxes:

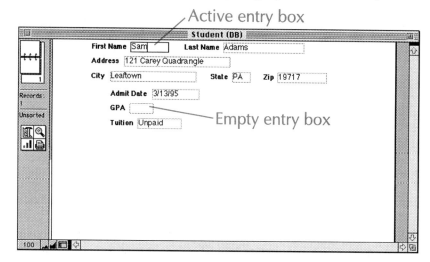

Data is entered in Browse view

The currently selected, or *active*, field contains a blinking cursor and has a solid border around its entry box, while the other fields have only dimmed entry boxes. *Empty fields* do not contain data and are indicated by empty entry boxes.

Data can only be typed in the active entry box. After typing the data, pressing the Tab key enters it into the field and makes the next field active. Pressing the Return key will not advance the cursor, but will instead make the entry box temporarily bigger. If you enter the wrong data or make a mistake, place the cursor in the correct entry box by either clicking on it with the pointer or pressing the Tab key until the field is selected again, and make the correction.

ClarisWorks can store hundreds of characters in a single field, but the number of characters displayed is limited to the size of the entry box. If an entry is too long to fit in the entry box, the box height temporarily changes to hold the data. When the field is no longer active, the entry box reverts back to its original size, displaying a limited number of characters. Selecting the field again displays its complete contents. To change the number of characters displayed in the field, switch to Layout view and resize its entry box.

5.14 The New Record Command

When all of the data for the current record has been entered, selecting the New Record command from the Edit menu (⌘R) displays an empty record below the first. The new record displays entry boxes indicating it is now the current, or active, record. A solid bar is also displayed to the

left of the current record. ClarisWorks keeps track of how many records have been entered and displays both the total number of records and the record number of the current record in the *Status panel* located in the upper-left corner of the window:

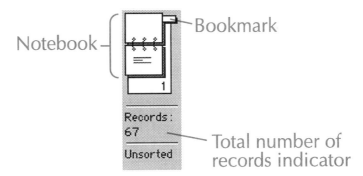

Use the Status panel to quickly move through a database

The Status panel contains an icon that looks like a small spiral-bound *Notebook*. Clicking once on the top "page" of the Notebook makes the previous record in the database current, and clicking on the bottom "page" makes the next record current. As each record is selected, ClarisWorks displays its record number below the Notebook. To quickly select a particular record, such as the last one in the database, place the pointer on the *Bookmark* and drag it down the length of the Notebook icon. As the Bookmark is moved, the current record indicator changes to reflect the active record. When the mouse button is released, the current record indicated in the Status panel is displayed.

Clicking on the New Record button on the Shortcuts palette also displays an empty record below the last one in the database.

5.15 Printing a Database

Before printing, it is a good practice to first save the database. To print the database, the Print command from the File menu is selected to display its dialog box. Selecting the **Print** button prints all records. To print only the active record, click on the **Current Record** option in the bottom of the dialog box before selecting **Print**.

A database can also be printed by clicking on the Print button (▦) on the Shortcuts palette. When the Print button is used, the Print dialog box is not displayed and every record in the database is printed.

The Page View command from the View menu (⇧⌘**P**) is used to determine how a database will look when printed. When this command is selected, a check mark is placed beside its name in the View menu, and the database layout is divided into page-sized sections. To return to normal view Page View is again selected, removing the check mark from beside its name.

As with the word processor, headers and footers can be included in the database to provide more informative printouts. Information such as the creator's name, the date of the printout, or the filename could be included. When the Insert Header or Insert Footer command from the Format menu is selected, the database is automatically displayed in Page View.

Practice 5

In this Practice you will enter two student records, use the New Record Command and the Status panel, and print the Student database. Start ClarisWorks and open the Student database if you have not already done so.

1) ENTER A STUDENT'S FIRST NAME

    a. From the Layout menu, select Browse if it is not already selected.

    b. Press the Tab key to display the entry boxes. The First Name entry box has a solid border and is selected. Note the "1" below the Notebook in the Status panel indicating that this is the first record in the database.

    c. Type Sam. If you make a mistake, use the mouse pointer, arrow keys, or Delete key to make any corrections. Press the Tab key when you are done to enter the data into the field and move the cursor to the next field, Last Name.

2) ENTER THE STUDENT'S LAST NAME

    a. Type Adams.

    b Press the Tab key. Adams is placed in the Last Name field and the cursor moved to the Address field.

3) COMPLETE THE STUDENT RECORD

Enter the following data for the remaining fields, pressing Tab to move the cursor to the next field:

Address: 121 Carey Quadrangle
City: Leaftown
State: PA
Zip: 19717
Admit Date: 3/13/95
GPA: 1.5
Tuition: Unpaid

4) DISPLAY AND ENTER DATA INTO A NEW RECORD

    a. If the Shortcuts palette is not already displayed, from the File menu, drag down to the Shortcuts command. In the submenu, select the Show Shortcuts command.

    b. On the Shortcuts palette, click on the New Record button (🗒). An empty record is inserted below the first. Note the two 2s in the Status panel indicating that this is the second record in the database which contains two records.

    c. Follow the instructions in the previous steps to enter the data for the second record into the file:

First Name: Roberta
Last Name: Poisson
Address: 8-P Corwin Place
City: Five Points
State: FL
Zip: 33434
Admit Date: 6/28/96
GPA: 4.0
Tuition: Unpaid

5) MAKE DIFFERENT RECORDS ACTIVE

a. Click on the top page of the Notebook in the Status panel. An entry box for record 1 becomes active. Also note the bar to the left of the record.

b. Click on the top page of the Notebook again. Nothing happens because there are no records above record number one.

c. Drag the Bookmark up and down. To move the Bookmark, you will need to drag it completely to the top or bottom of the Notebook. Notice that the current record indicator changes as the Bookmark moves. When the indicator changes to 2, release the mouse button to make Roberta Poisson's record the current record.

6) PRINT THE DATABASE

a. Save Student. The entered records are now stored in the database file.

b. From the File menu, select Print. The Print dialog box is displayed. Note the **Current Record** and **Visible Records** options in the bottom of the dialog box. The **Visible Records** option should be selected.

c. Select the **Print** button to print the database with the default option, **Visible Records**, selected. The database with two records is printed.

7) CLOSE STUDENT

5.16 Finding Records

    In addition to storing information in an organized manner, databases have the ability to quickly retrieve records that contain specific information. This is an invaluable feature, especially when a database contains hundreds or thousands of records.

    The Find command from the Layout menu (⇧⌘F) is used to display only those records that contain a specific entry in a particular field. Executing this command displays the Find screen. Note the Find options below the Notebook:

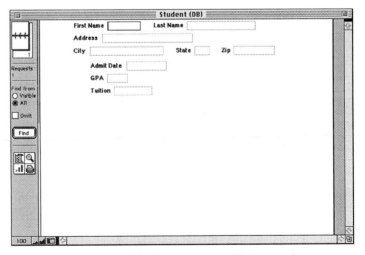

Data typed in this screen will be used to locate records with matching data

    The **All** button below the Notebook is automatically selected when the Find command is executed. This indicates that every record in the database will be searched for the find. Selecting the **Find** button displays all records that store the entry typed in the Find screen. To perform a find, first press the Tab key until the desired field entry box is selected. Next, type an equal sign (=) followed by the entry to search for. The equal sign is a *relational operator* that means "the same as." Selecting **Find** displays records with matching entries. Those records that do not match are hidden from view. For example, in the Student database, student records with a GPA of 1.5 are displayed by selecting the Find command, typing =1.5 in the GPA entry box, and then selecting the **Find** button. In this case, only Sam Adams record will be displayed.

To further limit the number of records displayed, data is entered in more than one field in the Find screen. For example, suppose we want to display records for those students from Florida who have not paid their tuition. Selecting the Find command displays the Find screen shown on the previous page. Typing =FL in the State entry box, =Unpaid in the Tuition entry box and selecting **Find** displays Roberta Poisson's record.

5.17   The Show All Records Command

The Find command displays records that contain specified data. Records that do not match the find are hidden from view. *Hidden records* have not been deleted, they are just no longer displayed. To again display all records the Show All Records command from the Organize menu (⇧⌘A) is selected.

Clicking on the Show All Records button on the Shortcuts palette (▤) also displays any records that are hidden from view.

Practice 6

In this Practice you will use the Find command to locate records in a large database called IVY STUDENT. The Show All Records command will be used to display hidden records.

1)   OPEN IVY STUDENT

Open IVY STUDENT. Note that there are 80 records in this database as indicated in the Status panel.

2)   FIND THE RECORDS FOR STUDENTS FROM PENNSYLVANIA

a.   From the Layout menu, select the Find command. The Find screen is displayed with an empty record.
b.   Press the Tab key until the State entry box becomes active. Type =PA.
c.   Click on the **Find** button in the Status panel below the Notebook. Two records are found as indicated on the Status panel.

3)   FIND THE RECORDS FOR STUDENTS WITH A GPA OF 3.9

a.   From the Layout menu, select the Find command.
b.   Click on the GPA entry box. Type =3.9.
c.   Press Return to select the **Find** button. Three records are displayed. Regardless of the number of records currently displayed, **Find** searches the entire database when **All** is selected.
d.   Scroll through the records and note each student's GPA.

4) DISPLAY ALL THE IVY STUDENT RECORDS

From the Organize menu, select the Show All Records command or click on the Show All Records button on the Shortcuts palette (▤). There are no longer any records hidden from view.

5) CREATE A MORE LIMITED FIND AND PRINT THE RESULTS

a. From the Layout menu, select the Find command.
b. Move to the State entry box and type =NC.
c. Move to the GPA entry box and type =3.9.
d. Select the **Find** button. The two records displayed are for students from NC with a GPA of 3.9.
e. Save and then print the database using the default **Visible Records** option in the Print dialog box. Note that only the records matching the find are printed.

6) SAVE IVY STUDENT

Show all records and then save IVY STUDENT.

5.18 Finding a Range of Records

Layout	
Browse	⇧⌘B
✓Find	⇧⌘F
Layout	⇧⌘L
List	⇧⌘I
Define Fields...	⇧⌘D
Insert Field...	
Insert Part...	
Tab Order...	
✓Show Multiple	
New Layout...	
Edit Layouts...	
✓Layout 1	

Other relational operators may also be used in a find. For example, Ivy U students with a GPA greater than 3.6 are placed on the Dean's List. To determine which students are eligible, >3.6 is typed in the GPA entry box in the Find screen. Selecting the **Find** button displays the records of those students with a GPA of 3.7 or higher. This type of find is said to contain a *range* because there are multiple values of GPA that meet this requirement (3.7, 3.8, 3.9, etc.).

There are several relational operators that may be used to define a find:

Operator	Meaning
=	Equal to
>	Greater than
<	Less than
<>	Not equal to
>=	Greater than or equal to
<=	Less than or equal to

Each of these operators may be used in any of the fields. For example:

How many students were admitted on or after 1/1/96?
    >=1/1/96   *in Admit Date field*

How many students have a GPA less than 2.0?
    <2.0   *in GPA field*

Which students are not from Florida?
    <>FL   *in State field*

Which students have last names that come after Kemp?
    >Kemp   *in Last Name field*

Note that text can be used in ranges. ClarisWorks recognizes that certain letters follow others in the alphabet. Ranges may be used in multiple fields to further limit the number of records displayed.

Practice 7

In this Practice you will use ranges to find records in IVY STUDENT. Start ClarisWorks and open IVY STUDENT if it is not already open.

1) FIND THOSE STUDENTS WITH A GPA GREATER THAN 3.6

    a. From the Layout menu, select the Find command. The Find screen is displayed.
    b. Move to the GPA field and type >3.6.
    c. Select the **Find** button. 14 records are displayed.
    d. Scroll through the displayed records and note the GPAs. What values are included in the range?

2) DETERMINE WHICH STUDENTS WERE ADMITTED ON OR AFTER 1/1/96

    a. From the Layout menu, select the Find command.
    b. Move to the Admit Date field and type >=1/1/96.
    c. Select the **Find** button. How many students were admitted on or after 1/1/96?

3) CREATE A MORE LIMITED FIND AND PRINT THE RESULTS

    a. From the Layout menu, select the Find command.
    b. Move to the Admit Date field. Type >=1/1/96.
    c. Move to the GPA field and type >3.8.
    d. Select the **Find** button. The records for those students admitted on or after 1/1/96 with a GPA greater than 3.8 are displayed. How many students meet these requirements?
    e. Save and then print the displayed records using the default **Visible Records** option in the Print dialog box.

4) SAVE IVY STUDENT

    a. Show all records and then save IVY STUDENT.
    b. Close IVY STUDENT and quit ClarisWorks.

Chapter Summary

The speed and storage capabilities of the computer make it an ideal tool for managing large amounts of information in the form of databases. Databases are used by many organizations (businesses, governmental agencies, educational institutions, etc.), and they can be used to organize information about almost any area.

A database is an organized collection of related information that is divided into records, each of which stores a complete set of data about a specific item. Each piece of data within a record is called a field and the arrangement of the fields within a record is called its layout. In a well-designed database the layout should not need to be changed frequently.

A field name and type is required for each field. Fields that store letters or a combination of letters and numbers are called text fields, while fields that store only numeric values are called number fields. ClarisWorks includes date and time fields which store dates or times. The data stored in an individual field in a single record is called an entry.

5

Before a database is created, a great deal of planning should go into its design. Who will use the database and how they will use it should be considered. Choosing appropriate field names, types, and field widths make a database complete and easy to use. Paper and pencil should be used to sketch record layouts. A hastily designed database usually requires a large amount of work to reorganize after it has been created.

When creating a new database, you must first define the fields by assigning them a name and type (text, number, time, date). The record layout is modified from Layout view. In Layout view, a field's entry box width is changed by clicking on the entry box to select it and then dragging the handles which appear around the entry box. Entire fields may also be moved in a layout.

It is best to enter data into records when in Browse view. Entering data into a record is done by typing the information in the active entry box. Clicking the mouse on an entry box or pressing the Tab key makes an entry box active. To display a new, blank record, the New Record command is selected or the New Record button is clicked on the Shortcuts palette. The Notebook in the Status panel indicates the number of the current record and the total number of records in the database and can be used to quickly select a desired record. Clicking on the top page of the Notebook displays the previous record while clicking on the bottom page displays the next record. The Bookmark can also be dragged to move through the database.

The Print command from the File menu is used to print records in a database. ClarisWorks prints all the records displayed unless the **Current Record** option is selected in the Print dialog box.

Records containing specific information can be quickly retrieved by using Find. The Find command enables specific information to be located in a database by typing the desired information in the Find screen. All records with that data in the same field are then displayed. A range of records can also be displayed by using relational operators. Using the Student database, if >3.7 were entered in the GPA field on the Find screen, ClarisWorks would display all those records with GPAs greater than 3.7 (3.8, 3.9, 4.0). All of the other records are hidden, but can be displayed again using the Show All Records command or by clicking the Show All Records button on the Shortcuts palette.

Vocabulary

Active field - The currently selected field.

Body - The part of the layout that contains all the fields for a single record.

Bookmark - Part of the Notebook which can be dragged to display a certain record.

Browse view - View in which data is entered into fields in a database. Field entries may be added, edited, and deleted in Browse view.

Database - A collection of related information.

Date field - A field that stores a date.

Entry - The information stored in one field in a specific record.

Entry box - Location where data for a field is entered and displayed.

Field - A specific piece of information stored in each record, such as Last Name.

Field name - Name by which the computer identifies a piece of information in a record.

Field type - A field is classified by the kind of data it holds, such as text, numeric, time, or date.

Field width - The amount of space left for data in a field.

Find command - Used to display records that contain specific information in a particular field.

Grid lines - Dotted lines used to help align fields in Layout view.

Handle - Used to resize a field name or entry box in Layout view.

Hidden records - Records that do not meet the current find requirements. Hidden records are not displayed, but remain in the database.

Layout - The order and placement of fields in a record.

Layout view - View in which fields can be moved, resized, and added.

New Record command - Adds a new, empty record at the bottom of the database.

Notebook - Icon in the upper-left corner of the screen used to quickly move through the database.

Number field - A field that contains only numbers (values).

Range - The set of values that meet the requirements of a find that uses relational operators such as >, <, >=, <=, or <>.

Record - A complete collection of data for one item.

Relational operator - Used to compare two values. Operators include =, <, >, <=, >=, <>.

Show All Records command - Used to display any hidden records. Usually applied after a find has been performed.

Status panel - Contains the Notebook and indicates the currently active record and the total number of records in the database.

Text field - A field that stores characters such as a name, address, or phone number.

Time field - A field that stores a time.

Reviews

Sections 5.1 — 5.3

1. Why do historians refer to our present time as the Information Age?

2. a) What is a database?
   b) What is a layout?
   c) What is a record?
   d) What is a field?
   e) What is an entry?
   f) What is a field name?

3. What capabilities of the computer make it an ideal tool for managing databases?

4. What determines the size of a single record in a database?

5. Can the following be stored as databases? Why or why not?
   a) the white pages in a phone book
   b) the yellow pages in a phone book
   c) patient files in a doctor's office
   d) a grocery list
   e) a school yearbook

6. The following information is found in the white pages of a phone book:

   ```
   Capeletti,Rod  17 Adams St. 212-0987
   Caputti,J.  80 Scarlet Ct. 123-4567
   Neldon,Karl  25 Potomac St. 555-1234
   ```

   a) What information would constitute a single record?
   b) Describe the separate fields in such a record.
   c) What information does each field store?

7. a) How would the information stored in a doctor's patient files be broken into records?
   b) Describe some of the possible fields and the data stored in them.

8. List three governmental agencies that might use a computerized database. Explain what information each agency would store in its database.

Sections 5.4 — 5.8

9. a) What is the difference between text and number fields?
   b) What is a date field? What is a time field?

10. How many text, number, and date fields are there in a single student record shown in Section 5.2?

11. Why is it important to plan a database before using the computer?

12. Why might it be better to store the first name and last name of students in separate fields rather than in the same field in the Ivy U student database?

13. a) What should be considered when choosing a field name?
    b) Why should abbreviations and numbers be avoided in field names?

14. Choose appropriate field names and types for the following data:
    a) a person's name
    b) a phone number
    c) the color of a car
    d) an item's price
    e) whether an item is on sale or not
    f) the day a person was born

15. a) What information should be stored in a computerized database listing the cars for sale at an automobile dealership?
    b) Describe a record from such a database, including the information to be stored in each of its fields.

Sections 5.9 — 5.12

16. List the steps required to create a new ClarisWorks database and enter three field names.

17. a) What is a database layout?
    b) What does the default database layout look like for a new database?

18. Using appropriate field names, sketch two different layouts for the database in Review question 15.

19. What is the difference between displaying the database in Browse view and Layout view? What actions can be performed in each view?

20. a) How can the width of an entry box be changed?
    b) Does changing the width of an entry box change the amount of data the field can store? Explain.

21. a) Can the design of a layout be changed after a database has been produced on the computer? If so, how?
    b) Why is it a good idea to move a field's entry box closer to its name?
    c) How can both the field name and field entry box be moved at the same time?

Sections 5.13 — 5.18

22. A database layout has been created which contains four fields—Item, Product Number, Price, and Department. Explain how data can be entered into each field in the first record of the database.

23. Is it possible to enter data into certain fields and leave others empty in the same record?

24. a) What is meant by an active entry box?
    b) If the name Joseph Josiah Kropeudopolis is entered into a field named Name, only part of the entry is displayed. What happens to the undisplayed part of the name?
    c) What can be done to display the complete name in part (b)?

25. What two methods can be used to create a new record?

26. a) How can you tell the number of the currently displayed record?
    b) The total number of records in the database?
    c) List two ways of using the Notebook to make another record active.

27. There are 5 records in a database. How can you print only record 2?

28. Give two examples of how the Find command could be used for the database described in Review 22.

29. List the steps required to display all records in the IVY STUDENT database for students who have not paid their tuition.

30. a) What happens to records that do not meet the Find requirements?
    b) How can hidden records be displayed?

31. What is meant by a range in a find? Give 2 examples.

32. Describe how to use Find to display the following IVY STUDENT database records:
    a) Students with GPAs greater than 2.5
    b) Students from NY
    c) Students with zip codes of 33432
    d) Students named Zoler

5 Exercises

1. Many people use a computerized database in place of an address book. You will create a database to store information about your friends.

   a) On a piece of paper create a list of categories for your address book. Be sure to include at least the full name, complete mailing address, and phone number for each person.

   b) It would be useful to store birthdays in your database. Add this category to the list.

   c) Using your categories, create a list of field names and types.

   d) Create two different sketches of the record layout experimenting with order, groupings, and spacing.

   e) Using ClarisWorks, create the database. Pick the best layout from part (d) and modify the record layout to match.

   f) Enter information for three of your friends.

   g) Save the database naming it Address and print a copy.

   h) Use the Find command to display the records of those friends who do not live in the same city as you, and then print the results.

2. Everybody wants to be an author. You will create a database to store information about books that your friends might someday write. For example, a friend who likes to talk on the phone may write a book entitled *Is There Life Beyond The Telephone?* The purpose of this database is to create a catalog of your friends and their works which will then be sent to different publishers.

   a) On a piece of paper create a list of categories for your author database. Publishers will want a phone number and a complete mailing address (address, city, state, zip code) where they can contact the author. They will also want to know how many years each friend has been an author. Be sure that these categories are included in the list along with each author's name and the title of his or her work.

   b) It would be helpful to know the subject area of each publication. Examples of subject areas include fiction, science fiction, mystery, education, humor, drama, romance, western, etc. Add this field to your list of categories.

   c) Using your categories, create a list of field names and types for each field.

   d) Create two different sketches of the record layout experimenting with order, groupings, and spacing.

   e) Using ClarisWorks, create the database. Pick the best layout from part (d) and modify the record layout to match.

   f) Enter records for three authors. Have a least one of your friends author a mystery.

   g) Save the database naming it Author Catalog and print a copy.

   h) Use the Find command to display the records of those authors who do not write mystery books, and then print the results.

3. The specialty store you announced in the Exercises for Chapters Two and Three needs a database for its inventory. Use the flyer you created in Chapter Three, Exercise 13 as a guide for the data to be included in the database.

    a) On a piece of paper create a list of data categories that describe the items in the inventory of your store. Categories could include item name, department, cost, price, etc.

    b) Be sure to include an item number, quantity on hand, amount ordered, and a price for each item in your inventory. If you have not included these categories, add them to your list created in part (a).

    c) Using your categories, create a list of field names and types.

    d) Create two different sketches of the record layout experimenting with order, groupings, and spacing.

    e) Using ClarisWorks, create the database. Pick the best layout from part (d) and modify the record layout to match.

    f) Enter information for four items in the store.

    g) Save the database naming it Store and print a copy.

    h) Use the Find command to display the records of those items that cost less than $50, and then print the results.

4. In the previous exercise you created a database file for the inventory of your store. Using the Store database as a guide, you will create a database to record the store's sales activity.

    a) On a piece of paper create a list of data categories for the store's daily sales log. Be sure there is a category for each of the following: item number, item name, department, price, quantity sold, method of payment (cash, credit card, check), and date of purchase.

    b) Using your categories, create a list of field names and types.

    c) Create two different sketches of the record layout experimenting with order, groupings, and spacing.

    d) Using ClarisWorks, create the database. Pick the best layout from part (c) and modify the record layout to match.

    e) Enter information for three different items that were sold today.

    f) Save the database naming it Store Log and print a copy.

An Introduction to Computing Using ClarisWorks

5

5. An adventure comic book company has hired you as a database consultant. They would like to use a database to organize the information about each character.

   a) On a piece of paper create a list of categories for the comic database. Be sure there is a category for each of the following: superhero name, "real life" name (i.e. Clark Kent is Superman), special power or advantage, partner, and the role of the character (i.e. crime fighter, villan, assistant, etc.).

   b) Most comic book characters have promotional items available for sale such as T-shirts, action figures, and other toys. The company would like to add a category that contains the best-selling promotional item for each character. Add this category to the list you created in part (a).

   c) Using your categories, create a list of field names and types.

   d) Create two different sketches of the record layout experimenting with order, groupings, and spacing.

   e) Using ClarisWorks, create the database. Pick the best layout from part (d) and modify the record layout to match.

   f) Enter information for four different comic book characters.

   g) Save the database naming it Comic and print a copy.

   h) Use the Find command to display the records of those characters who are villains, and then print the results.

6. Your insurance agent wants a database of all of your important belongings. Examples of the kind of information to include might be: music CDs, calculator, computer CDs, acoustic guitar, computer, etc.

   a) On a piece of paper create a list of categories that describes the items. Categories could include item name, original cost, and item type (i.e. electronics, art, clothing, jewelry, and equipment).

   b) The insurance agent forgot to tell you to include the age of the item. Add a category to your list that shows the date of purchase.

   c) Using your categories, create a list of field names and types.

   d) Create two different sketches of the record layout experimenting with order, groupings, and spacing.

   e) Using ClarisWorks, create the database. Pick the best layout from part (d) and modify the record layout to match.

   f) Enter data for four different items.

   g) Save the file naming it Insure and print a copy.

   h) Use the Find command to display the records of those items which cost over $50, and then print the results.

7. City Zoo needs your help to create a database of animals in the zoo. It may be helpful to refer to Chapter Three, Exercise 14.

a) City Zoo has determined that the categories of information should include the name of the staff member who cares for the animal, the kind of animal (American Black Bear, Asian Green Boa Constrictor, etc.), number of female animals, animal type (mammal, reptile, bird, etc.), location of animal (aquarium, rain forest, etc.), and number of male animals. On a piece of paper, create a list of field names and types for each of the categories.

b) Create two different sketches of the record layout experimenting with order, groupings, and spacing.

c) Using ClarisWorks, create the database. Pick the best layout from part (b) and modify the record layout to match.

d) The zoo has decided it wants the staff member field to be in the upper-left of the record, above the other fields. Move the staff member field, adjusting other fields as necessary.

e) Save the database naming it Zoo.

f) Enter the following records:

Staff	Animal	Type	Males	Females	Location
S. Smith	American Black Bear	Mammal	0	1	American West
T. Quay	Asian Green Boa	Reptile	1	2	Reptile Garden
S. Smith	Eastern Cotton Tail	Mammal	2	1	Eastern Forest

g) Save the modified Zoo and print a copy.

h) Use the Find command to display only the records of those animals that are mammals, and then print the results.

8. The research scientists have received the grant for the research proposal you helped write in Chapter Three, Exercise 12. They are living on the tropical island of Bashibashi and need a database to keep track of the movements of the island's gibbon population.

a) The research scientists have determined that the categories of information should include time of sighting, individual gibbon's name, gender (male or female), approximate age, the island's weather (sun, clouds, rain, wind, storm), temperature, location of the sighting, and gibbon's activity (eating, sleeping, grooming, playing, aggression). On a piece of paper, create a list of field names and types for each of the categories.

b) Create two different sketches of the record layout experimenting with order, groupings, and spacing.

c) Using ClarisWorks, create the database. Pick the best layout from part (b) and modify the record layout to match.

d) Save the database naming it My Gibbons and print a copy.

5

9. You will create a database of the colleges and universities you are interested in attending.

   a) On a piece of paper create a list of categories for the college database. Be sure to include the full name, complete mailing address, and phone number for each entry, as well as the school's enrollment, tuition, and room and board fees.

   b) It will be important to know if the school is public or private. Add a category to your list which indicates this.

   c) Using your categories, create a list of field names and types.

   d) Create two different sketches of the record layout experimenting with order, groupings, and spacing.

   e) Using ClarisWorks, create the database. Pick the best layout from part (d) and modify the record layout to match.

   f) Enter information for five of your favorite colleges. If you do not know the exact information concerning address, costs, etc., make up a realistic entry.

   g) Save the database naming it My College and print a copy.

   h) Use the Find command to display the records of those schools with tuition greater than $2,000 and then print the results.

10. Fantasy Wheels, Inc. is an automobile dealership that sells exotic used cars and wants to store their inventory of cars in a database. Below is the information to be stored in three records:

   1969 Maserati, blue exterior, black interior, 4-speed transmission, radio, and air conditioning. Originally paid $9,800. Now asking $21,600.

   1984 Ferrari, gray exterior, black interior, 4-speed transmission, convertible. Originally paid $22,000. Now asking $38,500.

   1972 Corvette, red exterior, green interior, automatic transmission, radio, and air conditioning. Originally paid $8,500. Now asking $25,800.

   a) Using the information above as a guide, create a list of categories for the car inventory database on a piece of paper.

   b) Using your categories, create a list of field names and types.

   c) Create two different sketches of the record layout experimenting with order, groupings, and spacing.

   d) Using ClarisWorks, create the database. Pick the best layout from part (c) and modify the record layout to match.

   e) Enter the information above for the three cars into the database. Each car should have its own record.

   f) Save the database naming it Wheels and print a copy.

   g) Use the Find command to display the records of those cars with black interiors and then print the results of the Find.

11. You are to use the survey form created in Chapter Three, Exercise 15 to produce a database.

   a) Open Survey Form. Print three copies and then close the file. Have three friends complete the survey.

   b) Using the questions on the survey form as categories, create a list of field names and types.

   c) Create two different sketches of the record layout experimenting with order, groupings, and spacing.

   d) Using ClarisWorks, create the database. Pick the best layout from part (c) and modify the record layout to match.

   e) Enter the data from the completed survey forms into the database. Each survey form should correspond to a separate record.

   f) Save the database naming it Student Survey and print a copy.

12. Holiday Airlines has weekly flights to the Bahamas and has decided to computerize its reservation system. Holiday owns one airplane which has 20 seats numbered as shown below:

Windows			Aisle			Windows
	1A	1B		1C	1D	
	2A	2B		2C	2D	
	3A	3B		3C	3D	
	4A	4B		4C	4D	
	5A	5B		5C	5D	

   a) On a piece of paper create a list of categories for the reservations database. Be sure to include a seat number, location (aisle or window), class (first or coach), and the name and phone number of each passenger on the plane.

   b) Using your categories, create a list of field names and types.

   c) Create two different sketches of the layout experimenting with order, groupings, and spacing.

   d) Using ClarisWorks, create the database. Pick the best layout from part (c) and modify the record layout to match.

   e) Add an empty record for each of the 20 seats on the plane. Enter the appropriate seat numbers. Enter the word "Empty" into the first name field of each record. In the appropriate field, enter the seat's location (window or aisle). Make all seats in rows 1 and 2 the first class section.

   f) Make the following reservations by updating the proper records in the database. Use the Find command to locate seats for passengers with preferences:

   Mr. and Mrs. Irplane
   Phone Number: (407) 555-6321
   Ada Irplane: window seat, first class
   Adam Irplane: aisle seat next to Ada

   Ms. McGuire
   Phone Number: (617) 555-5217
   Kerrin McGuire: aisle seat, coach

   g) Show all records and save the database naming it Holiday.

   h) Use the Find command to display both Mr. and Mrs. Irplane's records and print them.

13. A database is very useful for recording the data from experiments. Weather observation experiments require periodic data collection over a long period of time to establish trends and help meteorologists make predictions based on these trends.

   a) On a piece of paper create a list of categories for a weather experiment database. Each record should contain fields which store the date, time, temperature, amount of rainfall, and sky conditions for a single observation. Use the following data as a guide:

Date	Time	Temp. (C)	Rain (cm)	Sky
1/8/60	3:00 PM	22	0.0	partly cloudy
11/5/61	5:46 AM	19	0.0	sunny
4/20/62	6:19 PM	14	0.4	cloudy
6/5/65	5:26 PM	−3	0.2	cloudy

   b) Using your categories, create a list of field names and types for each field.

   c) Create two different sketches of the record layout experimenting with order, groupings, and spacing.

   d) Using ClarisWorks, create the database. Pick the best layout from part (c) and modify the record layout to match.

   e) Use the data above to create four new records.

   f) Save the database naming it Weather and print a copy.

   g) Use the Find command to display the records of those days where it did not rain, and then print the results.

An Introduction to Computing Using ClarisWorks

Chapter 6

Manipulating Data with the Database

Define Fields

Field Format

Alignment

Find

New Search

Edit Searches

List

Print

Page Setup

Page View

New Request

Delete Record

New Sort

Edit Sorts

Objectives

After completing this chapter you will be able to:

1. Use field entry options to limit the data a field will accept.

2. Update the data stored in a database.

3. Format fields.

4. Query the database for specific information using finds and the New Request command.

5. Create a named query using the Search pop-up menu.

6. Display, format, and print a database in List view.

7. Delete records from a database.

8. Sort records based on the data in a key sort field.

9. Create a named sort using the Sort pop-up menu.

6

This chapter describes the steps necessary to modify a ClarisWorks database and perform some common operations on it: query, update, and sort. Queries will be applied to determine which records meet certain criteria. Different ways of ordering records to make the database easier to use and options for making data entry more accurate are explained.

6.1 Field Entry Options

In ClarisWorks entry options can be included in a field's definition. *Field entry options* make it possible to limit the data a field will accept to only entries from within a specified range or to unique data. For example, an entry option could limit the GPA field in the Student database to entries that fall within the 0.0 to 4.0 range.

The best time to create entry options is when the database is created. Therefore, entry options should be considered while the database is being planned. The third step in planning a database is to create a list of field names and the type of data each will store. At this time, entry options for each field can also be planned.

6.2 Field Entry Options - Number

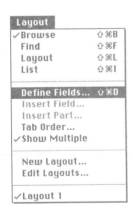

The Define Fields command from the Layout menu (⇧⌘**D**) displays the dialog box where fields are created. Field entry options are also defined here. To include entry options for an existing field, click on the field name to highlight it and then select the **Options** button to display the Options dialog box. The Options dialog box varies depending on the highlighted field's type. For number fields, entry options include defining a *data range*:

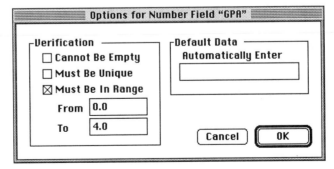

Only values between 0.0 and 4.0 will be accepted in the GPA field

In the Options dialog box on the previous page, the **Must Be In Range** option was selected and values entered in the **From** and **To** boxes to ensure that GPA field entries are within a specified range. Making a GPA entry that is not within the specified range displays a warning message when you attempt to make another record current or execute a command:

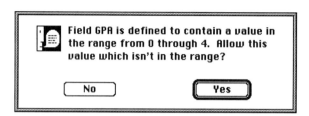

ClarisWorks can verify that data entries fall within a certain range

Selecting **No** highlights the invalid entry so that one within the acceptable range can be typed. Selecting **Yes** allows the entry outside the range.

Practice 1

In this Practice you will modify the field definition for the GPA field in the Student database. A data range will be created, and a new record will be added.

1) OPEN STUDENT

    a. Boot the System and start ClarisWorks.
    b. Open Student, the database created in Chapter Five.
    c. Be sure you are in Browse view.

2) CREATE A DATA RANGE FOR THE GPA FIELD

    a. From the Layout menu, select the Define Fields command (⇧⌘**D**). All fields in the database are listed in the Define Database Fields dialog box.
    b. Scroll through the field list to display GPA. Click once on GPA to highlight it. Notice that the **Options** button is no longer dim.
    c. Select the **Options** button to display the Options dialog box for a number field. Click on the **Must Be In Range** check box. The **From** and **To** boxes are no longer dim and a blinking cursor is displayed in the **From** box.
    d. Because we want ClarisWorks to verify that each GPA entry falls within the range of 0.0 and 4.0, type `0.0` in the **From** box. Click the mouse in the **To** box to place the cursor and type `4.0`.
    e. Select **OK** to return to the Define Database Fields dialog box. Select **Done** to remove the dialog box and return to Browse view. The GPA field definition has been modified.

3) ADD A NEW RECORD

From the Edit menu, select the New Record command to create a new record and then enter the following information:

First Name: `Matilda`
Last Name: `Rose`
Address: `435 Frelinghuysen Road`
City: `Leafville`
State: `NJ`
Zip: `08049`

An Introduction to Computing Using ClarisWorks

Admit Date: 12/14/96
GPA: 34 (this entry will be corrected in the next step)
Tuition: Paid

4) SAVE AND CLOSE THE MODIFIED STUDENT DATABASE

a. From the File menu, select the Save command. Because the GPA field contains an unacceptable entry (only values between 0.0 and 4.0 are acceptable as defined), ClarisWorks displays a warning.
b. Click on **No** in the error dialog box and notice that the invalid entry is highlighted. Type 3 . 4 to replace the incorrect entry.
c. Save and then close Student.

6.3 Field Entry Options - Text

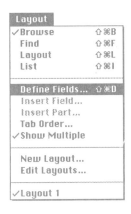

Like number field entry options, text field entry options are defined using the Options dialog box:

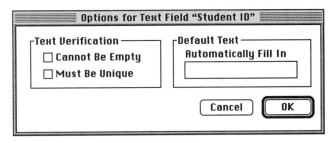

Text field entry options appear in this dialog box

When the **Must Be Unique** option is selected, ClarisWorks checks every record in the database for the same entry in that particular field. If the field's entry is not unique, a warning message is displayed when you attempt to make another record current or execute a command.

Practice 2

In this Practice you will add a record to the IVY STUDENT database, taking advantage of the field entry options. Ranges and unique fields have been incorporated into the database. Start ClarisWorks if it is not already running.

1) OPEN IVY STUDENT

a. Open IVY STUDENT.
b. Be sure the database is displayed in Browse view.

2) VIEW THE STUDENT ID FIELD OPTIONS

a. From the Layout menu, select the Define Fields command.
b. Select the Student ID field.
c. Select the **Options** button to display the Options dialog box. Note that the **Must Be Unique** option is selected. When planning the database, Ivy University decided that each student's ID must be unique. This entry option was used to help insure correct data.
d. Select **OK** to remove the dialog box.
e. Select **Done** to remove the Define Database Fields dialog box.

3) ADD A NEW RECORD

From the Edit menu, select the New Record command and then enter the following information:

Student ID: PS259
First Name: Paula
Last Name: Lutz
Address: 10 Daniel Drive
City: Squirrel Island
State: ME
Zip: 04570
Admit Date: 2/5/96
GPA: 3.5
Tuition: Paid

4) MOVE TO A DIFFERENT RECORD

a. Click on the top page of the Notebook to move to the previous record. A warning message is displayed because the entry in the Student ID field of the new record already exists in another record:

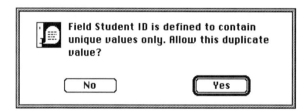

Field Student ID is defined to contain unique values only. Allow this duplicate value?

No   Yes

b. Click on **No** to remove the dialog box. The Student ID for Paula Lutz is highlighted.
c. Type the correct Student ID: PL259
d. Click on the top page of the Notebook to make the previous record active.

5) SAVE THE MODIFIED IVY STUDENT

6.4 Updating

Changing the information stored in a database is called *updating*. Updates are done from Browse view and examples include removing old information, changing existing information, and adding new information. The New Record command, discussed in the last chapter, is used to add new information. Removing old information is discussed later in this chapter. Existing information can be changed by replacing an entry or editing an entry.

The entry in a field can be replaced by triple-clicking the pointer in the desired field's entry box to highlight the contents, typing the new data, and then pressing the Tab key.

You can also edit the entry in a field. Clicking the mouse pointer in the desired field's entry box displays a cursor. The arrow keys and Delete key can then be used to edit the entry.

6

Because an update usually involves a specific record, the Find command can be used to locate the desired record. After updating, the file must be saved on disk. It is important to realize that simply changing the data on screen does not change it in the file. Should there be a power failure before you save the file, the change would not appear the next time the file is opened.

Practice 3

In this Practice you will update IVY STUDENT by modifying three records. Start ClarisWorks and open IVY STUDENT if you have not already done so. Be sure the database is displayed in Browse view because all updates must take place in this view.

1) LOCATE THE DESIRED RECORD

Student Roberta Poston needs to have the spelling of her last name corrected.

a. Roberta Poston's last name was entered into the database as Poisson. From the Layout menu, select the Find command. Type `=Poisson` in the Last Name entry box.

b. Select the **Find** button. ClarisWorks displays the Roberta Poisson record.

2) CORRECT THE STUDENT'S LAST NAME

a. Press the Tab key until the Last Name field is selected.
b. In the entry box, click the pointer before the second "s."
c. Drag the pointer over the second "s," highlighting just that letter.
d. Type the new character, `t`. The "t" is inserted at the current cursor position, replacing the highlighted "s" and the entry is now "Poisston."
e. Press the left-arrow key two times so that the cursor is to the right of the "i."
f. Press the Delete key to remove the "i." The proper last name, "Poston," is shown in the entry box.

3) SAVE IVY STUDENT TO RETAIN THE UPDATE

From the Organize menu, select Show All Records and then save IVY STUDENT.

4) LOCATE THE DESIRED RECORD

Student Jenny Lee has moved to 129 Amostown Road.

a. From the Layout menu, select the Find command. Type `=Lee` in the Last Name entry box.

b. Select the **Find** button. ClarisWorks displays two records that contain "Lee" as the last name.

c. Click on the bottom page of the Notebook to make Jenny Lee's record the current record. Press the Tab key to display the entry boxes.

5) ENTER THE NEW DATA FOR THE ADDRESS FIELD

a. Triple-click in the Address field to highlight the entry.
b. Type `129 Amostown Road`. Her new address is now stored in the field, replacing the old data.

6) SAVE IVY STUDENT TO RETAIN THE UPDATE

From the Organize menu, select Show All Records and then save IVY STUDENT.

7) LOCATE THE DESIRED RECORD

Student Bruce Bonner has paid his outstanding tuition bill.

a. From the Layout menu, select the Find command.

b. Type =Bonner in the Last Name field and then select the **Find** button.

8) ENTER THE NEW DATA

Press the Tab key to display the entry boxes. Select the Tuition field and change the entry to Paid.

9) SAVE IVY STUDENT TO RETAIN THE UPDATES

From the Organize menu, select Show All Records and then save IVY STUDENT.

6.5 Formatting Fields

ClarisWorks has a number of formatting options. When a field is formatted, the format is applied to that field in every record of the database. Formatting does not change what is stored in the field, only the way it is displayed.

To apply a format, the database must be in Layout view. The entry box of the field to be formatted is then clicked once to select it. Executing the Field Format command from the Options menu displays the Format dialog box. The contents of this dialog box change depending on the field type. For example, clicking on a number field such as GPA and then executing Field Format displays the following dialog box:

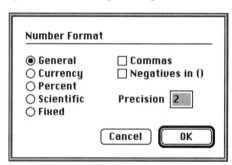

Numeric entries can be formatted in a variety of ways

In the Number Format dialog box, two commonly used formats are **Fixed** and **Currency**. A field formatted as fixed displays its entry to the number of decimal places specified in the **Precision** box. For example, the GPA field will be formatted for 1 decimal place if **Fixed** is clicked, a 1 typed in the **Precision** box, and **OK** selected. When in Browse view, all GPA values will be displayed with 1 decimal place (e.g., 3 will be displayed as 3.0, etc.).

Another useful formatting option for number fields is **Currency**. A value in a field formatted as **Currency** displays a dollar sign, such as $1000.00. The default **Precision** of 2 is usually used when a field is formatted for dollars. Selecting the **Commas** option inserts commas in a number, while selecting **Negatives in ()** places a number less than 0 in parentheses so that it is easier to recognize.

An Introduction to Computing Using ClarisWorks

When formatting a date field the following dialog box is displayed:

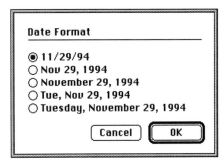

Date entries can be formatted in different ways

Dates can be displayed in short form (11/29/94) or long form (November 29, 1994). The day of the week can also be displayed. A similar dialog box is displayed when formatting a time field. Times can be displayed in either 12-hour (5:20 PM) or 24-hour format (17:20). Seconds can also be added to either time format.

6.6 Formatting - Alignment

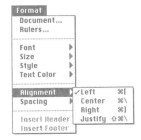

Database entries are left aligned unless formatted otherwise. In Layout view, the Alignment command from the Format menu can be used to change the way an entry is displayed. This is useful for right aligning numeric, date, and time entries.

To change the alignment of a field, first select its entry box by clicking on it once. Next, dragging down to the Alignment command in the Format menu displays a submenu from which Left, Center, Right, or Justify can be chosen. Selecting Right (⌘]) displays the selected field's entry right aligned.

6.7 Modifying Fields

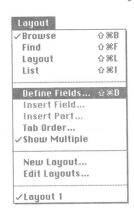

A field might need to be renamed, added, or deleted. Changes to a database's fields are made by selecting the Define Fields command from the Layout menu:

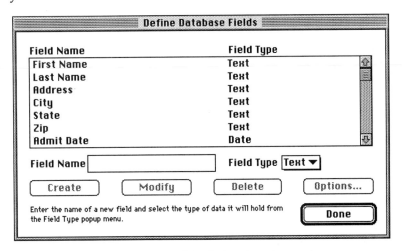

The Define Database Fields dialog box is used to rename, add, or delete a field

Renaming a Field   Clicking on a field in the field list selects it. Changes or corrections are made by editing the field name in the **Field Name** box. When the corrections have been made, selecting the **Modify** button renames the field in the list.

Adding a Field   A new field is added to a database by simply typing its name in the **Field Name** entry box, selecting its **Field Type**, defining any entry options using the **Options** button, and then selecting **Create**.

Deleting a Field   Selecting a field from the field list and then clicking on the **Delete** button displays the following warning:

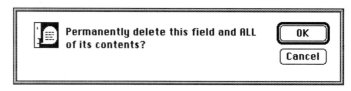

ClarisWorks warns you when a field is about to be deleted

If **OK** is selected, the field as well as any data in that field is removed from every record in the database. Selecting **Cancel** retains the field.

Practice 4

In this Practice you will modify records in IVY STUDENT by formatting, adding, renaming, and deleting fields. Start ClarisWorks and open IVY STUDENT if you have not already done so.

1) SCROLL THE DATABASE

    a. In the Status panel, drag the Bookmark until 25 is displayed on the Notebook.
    b. The records for Alma Lee and Al Monde are displayed. Note how the GPA for Alma Lee is displayed with no decimal places.

2) FORMAT THE GPA FIELD FOR 1 DECIMAL PLACE

    a. Switch to Layout view and click on the GPA entry box to select it.
    b. From the Options menu, select the Field Format command. The Number Format dialog box is displayed.
    c. Click on the **Fixed** radio button and then type a 1 to change the **Precision**. Select **OK** to apply the formatting.
    d. Switch to Browse view. The GPA field of each record is now displayed with 1 decimal place. For example, 4 is displayed as 4.0 in Alma Lee's record.

3) ADD A NEW FIELD TO THE DATABASE

    a. From the Layout menu, select the Define Fields command. The Define Database Fields dialog box is displayed, listing all the fields in the database.
    b. Type `Class` and then select **Create**. The new field is added to the field list as a **Text** field.
    c. Click **Done** to add the new field to the layout. The new field has been added to the database and placed below the last field, Tuition, in the record layout.

4) RENAME A FIELD

    a. From the Layout menu, select the Define Fields command.

    b. Scroll through the field list and click on Class. The field name is displayed in the **Field Name** entry box.

    c. Type `Status` to replace the current name. Click on **Modify**. Class then changes to Status in the list.

    d. Select **Done**. Notice that the field name has changed in the database.

5) DELETE THE STATUS FIELD

    a. From the Layout menu, select the Define Fields command.

    b. Highlight Status in the **Field Name** list and then select **Delete**. A warning is displayed about deleting the field.

    c. Click on **OK** to delete the field. If this field had stored any data, the data would have been removed from the database.

    d. Select **Done** to remove the Define Database Fields dialog box.

6) RIGHT ALIGN THE DATE AND NUMBER FIELDS

    a. Switch to Layout view.

    b. Click on the Admit Date entry box to select it.

    c. From the Format menu, drag down to the Alignment command. From the Alignment submenu, select Right. Note how the entry box name is now right aligned.

    d. Click on the GPA entry box to select it.

    e. Press ⌘] (the] key is located just above the Return key). The entry name is now right aligned in the box.

    f. Switch to Browse view.

    g. Press the Tab key to display the entry boxes of the current record. Note the alignment of the Admit Date and GPA entries.

7) SAVE THE MODIFIED IVY STUDENT

6.8 Querying a Database

In the last chapter, we used the Find command to display records that contained specified data. This type of database operation is called a *query*. To perform the query, we entered data, or *criteria*, in the Find screen. The **Find** button was then selected to search the database and display those records that matched the criteria. Records that did not match were hidden.

Query criteria can be specified using the conjunctions "and" and "or." For example, in the last chapter we queried IVY STUDENT for records with "GPA equal to 3.9 *and* State equal to NC." This kind of query is called a *complex query*.

Complex queries that use two or more fields joined by "and" can be done from the Find screen with the **All** button selected, as with the complex query performed in the last chapter. Complex queries that use only one field, like "GPA greater than 3.0 and GPA less than 3.5" require the Find screen's **Visible** button. When the **Visible** button is selected, **Find** searches only the displayed records. For example, to display records with GPAs between 3.0 and 3.5, Find is executed, `>3.0` typed in the GPA field, the **All** button clicked, and then the **Find** button selected. To complete the query, Find is executed again, <3 . 5 typed in the GPA field, the **Visible** button clicked, and then the **Find** button selected. Note that the first find for this query displays those records with GPAs greater than 3.0. However, GPAs greater than or equal to 3.5 are also displayed. To limit the range, a second find must be performed on the displayed records. The records not hidden meet the criteria GPA>3.0 and GPA<3.5.

6.9 Creating a Named Query

Below the Notebook are four pop-up menus:

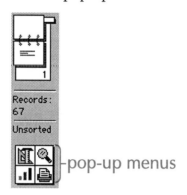
pop-up menus

Commands in the pop-up menus are accessed by pressing and holding the mouse button on a menu and then dragging down to the desired command to highlight it. When the mouse button is released, the highlighted command is executed.

The Search pop-up menu ([image]) is used to create a named query that is saved with the database. A named query can be applied at any time without having to redefine the query criteria.

Executing the New Search command from the Search pop-up menu displays the following dialog box:

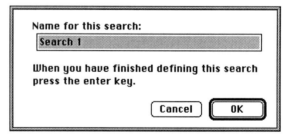

A query is given a name in this dialog box

A descriptive name should be typed in the **Name for this search** entry box. When **OK** is selected, the Find screen is displayed with a **Store** button in place of the **Find** button. After entering the criteria, **Store** is selected to save the query. Once a query has been saved, it can be applied to the database by simply selecting its name from the bottom of the Search pop-up menu.

An Introduction to Computing Using ClarisWorks

A query name is changed by selecting the Edit Searches command from the Search pop-up menu to display a dialog box similar to the following:

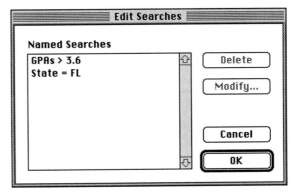

Query names can be changed using the Edit Searches dialog box

The query to be renamed must first be highlighted. Selecting the **Modify** button displays another dialog box where the new name for the query is entered. A highlighted query is deleted when the **Delete** button from the Edit Searches dialog box is selected.

Practice 5

In this Practice you will perform a complex query on IVY STUDENT. Named queries will also be created and saved with the database. Start ClarisWorks and open IVY STUDENT if you have not already done so.

1) APPLY A COMPLEX QUERY

Ivy University would like to know how many students were admitted in 1996.

a. From the Layout menu, select the Find command. The Find screen is displayed.
b. In the Admit Date field, type: `>=1/1/96`
c. The **All** button below the Notebook is already selected. Select the **Find** button to display those students admitted on or after January 1, 1996. The Status panel indicates 41 records have been found.
d. From the Layout menu, select the Find command again.
e. In the Admit Date field, type: `<1/1/97`
f. Click on the **Visible** button below the Notebook and then select the **Find** button. There are now only 24 records displayed. Each of these records has an Admit Date which is greater than or equal to 1/1/96 but also less than 1/1/97.
g. Scroll through the records and verify that the admit dates are within 1996.

2) CREATE A NAMED QUERY

a. From the Search pop-up menu (🔍), select the New Search command. A dialog box is displayed.
b. Type `Florida Students` for the query name.
c. Select **OK**. The Find screen is displayed.
d. In the State field, type: `=FL`
e. Select the **All** button and then select the **Store** button to save the query.

3) DETERMINE HOW MANY STUDENTS ARE FROM FLORIDA

From the Search pop-up menu, select Florida Students. The Florida Students query created in the previous step is applied to the database. Only the records of those students from Florida are displayed.

4) SAVE THE MODIFIED IVY STUDENT

Show all records and then save IVY STUDENT.

6.10 List View

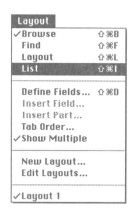

Selecting the List command from the Layout menu displays the records of a database in *List view*:

	Student ID	First Name	Last Name	Address	City	State	Zip	Admit Dat
	QS516	Quincy	Smith	2 Waterfall	Biminy	ME	04020	5/16/95
	SR228	Sonya	Rodd	100 NE	Fort Wayne	IN	46040	2/28/94
	BB139	Bruce	Bonner	35 Madison	Newark	DE	19312	1/3/97
	KK920	Kim	Kokonen	#5 Palm	Stans Valley	VI	00820	9/20/96
	AF939	Amy	Freitas	2841	Lantana	AL	36345	9/3/94
	RR489	Richie	Richman	6090 Gentry	Half Way	MO	65663	4/8/94
	SD825	Shanice	Drummond	5 Union	Darlington	ID	83231	8/25/97
	MR121	Matilda	Rose	435	Leafville	NJ	08049	12/14/94
	HH321	Homel	Hutchinson	2312	Jamaica	NY	11947	3/21/96
	SM517	Susan	Musa	721	Superstition	AZ	85220	5/17/94
	MO319	Megan	O'Toole	68902	Monticello	AR	71655	3/19/96
	DT119	Dorthy	Toto	1719 West	Mount Hope	KS	67108	1/1/96
	RW929	Richard	Wymore	Waterloo	Pickrell	NE	68422	9/2/96
	HR328	Harold	Rolls	30000	Wallace	IL	60616	3/28/97
	GG413	Gerri	Gurbuz	15 Beach	Mountainvie	HI	96771	4/13/94
	AH449	Adam	Hewgley	2 Cascade	Cayon City	OR	97820	4/4/95
	SA313	Sam	Adams	121 Carey	Leaftown	PA	19717	3/13/95
	TR511	Theodore	Ripley	789 Shady	Moss Point	MS	39563	5/11/95
	GB926	Galin	Baer	10 Gallon	Big Town	TX	75149	9/25/94
	JP622	Jack	Portillo	1585	Las Cruces	NM	88001	6/22/96
	CD130	Clare	Diningtable	9045	Clarance	OK	73601	1/30/94
	NR229	Nancy	Rohrma	291	Waumpum	IL	62920	2/2/97
	GG215	Gina	Golda	221	Buffalo	TN	37830	2/15/95
	YY328	Yin	Yang	1776	New	SD	57492	3/28/96
	AL889	Alma	Lee	713	Haddonfield	NJ	08033	8/8/96
	AM510	Al	Monde	88 West	Eighty Eight	KY	42130	5/10/96
	SS101	Steve	Settles	213 Mina	New	MA	03759	10/17/97
	EM424	Eric	Mariemont	5656	Diamond	MD	20878	4/24/96
	HC729	Hazel	Cruz	Ferncastle	Glade	VT	05906	7/29/94

IVY STUDENT (DB)

Records: 80   Unsorted   100

The List view screen

In List view, the records in a database are displayed as rows of data. Each row corresponds to a record, with approximately twenty-nine records being displayed at once. Each column corresponds to a field. This view is useful because it allows records to be compared to one another.

In List view, the active field has a solid outline. Pressing the Tab key makes the next field in the record active. The mouse can also be used to select an entry by clicking the pointer on it. Scroll bars at the bottom and right of the screen are used to view fields and records not currently visible.

The default field width in List view is about 1 inch. This may not be wide enough to display a field's contents in its entirety (i.e., the Address field shown above). In the next section we will describe how to increase the size of a field in List view to show all of the data stored in it.

It is possible to update a record in List view by selecting the desired entry and entering the new data. However, it is usually better to update records in Browse view because all of the fields for one specific record are visible. List view is best used for those operations which involve determining the relationships between records, such as querying.

6

6.11 Formatting List View

Formats applied to a database in Layout view are not automatically applied to List view. Field widths, the order in which fields appear, and the way entries are displayed can all be changed directly from List view.

Changing a Field's Width

Often the default field width of about 1 inch in List view is insufficient to display field entries in their entirety. A field's width is changed by dragging its right column divider bar. To do this, place the pointer on the bar separating the field names at the top of the screen. The pointer shape changes to a double-headed arrow:

Address	+City
129	Leaftown

Dragging the divider resizes the Address field

Next, drag the divider bar to the right to increase the width of the field. To decrease a field's width, drag the divider bar to the left.

It is important to note that changing a field's width has no effect on the data stored in that field, only its appearance on the screen. Also, changing field widths in List view has no effect on field widths in Browse view, and vice versa.

Moving Fields

The order in which fields appear in List view can be changed by dragging a field to a new location. To move a field, place the pointer on its field name. The pointer changes to a hollow double-headed arrow:

First Name	Last Name
Matilda	Rose

Field order is changed by dragging a field name to a new location

Next, drag the column of data to the new position. For example, placing the mouse pointer on the Last Name field name and then dragging displays an outline of the field column. Dragging the outline so that it is on top of the First Name field places the Last Name field column before the First Name field column.

Formatting Fields

To format a field in List view, it must first be selected by clicking once on the field name at the top of the screen. When a field is selected, the Alignment command from the Format menu can be used to change the alignment of the field's entries. Double-clicking on a number field name displays the Number Format dialog box. The Date Format or Time Format dialog box is displayed when a date or time field name is double-clicked.

6.12 Printing in List View

A database in List view can be printed by selecting the Print command from the File menu to display its dialog box and then selecting the **Print** button or by clicking on the Print button on the Shortcuts palette. Databases in List view are often too wide to print on a single sheet of paper. In this case the database is printed on consecutive sheets starting from the leftmost columns and proceeding to the right.

The Page Setup command from the File menu displays a dialog box that contains the **Orientation** options:

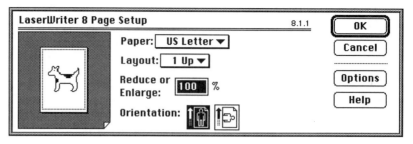

The Orientation option is available from the Page Setup dialog box

Clicking on the rightmost option (⬛) prints the database across the widest part of the page in *landscape orientation*. This is useful when printing a database in List view because more fields fit on a page.

The Page View command from the View menu (⇧⌘**P**) is used to determine how a database will look when printed. When Page View is selected, a check mark is placed beside its name in the View menu and the database is divided into page-sized sections. To view each page entirely, use the Zoom controls. To return to normal view select Page View again.

As with the word processor, headers and footers can be included in a database to provide more informative printouts. Information such as a person's name, the date of the printout, or the filename can be included. When the Insert Header or Insert Footer command from the Format menu is selected, the database is automatically displayed in Page View.

Practice 6

In this Practice you will query IVY STUDENT and then display the results in List view. Start ClarisWorks and open IVY STUDENT if you have not already done so.

1) DISPLAY IVY STUDENT IN LIST VIEW

From the Layout menu, select the List command. The first few fields of many records are displayed. If necessary, scroll until the Address field is visible.

2) FORMAT LIST VIEW

a. Place the pointer on the divider bar between the Address and City fields. The pointer changes to a solid double-headed arrow.
b. Drag the divider bar about ½ inch to the right. The column is widened. Continue to widen the column until all the Address field entries are displayed entirely.
c. Change the widths of the remaining fields so that all of the entries in the fields are displayed entirely. Narrow fields that are unnecessarily wide.
d. Double-click on the GPA field name at the top of the screen. The Number Format dialog box is displayed.
e. Format the GPA field as **Fixed** with 1 as the **Precision**. Select **OK**.

3) CREATE AND APPLY A QUERY

a. From the Search pop-up menu, select the New Search command. A dialog box is displayed.
b. Type GPAs > 3.6 for the query name.

c. Select **OK**. The Find screen is displayed.
d. In the GPA field, type: >3 . 6
e. Select the **All** button and then select the **Store** button to save the query.
f. From the Search pop-up menu, select GPAs > 3.6. Only the records of those students with GPAs greater than 3.6 are displayed.

4) VIEW THE QUERY RESULTS IN LIST VIEW

From the Layout menu, select the List command. Only those records matching the query criteria are visible. Scroll if necessary, and note how easy it is to see that the records displayed have a GPA greater than 3.6.

5) SAVE AND PRINT IVY STUDENT

a. From the View menu, select the Page View command. The database is divided into page-sized sections.
b. If necessary, scroll until page 2 is visible. Note how the Admit Date, GPA, and Tuition fields appear on page 2.
c. From the File menu, select the Page Setup command. A dialog box is displayed.
d. Click on the landscape **Orientation** option (⊞). Select **OK**.
e. Note how only one page is now required to print the query results in List view.
f. Save IVY STUDENT and then print a copy.
g. From the View menu, select Page View again to deselect it.
h. Show all records and then save IVY STUDENT.

6.13 The New Request Command

Complex queries that use fields joined by "or" require the New Request (⌘**R**) command from the Edit menu to perform the query. Selecting New Request displays an empty record below the existing record in the Find screen. Additional criteria can then be entered in the empty record and **Find** selected to execute the query. For example, to display the records of those students from Pennsylvania *or* Florida, the Find command is executed and =PA is typed in the State field. Executing the New Request command displays a new record where =FL is typed:

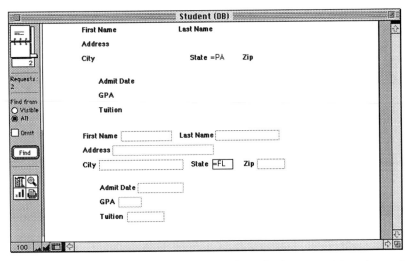

Students from PA or FL will be displayed when Find is selected

Selecting **Find** displays only records that have PA or FL in the State field.

Ranges may also be used in each request. To display the records of those students with a GPA less than 1.0 or greater than 3.5, the Find command is executed and `<1.0` typed in the GPA field. New Request is then selected and `>3.5` typed in the new record's GPA field. Selecting Find displays the appropriate records from the database.

6.14 Defining Query Criteria

The most important step in querying a database is carefully defining the criteria. Some guidelines to follow when creating query criteria are as follows:

1. **Determine which fields are required in the query.** For example, suppose the college admissions office wants to know which students on the Dean's list are from Arizona. The GPA field will be used in this query because Dean's list students must have a GPA greater than 3.5. The State field will also be used in this query to determine which students are from Arizona.

2. **Determine which values are required in the query.** Continuing with the example in Step 1, >3.5 is used because we are interested in a range of GPA values. AZ is used to determine the appropriate state.

3. **Carefully create the criteria using the proper relationships.** Because we want student records which contain a value of 3.5 or greater in the GPA field and the text AZ in the State field, our criteria is GPA>3.5 *and* State=AZ.

4. **Before using the computer, think about the data a record must contain in order to be displayed.** For example, if the criteria is GPA>3.5 and State=AZ, does this mean that a record storing 3.5 in the GPA field will be displayed? What about a record storing 3.6 in the GPA field and RI in the State field?

After carefully defining the criteria, the following guidelines can be used to execute the query in ClarisWorks:

One Field

If the criteria contains only one value or an open-ended range of values for one field, one Find is used. For example:

Paid=No   Type `=No` in the Paid field, select **All**, then select **Find**

GPA>3   Type `>3` in the GPA field, select **All**, then select **Find**

6

Multiple Fields with "And"

If the criteria contains an "and" that joins different fields or an open-ended range of values, again only one Find is used. For example:

> **Name=Connie and State=CA**
>> Type =Connie in the Name field, =CA in the State field, select **All**, then select **Find**

> **GPA>2.5 and State=AZ**
>> Type >2.5 in the GPA field, =AZ in the State field, select **All**, then select **Find**

Same Field with "And"

If the criteria contains an "and" that joins the same field, multiple finds and the **Visible** button are used. For example:

> **GPA>2.0 and GPA<3.0**
>> Type >2.0 in the GPA field, select **All**, then select **Find**. Execute Find, type <3.0 in the GPA field, select **Visible**, then select **Find**

> **GPA>3.0 and GPA<3.5 and Tuition=Unpaid**
>> Type >3.0 in the GPA field, select **All**, then select **Find**. Execute Find, type <3.5 in the GPA field, =Unpaid in the Tuition field, select **Visible**, then select **Find**

"Or"

If the criteria contains an "or," New Request is used. For example:

> **State=GA or State=TX**
>> Type =GA in the State field. Execute New Request, type =TX in the State field, select **All**, then select **Find**

> **GPA<1.5 or Tuition=Unpaid**
>> Type 1.5 in the GPA field. Execute New Request, type =Unpaid in the Tuition field, select **All**, then select **Find**

Practice 7

In this Practice you will use the New Request command to apply queries to the IVY STUDENT database. Start ClarisWorks and open IVY STUDENT if you have not already done so.

1) DETERMINE WHICH STUDENTS ARE FROM CA OR NV

    a. From the Layout menu, select the Find command.
    b. Type =CA in the State field.
    c. From the Edit menu, select the New Request command. An empty record is displayed. Note the entry boxes indicating it is active.
    d. Type =NV in the State field of the new record.
    e. Select the **All** button and then select the **Find** button. Four records are displayed.
    f. Display the database in List view and verify that the State field for each record contains CA or NV.

2) DISPLAY TWO RANGES OF RECORDS

    a. From the Layout menu, select the Find command.
    b. Type `<2.0` in the GPA field.
    c. From the Edit menu, select the New Request command.
    d. Type `>3.8` in the GPA field of the empty record.
    e. Select the **All** button and then select the **Find** button. Records for those students with a GPA less than 2.0 or greater than 3.8 are displayed.
    f. Display the database in List view. How many students meet the query criteria?

3) SAVE THE MODIFIED IVY STUDENT

Show all records and then save IVY STUDENT.

6.15 Deleting Records

Just as it is necessary to add new records to a database, records must often be deleted: a student graduates or transfers out of school, a store decides to no longer carry an item, etc. In ClarisWorks, the Delete Record command from the Edit menu deletes the active record.

Selecting Undo from the Edit menu (⌘Z), before any other command is executed, recovers the deleted record. The Undo button on the Shortcuts palette (▣) can also be used. As when updating a record, there is often a need to first use the Find command to locate the record to be deleted. When the file is saved on disk, the deleted record is no longer stored.

Practice 8

In this Practice you will delete a record. Start ClarisWorks and open IVY STUDENT if you have not already done so.

1) FIND THE RECORD TO BE DELETED

    a. Note the Status panel indicates there are 81 records in this database.
    b. From the Layout menu, select the Find command.
    c. Type `=Morrison` in the Last Name field.
    d. Select the **Find** button. The record for Ian Morrison is displayed.

2) DELETE A RECORD

From the Edit menu, select the Delete Record command. The current record is removed.

3) SAVE IVY STUDENT

    a. Show all records. Note the Status panel indicates there are now only 80 records in the database.
    b. Save IVY STUDENT.

An Introduction to Computing Using ClarisWorks

6.16 Sorting Records

Placing the records in a database in a specified order is called *sorting*. For example, it is easier to locate students in the IVY STUDENT database if the records are in order alphabetically by last name. In ClarisWorks, records can be sorted based on the data stored in a specified field called the *key sort field*. In the example, Last Name would be the key sort field.

The Sort pop-up menu (⬚⬚) is used to create a named sort that is saved with the database. A named sort can be applied at any time without having to redefine the key sort field.

Executing the New Sort command from the Sort pop-up menu displays the Sort Records dialog box:

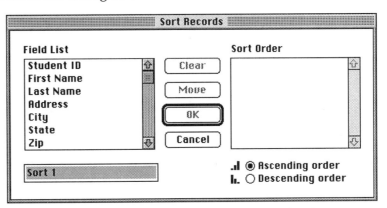

The key sort field is chosen in this dialog box

A descriptive sort name should be typed in the entry box. The desired key sort field is then highlighted and **Move** clicked to place the field name in the **Sort Order** list. The sort order is indicated beside the field name. Ascending (.⬚) means records will be sorted from lowest to highest. Descending (⬚.) means sorting will be done from highest to lowest. To change the order of the sort, the **Ascending order** or **Descending order** button is clicked. For example, when an ascending sort based on the GPA field is specified, the Sort Records dialog box appears like the following:

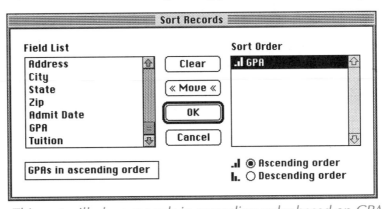

This sort will place records in ascending order based on GPA

OK is selected to save the sort. Once a sort has been saved, it can be applied to the database by simply selecting its name from the bottom of the Sort pop-up menu. Performing a sort reorders all the records in the database, even those that are hidden as a result of a query.

A sort can be modified by selecting the Edit Sorts command from the Sort pop-up menu. The Edit Sorts dialog box appears and the sort to be modified must be highlighted. Clicking on the **Modify** button displays the Sort Records dialog box. After making the desired changes, **OK** is selected to close the dialog box. **OK** is again selected to close the Edit Sorts dialog box. A sort is deleted by clicking **Delete** in the Edit Sorts dialog box.

Sorts can also be performed on a database using the Sort buttons on the Shortcuts palette. Clicking on the Sort Ascending button (▦) or the Sort Descending button (▦) sorts the database by the field which is currently selected. Clicking on the Sort Again button (▦) repeats the last sort.

Practice 9

In this Practice you will sort IVY STUDENT. Start ClarisWorks and open IVY STUDENT if you have not already done so.

1) CREATE A DESCENDING SORT BASED ON THE GPA FIELD

    a. Switch to List view.

    b. From the Sort pop-up menu (▣), select the New Sort command. The Sort Records dialog box is displayed.

    c. Type GPAs in descending order in the entry box.

    d. If there are any fields in the **Sort Order** list, click on the **Clear** button.

    e. Scroll through the **Field List** until GPA is visible.

    f. Click on GPA and then click on the **Move** button. The field name is added to the **Sort Order** list.

    g. Click on the **Descending order** radio button. The icon next to GPA in the **Sort Order** box changes.

    h. Select **OK** to save the sort named GPAs in descending order.

2) SORT THE RECORDS AND VERIFY THE RESULTS

    a. From the Sort pop-up menu, select GPAs in descending order to sort the records from high to low based on the data stored in the GPA field. After a slight pause the records are rearranged and displayed in their new order on the screen.

    b. Scroll so that the GPA field is visible. Note how the records are now in descending order by GPA.

3) SORT THE DATABASE IN ASCENDING ORDER ON THE LAST NAME FIELD

    a. Display the Shortcuts palette if it is not already displayed.

    b. Click on an entry in the Last Name field.

    c. On the Shortcuts palette, click on the Sort Ascending button (▦). The records are displayed in their new order. Scroll through the database to verify that the records are in alphabetical order by Last Name.

4) PRINT A RECORD

    a. Click once on the number just below the Notebook to highlight it. Type 5 and press Return to make the fifth record current. A box to the left of the record is highlighted indicating that it is the active record.

    b. Save IVY STUDENT.

    c. From the File menu, select Print. The Print dialog box is displayed.

    d. Select the **Current Record** option.

    e. Select **Print** to print the fifth record only.

5) CLOSE IVY STUDENT

    Close IVY STUDENT and quit ClarisWorks.

Chapter Summary

Errors in data entry can be avoided by using entry options. Field entry options include data ranges and unique entries. For example, a field can be defined to only accept values between 2.0 and 4.0. Data entry options are defined using the Define Fields command in the Layout menu.

A database is updated by changing the information it stores. Changes to the contents in a field are made by moving the cursor to the entry box and using the mouse, arrow keys, and Delete key to make the correction. A field's entry can also be replaced by triple-clicking in the entry box to highlight the contents and then typing the new entry. The Find command can be used to quickly locate the records that need to be updated. Existing records are deleted with the Delete Record command from the Edit menu. When a change has been made to a database, the database file must again be saved on disk to ensure that the change will be present the next time the file is used.

To change the way fields are displayed in Browse view, they must be formatted from Layout view. The Field Format command from the Options menu can be used to display numeric entries with a fixed number of decimal places or as currency. Times and dates can also be formatted in different ways (long or short form). The alignment of both field names and entries can be changed using the Alignment command in the Format menu.

Once a database has been created, new fields can be added, and existing fields can be renamed or deleted using the Define Fields command in the Layout menu.

When you use the Find command to locate specific records in a database, you are querying the database. ClarisWorks uses criteria that you supply to query a database. Complex queries are specified using the conjunctions "and" and "or." Complex queries that use only one field require the Find screen's **Visible** button which searches only the currently displayed records. The New Request command is used when a complex query contains an "or." For example, two requests must be made to find all students with GPAs of either 3.0 or 4.0. Careful planning will help you create the correct criteria for any query.

Named queries are created using the New Search command from the Search pop-up menu. Named queries are saved with the database and are applied by selecting its name from the bottom of the Search pop-up menu.

The List command from the Layout menu displays the database in List view, where records are displayed in rows. List view is useful for determining relationships between records, such as querying and sorting. In List view, field widths are changed by dragging the divider bar at the top of the screen. Fields in List view are not automatically formatted. Double-clicking on a field name displays the Format dialog box.

Placing a database in a particular order is called sorting and is accomplished by selecting the New Sort command from the Sort pop-up menu. The records are reordered, or sorted, in either ascending or descending order based on the data stored in the desired key sort field. The New Sort command creates named sorts that are saved with the database. A named sort is applied by selecting its name from the bottom of the Sort pop-up menu. The Shortcuts palette can also be used to sort a database.

Vocabulary

Ascending order - In order from low to high.

Complex query - Criteria specified using the conjunctions "and" and "or."

Criteria - Description of the data in specific fields that records must contain to be displayed by a query.

Data range - The range of values allowed in a number field.

Define Fields command - Used to add, delete, and modify fields. Also used to define field entry options.

Delete Record command - Removes the highlighted record from the database.

Descending order - In order from high to low.

Field entry options - Used to have a field accept only entries from a specified range or only unique data.

Key sort field - Field whose entries are used to determine the order of the records during a sort.

Landscape orientation - A printing orientation that indicates the document is to be printed across the widest part of the paper.

List view - Viewing the database with the records placed in rows. The active field has a solid outline.

New Request command - Adds another empty record on the Find screen, enabling more query criteria to be entered for complex queries involving "or."

Query - Limiting the records displayed to those that contain specified data called criteria.

Range - Criteria that include an operator such as less than (<) or greater than (>).

Sort - To place records in a specific order based on the data stored in a key sort field.

Unique field - A field that must have a different entry in each record of the database.

Updating - Changing the information stored in a database.

An Introduction to Computing Using ClarisWorks

6 | Reviews

Sections 6.1 — 6.3

1. How can a GPA field be made to accept only values between 0.0 and 4.0?

2. a) How can a field be made to accept only unique entries?
   b) Why would a unique field be used in a National Patent Office database?

3. A database for the Under 21 Year Old Ivy University Ski Club contains the following fields: Last Name, Membership Number, Age, Skill Level, and Specialty (cross country, downhill, etc.). Which fields should use entry options?

Sections 6.4 — 6.7

4. a) Describe two ways in which an entry can be updated in a record.
   b) How can a desired record be located quickly so that an update can be made?

5. Sam Adams has moved to 35 Cleve Street in Lawrenceville, NJ, 08618. List the steps required to change his address in the IVY STUDENT database.

6. List the steps required to format a field containing numeric data so that it will display:
   a) three decimal places.
   b) dollars with commas and two decimal places.

7. What type of entries are best displayed right aligned? In parentheses?

8. a) What does ClarisWorks do to verify that a field is to be deleted?
   b) List the steps required to change the field name Years to Age.
   c) Can a new field be added to an existing database? If so, how? If not, why?

Sections 6.8 — 6.16

9. Give an example of why the Admissions office of Ivy U would query the IVY STUDENT database.

10. a) What is meant by the term criteria? Give two examples.
    b) What is a complex query? Give two examples.

11. a) How is a named query created?
    b) How is a named query applied?

12. How do the records of a database appear in List view?

13. How can the GPA field be formatted for 1 decimal place in List view?

14. When is the New Request command used?

15. List the steps required to display all records in a database that contain the name Molly or Marguerite in their First Name field.

16. Can query criteria include more than one field? If yes, give an example using the IVY STUDENT database. If no, why not?

17. Describe how a record can be deleted.

18. Ivy University is planning a mailing to its students and wants its database arranged in ascending order by zip code. Describe how a named sort would be created to do this.

19. How is a named sort applied to a database?

20. How can the Shortcuts palette be used to sort a database by Last Name?

Exercises

1. Print seven more copies of Survey Form, the questionnaire you designed in Chapter Three, Exercise 15 and distribute them to your friends. The data from your surveys will be entered into the Student Survey database along with the three previously entered records.

   a) Open Student Survey and modify any fields that would benefit from data ranges or unique entries.

   b) Format fields appropriately. Save the modified Student Survey.

   c) Enter the data from the completed survey forms into the database. Each form should correspond to a separate record.

   d) Display the database in List view. Format List view appropriately.

   e) Create and apply a sort named `Course - Alphabetical` that sorts the database alphabetically by the favorite course.

   f) Save the modified Student Survey and print a copy in List view.

2. In Chapter Five, Exercise 2 you created an author database named Author Catalog and entered three records. Open Author Catalog and make the following changes.

   a) Modify any fields that would benefit from data ranges or unique entries.

   b) Format fields appropriately. Save the modified Author Catalog.

   c) Enter seven records for books that your friends might someday write. Be sure to use a wide variety of names, states, subject areas, etc. Have at least one friend author a romance.

   d) Display the database in List view. Format List view appropriately.

   e) Create and apply a query named `Mysteries or Romances` that displays the records of mystery or romance books. Print the results in List view.

   f) Show all records, then create and apply a sort named `Last Name - Alphabetical` that sorts the database alphabetically by the author's last name.

   g) Save the modified Author Catalog and print a copy in List view.

3. Fantasy Wheels would like you to modify and update the database created in Chapter Five, Exercise 10. Open Wheels and make the following changes.

   a) Modify any fields that would benefit from data ranges or unique entries.

   b) Format fields appropriately. Save the modified Wheels.

   c) Add these additional records:

      1975 Aston Martin, red exterior, black interior, automatic transmission, radio, and air conditioning. Originally paid $56,000. Now asking $120,000.

      1987 Porsche, black exterior, white interior, 4-speed transmission, and air conditioning. Originally paid $22,300. Now asking $46,000.

1988 Ferrari, red exterior, black interior, 4-speed transmission, radio, and air conditioning. Originally paid $72,300. Now asking $102,000.

1985 Porsche, red exterior, blue interior, 4-speed transmission, and radio. Originally paid $31,000. Now asking $62,000.

1978 Triumph, green exterior, white interior, 4-speed transmission, and air conditioning. Originally paid $4,560. Now asking $7,200.

1958 Thunderbird, white exterior, red interior, automatic transmission, radio, and air conditioning. Originally paid $14,500. Now asking $31,000.

1969 Maserati, red exterior, black interior, 4-speed transmission, radio, and air conditioning. Originally paid $9,800. Now asking $21,600.

1978 Nova, yellow exterior, orange interior, automatic transmission, and air conditioning. Originally paid $4,200. Now asking $6,600.

d) Display the database in List view. Format List view appropriately.

e) Fantasy Wheels has had a great day and sold the 1985 Porsche. Delete this record from the database.

f) A customer has come into Fantasy's show room and wants to buy her husband a red sports car as a Valentine's Day present. Display a listing of only red cars. Which are they?

g) Fantasy has had the blue 1969 Maserati painted purple, its radio removed, and its asking price raised to $29,000. Update the appropriate Maserati record accordingly.

h) Query the database for all cars with black interiors that originally cost under $25,000. Display these records in List view and then sort by price.

i) Save the modified Wheels database and then print the results of the query in part (h) in List view.

4. In Chapter Five, Exercise 12, you created a database for Holiday Airlines. Open Holiday and modify and update the database following the steps below. It may be helpful to refer to the seating chart in Chapter Five.

a) Modify any fields that would benefit from data ranges or unique entries.

b) Format fields appropriately. Save the modified Holiday.

c) Make the following reservations by updating the proper records in the database. Use queries to locate seats for passengers with preferences.

Mr. and Mrs. Kemp
Phone Number: (407) 555-2475
Katie Kemp: window seat, first class
Tristan Kemp: aisle seat next to Katie

Mr. and Mrs. Morawski
Phone Number: (508) 555-3197
Susan Morawski: window seat, coach
Steve Morawski: aisle seat next to Susan

Mr. Presley
Phone Number: (305) 555-7847
Bruce Presley: aisle seat, first class

Ms. Crane
Phone Number: (609) 555-9165
Heidi Crane: window seat, first class

Mr. Borelli
Phone Number: (413) 555-8857
John Borelli: window seat, coach

Mrs. Wagy
Phone Number: (217) 555-3500
Ruth Wagy: No preference

d) Display the database in List view. Format List view appropriately.

e) The reservation desk at Holiday needs to know the seat numbers of all empty seats. Create and apply a query named `Empty Seats` that displays the records of available seats. Print the results in List view.

f) Holiday Airlines has held a promotional contest and you have won five free trips to the Bahamas. Make five reservations using the names and phone numbers of friends. No first class seating is allowed for these free seats.

g) Ms. McGuire has changed her mind and would now like a seat in first class. Use the Find command to list all empty seats in first class. If such a seat is available, change Ms. McGuire's record.

h) Save the modified Holiday and then print in List view the records of those passengers in first class who have a window seat.

5. In Chapter Five, Exercise 13 you created a database for a weather experiment and entered four records. Open Weather and update the database by following the steps below.

a) Modify any fields that would benefit from data ranges or unique entries.

b) Format fields appropriately. Save the modified Weather.

c) Add these additional records:

Date	Time	Temp. (C)	Rain (cm)	Sky
12/21/67	10:59 PM	8	0	clear
10/15/69	7:15 AM	27	0.2	windy
3/16/70	4:00 PM	9	0	partly cloudy
7/12/72	1:00 PM	26	0	sunny
12/11/73	12:59 AM	8	0	hazy
7/19/74	6:49 AM	13	0	sunny
10/31/75	9:15 AM	9	0.3	windy
11/16/77	11:50 PM	23	0	clear
1/1/80	3:43 PM	0	0	partly cloudy
2/6/81	6:55 PM	−6	0.1	cloudy
2/27/82	8:20 PM	32	1.2	partly cloudy
5/19/84	7:46 PM	17	0	sunny
6/27/85	2:28 PM	20	0.3	cloudy
12/23/86	12:59 PM	2	0	clear
8/24/87	5:33 AM	24	0.5	hazy
11/5/88	6:45 AM	7	0.1	windy
3/2/89	2:33 PM	19	0.7	cloudy
10/22/90	10:15 AM	28	0.2	windy
2/24/91	7:32 AM	26	0	sunny
3/22/91	2:45 PM	22	0.5	windy
5/24/92	5:03 AM	21	1.5	cloudy
8/22/92	9:30 PM	27	0.3	windy

d) Add a record to the database describing today's weather.

e) Display the database in List view. Format List view appropriately.

f) Create and apply queries to answer the questions below. Be sure to name the queries appropriately. Write your answers on a separate piece of paper.

- On which days was it sunny or hazy?
- On which days was the temperature exactly –6 degrees or above 26 degrees?
- On which days was it windy and colder than 15 degrees?
- When the temperature was lower than 10 degrees, what days were not sunny or were not clear?

g) Save the modified Weather and print the results of the last query in List view.

6. Open CAR PRICE which contains information about the prices of new cars.

a) Format each price field for currency and commas with 0 decimal places. Right align all numeric fields. Save the modified CAR PRICE.

b) Sort the database alphabetically by the Make field. What is the first and last car on the list? Write your answer on a separate piece of paper.

c) The price for a Porsche 944S with sunroof has gone up $200. Find this car and then update the record to reflect this change.

d) Create and apply queries to answer the questions below. Be sure to name the queries appropriately. Write your answers on a separate piece of paper.

- How many cars have a base price under $12,000?
- Your friend needs a new car but does not have much money. How many cars with a stereo cost under $9,000?
- How many cars have air conditioning for under $6,500?

e) Save the modified CAR PRICE and print the results of the last query in List view.

7. Open COUNTRY which contains information about the countries of the world.

a) Format the Area and Population fields as fixed with commas and 0 decimal places. Right align all numeric fields. Save the modified COUNTRY.

b) What country is the fifth most populated? Write your answer on a separate piece of paper.

c) Create and apply queries to answer the questions below. Be sure to name the queries appropriately. Write your answers on a separate piece of paper.

- How many countries use the ruble or the pound as their currency?
- Which countries with areas over 3 million use the dollar as their currency?
- Which countries have populations under 100,000?
- Which countries using the franc have areas less than 15,000?

d) Save the modified COUNTRY and print the results of the last query in List view.

8. In Chapter Five, Exercise 7 you created a database for City Zoo. Open Zoo and update the database by following the steps below.

    a) Modify any fields that would benefit from data ranges or unique entries.

    b) Format fields appropriately. Save the modified Zoo.

    c) Enter the remaining records:

Staff	Animal	Type	Males	Females	Location
L. Wrighte	Blue-faced Angelfish	Fish	1	1	Aquarium
M. Rolls	Barn Owl	Bird	0	1	Aviary
M. Rolls	S. American Fruit Bat	Mammal	2	5	Aviary
W. Carr	Locust	Insect	12	25	Insect Room
T. Quay	Eastern Indigo	Reptile	2	0	Reptile Garden
W. Carr	Egyptian Scarab Beetle	Insect	4	0	Insect Room
S. Smith	Mountain Cougar	Mammal	1	1	American West
L. Wrighte	Nurse Shark	Fish	0	1	Aquarium
W. Carr	Praying Mantis	Insect	3	7	Insect Room
S. Smith	Eastern Red Fox	Mammal	1	2	Eastern Forest
M. Rolls	Zebra Finch	Bird	6	14	Aviary
M. Rolls	Red Shoulder Hawk	Bird	1	0	Aviary

    d) Create and apply queries to answer the questions below. Be sure to name the queries appropriately. Write your answers on a separate piece of paper.

        • How many mammals and insects are at the zoo?
        • What is the total number of animals in the Aviary and American West?
        • Which animals have more than 5 females and more than 5 males?
        • How many animals are cared for by S. Smith and W. Carr?

    e) Sort the modified database by the animal and then print the results of the last query in List view.

    f) A female Red Shoulder Hawk has been added to the Aviary display. Update this record in the database and save the modified Zoo. Print only this updated record in Browse view.

9. Open COLLEGES which contains information about colleges and universities in the United States.

    a) Format the Enrollment field as fixed with 0 decimals and commas. Format the Tuition and Room and Board fields for currency with 0 decimal places and commas. Right align all numeric fields.

    b) Save the modified COLLEGES.

    c) Which college or university is located in Kalamazoo?

    d) Based on tuition only, what are the three most expensive and inexpensive schools in the database?

6

e) Create and apply queries to answer the questions below. Be sure to name the queries appropriately. Write your answers on a separate piece of paper.

- How many public schools are in Massachusetts?
- How many public schools enroll more than 10,000 students?
- Which California and Illinois public schools enroll less than 20,000 students?

f) Save the modified COLLEGES. Find your favorite college and print only that record.

10. Open INVENTOR which contains a list of inventors and their inventions. Answer the questions below on a separate piece of paper.

   a) Which French inventors produced their inventions in the 1800s?

   b) What inventions did Galileo invent?

   c) Which inventions were produced in Russia after 1960?

   d) How many inventions were invented in England and Italy between 1600 and 1830, inclusively?

   e) Last week your friend Molly McVention from Ireland invented a Peanut butter and Tuna fish sandwich. Add a new record to INVENTOR which chronicles this event. Resize the Invention field entry box so the entire name contents are displayed.

   f) Save the modified INVENTOR.

   g) Find all inventors from the United States with inventions made before 1840.

   h) Sort the results of part (g) in ascending order by year. Save the modified INVENTOR and then print the database in List view with the query still applied.

11. Open the Address database you created in Chapter Five, Exercise 1.

   a) Modify any fields that would benefit data ranges or unique entries.

   b) Format fields appropriately. Save the modified Address.

   c) Enter data for at least seven more of your friends.

   d) Display the database in List view. Format List view appropriately.

   e) Apply a query to display only friends born during the year you were born.

   f) Save the modified Address and print the results of the query in List view.

   g) You've made a new friend, Amy Eppelman. Add her record to the database:

   > Amy Eppelman
   > 713 Graisbury Avenue
   > Haddonfield, NJ 08033
   > (213) 555-1324
   > Born 7/5/80

   h) You have decided that the first person in the file is no longer your friend. Delete that record from the database.

   i) Sort the database alphabetically by last name, save Address, and then print only record 5.

12. In Chapter Five you created a gibbon observation database. Open GIBBON RESEARCH which already contains a number of observations of the gibbons.

a) Sort the database in descending order by the age of the animal. Print the record of the oldest gibbon in the database.

b) Create and apply queries to answer the questions below. Be sure to name the queries appropriately. Write your answers on a separate piece of paper.

- When the temperature was above 80 degrees, which gibbons were observed either playing or eating?
- How many observations were made between 6 AM and 9 AM? 3 PM and 6 PM?
- What is the most common activity of the animals when it is raining?
- How many gibbons under the age of 10 are female?
- Find the record of the animal who was in Base Camp. What was the name of this animal, and what was it doing when it was being observed?
- Which male gibbons older than 7 years old have female companions?
- Which gibbons are under 5 years old?

c) Sort the results of the last query alphabetically by name. Save GIBBON RESEARCH and print the database with the query still applied.

13. Open ACADEMY AWARDS which contains information about the Academy Award winners since the Awards started in the late 1920s. Each record contains the winners in each category for each year. Answer the following questions on a separate piece of paper.

a) How many winning films has United Artists produced?

b) Which winning movies did Columbia produce between the years 1960 and 1990?

c) What movies won in the 1940s?

d) How many total times did Katherine Hepburn or Bette Davis win the Academy Award for Best Actress?

e) Sort the results of part (d) by Actress. Save the file and then print the database in List view with the last query still applied.

Chapter 7

Reports and Advanced Database Techniques

New Layout

Insert Field

Document

Edit Layouts

New Report

Edit Reports

Define Fields

Objectives

After completing this chapter you will be able to:

1. Plan and create new Layouts.

2. Format, rename, and delete Layouts.

3. Display and modify previously created Layouts.

4. Plan and create database reports.

5. Edit reports.

6. Create and add a calculation field to a database.

7. Create summary and sub-summary fields to produce totals, subtotals, and averages.

7

One of the most powerful features of a database is the ability to produce printed reports detailing the information stored in its records. In this chapter the commands necessary to produce reports are discussed. Special fields that make calculations based on the data stored in other fields are also introduced.

7.1 Using Different Layouts

A database is often used by many people, each with different needs. For example, Ivy University's billing department uses the name, address, and tuition fields of the IVY STUDENT database for preparing student bills. The office of the academic dean uses the name and GPA fields. To meet the needs of different users, a ClarisWorks database can have many *Layouts*. Each Layout can contain as few as one field or all the fields in a database. Having the ability to view information in a database in different ways (through multiple Layouts) increases the database's flexibility.

Standard Layout

There are several types of Layouts that can be created in a ClarisWorks database. Two commonly used Layouts are Standard Layout and Labels Layout. The *Standard Layout* automatically places all the fields in the database in a column:

Student ID	LA329
First Name	Lorna
Last Name	Acenbrack
Address	30 Ship Down Manor
City	Loxahatchee
State	FL
Zip	33470
Admit Date	3/2/96
GPA	3.8
Tuition	Paid
Student ID	SA313
First Name	Sam
Last Name	Adams
Address	121 Carey Quadrangle
City	Leaftown
State	PA
Zip	19717
Admit Date	3/13/95
GPA	1.5
Tuition	Unpaid

A Standard Layout arranges all the fields in the database in a column

The Layout can then be customized by deleting and moving fields to create the desired record layout.

When a Labels Layout is created, selected fields are automatically displayed without their corresponding field names:

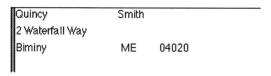

Field names are not displayed in Labels Layouts

It is important to understand that the First Name field in one Layout for a particular record is the same as the First Name field in another Layout for the same record. Therefore, changing a field's entry changes it for the entire database no matter what Layout is currently displayed. The diagram below shows the relationship between a database and its Layouts:

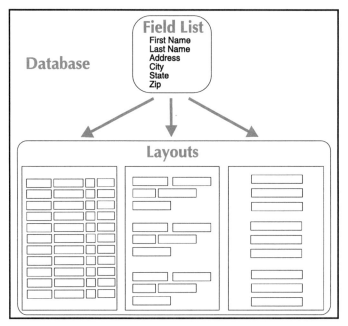

The records in a database can be displayed differently using Layouts

7.2 Planning a New Layout

A new Layout should be carefully planned before it is created by answering two of the questions posed when first creating a database:

1. What information should be included?
2. How should that information appear?

The information to be included is determined by analyzing the needs of the person for whom the Layout is being created. Including unnecessary information makes it harder to find desired information. To determine how the information should appear, a sketch of a record layout should be made using paper and pencil.

7

Practice 1

In this Practice you will design Layouts using paper and pencil for three different users of the IVY STUDENT database. For each Layout, determine which fields are needed and then make a sketch of the record layout.

    a. The accounting department at Ivy University will be using the IVY STUDENT database to maintain tuition status.

    b. The dean wants to be able to view student GPAs.

    c. The IU public relations department is creating a mailer that will list upcoming activities. They need a Layout containing mailing information for each student.

7.3 Creating a New Layout

The New Layout command from the Layout pop-up menu (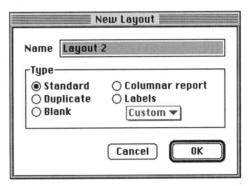) displays the following dialog box:

Layouts are created using the New Layout command

A name describing the new Layout should be typed in the **Name** box. Selecting **Standard** as the **Type** and then selecting **OK** displays a layout that contains all the fields of the database arranged in a column as displayed in Section 7.1.

The names of a database's Layouts are listed at the bottom of the Layout pop-up menu. When a database is created the default Layout is named Layout 1. Selecting a Layout places a check mark beside its name and displays it on the screen.

Practice 2

In this Practice you will create a new Standard Layout in the IVY STUDENT database. You will also update the database from the new layout.

1) OPEN IVY STUDENT

    a. Boot the System and start ClarisWorks.
    b. Open IVY STUDENT and display the database in Browse view.

2) CREATE A NEW LAYOUT

The dean wants to use the IVY STUDENT database to keep track of student GPAs.

a. From the Layout pop-up menu (), select the New Layout command. The New Layout dialog box is displayed.
b. Type `Name and GPA` in the **Name** box.
c. **Standard** should already be selected. Select **OK** to display the new Layout. Note how each record contains all the fields in the database arranged in a column.

3) UPDATE SHERMAN TAO'S RECORD

a. From the Layout menu, select the Find command.
b. Enter `=Tao` in the Last Name field and then select the **Find** button. Sherman Tao's record is displayed.
c. Press Tab to display the entry boxes. In the GPA entry box replace the current value, 1.6, with 2.1.
d. From the Organize menu, select the Show All Records command.

4) SWITCH TO LAYOUT 1

From the Layout pop-up menu, select Layout 1. Note that Sherman Tao's record is updated in this Layout as well. Updating a record in one Layout affects every Layout in the database.

5) SAVE IVY STUDENT

7.4 Formatting a Layout

Fields are not automatically formatted in a new Layout. Therefore, when a new Layout is created it is often necessary to move, resize, and format fields. A new Layout is modified the same way the original Layout was modified. With the new Layout displayed in Layout view, a selected field can be resized by dragging its handle. To move a field use the arrow keys or drag. The Field Format and Alignment commands are used to format a field's contents.

When a Standard Layout is created, every field in the database is automatically added to the Layout. Therefore, it is necessary to remove fields that are not required for the purpose of the Layout. In Layout view, a field is deleted by first selecting both its field name and entry box. Next, pressing the Delete key removes the field and its contents from the Layout.

When a field is deleted from a Layout using the Delete key it is still part of the database and can be added back to a Layout. To add a field to a Layout, the Insert Field command from the Layout menu is selected. A dialog box is displayed that lists all the fields in the database that are not included in the current Layout. Simply highlighting the desired field name and selecting **OK** adds the field to the Layout.

When a new Layout is created, the margins may not be wide enough for records to be printed entirely. Like the word processor, margins can be increased using the Document command from the Format menu. Margin settings affect only the displayed Layout.

An Introduction to Computing Using ClarisWorks

7.5 Renaming and Deleting a Layout

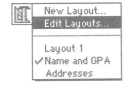

The Edit Layouts command from the Layout pop-up menu is used to change a Layout's name. Selecting this command displays a dialog box similar to the following:

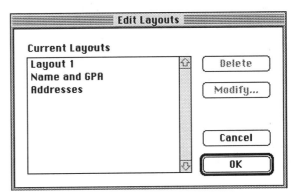

A Layout's name can be changed using the Edit Layouts dialog box

To change the name of a Layout, highlight the name and then click the **Modify** button to display the Layout Info dialog box:

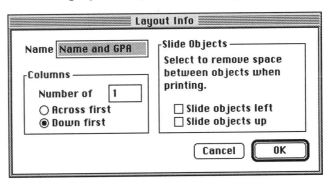

A Layouts name is changed from the Layout Info dialog box

Type the new Layout name in the **Name** box and then select **OK** to remove the dialog box. Select **OK** again to remove the Edit Layouts dialog box.

In the Edit Layouts dialog box, the highlighted Layout is deleted by clicking on the **Delete** button. When a Layout is deleted a warning is first displayed:

ClarisWorks warns you before a Layout is deleted

Selecting **OK** removes the Layout, and **Cancel** leaves the database unchanged. Deleting a Layout does not delete the fields in the database. If there is only one Layout in a database, it cannot be deleted.

Practice 3

In this Practice you will format the Name and GPA Layout created in the previous Practice. Start ClarisWorks and open IVY STUDENT if you have not already done so.

1) DISPLAY THE CORRECT LAYOUT

From the Layout pop-up menu, select Name and GPA.

2) CHANGE THE NAME OF THE LAYOUT

a. From the Layout pop-up menu, select the Edit Layouts command. A dialog box is displayed.
b. Highlight Name and GPA in the **Current Layouts** list.
c. Click on the **Modify** button. The Layout Info dialog box is displayed.
d. Type Student GPAs in the **Name** box and then select **OK** to rename the Layout.
e. Select **OK** to remove the Edit Layouts dialog box.
f. Display the Layout pop-up menu. Note how Student GPAs now appears instead of Name and GPA at the bottom of the menu.

3) DELETE FIELDS

Only the first name, last name, and GPA fields are needed in this Layout.

a. Switch to Layout view.
b. Click on the Student ID field name to select it.
c. Press and hold the Shift key and then click on the Student ID entry box. Both the Student ID field name and entry box are selected together.
d. Press the Delete key. The Student ID field is removed from the Layout.
e. Use steps (b) through (d) to delete all but the First Name, Last Name, and GPA fields.

4) RESIZE AND MOVE FIELDS

a. Click on the GPA field name to select it.
b. Drag one of the right handles so that the field name box is just the width of the field name.
c. Repeat the procedure in steps (a) and (b) to resize the First Name and Last Name field name boxes.
d. Resize field entry boxes and move fields so that your record layout looks like the one below. Drag the Body marker up so that there is less room between records:

5) FORMAT THE GPA FIELD

a. Click on the GPA entry box to select it.
b. From the Options menu, select Field Format. The Number Format dialog box is displayed.
c. Click on **Fixed** and type 1 for the **Precision**. Select **OK** to apply the formatting.
d. With the GPA entry box still selected, select Right from the Alignment submenu in the Format menu.

6) VIEW THE FORMATTED LAYOUT

From the Layout menu, select Browse. The new Layout is displayed with only the name and GPA fields.

7) CHANGE THE LAYOUT'S MARGINS

a. From the Format menu, select the Document command. The Document dialog box is displayed.
b. Change the **Top**, **Bottom**, **Left**, and **Right** margins to 0.5. Select **OK**.

8) SAVE IVY STUDENT

7.6 Creating Database Reports

Querying and sorting are two database applications already discussed. Reports are another powerful application of computerized databases. A database *report* uses a specified Layout, sort, and query to organize database records for a specific purpose. For example, the dean of Ivy U could request a report that details those students eligible for the dean's list. The report would use a layout displaying the name and GPA fields, a sort that places the records in alphabetical order, and a query that limits the records displayed to those with GPAs greater than 3.6.

The four steps for creating a report are:

1. **Determine the appropriate Layout for the report.** A report should include only the necessary fields. For example, if the dean wants a report listing those students who are eligible for the dean's list, a Layout containing only First Name, Last Name, and GPA fields is needed. If an appropriate Layout does not exist then it must be created.

2. **Determine the appropriate query for the report.** A report should display only the necessary records. For example, because the dean's report is to list students eligible for the dean's list, a named query that will display only those students that have a GPA greater than 3.6 would be used. If the appropriate named query does not exist then it must be created.

3. **Determine the appropriate sort for the report.** To make the report easier to read, a named sort that arranges the records in order by GPA is needed. For example, the dean's report should list students eligible for the dean's list in alphabetical order. If the appropriate named sort does not exist then it must be created.

4. **Use the New Report command from the Report pop-up menu to create and generate the report.**

A report is created by executing the New Report command from the Report pop-up menu (). New Report displays the following dialog box:

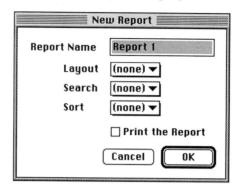

A report's components are defined from the New Report dialog box

A descriptive name should be typed in the **Report Name** entry box. The **Layout**, **Search**, and **Sort** drop-down lists contain the names of Layouts, named queries, and named sorts that have been previously created in the database. Selecting the appropriate Layout, query, and sort and then selecting **OK** creates the report. After a report is created, it can be generated by selecting its name from the bottom of the Report pop-up menu.

To print a report, simply display it and then use the Print command from the File menu. If the **Print the Report** option in the New Report dialog box is selected when a report is created, the print dialog box is automatically displayed when the report name is selected from the Report pop-up menu.

7.7 Editing a Report

The Edit Reports command from the Report pop-up menu is used to modify a report. Selecting this command displays a dialog box similar to the following:

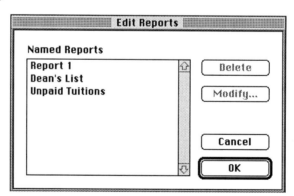

A report can be modified using the Edit Reports dialog box

The report to be modified must first be highlighted and then the **Modify** button clicked to display the Modify Report dialog box where the Layout, query, sort, and report name can be changed.

In the Edit Reports dialog box, the highlighted report is deleted by clicking on the **Delete** button.

7

Practice 4

In this Practice you will create a report which shows the students eligible for the dean's list. Start ClarisWorks and open IVY STUDENT if you have not already done so.

1) CREATE THE DEAN'S LIST REPORT

The dean needs a report that lists in alphabetical order only those students with GPAs greater than 3.6. The records for each of these students need only contain name and GPA fields.

a. The components necessary for the dean's report have already been created in earlier practices. From the Report pop-up menu (▤), select the New Report command. A dialog box is displayed.
b. In the **Report Name** entry box, type: Dean's List
c. Press and hold the mouse button on the triangle in the **Layout** drop-down list to display the database Layouts. From the **Layout** drop-down list, select Student GPAs.
d. From the **Search** drop-down list, select GPAs > 3.6.
e. From the **Sort** drop-down list, select GPAs in descending order.
f. Select **OK**. The Dean's List report has been created.

2) DISPLAY THE DEAN'S LIST REPORT

From the Report pop-up menu, select Dean's List. The report requested by the dean is displayed on the screen.

3) PRINT THE REPORT

a. From the File menu, select the Page Setup command. A dialog box is displayed.
b. Click on the portrait **Orientation** option (▯) and then select **OK**.
c. Save IVY STUDENT.
d. From the File menu, select the Print command. Select the **Visible Records** option if it is already not selected and then select **Print** to print the report.

4) SAVE AND CLOSE IVY STUDENT

a. From the Layout pop-up menu, select Layout 1.
b. From the Organize menu, select Show All Records.
c. Save IVY STUDENT and then close the database.

7.8 Calculation Fields

Database fields can store more than just information entered from the keyboard. A *formula* is a mathematical statement used to calculate a value. A *calculation field* displays the result of a formula that is defined when the field is created. The formula in a calculation field uses the data contained in other fields of the record to calculate the value it displays.

The usefulness of a calculation field can be illustrated by examining the partial database on the next page. This database lists all items sold at the Ivy Bookstore, how many of each are in stock, and the price of each item:

Item Name	Department	In Stock	Price
Aspirin	Pharmacy	168	$1.99
Ball Point	Pens/Pencil	150	$0.89
Band Aids	Pharmacy	12	$1.39
Calculator	Electronics	136	$17.88
Cheetos	Food	280	$0.97
Chips	Food	77	$0.65

The Bookstore manager wants to know the cash value of the stock of each item. To find this, she would multiply the number in stock by its price. For example, there are 50 class rings in stock and each one is priced $198.95. To find the cash value of the stock of class rings, 50 would be multiplied by $198.95, producing $9,947.50. This operation can be performed automatically by a calculation field in the database.

To create a calculation field, select the Define Fields command from the Layout menu to display the Define Database Fields dialog box. Next, type a field name and then select **Calculation** as the **Field Type**. When the **Create** button is selected, the Enter Formula dialog box is displayed:

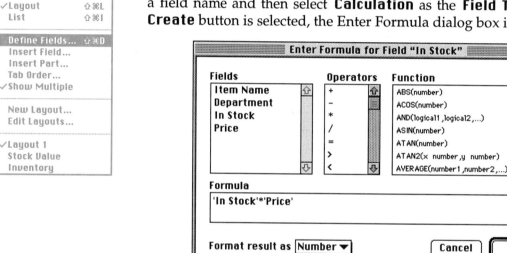

A calculation field's formula is entered in this dialog box

Clicking on or typing the proper fields, operators, and other data displays the field's formula in the **Formula** box. The formula for the Value field is shown in the dialog box above. (The * symbol is used for multiplication.) Select **OK** when the formula is complete to again display the Define Database Fields dialog box. Select **Done** to add the field to the current Layout:

Item Name	Department	In Stock	Price	Value
Aspirin	Pharmacy	168	$1.99	$334.32
Ball Point	Pens/Pencil	150	$0.89	$133.50
Band Aids	Pharmacy	12	$1.39	$16.68
Calculator	Electronics	136	$17.88	$2431.68
Cheetos	Food	280	$0.97	$271.60
Chips	Food	77	$0.65	$50.05

A calculation field named Value has been added to the database

The calculation field may be added to other Layouts using the Insert Field command from the Layout menu.

While the formula in a calculation field remains constant and does not change, the result displayed is updated when any value in the formula changes. For example, if 20 ball point pens were sold one day and the In Stock field updated to 130, the Value field would automatically display $115.70 to reflect this change (130*0.89).

It is also possible to include numeric constants in a calculation field's formula. For example, to quickly figure a 5% tax on each item, a new calculation field called Tax that stores the formula `'Price'*0.05` could be added to the database. ClarisWorks multiplies each item's price by 0.05 and displays the product in the Tax field. The tax on a class ring, for example, would be $198.95*0.05, or $9.95.

Practice 5

In this Practice you will add a calculation field which displays the value of each item in Ivy Bookstore's inventory. Start ClarisWorks if you have not already done so.

1) OPEN IVY BOOKSTORE

   a. Open IVY BOOKSTORE which stores inventory data for Ivy University.
   b. Display the Stock Value Layout in Browse view.

2) CREATE A CALCULATION FIELD

   a. From the Layout menu, select the Define Fields command. The Define Database Fields dialog box is displayed.
   b. Type `Value` as the **Field Name**, select Calculation as the **Field Type**, and then select **Create**. The Enter Formula dialog box is displayed.
   c. In the **Fields** list click on In Stock. In the **Operators** list click on *. Again in the **Fields** list, click on Price. The **Formula** box displays: `'In Stock'*'Price'`
   d. Select **OK** to display the Define Database Fields dialog box again. Notice that the calculation field has been added to the list of fields.
   e. Select **Done** to return to the Layout. The new field has been added to the Layout.

3) SWITCH TO LAYOUT 1

   a. From the Layout pop-up menu, select Layout 1. Note how the Value field has not been automatically added to the Layout.
   b. Switch back to the Stock Value Layout.

4) FORMAT THE VALUE FIELD

   a. Switch to Layout view.
   b. Select the Value field name. Decrease the size of the field name box by dragging.
   c. Select the Value entry box. Decrease the size of the entry box by about one-fourth.
   d. Double-click on the Value entry box to display the Number Format dialog box. Format the Value entry box for **Currency** with **Precision** of 2 and **Commas** and then select **OK**.
   e. Press ⌘] to right align the field entry box.
   f. Move the Value field name and entry box so they are aligned under the Price field.

Check - Your Layout should be similar to the one shown on the next page:

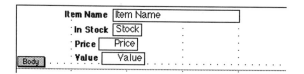

g. Switch to Browse view. The Value entry is automatically calculated for each record.

Check - Your database should be similar to the following:

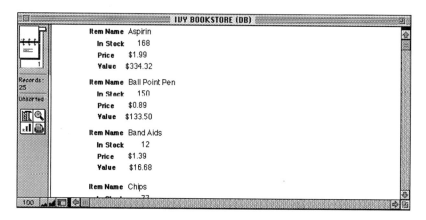

5) UPDATE A RECORD

a. Press the Tab key to display the entry boxes for the first record. An entry box is not displayed for the Value field because Value is a calculation field and its entry is automatically calculated by ClarisWorks.

b. Note the current entry in the Value field of the Aspirin record. In the In Stock field of the Aspirin record type 105. Press Tab to enter the new value. Note how the Value entry is automatically recalculated.

6) SAVE IVY BOOKSTORE AND PRINT A RECORD

a. Save IVY BOOKSTORE.

b. Print only the first record by using the **Current Record** option in the Print dialog box.

7.9 Adding Summaries to a Layout

Summary fields are used to make a Layout more informative. For example, a summary field can be used to total the Value field in the IVY BOOK-STORE database. Summary fields are similar to calculation fields because data is not directly entered into them. They contain *functions* that perform a set of calculations using the data stored in other fields.

Summary fields make their calculations based only on the values in displayed records. Functions such as SUM, AVERAGE, MAX, and MIN are used in a summary field to total, compute the average, or find the highest or lowest value in a particular field from the records displayed. The COUNT function can be used to count the number of records displayed.

Selecting the Define Fields command from the Layout menu displays a dialog box. Here the summary field name is typed in the **Field Name** box and **Summary** selected as the **Field Type**. Selecting the **Create** button displays the Enter Formula dialog box, the same dialog box used to create a calculation field. The **Fields**, **Operators**, and **Function** lists can be used to create the summary field's formula. For example, if the Ivy Bookstore wanted to determine the total number of items in stock the following formula would be stored in a summary field:

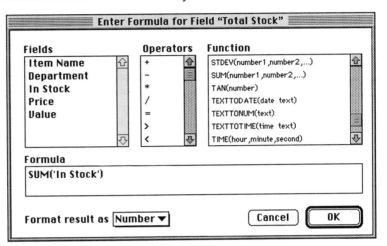

The SUM function is used to find the total number of items in stock

Selecting **OK** creates the new summary field and adds it to the list of field names in the Define Database Fields dialog box.

To display the new summary information, a *Grand Summary* must be added to the Layout. To do this, the desired Layout must be displayed in Layout view. The Insert Part command is then executed from the Layout menu, displaying a dialog box similar to the following:

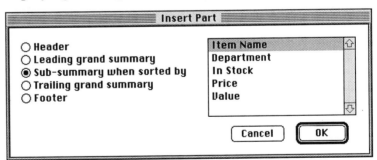

Grand Summary may be added to a Layout using this dialog box

A Grand Summary part is placed below the Body by selecting **Trailing grand summary** and then **OK**:

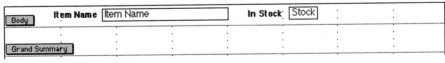

The Grand Summary is added below the Body in a Layout

Next a summary field is added to the Layout with the Insert Field command. Both the summary field name and entry box must be moved into the Grand Summary part of the record layout in order for the totaling to occur:

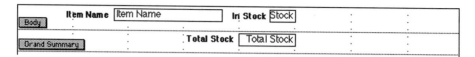

To see the summary, switch to Browse view and select Page View from the View menu. The summary is displayed at the end of the Layout after the last record.

Creating a Summary

1. Use the Define Fields command to create the summary field.
2. Display the Layout that is to include the summary field.
3. Switch to Layout view and select the Insert Part command from the Layout menu to add the Grand Summary part to the Layout.
4. Insert the summary field created in step 1 by selecting the Insert Field command from the Layout menu.
5. Move the summary field name and entry box into the Grand Summary part of the Layout (above the Grand Summary boundary line).
6. Switch to Browse view and select Page View or print the database to view the summary.

Practice 6

In this Practice you will create and print a report that finds the total number of items in stock in the database used by Ivy Bookstore. Start ClarisWorks and open IVY BOOKSTORE if you have not already done so.

1) CREATE A TOTAL STOCK SUMMARY FIELD

a. From the Layout menu, select Define Fields. A dialog box is displayed.
b. Type Total Stock and select **Summary** as the **Field Type**. Select the **Create** button to display the Enter Formula dialog box.
c. Scroll through the **Function** list and click on SUM(number1,number2,...) to display it in the **Formula** box.
d. Highlight everything in the parentheses and then click on In Stock in the **Fields** list. Your formula should look like:

```
SUM('In Stock')
```

e. Select **OK** and notice that the Total Stock field has been added to the list of field names in the Define Database Fields dialog box, along with its formula.
f. Select **Done**. ClarisWorks does not automatically add summary fields to a Layout.

2) INSERT THE GRAND SUMMARY PART

a. Display the Inventory Layout and then switch to Layout view.
b. From the Layout menu, select the Insert Part command. A dialog box is displayed.
c. To have ClarisWorks total the In Stock field, select **Trailing grand summary** and then **OK**. Grand Summary is added to the Layout.

An Introduction to Computing Using ClarisWorks

3) INSERT THE SUMMARY FIELD

a. From the Layout menu, select the Insert Field command. A dialog box is displayed listing the fields not already in the Layout.

b. Highlight Total Stock and then select **Insert**. The Total Stock field name and entry box are inserted in the Body of the Layout.

c. Resize the Total Stock field name so that it is just the width of the field name.

d. Move the Total Stock field name and entry box into the Grand Summary. Be sure the right edges of the Total Stock and In Stock entry boxes line up evenly. Right align the Total Stock entry box and format it as **Fixed** with **Precision** as 0 and **Commas**.

e. Drag the Body marker up so the space between records is reduced. Drag the Grand Summary marker up as well.

Check: Your Layout should look similar to:

4) DISPLAY THE SUMMARY

a. Switch to Browse view.

b. From the View menu, select the Page View command.

c. Scroll to the bottom of the database and note the Summary field. The value displayed by the Total Stock field is the sum of the values in the In Stock fields of all the records in the database.

5) CREATE AND DISPLAY A REPORT

Ivy Bookstore needs to know how much stock there is in the Clothing department.

a. Display Layout 1.

b. From the Search pop-up menu, select the New Search command. A dialog box is displayed.

c. Type Clothing Items and then select **OK**. The Find screen is displayed.

d. In the Department entry box, type: =Clothing

e. Select **Store** to save the query.

f. From the Sort pop-up menu, select the New Sort command. The Sort Records dialog box is displayed.

g. In the entry box, type: Item Names - Alphabetical

h. Click on Item Name in the **Field List** and then click on **Move**. Item Name is moved to the **Sort Order** list with ascending indicated as the sort order.

i. Select **OK** to save the sort.

j. From the Report pop-up menu, select New Report. A dialog box is displayed.

k. Type Clothing Stock as the **Report Name**. Select Inventory for the **Layout**, Clothing Items for the **Search**, and Item Names - Alphabetical for the **Sort**.

l. Select **OK** to create the Report.

m. From the Report pop-up menu, select Clothing Stock. The new report is displayed.

6) PRINT THE REPORT

a. Save IVY BOOKSTORE.

b. Print the report using the **Visible Records** option. Note the summary information below the records on the printout.

c. From the View menu, deselect Page View.

d. Show all records and then save IVY BOOKSTORE.

7.10 Including Sub-summaries in a Layout

A database and its reports become even more useful when records are grouped together and summarized. To do this, a *sub-summary* is added to a Layout:

Item Name	Dictionary	**In Stock**	22
Item Name	Thesaurus	**In Stock**	12
	Department Stock		34
Item Name	Class Ring	**In Stock**	50
Item Name	School Logo T-Shirt	**In Stock**	250
Item Name	School Book bag	**In Stock**	125
Item Name	School Jacket	**In Stock**	100
Item Name	School Tie	**In Stock**	15
Item Name	School Umbrella	**In Stock**	26
	Department Stock		566
Item Name	Calculator	**In Stock**	136
	Department Stock		136
Item Name	Chips	**In Stock**	77
Item Name	Pepsi	**In Stock**	444
Item Name	Cheetos	**In Stock**	280

Subtotals make a database more informative

A new field called Department Stock has been added to the Layout above to subtotal the items in each department. The Department Stock field is a summary field that contains the formula `SUM('In Stock')`. The summary field summarizes each Department because it has been added to the Sub-summary part of the Layout and then the Layout sorted by Department. To add a Sub-summary part to a Layout, select the Insert Part command from the Layout menu to display a dialog box similar to the following:

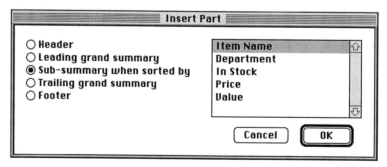

A new part can be added to a Layout using this dialog box

Next, click on the **Sub-summary when sorted by** option and then the field that the database will be sorted on. Selecting **OK** displays a message asking where the subtotal should be placed in relation to its records:

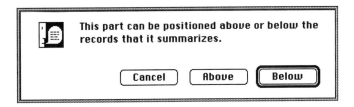

Selecting **Below** inserts the new part into the Layout below the Body. The last step is to insert the summary field using the Insert Field command from the Layout menu. The subtotal field name and entry box must then be moved into Sub-summary in order to be displayed properly:

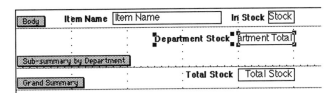

When sorted by department, the report will display subtotals for each department

To see the sub-summaries, switch to Browse view, sort the database on the appropriate field, and select Page View. In our example, the database must be sorted by Department to calculate the subtotals. Sub-summaries will not be displayed or printed if the proper sort has not been applied.

Creating a Sub-Summary

1. Use the Define Fields command to create the summary field.
2. Display the Layout that is to display the sub-summary.
3. Switch to Layout view and select the Insert Part command from the Layout menu. Select **Sub-summary when sorted by** and then highlight the field the database is to be sorted by to display the sub-summary information.
4. Insert the summary field created in step 1 by selecting the Insert Field command from the Layout menu.
5. Move the field name and entry box into the Sub-summary part of the Layout (above the Sub-summary marker).
6. Switch to Browse view and sort the database on the appropriate field.
7. Select Page View or print the report to view the sub-summary.

Practice 7

In this Practice you will subtotal the In Stock field by Department. Start ClarisWorks, open IVY BOOKSTORE, and display the Inventory Layout if you have not already done so.

1) CREATE THE SUBTOTAL SUMMARY FIELD

a. Switch to Layout view. This Layout currently has two parts, Body and Grand Summary.
b. From the Layout menu, select Define Fields.
c. Type Department Total in the **Field Name** box. Select **Summary** as the **Field Type**. Select **Create** to display the Enter Formula dialog box.
d. Scroll through the **Function** list and click on SUM(number1,number2,...) to display it in the **Formula** box.

e. Highlight everything in the parentheses and then click on In Stock in the **Fields** list. This field will add up all the items in stock. Your formula should look like:

```
SUM('In Stock')
```

f. Select **OK** and then **Done** to create the new field.

2) INSERT THE SUB-SUMMARY INTO A LAYOUT

Ivy Bookstore would like to subtotal the stock by Department.

a. From the Layout menu, select the Insert Part command. A dialog box is displayed.
b. Select **Sub-summary when sorted by** and then click on Department to highlight it.
c. Select **OK**. In the displayed dialog box, select the **Below** button to position the subtotal below each set of records. A Sub-summary by Department part is inserted into the Layout below the Body.

3) INSERT THE SUMMARY FIELD

a. From the Layout menu, select the Insert Field command. A dialog box is displayed listing the available fields not already in the report.
b. Highlight Department Total and then select **Insert**. The field name and entry box are inserted in the Body of the Layout.
c. Increase the width of the Department Total field name so that the entire name is visible on one line.
d. Move both the Department Total field name and entry box into Sub-summary. Be sure the Department Total entry box lines up evenly with the In Stock and Total Stock entry boxes.
e. Drag the Body marker up so the space between records is reduced.

4) FORMAT THE SUB-SUMMARY

Right align the Department Total field entry box and format the field so the entry is displayed with **Fixed**, with 0 **Precision** and **Commas**.

Check: Your Layout should look similar to:

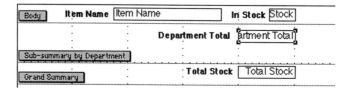

5) VIEW THE SUB-SUMMARY

a. Switch to Browse view and select Page View from the View menu if it is not already selected. Because the database is not yet sorted by Department, the subtotals do not appear.
b. From the Organize menu, select the Sort Records command. Click on **Clear** to remove fields from the **Sort Order** list, if necessary.
c. Click on Department and then **Move**. Select **OK** to sort the database in ascending order by Department. A subtotal now appears for each group of items in each department.
d. Deselect Page View.

6) PRINT THE DATABASE

    a. Save IVY BOOKSTORE.

    b. Print the database.

    c. Close IVY BOOKSTORE.

7.11 Where can you go from here?

The last three chapters introduced the concepts of databases: their design, creation, and use. The ClarisWorks database has a number of other options not discussed in this text which you may want to explore on your own. One of the best places to begin is by reading the database sections of the *ClarisWorks User's Guide* supplied by Claris.

A powerful feature of ClarisWorks is its ability to integrate the information stored in a database with a word processor document to produce personalized form letters. This process is called *mail merge* and is described in Chapter Eleven. Chapter Twelve describes how to add graphics to database Layouts.

Larger, more powerful database programs have even more options for generating reports and performing various operations with the data. Several of the most widely used packages are dBASE, FoxBase, and FileMaker Pro. Because you have learned how to use the ClarisWorks database it will be easier to learn a new package.

As the use of computerized databases becomes more widespread the knowledge of what a database is and what it can be used for will be an important skill. There are many job opportunities for people to work with computer databases. Information about careers involving computers and databases is given in Chapter Thirteen.

Chapter Summary

A database can have many different Layouts that contain all or some of the fields in the database. These Layouts may be used by different people who are only concerned with certain information in the database. The Standard Layout arranges all the fields in a column while the Labels Layout arranges selected fields to create mailing labels. When a record is updated in one Layout, it is automatically updated in all Layouts.

Careful planning should take place before a new Layout is created. Layouts are listed at the bottom of the Layout pop-up menu and the currently displayed Layout is indicated with a check mark. Layouts can be renamed and deleted using the Edit Layouts command.

In Layout view, fields can be deleted from a Layout by simply selecting the field and pressing the Delete key. The field is removed from the Layout, but not the database. Fields can also be added to a Layout by using the Insert Field command. Fields in a new Layout are not automatically formatted and must be resized, moved, aligned, etc.

This chapter covered one of the most important aspects of the computerized database: producing printed reports detailing the information it stores. A report uses a specified Layout, sort, and query to organize records for a specific purpose. The New Reports command from the Report pop-up menu is used to create a report. The Edit Reports command, also from the Report pop-up menu, is used to modify or delete a report.

A calculation field displays a value that is automatically computed. This value is calculated from a mathematical formula that is stored in the field. For example, the formula `'In Stock'*'Price'` displays the product of the value stored in the In Stock field and the value stored in the Price field. Calculation fields are created using the Define Fields command.

Summaries and Sub-summaries can be added to a Layout. To add a summary, a summary field must first be created using the Define Fields command. A corresponding summary part must be added to the desired Layout and then the summary field placed in it. When the database is displayed in Page view or printed, a summary is displayed at the end. Sub-summaries are displayed when the database is sorted on the required field and then displayed in Page view or printed. For example, this feature can be used to total the sales separately for each department of a store.

Vocabulary

Calculation field - Numeric field that displays a value based on a calculation. The calculation can be based on values stored in other fields or constants.

Formula - A mathematical statement used to calculate a value.

Functions - Used in calculation and summary fields to perform mathematical calculations. SUM, AVERAGE, and MAX are functions.

Grand Summary - Added to a report to display summary field information, usually at the end of a report.

Insert Field command - Adds a field to a Layout.

Labels Layout - Automates the procedure for producing mailing labels.

New Layout command - Selected when a new Layout of the database is desired. Standard and Labels are two kinds of Layouts that can be created.

Report - Using a specified Layout, sort, and query to organize database records for a specific purpose. A report is usually printed on paper.

Standard Layout - Layout which includes all of the fields in the database placed in a column.

Sub-summary - Displays a summary for a group of records when the database is sorted on a specific field.

Summary fields - Used to make a Layout more informative by summarizing certain fields, as in totaling, counting, and finding the highest or lowest value.

7 Reviews

1. a) Why would a database have more than one Layout?
   b) Describe two types of Layouts that you can create with ClarisWorks.

2. There are three Layouts for a single database. If the entry for one record changes in Layout 1, what happens to the entry stored in the same record in Layout 2 and Layout 3?

3. List 2 questions that should be asked when planning a new Layout.

4. a) How is a previously created Layout displayed?
   b) Explain how you would rename Layout 2 as Financial Report.
   c) What happens when a Layout is removed from the database? Are all the fields in that Layout deleted from the database?

5. Explain how a report named Unpaid Students would be produced for Ivy University.

6. How can the name of the report in Review question 5 be changed?

Section 7.8

7. a) How is the entry in a calculation field computed?
   b) What is an advantage of adding a calculation field to a database? Give an example where a calculation field would be useful.

8. A database stores each student's grades in fields named Grade 1, Grade 2, Grade 3, Grade 4, and Grade 5. The grades are numeric values from 0 to 100. Explain how a field named Average can be added to the database which calculates and stores the grade average for each student.

Sections 7.9 — 7.11

9. a) What is a summary field?
   b) If a summary field is placed in the Grand Summary, where is the information displayed?

10. a) What is a sub-summary field?
    b) What two things must be done for a Sub-summary to be displayed?

11. A database named CAR PRICE lists makes, models, and prices for more than 100 different automobiles.
    a) Explain the steps required to produce a Layout that lists the total of all the car prices.
    b) Explain the steps needed to total the prices for each make of car.

12. A banking database contains the following fields:

    First Name
    Last Name
    Acct Number
    Deposit Date
    Withdrawal Date
    Acct Balance

    a) List the steps required to produce a Layout named Balance. Balance should display only the First Name, Last Name, Acct Number, and Acct Balance for each depositor.
    b) What additional steps are required to add a summary to the Layout in part (a) so that the sum of all of the account balances is displayed?
    c) What formula would be used to calculate the interest in each account if interest is computed as 5% of the account balance?
    d) What steps are necessary to create a new calculation field named Interest that contains the formula from part (c).
    e) What steps are necessary to print a copy of the Balance report for only those customers having more than $10,000 in their account?

Exercises

1. The CAR PRICE database stores prices for a number of foreign and domestic cars. Open CAR PRICE.

   a) Plan and then create a new Layout named `Base Prices` that includes only the Make, Model, and Base Price fields. Format the fields appropriately. Change the margins of the Layout to 0.5".

   b) Create a summary field named `Average Price` that calculates the average base price (use the AVERAGE function, replacing its placeholders with 'Base Price'). Place the new field in the Grand Summary part of the Base Prices Layout and then format it appropriately.

   c) Using the Base Prices Layout, create a report named `Less than $9,000` that lists in alphabetical order those cars with a base price under $9,000. Save CAR PRICE and then print the report.

   d) Plan and then create a new Layout named `With Stereos` that includes only the Make, Model, and With Stereo fields. Format the fields appropriately. Change the margins of the Layout to 0.5".

   e) Create a summary field named `Subtotal` that computes the total number of makes (use the COUNT function, replacing its placeholders with 'Make'). Place the field in the Sub-summary of the With Stereos Layout so that subtotals are displayed when the database is sorted by Make. Format the field appropriately.

   f) Using the With Stereos Layout, create a report named `Cheap Chev & Ply w/Stereos` that lists in ascending order by Make all Chevrolets and Plymouths with stereos that cost under $10,000. Save CAR PRICE and then print the report.

2. The Address database stores information about your friends. Open Address which you last modified in Chapter Six, Exercise 11.

   a) Plan and then create a new Layout named `Birthdays` that includes only the name, birth date, and city fields. Format the fields appropriately. Change the margins of the Layout to 0.5".

   b) Using the Birthdays Layout, create a report named `Older Friends` that lists in ascending order by birth date only friends that were born before you. Save Address and print the report.

   c) Using the Birthdays Layout, create another report named `Friends in My Town` that lists in descending order by last name your friends that live in the same town as you. Save Address and print the report.

3. Open INVENTOR which you last modified in Chapter Six, Exercise 10.

   a) Plan and then create a new Layout named `Inventions` that includes the Invention, Country, and Year fields. Format the fields appropriately. Change the margins of the Layout to 0.5".

   b) Create a summary field named `Total Number of Inventions` that counts the number of inventions (use the COUNT function, replacing its placeholders with 'Invention'). Place the new field in the Grand Summary part of the Inventions Layout.

   c) Using the Inventions Layout, create a report named `French Inventions` that lists in alphabetical order those inventions from France. Save INVENTOR and then print the report.

   d) Modify the report to display only those French inventions from this century. Save INVENTOR and print the modified report.

4. Fantasy Wheels, Inc. would like reports generated from their Wheels database. Open Wheels which you last modified in Chapter Six, Exercise 3.

   a) Plan and create a new Layout named `Auto Profit` that includes the Make, Price Paid, and Asking Price fields. Format the fields appropriately. Change the margins of the Layout to 0.5".

   b) From the Auto Profit Layout, create a calculated field named `Profit` that calculates the profit on each sale (asking price minus the price paid). Format the field appropriately.

   c) Create a summary field named `Total Asking Price` that totals the Asking Price field (use the SUM function, replacing its placeholders with 'Asking'). Create another summary field named `Total Profit` that totals the Profit field.

   d) Add the summary fields created in part (c) to the Grand Summary of the Auto Profit Layout. Format the fields appropriately. Save Wheels and print a copy of the database.

   e) Plan and create a new Layout named `Sticker Price` that includes the Year, Make, Exterior, Accessories, and Asking Price fields. Format the fields appropriately. Change the margins of the Layout to 0.5".

   f) Using the Sticker Price Layout, create a report named `Asking < $10,000` that lists in ascending order by price those cars with an Asking Price under $10,000. Save Wheels and print the report.

5. Reports can be used to learn more from the temperature data you entered in the Weather database. Open Weather which you last modified in Chapter Six, Exercise 5.

   a) Create a calculated field named `Temp. (F)` that converts degrees Celsius (C) to degrees Fahrenheit (F). The conversion formula is Fahrenheit=9/5 × Celsius + 32.

   b) Plan and create a new Layout named `Sky Conditions`. Include the Date, Time, Sky, and both temperature fields. Format the fields appropriately. Temperatures should be displayed with 0 precision. Change the margins of the Layout to 0.5".

c) Using the Sky Conditions Layout, create a report named `Sunny and Over 65` that lists in ascending order by temperature (F) those days when it was warmer than 65° F and sunny. Save Weather and print the report.

d) Modify the report to display those days when it was cloudy with a temperature below 40° F. Save Weather and print the report.

6. Open the ACADEMY AWARDS database which contains information about Academy Award winners since 1928.

a) Plan and create a new Layout named `Studio`. Include the Year, Picture, and Studio fields. Format the fields appropriately. Change the margins of the Layout to 0.5".

b) Using the Studio Layout, create a report named `United Artists Films` that displays in alphabetical order by Picture those films produced by United Artists. Save ACADEMY AWARDS and print the report.

c) Using Layout 1, create a report named `1985 to Present` that displays in ascending order by Year those films from 1985 to the present. Save ACADEMY AWARDS and print the report.

7. Open COLLEGES which contains information about U.S. colleges and universities.

a) Plan and create a new Layout named `School with Total Costs` and include the Name, Enrollment, and Total Cost fields. Format the fields appropriately. Change the margins of the Layout to 0.5".

b) From the School with Total Costs Layout, create a calculated field named `Total Cost` that displays the total cost of attending each school (tuition plus room and board). Format the field appropriately.

c) Using the Layout from part (a), create a report named `Students<8000 and Cost>$15000` that lists in alphabetical order by name those schools with less than 8,000 students and whose total cost is more than $15,000. Save COLLEGES and print the report.

d) Plan and create a new Layout named `Schools by State` that includes the Name, State, and Private/Public fields. Format fields appropriately. Change the margins of the Layout to 0.5".

e) Using the Schools by State Layout, create a report named `CA and MA Schools` that lists in alphabetical order by State those schools in California or Massachusetts. Save COLLEGES and print the report.

8. Open COUNTRY which contains information about the countries of the world.

a) Plan and create a new Layout named `Currency` that includes the Country, Capital, and Currency fields. Format fields appropriately. Change the margins of the Layout to 0.5".

b) Using the Currency Layout, create a report named `Pounds or Pesos Countries` that lists in alphabetical order by Country those countries that use the pound or peso for their currency. Save COUNTRY and print the report.

c) Plan and create a new Layout named Population that includes only the country and population fields. Format the fields appropriately. Change the margins of the Layout to 0.5".

d) Using the Population Layout, create a report named Less than 1 Million that lists in alphabetical order by Country only those countries who have a population of less than one million. Save COUNTRY and print the report.

9. Open GIBBON RESEARCH which contains a number of observations of gibbons.

a) Plan and create a new Layout named Gibbons that includes the Name, Age, Companion, and Location, and Gender fields. Format the fields appropriately. Change the margins of the Layout to 0.5".

b) Using the Gibbons Layout, create a report named Male Gibbons that lists only male gibbons in alphabetical order by Name. Save GIBBON RESEARCH and print the report.

c) Using the Gibbons Layout, create a report named Female Gibbons that lists only female gibbons in alphabetical order by Name. Save GIBBON RESEARCH and print the report.

An Introduction to Computing Using ClarisWorks

Chapter 8
Introducing the Spreadsheet

Save

Page View

Print

Clear

SUM

AVERAGE

ROUND

Number

Alignment

Objectives

After completing this chapter you will be able to:

1. Define a spreadsheet.

2. Create a spreadsheet and enter data into it.

3. Save and print a spreadsheet.

4. Use formulas and functions to perform calculations.

5. Use the SUM, AVERAGE, and ROUND functions.

6. Change the width of columns.

7. Format a spreadsheet.

8. Select cell ranges by highlighting blocks of cells.

8

This chapter explains what a spreadsheet is and how to use one. The components of a spreadsheet are presented first, then the commands needed to produce a simple ClarisWorks spreadsheet are covered. The next chapter explains how to create larger and more powerful spreadsheets.

8.1 What is a Spreadsheet?

A *spreadsheet* is simply rows and columns of data. The term comes from the field of accounting where accountants keep track of business activities on large sheets of paper that spread out to form a "spreadsheet." Accounting spreadsheets contain rows and columns of figures that relate to the flow of money, but spreadsheets can be used to organize any type of numeric data.

Spreadsheets are record keeping tools that work primarily with numbers. An example of a simple spreadsheet is the grade book used by Ivy University's chemistry professor, Dr. Sulfuric. In her grade book, the names of her students run down the left side of the page and labels run across the top of the page to indicate each test and test date:

Name	Test 1	Test 2	Test 3	Test 4
	9/12/97	10/17/97	11/14/97	12/12/97
C. Bowser	50	83	68	64
D. Warheit	86	89	78	88
M. Porter	78	100	90	89
B. Presley	45	78	66	78
D. Sophocles	66	76	78	55
T. Hogan	85	74	83	66

Dr. Sulfuric's grade book

The grade book is organized into rows and columns. A row runs horizontally and stores both the name and grades for one student. The name T. Hogan and the grades 85, 74, 83, and 66 form a row. A column runs vertically and stores a title, date, and all of the grades for a single test. The title Test 1, the date 9/12/97, and the grades from 50 to 85 form a column.

Computerized spreadsheets allow the user to perform calculations on data. Dr. Sulfuric could use a computerized spreadsheet for her gradebook and have it calculate grade averages. The computer would then automatically recalculate the average if she changed a grade. This is the primary advantage of a computerized spreadsheet; the ability to perform calculations on data and to automatically recalculate when changes are made.

8.2 The Spreadsheet Screen

 A new spreadsheet document is created by clicking on the **Spreadsheet** option and then selecting **OK** in the New Document dialog box. The Spreadsheet button on the Shortcuts palette can also be used.

The ClarisWorks spreadsheet screen has columns, rows, and a few other features:

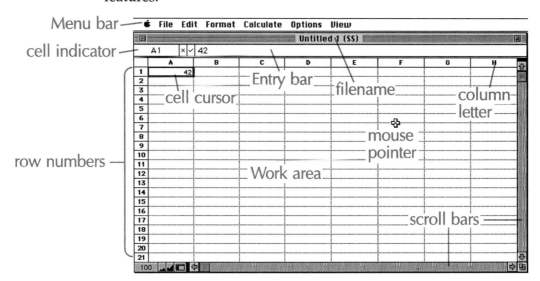

The ClarisWorks spreadsheet screen

Columns are identified by letters which run horizontally across the top of the screen, and rows are identified by numbers which run vertically down the left side. In ClarisWorks, a spreadsheet has letters that run from A to Z, and then AA to AN for 40 columns. Rows are numbered from 1 to 500. However, only a limited number of rows and columns can be displayed on the screen. For example, the screen above displays only columns A to H and rows 1 to 21. Other columns and rows can be displayed by scrolling the spreadsheet with the scroll bars.

Data is entered into a spreadsheet on the screen shown above. The intersection of a row and column is called a *cell*. A single cell is identified by its column letter and row number, which together is called a *cell name*. For example, the third cell from the top in column C is named C3. Each cell can store a single item of data. This system is similar to mailboxes at the post office where each box (or cell) has a name and can store information. Be careful not to confuse the name of a cell with the data it stores. The heavy outline appearing around cell A1 is called the *cell cursor*. Data can only be entered into the cell where the cell cursor is located, also called the *selected cell*. The *cell indicator* at the top of the screen shows the current location of the cell cursor, in this case A1.

Commands are accessed from menus in the Menu bar at the top of the screen. Below the Menu bar, the filename is displayed. The contents of the selected cell are displayed on the Entry bar. Spreadsheet cells and the data they store are in the Work area.

8.3 Types of Data

Spreadsheets can store three types of data in cells: labels, values, and times/dates. *Labels* are text and cannot be used in calculations. *Values* are numeric and can be used in calculations. *Times/dates* are either a time, such as 12:10 PM, or a calendar date such as 6/4/96. A time/date entry may be used in some calculations. In the grade book spreadsheet, student names and titles (e.g., T. Hogan and Test 1) are labels, a grade such as 50 is a value, and a date such as 9/12/97 is a time/date. When planning a computerized spreadsheet it is important to first determine what the data will be stored as: labels, values, or times/dates.

8.4 Moving Through the Spreadsheet

The mouse pointer is displayed as a plus sign (✛) when it is placed over the Work area. Moving it to a cell and clicking once moves the cell cursor to that cell, selecting it for data entry. The cell indicator, in the upper-left corner of the screen, displays the selected cell's name.

The scroll bars can be used to bypass rows and columns before placing the cell cursor with the mouse pointer. Clicking the mouse once on one of the scroll arrows moves the spreadsheet one row or column in the direction of the arrow. Holding the mouse button down continues the scroll. Dragging the scroll box within the scroll bar moves the spreadsheet in the window a greater distance. Another way to move the cell cursor is to use the arrow keys to move the cursor from cell to cell. When the arrow keys are used, the spreadsheet scrolls automatically if necessary.

Some Macintosh keyboards have additional keys that can be used for scrolling. Pressing the Home key brings the start of the spreadsheet into view, with cell A1 visible in the upper-left corner of the screen. The End key can be used to scroll the screen so that the very end of the spreadsheet is in view. Pressing the Page Up key scrolls the spreadsheet up one screen while pressing the Page Down key scrolls it down one screen.

Practice 1

In this Practice you will create a new spreadsheet, use the mouse to move the cell cursor around, and scroll through the empty spreadsheet.

1) START CLARISWORKS

Following the steps given in Chapter Two, boot the System and start ClarisWorks.

2) CREATE A NEW SPREADSHEET

    a. In the New Document dialog box, click on **Spreadsheet**.
    b. Select **OK**. A new empty spreadsheet is displayed.

3) SELECT CELL D8

Select cell D8 by moving the mouse pointer to cell D8 and clicking once. Note that the cell indicator in the upper-left corner of the screen displays D8.

4) SCROLL THE SCREEN USING THE SCROLL BARS

a. Click once on the right horizontal scroll arrow. Note how column A moves off the screen and another column moves onto the screen.

b. Click and hold the mouse on the right horizontal scroll arrow until cell Z8 becomes visible. When scrolling with the mouse, the cell cursor does not move from the currently selected cell. Click on cell Z8 to select it.

c. Click once on the down vertical scroll arrow. Note how the top row moves off the screen. Click and hold the mouse on the down vertical scroll arrow until cell Z50 becomes visible. Click on cell Z50 to select it.

5) RETURN THE CELL CURSOR TO CELL A1 USING THE SCROLL BOXES

a. Drag the scroll box to the far left of the horizontal scroll bar. Column A should be visible.

b. Drag the scroll box in the vertical scroll bar upwards to display Row 1. Note that the cell indicator still displays Z50 because scrolling only changes what is displayed, not which cell is selected. Click on cell A1 to select it.

8.5 Entering Data into the Spreadsheet

Data in entered into a cell by moving the cell cursor to that cell and entering the data from the keyboard. When the data is typed, it first appears on the Entry bar:

Clicking on the Check box enters the label "Jodi" into cell A1

Clicking on the *Check box* (☑) transfers the data from the Entry bar to the selected cell. Clicking on the *X box* erases the data from the Entry bar and the current cell is left unchanged.

Data can also be transferred from the Entry bar to the selected cell by pressing the Return key, which then moves the cell cursor to the next cell below. To enter data and move to the cell to the right, type the data and press the Tab key.

If a mistake is made when entering data, it can be corrected by returning the cell cursor to the cell and entering the correct data. The new data then replaces any previous data. If the mistake is noticed before transferring the data from the Entry bar to the cell, the Delete key can be used to delete one character at a time. The whole entry may be canceled by clicking on the X box in the Entry bar, or by pressing the Escape key.

ClarisWorks automatically displays values up to 11 digits long in a single cell. When the value exceeds 11 digits it is expressed in scientific notation. For example, the number 333344445555 is displayed as 3.33344e+11. However, labels are displayed in their entirety until they encounter another cell containing data.

8.6 Saving, Printing, and Viewing a Spreadsheet

Selecting the Save command from the File menu (⌘**S**) transfers a copy of the spreadsheet from the computer's memory to disk. To maintain the most recent version of a document, the Save command should be executed after making changes to the spreadsheet. A spreadsheet should also be saved before printing.

The Page View command from the View menu (⇧⌘**P**) is used to determine how a spreadsheet will look when printed. When Page View is selected, a check mark is placed beside its name in the View menu and the spreadsheet is divided into page-sized sections. To view each page entirely, use the Zoom controls. To return to normal view select Page View again.

A spreadsheet can be printed by first selecting the Print command from the File menu to display its dialog box. Then, selecting the **Print** button prints the portion of the spreadsheet that contains data. The dialog box also contains options for including the column headings, row headings, and cell grid in the printout.

Spreadsheets are often too wide to print on a single sheet of paper. In this case the spreadsheet is printed on consecutive sheets starting from the leftmost columns and proceeding to the right. The separate sheets can then be taped together if desired.

On the Shortcuts palette, clicking the Save button saves the file to disk. The Print button on the Shortcuts palette can be used to print one copy of the displayed spreadsheet using the default print options.

As with the word processor, headers and footers can be included in spreadsheets to provide more informative printouts. Information such as a person's name, the date of the printout, or the filename can be included. Note that when the Insert Header or Insert Footer command from the Format menu is selected, the spreadsheet is then automatically displayed in Page View.

Practice 2

In this Practice you will enter the data from Dr. Sulfuric's grade book into the spreadsheet created in the last Practice. If the spreadsheet is not open, create a new one following the steps given in Practice 1.

1) ENTER THE COLUMN TITLES IN ROW 1

a. Move the pointer to cell A1 and click once to select it, if it is not already selected. Type Name and click on the Check box. Cell A1 now contains the label Name. Note that the Entry bar displays the currently selected cell's contents.

b. Select cell B1 and type Test 1. Click on the Check box.

c. Press the right-arrow key to move the cell cursor to cell C1, then type Test 2.

d. Press the Tab key. The label is entered and the cell cursor moved to the next cell in the row, D1.

e. Continue this procedure to place the headings Test 3 in cell D1 and Test 4 in cell E1.

2) ENTER THE TEST DATES

a. Select cell B2 and type the date 9/12/97. Click on the Check box. ClarisWorks right aligns a date when entered into a cell.

b. Select cell C2 and type the date 10/17/97. Press the Tab key. The cell cursor is moved to the next cell in the row, D2.

c. Enter the date 11/14/97 in cell D2 and the date 12/12/97 in cell E2.

3) ENTER THE STUDENT NAMES

a. Select cell A3. Type the name C. Bowser and press the Return key. The cell cursor moves to the next cell in the column, A4.

b. Type the name D. Warheit and press the Return key.

c. Continue this process to place the names:

    M. Porter   into cell A5
    B. Presley   into cell A6
    D. Sophocles   into cell A7
    T. Hogan   into cell A8

4) ENTER THE GRADES

Move the cell cursor to cell B3 and enter the first grade for C. Bowser, a 50. Continue entering the grades from Dr. Sulfuric's grade book as shown in Section 8.1. If a mistake is noticed before a cell's data has been entered, use the Delete key to erase data on the Entry bar, then type the correction. Incorrect data that has already been entered may be corrected by moving the cell cursor to the cell and entering new data. When complete your spreadsheet should look like the one below:

	A	B	C	D	E
1	Name	Test 1	Test 2	Test 3	Test 4
2		9/12/97	10/17/97	11/14/97	12/12/97
3	C. Bowser	50	83	68	64
4	D. Warheit	86	89	78	88
5	M. Porter	78	100	90	89
6	B. Presley	45	78	66	78
7	D. Sophocles	66	76	78	55
8	T. Hogan	85	74	83	66

5) SAVE THE SPREADSHEET AND VIEW IT

a. From the File menu, select the Save command.

b. Type Grades and then select **Save**. Your spreadsheet is now saved on disk using the name Grades.

c. From the View menu, select Page View. Margins are visible around the spreadsheet.

d. Click twice on the Zoom-out control (▣). The view scale changes to 50 percent and two pages of the spreadsheet can be seen.

e. Click on the Zoom-in control (▣) until the view scale indicates 100.

f. From the View menu, select Page View again to return to normal view.

6) PRINT AND CLOSE GRADES

a. From the File menu, select the Print command. A dialog box is displayed. Note the options available at the bottom of the dialog box.

b. Select **Print** to print the spreadsheet. The printout contains only the portion of the spreadsheet that contains data.

c. Close Grades.

8.7 Using Formulas to Perform Calculations

We have stated that the primary benefit of a spreadsheet is its ability to perform calculations. To perform these calculations, *formulas* are used. Formulas are mathematical statements used to calculate values. For example, entering the formula =25 * 3 will display the value 75 in the cell. Note that every formula in ClarisWorks must begin with an equal sign (=).

The following mathematical operators can be used in writing a formula:

Addition	+
Subtraction	−
Multiplication	*
Division	/
Exponentiation	^

Exponentiation means to raise to a power and is represented by the caret (^) symbol. For example, $2^2 = 4$ and $5^3 = 125$.

When ClarisWorks evaluates a formula, it follows the rules of *order of operations* which indicate the priority of operators. For example, what value is displayed when the formula

=9+12/3

is evaluated? Is the sum of 9 and 12 divided by 3? If so, the answer is 7. Or is the result of 12 divided by 3 added to 9 to produce 13? Entering the formula we discover that 13 is displayed. Division is performed first and then addition because a specific order of operations is followed.

ClarisWorks evaluates a formula from left to right. If a formula contains two operators of equal priority, the leftmost operator is used first. The following order of operations is used when a formula is evaluated:

Exponents

1. Any number raised to a power is calculated first.

   =4+3^2   produces the value 13

Multiplication & Division

2. Calculations involving multiplication and division, which are of equal priority, are performed next.

   =3+5*6/2   produces the value 18

   Here, ClarisWorks first computes the product of 5 and 6 to get 30, and then divides by 2 to produce 15. Finally, 3 is added to 15 to produce 18. Operations of the same priority are performed in order from left to right.

Addition & Subtraction

3. Third in the order of operations is addition and subtraction which are of equal priority.

   =7+4*2   produces the value 15

   Here, ClarisWorks first multiplies 4 and 2 to get 8. The final result is computed by adding 7 to 8 to get 15.

When parentheses are used, whatever operations are within them are performed first. By using parentheses you can change the order of operations. For example, to add 7 and 4 and then multiply the result by 2, parentheses must be used:

$$=(7+4)*2 \qquad\qquad \text{produces the value } 22$$

Here are a number of example formulas and their results:

Formula	Resulting value
=2*2+3*2	10
=25*8/4	50
=35+12/3	39
=3+5*8+7	50
=(3+5)*(8+7)	120
=3^2*8+4	76
=6+2^2	10
=(6+2)^2	64

Entering an improper formula in a cell causes ClarisWorks to display an error message in that cell. Error messages begin with a pound sign (#) and end with an exclamation point (!). For example, a number cannot be divided by zero because the result is mathematically undefined. Therefore, entering =10/0 displays: #DIV/0!

··

Practice 3

In this Practice you will enter formulas into the cells of a new spreadsheet to perform calculations. Boot the System and start ClarisWorks if you have not already done so.

1) CREATE A NEW SPREADSHEET

Use the New Document dialog box to create a new empty spreadsheet.

2) ENTER A FORMULA INTO CELL A1 OF THE SPREADSHEET

a. Select cell A1 if it is not already selected.
b. Type =35*12/3. Click on the Check box. The result 140 is displayed in cell A1. Note that the formula is shown on the Entry bar, but the result of the formula is shown in the cell:

A1	x ✓	=35*12/3

	A	B
1	140	

3) ENTER FORMULAS

a. Move the cell cursor to cell B1.
b. Enter each of the formulas shown on the next page by typing the formula and then pressing the Return key to move the cell cursor to the next cell in the column. Note the resulting values:

Formula	Resulting value
=20/50	0.4
=20*50	1000
=20-50	-30
=2+20*5+50	152
=(2+20)*(5+50)	1210
=20/0	#DIV/0!
20+50	20+50

In the last example, the result is a *label* because it is not preceded by an equal sign.

4) SAVE THE SPREADSHEET

Save the spreadsheet naming it Test.

8.8 Using Cell Names in Formulas

A cell name may be used in a formula. When ClarisWorks evaluates the formula, it uses the cell name to locate the value needed in the calculation. For example, if cell B3 stores the value 20 and cell C2 stores the value 50:

Formula	Resulting value
=B3/C2	0.4
=B3*C2	1000
=B3-C2	-30
=2*B3+5*C2	290
=B3+5*C2+8	278
=B3+5*(C2+8)	310
=(B3+5)*(C2+8)	1450

If the cell contains a label, 0 is used for its value.

It is important to realize that a formula cannot reference the cell it is stored in. For example, the formulas above cannot be stored in cells B3 or C2 because this would cause an error.

Formulas are commonly used to sum values. For example, the sum of the values stored in cells C1 to C6 can be calculated using the formula:

=C1+C2+C3+C4+C5+C6

To average the values stored in cells C1 to C6, the following formula can be used:

=(C1+C2+C3+C4+C5+C6)/6

8.9 Editing Entries

A cell's entry, including formulas, can be edited by first selecting the cell to display its contents on the Entry bar. Next, clicking the pointer on the Entry bar displays a cursor and then characters can be entered or deleted. When the entry has been corrected it is entered into the selected cell by clicking on the Check box, or by pressing Return.

Entering an improper formula displays the following dialog box:

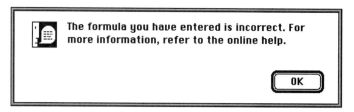

ClarisWorks displays this error dialog box when an improper formula has been entered

Selecting **OK** removes the box so that the formula can be corrected.

The contents of a selected cell can be erased by selecting the Clear command from the Edit menu. Pressing the Delete key also clears a selected cell. If a cell is cleared by mistake, immediately executing the Undo command (⌘Z), also from the Edit menu, restores the cell's contents.

Practice 4

In this Practice you will enter values and formulas into the cells of a new spreadsheet and perform calculations. Start ClarisWorks and open the Test spreadsheet created in Practice 3 if it is not already displayed.

1) ENTER VALUES INTO THE SPREADSHEET

    a. Move the cell cursor to cell C1 and enter the value 20.
    b. Move the cell cursor to cell D2 and enter the value 50.

2) ENTER FORMULAS

    a. Move the cell cursor to cell D5.
    b. Enter each of the formulas below by typing the formula and then pressing the Return key to move the cell cursor to the next cell in the column. Note the resulting values:

Formula	Resulting value
=C1/D2	0.4
=C1*D2	1000
=C1-D2	-30
=2+C1*5+D2	152
=(2+C1)*(5+D2)	1210
=C1^2+D2^2	2900
=(C1+D2)^2	4900
=C1/0	#DIV/0!
C1+D2	C1+D2

In the last example, the result is a *label* because it is not preceded by an equal sign.

3) ENTER A NEW VALUE IN CELL C1

    a. Move the cell cursor to cell C1.
    b. Enter 30 to replace the current value. Every formula in the spreadsheet referencing cell C1 is automatically recalculated. A major advantage of using a computerized spreadsheet is that formulas are automatically recalculated when necessary.
    c. Enter 20 in cell C1. Note how the values are again automatically recalculated.

4) CLEAR THE CONTENTS OF EACH CELL

    a. Move the cell cursor to cell D5.

    b. From the Edit menu, select the Clear command. The cell's contents are now cleared and the Entry bar is blank.

    c. Clear each cell displaying data using either the Clear command or the Delete key. The spreadsheet Work area should now be blank.

5) ENTER NEW VALUES

    a. Move the cell cursor to cell C1 and enter the value 50.

    b. Move the cell cursor to cell C2 and enter the value 85.

    c. Continue entering the values:

        75   in cell C3
        83   in cell C4
        34   in cell C5
        55   in cell C6

6) CALCULATE THE SUM OF THE VALUES IN COLUMN C

    a. Move the cell cursor to cell C8.

    b. Enter the formula:

        =C1+C2+C3+C4+C5+C6

Cell C8 displays the sum of the values stored in cells C1 through C6, 382.

7) CALCULATE THE AVERAGE OF THE VALUES IN COLUMN C

    a. Move the cell cursor to cell C9.

    b. Enter the formula:

        =(C1+C2+C3+C4+C5+C6)/6

The average of the values, 63.66666666, is shown in cell C9.

8) EDIT THE FORMULA TO AVERAGE THE FIRST 3 CELLS ONLY

    a. Move the cell cursor to cell C9.

    b. Move the pointer to the right of the divisor 6 on the Entry bar and click the mouse to place the cursor. Press the Delete key to delete the 6. Type a 3.

    c. Press the left-arrow key 3 times to place the cursor to the right of the cell name C6.

    d. Press the Delete key 9 times. The formula should now read =(C1+C2+C3)/3. Click on the Check box or press the Return key. The average of the first three cells only is shown in cell C9. What is it?

Check - Your spreadsheet should be similar to:

C9	×✓	=(C1+C2+C3)/3	
	A	B	C
1			50
2			85
3			75
4			83
5			34
6			55
7			
8			382
9			70
10			

9) ENTER A NEW VALUE IN CELL C1

a. Move the cell cursor to cell C1.
b. Enter 20 to replace the current value. Every formula in the spreadsheet referencing cell C1 is automatically recalculated.
c. Enter 50 in cell C1. The values are again automatically recalculated.

10) SAVE AND CLOSE TEST

8.10 Using Functions to Perform Calculations

To perform common calculations ClarisWorks contains built-in *functions* that can be used as part of a formula. A function performs a set of calculations and then returns a single value. To better understand this, consider the formula =C1+C2+C3+C4+C5+C6 used in Practice 4. We could also have used a formula that contained ClarisWorks' built-in SUM function:

=SUM(C1..C6)

The SUM function requires the first and last cell names of the cells to be summed. The dots (..) are used to indicate a *range* of cells. For example, C1..C6 refers to cells C1, C2, C3, C4, C5, and C6. Functions are useful because they often make a formula shorter and are less error-prone, especially when a large range of cells is involved.

Values stored in a row of cells can also be added together. For example, the formula

=SUM(B2..E2)

adds the values in cells B2, C2, D2, and E2 together. It is important to realize that only a section of adjacent cells can be used to define a range.

In Practice 4, we could replace the formula in cell C9 used to average the column of grades with:

=SUM(C1..C6)/6

Note that we must still divide the sum by 6 to obtain the average. An easier method is to use ClarisWorks' AVERAGE function:

=AVERAGE(C1..C6)

....

Practice 5

In this Practice you will enter formulas to calculate the average grade on each test and the term averages for each of Dr. Sulfuric's students in the Grades spreadsheet created in Practices 1 and 2. Start ClarisWorks if you have not already done so.

1) OPEN THE GRADES SPREADSHEET

2) USE A FUNCTION TO SUM THE GRADES FOR TEST 1

a. Move the cell cursor to cell B9.

An Introduction to Computing Using ClarisWorks

b. Enter the following formula:

`=SUM(B3..B8)`

The sum 410 is displayed.

3) ENTER THE FORMULA TO AVERAGE THE GRADES FOR TEST 1

Dr. Sulfuric needs the average of the grades, not the sum. Move the cell cursor to cell B9 and enter the formula:

`=AVERAGE(B3..B8)`

The average grade on Test 1, 68.33333333, is displayed in cell B9.

4) ENTER FORMULAS TO CALCULATE THE OTHER TEST AVERAGES

`=AVERAGE(C3..C8)`	into cell C9
`=AVERAGE(D3..D8)`	into cell D9
`=AVERAGE(E3..E8)`	into cell E9

5) CALCULATE EACH STUDENT'S TERM AVERAGE

a. Move the cell cursor to cell F3.
b. Enter the formula:

`=AVERAGE(B3..E3)`

The average for C. Bowser, 66.25, is displayed in cell F3.
c. Repeat this process by entering the formulas:

`=AVERAGE(B4..E4)`	into cell F4
`=AVERAGE(B5..E5)`	into cell F5
`=AVERAGE(B6..E6)`	into cell F6
`=AVERAGE(B7..E7)`	into cell F7
`=AVERAGE(B8..E8)`	into cell F8

6) ADD TITLES FOR THE NEW INFORMATION

a. Move the cell cursor to cell F1 and enter the label: `Average`
b. Select cell A9 and enter the label: `Test Average:`

7) SAVE THE MODIFIED GRADES SPREADSHEET

<u>Check</u> - Your spreadsheet should be similar to:

	A	B	C	D	E	F
1	Name	Test 1	Test 2	Test 3	Test 4	Average
2		9/12/97	10/17/97	11/14/97	12/12/97	
3	C. Bowser	50	83	68	64	66.25
4	D. Warheit	86	89	78	88	85.25
5	M. Porter	78	100	90	89	89.25
6	B. Presley	45	78	66	78	66.75
7	D. Sophocles	66	76	78	55	68.75
8	T. Hogan	85	74	83	66	77
9	Test Average:	68.33333333	83.33333333	77.16666666	73.33333333	

8.11 The ROUND Function

The ROUND function rounds a value to a specific number of decimal places. In the spreadsheet containing Dr. Sulfuric's grades, the test averages are printed to 8 decimal places, but only 1 place is desired. For example, the class average on Test 1 appears as 68.33333333, but Dr. Sulfuric wants it computed as 68.3.

To round a stored value, the cell name is used in the ROUND function followed by the number of decimal places that the result is to be rounded. For example, to round the value stored in cell C16 to 2 places, the formula is written:

=ROUND(C16,2)

If the value stored in C16 is 42.865 the rounded result is 42.87.

To round the result of a formula, the formula followed by the number of decimal places desired is used in the ROUND function. For example, C. Bowser's average can be rounded to 1 place with the formula:

=ROUND(AVERAGE(B3..E3),1)

To round a value to the nearest integer, a 0 is used to indicate no decimal places:

=ROUND(AVERAGE(B3..E3),0)

It should be noted that rounding changes the actual value stored in the cell, not just the way the original value is displayed. Therefore, the result of a calculation involving a rounded value may be different from the same calculation using the value before rounding. ClarisWorks includes a number of other functions which are listed in Appendix A.

Practice 6

In this Practice you will round the averages in the Grades spreadsheet by editing the existing formulas. The modified spreadsheet will then be printed. Start ClarisWorks and open the Grades spreadsheet if you have not already done so.

1) DISPLAY THE RESULT OF A FORMULA TO 2 DECIMAL PLACES

    a. Select cell B9.
    b. Move the pointer to the formula on the Entry bar, placing it before the A in AVERAGE, and type: ROUND(
    c. Place the cursor at the end of the formula and type ,2) so that the formula on the Entry bar appears:

        =ROUND(AVERAGE(B3..B8),2)

Click on the Check box or press Return and note that the average is now rounded to 2 decimal places, 68.33.

2) ROUND ALL TEST AVERAGES TO 2 DECIMAL PLACES

Repeat step 1 for cells C9, D9, and E9.

3) ROUND C. BOWSER'S AVERAGE TO 1 DECIMAL PLACE

a. Move the cell cursor to cell F3.
b. Place the cursor before the A in AVERAGE and type: ROUND(
c. Place the cursor at the end of the formula and type ,1) so that the formula is:

   =ROUND(AVERAGE(B3..E3),1)

Click on the Check box or press Return and note that the average is rounded to one decimal place, 66.3.

4) ROUND ALL STUDENT AVERAGES TO 1 DECIMAL PLACE

Repeat step 3 for cells F4, F5, F6, F7, and F8.

5) SAVE THE MODIFIED GRADES

<u>Check</u> - Your spreadsheet should be similar to the one below:

	A	B	C	D	E	F
1	Name	Test 1	Test 2	Test 3	Test 4	Average
2		9/12/97	10/17/97	11/14/97	12/12/97	
3	C. Bowser	50	83	68	64	66.3
4	D. Warheit	86	89	78	88	85.3
5	M. Porter	78	100	90	89	89.3
6	B. Presley	45	78	66	78	66.8
7	D. Sophocles	66	76	78	55	68.8
8	T. Hogan	85	74	83	66	77
9	Test Average:	68.33	83.33	77.17	73.33	

8.12 Changing a Column's Width

Often the default column width of 1 inch is insufficient to display a column's data. A column's width is changed by dragging its right column divider bar. To do this, place the pointer on the bar separating the column letters at the top of the screen. The pointer shape changes to a double-headed arrow:

*The width of column G will be changed
when the divider bar is dragged*

Next, drag the divider bar to the right to increase the width of the field. To decrease a field's width, drag the divider bar to the left.

It is important to realize that the width of single cells cannot be changed, only whole columns. If a cell is not wide enough to display its value, scientific notation is used. For example, the value 123456789012 is displayed as 1.23456e+11. Pound signs (#) are displayed if a cell is not wide enough to display a formatted value.

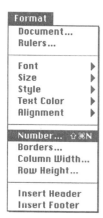

How a spreadsheet is displayed is called its *layout*. Column widths, value formats, and label formats all relate to layout. Choosing a proper layout not only makes a spreadsheet easy to use, but also easier to expand so that it can perform additional tasks.

Changing a column's width affects every cell in the column. However, other formatting commands affect only the selected cell. To format a cell that stores a number, time, or date, the cell is highlighted and the Number command from the Format menu (⇧⌘N) selected. A dialog box is then displayed:

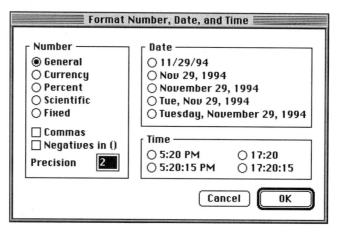

Number formats can be selected from this dialog box

To display the value in the selected cell with a specific number of decimal places, **Fixed** is selected and then the desired number of decimal places typed in the **Precision** box. Unlike the ROUND function, fixing a value to a specific number of decimal places only changes how the value is displayed, not the value itself. For example, a cell containing a value of 27.8 fixed to 0 decimal places displays 28. Adding 10 to the value of this cell produces 37.8, not 38.

Cells that store dollar amounts should be formatted for **Currency**. **Commas** and **Negatives in ()** may be selected in addition to any of the other options in the **Number** section and are commonly used when displaying dollar amounts. The **Percent** option displays the value stored in the cell as a percentage. For example, a cell storing the value 0.15 formatted as **Percent** with 0 as the **Precision** displays 15%. As with the **Fixed** format, **Currency** and **Percent** do not change the value that is stored in the selected cell, only how that value is displayed.

The Shortcuts palette can also be used to apply some number formats:

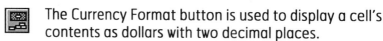

The Currency Format button is used to display a cell's contents as dollars with two decimal places.

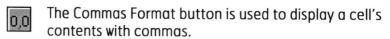

The Commas Format button is used to display a cell's contents with commas.

The Percent Format button is used to display a cell's contents as a percentage with two decimal places.

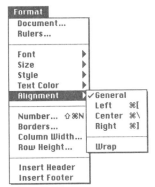

Unless formatted otherwise, cells containing labels are left aligned, while values and dates are right aligned. For this reason labels and values displayed in the same column do not line up. The Test labels and dates in the Grades spreadsheet demonstrate this. To line up label headings over columns of values, the cell storing the label is selected. Dragging down to the Alignment command in the Format menu displays a submenu where Right is selected (⌘]). Selecting the General command in the Alignment submenu formats a cell's data for the default alignment, which is left aligned for labels and right aligned for numbers, dates, and times.

Some of the alignment formats can also be applied to a selected cell by using buttons on the Shortcuts palette:

   Align Left

   Align Center

   Align Right

The Font, Size, and Style commands in the Format menu may also be used to change the way cell data is displayed. The Bold, Italic, and Underline buttons on the Shortcuts palette can be used to change the style of a cell's contents. There are many different ways to use these formats: titles and section names could be bold, important numbers might be italic, and so on. It is also possible to apply more than one style to a cell. For example, a cell can be formatted as both bold and italic.

8.14 Highlighting

In a spreadsheet, several cells can be selected together to form a *highlighted block*. This is helpful when applying formatting or using the editing commands because the entire highlighted block is affected. To highlight a block of cells, the mouse is dragged from one cell to another:

The mouse pointer was placed on cell B2 and then dragged to cell D4 to create this highlighted block

An entire row, column, or block of adjacent cells can be highlighted.

Another way of creating a highlighted block is by first selecting the starting cell, then holding down the Shift key and clicking the mouse on the last cell in the block. An entire row is selected by clicking on the row number, and clicking on a column letter highlights a column. Clicking in the box above row 1 and to the left of column A selects the entire spreadsheet.

In this Practice you will format the Grades spreadsheet. Start ClarisWorks and open the Grades spreadsheet if you have not already done so. If it is not already displayed, display the Shortcuts palette and move it so that all data is displayed.

1) BOLD THE NAME LABEL

    a. Select cell A1.

    b. From the Format menu, drag down to the Style command. In the submenu, select Bold. The label is now bold.

2) RIGHT ALIGN AND BOLD THE TEST AVERAGE LABEL

    a. Select cell A9.

    b. From the Format menu, drag down to the Alignment command. In the Alignment submenu, select Right. The label is now right aligned in the cell.

    c. From the Format menu, select Bold. The label is now bold, but only partially displayed because the column is not wide enough for the formatted label.

3) WIDEN COLUMN A BY DRAGGING

    a. Place the pointer on the line separating the column letters A and B at the top of the spreadsheet. The pointer changes to a double-headed arrow.

    b. Slowly drag the line to the right approximately 3 spaces. Column A should be wide enough to display the entire label in cell A9. If not, drag the column divider farther to the right.

4) CHANGE THE AVERAGE LABEL

    a. Move the cell cursor to cell F1.

    b. Enter the label Student Average replacing the current label. Notice how the label extends into the next column because there is no data in the next cell.

5) RIGHT ALIGN AND BOLD THE STUDENT AVERAGE LABEL

    a. Select cell F1 if it is not already selected.

    b. On the Shortcuts palette, use the Align Right button to change the alignment of the label.

    c. On the Shortcuts palette, use the Bold button to change the style of the label.

6) WIDEN COLUMN F

    Use the procedure described in Step 2 to widen column F so that label fits entirely in cell F1.

7) RIGHT ALIGN AND BOLD THE TEST LABELS USING KEYBOARD SHORTCUTS

    a. Place the mouse pointer on cell B1.

    b. Drag the mouse pointer from cell B1 to cell E1. Cells B1, C1, D1, and E1 are highlighted as a block.

    c. Press ⌘B to bold the labels.

    d. Press ⌘] (the] key is located above the Return key) to right align the labels.

8) FORMAT AVERAGES TO DISPLAY 1 DECIMAL PLACE

a. Place the mouse pointer on cell F3.
b. Drag the mouse pointer from F3 to F8. The averages are highlighted as a block.
c. From the Format menu, select the Number command. The dialog box is displayed.
d. Click on **Fixed**. Type 1 for the **Precision**.
e. Select **OK**. Notice how the value in cell F8 is displayed with a trailing zero in order to display it to 1 decimal place. When the ROUND function was applied to the value in this cell in Practice 6, there was no change in the display because the value remained the same. Fixing the number of decimal places changes the display; the ROUND function changes the value.

9) CHANGE C. BOWSER'S GRADE

a. Select cell C3.
b. An error was made in recording C. Bowser's score for Test 2. Enter the correct test score, 82. Both the Student Average and Test Average have been updated. The trailing zero is displayed in the Student Average because the cell was formatted as fixed to one decimal place.

Check - Your spreadsheet should be similar to:

	A	B	C	D	E	F
1	Name	Test 1	Test 2	Test 3	Test 4	Student Average
2		9/12/97	10/17/97	11/14/97	12/12/97	
3	C. Bowser	50	82	68	64	66.0
4	D. Warheit	86	89	78	88	85.3
5	M. Porter	78	100	90	89	89.3
6	B. Presley	45	78	66	78	66.8
7	D. Sophocles	66	76	78	55	68.8
8	T. Hogan	85	74	83	66	77.0
9	Test Average:	68.33	83.17	77.17	73.33	

10) SAVE GRADES AND PRINT THE SPREADSHEET

11) CLOSE GRADES AND EXIT CLARISWORKS

Chapter Summary

This chapter covered the basics of planning and creating a computerized spreadsheet. A spreadsheet is simply rows and columns of data, with rows running horizontally and columns vertically. The primary advantage of a computerized spreadsheet is that it has the ability to perform calculations on the data it stores, with the calculations automatically changing to reflect any changes in the data.

In a ClarisWorks spreadsheet the rows are numbered on the left side and the columns identified by letters which run along the top. Where a row and column intersect is called a cell. A single cell is identified by its column letter and row number, which is called its cell name. For example, C3 is the name of the cell located at column C and row 3.

Spreadsheet cells can store three types of data: labels, values, and times/ dates. Labels are text and cannot be used in calculations. Values are numeric and can be used in calculations. Time/Date entries are either times (12:30 AM) or calendar dates (9/21/95) and both can be used in certain types of calculations.

A new spreadsheet is created by double-clicking on **Spreadsheet** in the New Document dialog box or by clicking on the Spreadsheet button on the Shortcuts palette. Data is entered into a spreadsheet by moving the cell cursor to a cell, typing the data and clicking on the Check box or pressing Return. The cell indicator in the upper-left corner of the screen shows the current location of the cell cursor. The Entry bar shows the contents of the cell. To move through a spreadsheet, either the scroll arrows or the arrow keys can be used.

A spreadsheet is saved on disk by selecting the Save command from the File menu. It is printed by selecting the Print command also from the File menu. Both of these actions can be performed by using the Shortcuts palette. The Page View command from the View menu can be used to divide the spreadsheet into page-sized sections.

Formulas are mathematical statements used to calculate values which can be stored in cells. All formulas must begin with an equal sign (=) and may contain cell names. For example, if cell B5 stores the value 12 and cell C8 stores 10, the formula =B5*C8 would display 120.

ClarisWorks uses an order of operations when evaluating a formula. First it performs exponentiation, then multiplication and division, and finally addition and subtraction. Operations of the same priority are performed from left to right. The order of operations can be changed by using parentheses. For example:

=3+5*8+7   *displays* 50
=(3+5)*(8+7) *displays* 120

Functions are predefined formulas that are used by the computer to perform common calculations. The formula =SUM(B3..B8) includes the SUM function. B3..B8 is called a range and defines a portion of a row or column. This chapter covered the following three functions:

SUM   =SUM(B3..B8)

sums the values in the column of cells B3, B4, B5, B6, B7, and B8.

=SUM(A5..E5)

sums the values in the row of cells A5, B5, C5, D5, and E5.

AVERAGE   =AVERAGE(C3..C8)

averages the values in the column of cells C3, C4, C5, C6, C7, and C8.

=AVERAGE(B7..F7)

averages the values in the row of cells B7, C7, D7, E7, and F7.

ROUND

=ROUND(C5,2)

rounds the value stored in cell C5 to 2 decimal places.

=ROUND(AVERAGE(B7..F7),1)

rounds the average of the values in the range B7..F7 to 1 decimal place.

The width of a column can be changed by dragging its column divider bar. Commands from the Format menu are used to change the layout of a spreadsheet. Cells can be formatted to display currency, percent, or a fixed number of decimal places by using the Number command. The Style and Alignment commands allow the style of labels or values to be changed. Many formatting buttons are available on the Shortcuts palette.

Formatting and editing commands can be applied to a highlighted block. A block of highlighted cells is formed by dragging the mouse from one cell to another cell. A row is highlighted by clicking on its row number, while a column is highlighted by clicking on its column letter.

Vocabulary

Block - A group of adjoining cells. Formatting commands can be applied to a highlighted block, affecting every cell in the selection.

Cell - Where a row and column intersect. A cell is identified by its column letter and row number, for example C3.

Cell cursor - Rectangular outline on the screen which is used to indicate the current cell. It can be moved from cell to cell by using the mouse or the arrow keys. Data can be entered into a cell when the cell cursor is located on it.

Cell indicator - Location at the top of the screen that displays the current location of the cell cursor.

Cell name - The column letter and row number used to identify a cell (i.e., B3).

Check box - A box on the Entry bar containing a check. Clicking on this box moves data from the Entry bar to the selected cell.

Column - Vertical line of data identified by a letter.

Date - Entry in the form of a date (i.e., 9/5/96).

Entry bar - Area at the top of the screen where data entered from the keyboard is displayed before it is entered into a cell. Also displays the contents of the selected cell.

Formulas - Mathematical statements used to calculate values which are stored in cells. The statement =C5+D7+E8 is a formula.

Functions - Used in formulas to perform common calculations. =SUM(B3..B8) is a function.

Label - Words or characters stored in a cell that cannot be used in calculations.

Layout - The way in which cells are formatted and data displayed in a spreadsheet.

Order of operations - The rules the computer uses to evaluate a formula.

Range - Partial row or column of adjacent cells. B3..B8 is a range.

Row - Horizontal line of data identified by a number.

Selected cell - The spreadsheet cell containing the cell cursor as indicated by a heavy outline.

Scroll - Moving the cell cursor to view different parts of a spreadsheet.

Spreadsheet - Rows and columns of data on which calculations can be performed.

Time - Entry in the form of a time (i.e., 12:30 PM).

Values - Numeric data that can be stored in cells and used in calculations.

X box - A box on the Entry bar containing an X. Clicking on this box erases data from the Entry bar and leaves the selected cell unaffected.

Reviews

Sections 8.1 — 8.5

1. What is the primary advantage of using a computerized spreadsheet over a spreadsheet produced using paper and pencil?

2. a) What is a cell in a spreadsheet?
   b) What is the difference between a row and a column?
   c) What is the difference between the cell cursor and cell indicator?

3. a) What is the difference between a label and a value entry?
   b) What is a date entry? Give an example.
   c) What is a time entry? Give an example.

4. What information is displayed on the screen by the:
   a) Entry bar
   b) Cell indicator
   c) Menu bar

5. How many of each of the following types of entries are stored in the Grades spreadsheet shown in Practice 2?
   a) labels
   b) values
   c) dates
   d) times

6. a) How can spreadsheet columns that are off the screen be moved on to the screen?
   b) What is this action called?

7. How can the screen be moved to show:
   a) cell A1?
   b) the last cell in a spreadsheet that contains data?

8. a) What is the difference between a cell name and the data stored in a cell? Give an example.
   b) Can the name of a cell be changed? If so, how?

9. Draw a diagram that shows all of the cells in the first three columns and five rows of a spreadsheet. Show the name of each cell and store the value 27 in cell B3.

10. What is the maximum number of digits that may be displayed in a single cell without using special commands?

11. What steps would you take to enter the value 65 into cell C4 of the spreadsheet produced in Practice 2?

12. If a mistake has been made entering data into a cell, how can it be corrected?

Sections 8.6 — 8.9

13. How do you transfer a copy of a spreadsheet from the computer's memory to disk?

14. What happens when you print a spreadsheet that is too large to fit on a single piece of paper?

15. How can a spreadsheet be displayed on the screen as it will appear when printed?

16. Briefly explain what a formula is and give two examples.

17. a) What is meant by order of operations?
    b) Which operation is performed first?
    c) Which operation is performed last?
    d) How can the order of operations be changed?

18. If a formula contains 3 operations, all of the same order, which will be performed first?

19. If 10/20 is entered into a cell, ClarisWorks considers it a label. How must the entry be changed so that 10 will be divided by 20?

20. Write formulas for each of the following calculations:
    a) The product of the values stored in cells A1, B3, and C4.
    b) The sum of the values stored in cells A3, A4, A5, A6, A7, and A8.
    c) The average of the values stored in cells B5, B6, and B7.
    d) The average of the values stored in cells A1, B3, and C4.

21. What value would be calculated by Claris-Works for each of the following formulas?
    a) =2+7*5+4
    b) =(2+7)*(5+4)
    c) =5+10/5
    d) =(5+10)/5
    e) =2^3+4
    f) =15+(12/4)

22. What value would be calculated by Claris-Works for each of the following formulas if cell C15 stores a value of 16 and cell D8 a value of 4?
    a) =C15*D8
    b) =C15+5+D8
    c) =C15*5+D8
    d) =C15*(5+D8)
    e) =C15/D8
    f) =C15+4/D8
    g) =C15+(4/D8)

23. If a mistake has been made in a formula what are two ways it can be corrected?

24. How can the value stored in a cell be erased?

Sections 8.10 — 8.14
25. a) What is meant by a range of cells?
    b) Give an example of a range of cells contained in a row.
    c) Give an example of a range of cells contained in a column.

26. Write a formula which calculates the average of the values stored in cells B3, B4, B5, C5, D5, and E5.

27. What is the difference between a formula and a function?

28. Write formulas using functions that will calculate each of the following:
    a) The sum of the values stored in cells B4, B5, B6 and B7.
    b) The sum of the values stored in cells B4, C4, D4, and E4.
    c) The average of the values stored in the column of cells D7 to D35.
    d) The average of the values stored in the row of cells F3 to J3.

29. Using functions, write formulas to calculate each of the following:
    a) The sum of the values in cells C5, C6, C7, C8, and C9 rounded to 2 decimal places.
    b) The sum of the values in cells B5, C5, D5, and E5 rounded to the nearest integer.
    c) The average of the values in cells A1, A2, A3, B1, B2, B3 rounded to 1 decimal place.

30. Is it possible to change the width of only a single cell?

31. Explain how the width of a column is increased.

32. List all of the differences between using the ROUND function or fixing a value to display 2 decimal places using the Number command.

33. List the steps required to perform the following operations:
    a) Format a cell to display a fixed value to 3 decimal places.
    b) Bold and right align the contents of a cell.
    c) Format a cell to display a value in dollars to 2 decimal places.

34. a) Why should the label headings over columns of values be right aligned?
    b) Explain how all of the column headings in a spreadsheet can be right aligned at one time.

35. List two ways to highlight cells B3 through C12.

Exercises

1. The Ivy U Meteorology department has asked you to create a spreadsheet that converts a Fahrenheit temperature to the equivalent Celsius temperature.

   a) The formula for converting from degrees Fahrenheit (F) to degrees Celsius (C) is Celsius = 5/9× (Fahrenheit – 32). Enter the following data into a new spreadsheet as shown, making sure to enter the appropriate formula into cell E3:

	A	B	C	D	E
1			Temperature Conversion		
2					
3	Fahrenheit Temp:	20.0		Celsius Temp:	-6.7

   Format cell C1 as bold and resize columns if necessary to display all data. Format the cells displaying temperature values as **Fixed** to 1 decimal place.

   b) Save the spreadsheet naming it Temp Convert.

   c) In row 5 have the spreadsheet convert temperatures from a Celsius temperature entered in cell B5 to a Fahrenheit temperature displayed in cell E5. Be sure to use the correct formula and appropriate labels.

   d) Save the modified Temp Convert and print a copy.

2. The Ivy U Auto Club is testing different sports cars and wants to store the results in a spreadsheet.

   a) In a new spreadsheet, enter the data as shown below. Resize columns as necessary so that all data is displayed entirely:

	A	B	C
1		Track Test	
2			
3	Car	Distance (meters)	Time (seconds)
4	Porsche	37.44	6.78
5	Ferrari	44.18	7.77
6	Lotus	37.51	5.99
7	Aston-Martin	45.19	7.89
8	Corvette	47.42	6.68
9	Jaguar	37.57	5.34
10	Supra	41.55	7.11

   b) Save the spreadsheet naming it Track Test:

   c) In cell D3, enter the label `Velocity (m/sec)`. Velocity is calculated by dividing distance travelled by time. Use a formula to calculate the velocity for each car. Be sure that any change made to a distance or time will automatically change the corresponding velocity.

   d) In cell D12 have the spreadsheet calculate the average velocity. Include a label in cell C12 for the average.

   e) Edit the formulas for velocity and average velocity to round the results to 2 decimal places. Resize column D as necessary to display all data.

   f) Save the modified Track Test and print a copy.

3. Dorothy Sophocles has recently graduated from Ivy University and has decided to keep track of her personal finances using a spreadsheet.

a) In a new spreadsheet, enter D. Sophocles' expenses for three months as shown below. Resize columns as necessary so that all data is displayed entirely:

	A	B	C	D
1		D. Sophocles Expenses		
2				
3	Expense	June	July	August
4	Rent	500	500	500
5	Groceries	120	135	110
6	Transportation	100	90	88
7	Clothes	100	120	150
8	Savings	50	50	50
9	Misc.	80	50	75

b) Save the spreadsheet naming it Expenses.

c) Enter the label Total in cell A11. In cell B11, enter a formula to total the expenses for June. Add similar formulas to total the expenses for July and August.

d) In column E, add a label and the appropriate formulas to display the average for each of the expenses over the three months.

e) Format the values in columns B, C, D, and E as currency with 0 decimal places. Format all the titles to be bold. Right align the month and average titles. Your spreadsheet should be similar to:

	A	B	C	D	E
1		D. Sophocles Expenses			
2					
3	Expense	June	July	August	Average
4	Rent	$500	$500	$500	$500
5	Groceries	$120	$135	$110	$122
6	Transportation	$100	$90	$88	$93
7	Clothes	$100	$120	$150	$123
8	Savings	$50	$50	$50	$50
9	Misc.	$80	$50	$75	$68
10					
11	Total	$950	$945	$973	

f) Save the modified Expenses and print a copy.

4. Create a spreadsheet that displays a multiplication table. The table should be set up so that when a number is entered into cell C3, it is automatically multiplied by 1 through 10:

	A	B	C	D
1			Multiplication Table	
2				
3	Number:		10	
4	10	*	1	10
5	10	*	2	20
6	10	*	3	30
7	10	*	4	40
8	10	*	5	50
9	10	*	6	60
10	10	*	7	70
11	10	*	8	80
12	10	*	9	90
13	10	*	10	100

a) Resize the columns as shown. The formulas in column D should use cell references for both the multiplier and the multiplicand.

b) Save the spreadsheet naming it Multiply and print a copy.

5. Mr. Hernandez, owner of the Aztec Café, has decided to use a spreadsheet to keep track of the number of hours his employees work.

a) In a new spreadsheet, enter the employee data, resizing the days of the week columns as shown:

	A	B	C	D	E	F	G	H
1			Aztec Cafe Employee Hours					
2								
3	Employee	Sun	Mon	Tue	Wed	Thu	Fri	Sat
4	H. Berry	10	0	0	10	8	8	4
5	G. Diez	0	8	8	8	8	10	0
6	K. Martin	4	4	4	0	4	0	4
7	D. Romani	8	10	9	10	0	10	0

b) Save the spreadsheet naming it AC Employees.

c) In column I, enter formulas to display the total number of hours worked by each employee. Enter an appropriate label in cell I3.

d) Bold all the titles. Format the day and total titles to be right aligned.

e) Save the modified AC Employees and print a copy.

6. Mr. Horatio von Money, Ivy University's major benefactor, keeps track of his stock portfolio in a spreadsheet named STOCKS. Open STOCKS. Note that the spreadsheet displays the price of each stock and the number of shares Mr. von Money owns.

a) You are to assist Mr. von Money by having the spreadsheet calculate the value of each stock he owns. Title the column Value. The value is calculated by multiplying the price of the stock by the number of shares owned. Add formulas to compute the value of each stock. Format the values appropriately.

b) Mr. von Money has decided that he will donate one fourth of his portfolio to Ivy University. Add formulas to total the value of all of his stocks and to compute the amount of his donation. Be sure to label both figures.

c) Format the labels to be right aligned and bold. Format the calculations appropriately.

d) Save the modified STOCKS and print a copy.

7. Varsity baseball coach Slugger Ryan needs to store his player's statistics in a spreadsheet.

a) Enter the following statistics into a new spreadsheet, including proper labels:

Player	At bats	Hits	Player	At bats	Hits
Attis	10	3	Fritz	10	6
Baker	11	3	Gold	14	4
Connelly	9	5	Hernandez	12	6
Doucette	12	4	Li	11	5
Enders	15	2			

b) Save the spreadsheet naming it Baseball.

c) Batting averages are calculated by dividing the number of hits by the number of times at bat. Add a column to Baseball that calculates and displays each player's batting average rounded to 3 decimal places. Be sure to title the column.

d) Coach Ryan would like to know the overall team batting average. Use the average function to produce the calculation for him. Be sure to include rounding and an appropriate label.

e) Bold all the labels and right align the labels describing the At Bats, Hits, and Average columns.

f) Save the modified Baseball and print a copy.

8. You are to produce a spreadsheet to help determine your caloric intake for a week.

a) In a new spreadsheet, enter data for the calories you consume in a typical week. Include appropriate labels and formatting. Your spreadsheet will have different numbers but should look similar to:

	A	B	C	D	E	F	G	H
1		Calories Consumed in 1 Week						
2								
3		Sun	Mon	Tue	Wed	Thu	Fri	Sat
4	Breakfast	500	0	0	0	0	0	520
5	Lunch	500	510	660	740	590	710	530
6	Afternoon Snack	0	150	0	100	0	0	300
7	Dinner	910	1190	1210	930	1000	1130	1020
8	Midnight Snack	110	0	0	100	0	0	250
9	Other	230	0	0	300	170	0	40

b) Save the spreadsheet naming it Diet.

c) Have the spreadsheet calculate the total number of calories consumed each day, the total for the week, and the average number of calories consumed per day. Round the totals and averages to 1 decimal place. Be sure to include appropriate labels and proper formatting.

d) It has been determined that aerobic exercise burns 360 calories per hour. Have the spreadsheet calculate the number of hours for a workout to burn off half of the total calories consumed for each day. Round the number of hours to 1 decimal place. Be sure to include an appropriate label and proper formatting.

e) Save the modified Diet and print a copy.

9. Spreadsheets can be helpful in personal time management. You are to create a spreadsheet to help determine the time spent on different activities during a week.

   a) In a new spreadsheet store the number of hours you spend each day of the week at each of the following activities:

   - school classes
   - athletics
   - extracurricular groups and clubs
   - studying and doing homework
   - eating
   - sleeping
   - watching television or listening to music
   - talking on the phone
   - doing chores at home
   - working at a part-time job

   b) Save the spreadsheet naming it Activity.

   c) Have the spreadsheet calculate the total hours spent for the week on each activity. Also calculate the average number of hours spent per day on each activity for the week.

   d) Most people's schedules do not account for all 24 hours in a day. Add a row that calculates and displays the amount of unaccounted time in your schedule for each day.

   e) Save the modified Activity and print a copy.

Chapter 9
Manipulating Data with the Spreadsheet

Paste Function

Fill Right

Fill Down

Find/Change

Go To Cell

MAX

MIN

Cut, Copy, Paste, Show Clipboard

Insert Cells

Delete Cells

IF

Document

Page Setup

Make Chart

Modify Chart

9

Objectives

After completing this chapter you will be able to:

1. Plan a large spreadsheet including its layout.

2. Enter formulas by pointing.

3. Copy labels, values, and formulas using relative and absolute copying.

4. Display the formulas in cells.

5. Use the MAX, MIN, and IF functions.

6. Insert and delete rows and columns.

7. Change the margins and print orientation of a spreadsheet.

8. Create charts and graphs of spreadsheet data.

9. Modify charts and graphs.

9

This chapter discusses how to plan and produce a large spreadsheet on the computer. Techniques for modifying a spreadsheet will be explained and commands will be introduced which enable you to copy formulas from one set of cells to another. The chapter ends by teaching you how to produce graphs and charts using the data stored in a spreadsheet.

9.1 Planning a Large Spreadsheet

The spreadsheets produced in Chapter Eight did not require much planning because they were small and easy to understand. In this chapter, planning is more important as we develop large spreadsheets that will be continually modified and expanded.

Before using ClarisWorks, a spreadsheet should be carefully planned by answering the following questions:

1. What new information should the spreadsheet produce?

2. What data must the spreadsheet store to produce the new information?

3. How would the new information be produced without using a computer?

4. How should the spreadsheet be organized and displayed on the computer?

In this chapter we will produce a spreadsheet for Ivy University's accounting department to assist it in calculating the weekly payroll. The first step in producing a spreadsheet is to plan by answering the four questions described above:

1. The spreadsheet should produce each employee's gross pay for the week. Gross pay is the pay earned before any deductions (such as taxes) are made.

2. The spreadsheet needs to store the following data:
   • Employee name
   • Pay rate per hour
   • Hours worked per day for each weekday

3. The gross pay can be produced by multiplying the total number of hours worked for the week by the employee's pay rate.

4. The spreadsheet should appear on the computer screen with each employee's data in a separate row. That way, related data will be grouped by columns.

The fourth question is best answered by drawing a sketch of the spreadsheet showing each column heading and the type of data it will store:

Name	Rate/hr	Mon	Tue	Wed	Thu	Fri	Gross Pay
text	dollars	fixed for 1 decimal place					dollars

Practice 1

In this Practice you will create a new spreadsheet named Payroll that stores the names, hourly wages, and hours worked each day for three Ivy University employees.

1) CREATE A NEW SPREADSHEET

a. Boot the System and start ClarisWorks.
b. In the New Document dialog box, select **Spreadsheet** and then **OK**. A new spreadsheet is displayed.

2) ENTER THE SPREADSHEET DATA

Enter data into the spreadsheet as shown below. Be sure to include the names and column headings:

	A	B	C	D	E	F	G
1	Employee Name	Rate/Hr	Mon	Tue	Wed	Thu	Fri
2	Hert, N.	4.75	6	7.5	3	8	7
3	Esser, C.	5.8	5	8	6	5	7.5
4	McMasters, J.	7.65	6.5	7	0	8	8

3) FORMAT CELLS B2 TO B4 TO DISPLAY DOLLARS

a. Drag the mouse pointer from B2 to B4. Cells B2, B3, and B4 are highlighted.
b. From the Format menu, select Number. A dialog box is displayed.
c. In the **Number** section, select **Currency** and **Commas**. The **Precision** should already be set at 2.
d. Select **OK**. The format has been applied to all three cells at once.

4) FORMAT A BLOCK TO DISPLAY 1 DECIMAL PLACE

a. Drag from cell C2 to cell G4. A block of 15 cells is now highlighted.
b. Press ⇧⌘**N** to display the Format Number dialog box.
c. Click on **Fixed**. Type 1 for the **Precision**.
d. Select **OK** to apply the format to all 15 cells.

5) RIGHT ALIGN THE COLUMN HEADINGS

The column headings in your spreadsheet need to be right aligned to line up with the numbers in the columns.

a. Select cell B1.
b. Move the mouse pointer so that it is on cell G1. Press and hold the Shift key and then click the mouse button. Cells B1, C1, D1, E1, F1, and G1 should be highlighted.
c. From the Format menu, drag down to the Alignment command. Select Right from the submenu. The headings are now right aligned.

6) CHANGE THE WIDTH OF COLUMNS C THROUGH G

   a. Click on the column letter of column C. The entire column is highlighted.

   b. Drag from column letter C to column letter G. All the cells in columns C through G are highlighted.

   c. Place the pointer on the column divider for columns G and H. The pointer shape changes to a double-headed arrow.

   d. Drag the divider bar to the left until it is over the column's letter "G" and release the mouse button. All of the highlighted columns have been resized.

<u>Check</u>: Your spreadsheet should look similar to the following:

C1	×✓	Mon					
	A	**B**	**C**	**D**	**E**	**F**	**G**
1	Employee Name	Rate/Hr	Mon	Tue	Wed	Thu	Fri
2	Hert, N.	$4.75	6.0	7.5	3.0	8.0	7.0
3	Esser, C.	$5.80	5.0	8.0	6.0	5.0	7.5
4	McMasters, J.	$7.65	6.5	7.0	0.0	8.0	8.0

7) SAVE PAYROLL

   a. Click anywhere in the spreadsheet to remove the highlight.

   b. Save the spreadsheet naming it `Payroll`.

9.2 Entering Formulas - Pointing

When creating a formula, cell names can be entered using a process called *pointing*. This is accomplished by first typing the formula up to where a cell name should appear and then using the mouse to select, or point to, the desired cell. Clicking on the cell places its name in the formula. This process is continued until the formula is complete. Ranges can be entered in the same manner by selecting a block of cells.

To demonstrate pointing, consider the formula needed to compute the gross pay of an employee in Ivy's payroll spreadsheet. Gross pay is calculated by multiplying the pay rate by the total number of hours worked for the week. In the Payroll spreadsheet, the following formula would be needed to calculate N. Hert's gross pay:

```
=B2*SUM(C2..G2)
```

This formula can be entered by first selecting cell H2 and typing an equal sign. Next, clicking on cell B2 automatically places it in the formula. An asterisk (*) and SUM(are then typed. Dragging the mouse from cell C2 to cell G2 places the range in the formula. The two dots (. .) are automatically inserted by ClarisWorks. A right parenthesis is typed and the Check box clicked to enter the completed formula.

Pointing helps avoid the error of including wrong cell names in the formula. This is especially useful when the cells to be included in the formula are not currently shown on the screen.

9.3 Using the Paste Function Command

An alternative to typing a function name is selecting one using the Paste Function command from the Edit menu. Executing this command displays the following dialog box:

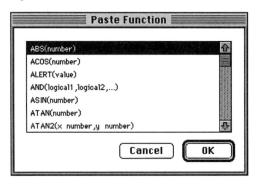

A function name can automatically be inserted into a formula using the Paste Function dialog box

Here, ClarisWorks lists all of the available functions in alphabetical order. Selecting **OK** transfers the highlighted function to the Entry bar. Pasted functions are automatically preceded by an equal sign and contain *placeholders* which are a reminder that cell names, ranges, or values must be included in the function. In the dialog box above, the word number in the ABS function is a placeholder. Highlighting the placeholders of the pasted function and then typing or pointing to a range of cells replaces the placeholders with the cell range.

When the Paste Function dialog box is displayed the keyboard may be used to scroll the function list. Pressing a letter scrolls to the first function in the list that begins with that letter. This method of scrolling can be much faster than using the scroll bar.

Practice 2

In this Practice you will add a Gross Pay column to Payroll and calculate N. Hert's gross pay for the week. Start ClarisWorks and open Payroll if you have not already done so. Display the Shortcuts palette (⇧⌘**H**) if it is not already visible.

1) ENTER THE GROSS PAY HEADING AND RIGHT ALIGN IT

    a. Select cell H1.
    b. Type the label Gross Pay and then click on the Check box to enter it.
    c. The cell cursor should still be located on cell H1. Use the Shortcuts palette to right align the heading.

2) ENTER GROSS PAY FORMULA IN CELL H2

    a. Select cell H2.
    b. Type an equal sign (=).
    c. Click on cell B2. Note how the cell reference B2 is inserted into the formula displayed on the Entry bar.
    d. Type an asterisk (*).

An Introduction to Computing Using ClarisWorks

e. From the Edit menu, select the Paste Function command. A dialog box is displayed.

f. Press the S key once to display the first function name that begins with an S. Note that SUM(number1,number2,...) is visible. Click on the SUM function.

g. Select **OK** to enter the function into the formula. Note the formula on the Entry bar. The placeholder, number1, is highlighted because you are expected to enter a valid cell name or range.

h. Place the pointer on the Entry bar and drag to highlight everything within the parentheses.

i. Place the pointer on cell C2 and drag from C2 to G2. The formula on the Entry bar should appear like the following:

H2	×✓	=B2*SUM(C2..G2)

j. Click on the Check box to enter the formula. The calculated gross pay for N. Hert, 149.625, is shown in cell H2.

3) FORMAT CELL H2 TO DISPLAY DOLLARS

a. The cell cursor should already be on cell H2.

b. On the Shortcuts palette, click on the Currency Format button (). The gross pay is now displayed as dollars with 2 decimal places.

4) SAVE THE MODIFIED PAYROLL

<u>Check</u> - Your spreadsheet should be similar to:

H2	×✓	=B2*SUM(C2..G2)					

	A	**B**	**C**	**D**	**E**	**F**	**G**	**H**
1	Employee Name	Rate/Hr	Mon	Tue	Wed	Thu	Fri	Gross Pay
2	Hert, N.	$4.75	6.0	7.5	3.0	8.0	7.0	$149.62
3	Esser, C.	$5.80	5.0	8.0	6.0	5.0	7.5	
4	McMasters, J.	$7.65	6.5	7.0	0.0	8.0	8.0	

9.4 Using Fill Right and Fill Down

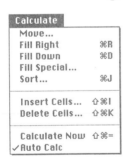

The Fill Right and Fill Down commands from the Calculate menu are used to copy a cell's contents to an adjacent row or column of cells. The cell with the contents to be copied is called the *source cell*. Dragging from the source cell selects the cells into which copies are to be made. The Fill Right command (⌘**R**) is used if the cells are in a row; the Fill Down command (⌘**D**) is used if cells are in a column.

When using the Fill Right or Fill Down commands, a cell's format is copied as well as its contents.

9.5 Relative Copying

Another useful application of the Fill Down and Fill Right commands is for copying formulas. In the Payroll spreadsheet the formula to calculate N. Hert's gross pay, =B2*SUM(C2..G2) is stored in cell H2. To calculate C. Esser's and J. McMasters' gross pay, the formula must be entered into rows 3 and 4 with the cell names adjusted for the new row numbers. For example, because C. Esser's data is stored in row 3, the formula must be changed: =B3*SUM(C3..G3)

When copying a formula, ClarisWorks automatically changes the cell references to apply to the new row or column. This is called *relative copying*. To produce relative copies in a column of cells the formula is entered into the source cell. A highlight is then created from the source cell to the last cell in the column into which relative copies will be made. When Fill Down is executed, formulas are automatically copied with the cell references changed. Fill Right is used to make relative copies in a row.

If we copy the formula that calculates N. Hert's wage

    =B2*SUM(C2..G2)

from cell H2 into cells H3 and H4, the formula in H3 will be

    =B3*SUM(C3..G3)

and in H4:

    =B4*SUM(C4..G4)

Although this technique is useful for making copies of formulas into only two cells, think how much time it would save if the spreadsheet contained a larger number of employees. Another important advantage of this approach is that it avoids the possible errors that would be made if each formula were typed separately.

9.6 Displaying Formulas

It is helpful to view a spreadsheet's formulas at their cell locations. Clicking on the Show Formulas button on the Shortcuts palette does this. A formula that is longer than the cell width can be displayed in its entirety by increasing the cell width.

Printing when formulas are displayed prints the formulas stored in the cells rather than the values. To return to the regular spreadsheet screen select the Show Formulas button again.

•••

Practice 3

In this Practice you will create copies of the wage formula in cell H2 for cells H3 and H4 in the Payroll spreadsheet. Start ClarisWorks and open Payroll if you have not done so already.

1) COPY THE FORMULAS USING FILL DOWN

   a. Highlight cells H2 to H4 as a block.
   b. From the Calculate menu, select Fill Down.

c. Select cell H4. The formula displayed on the Entry bar shows how the cell names have been automatically changed due to relative copying.

2) VIEW THE FORMULAS ON SCREEN

a. Display the Shortcuts palette if it is not already shown.
b. On the Shortcuts palette, click on the Show Formulas button (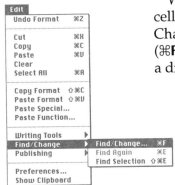). Partial formulas are displayed in cells H2 through H4. You may need to move the palette to display cells H2 through H4.
c. Widen column H until the formulas can be seen entirely. Note how the cell references were changed during the copy.

3) RETURN TO THE REGULAR DISPLAY

a. On the Shortcuts palette, click on the Show Formulas button. The formulas are replaced on screen by the values they calculate.
b. Decrease the width of column H. Be sure the label in cell H1 can be entirely seen.

<u>Check</u> - The gross pay amounts for C. Esser and J. McMasters now appear in cells H3 and H4:

H4	✕ ✓	=B4*SUM(C4..G4)						
	A	**B**	**C**	**D**	**E**	**F**	**G**	**H**
1	Employee Name	Rate/Hr	Mon	Tue	Wed	Thu	Fri	Gross Pay
2	Hert, N.	$4.75	6.0	7.5	3.0	8.0	7.0	$149.62
3	Esser, C.	$5.80	5.0	8.0	6.0	5.0	7.5	$182.70
4	McMasters, J.	$7.65	6.5	7.0	0.0	8.0	8.0	$225.68

4) CHANGE THE PAY RATE OF J. MCMASTERS

a. Move the cell cursor to cell B4.
b. Enter 7.5, replacing the current value. $7.50 is displayed in the cell. Note how ClarisWorks automatically recalculates the gross pay, $221.25.

5) SAVE, PRINT, AND CLOSE PAYROLL

9.7 The Find/Change Command

When working with a large spreadsheet it can be difficult to locate the cell or cells that contain a particular value, label, or formula. The Find/Change command from the Find/Change submenu from the Edit menu (⌘**F**) can be used to assist in such a search. Executing Find/Change displays a dialog box where the cell contents to be searched for is typed:

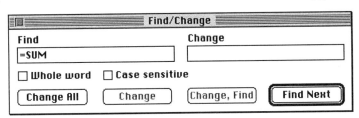

Search text is typed in the Find box

In this case "=SUM" has been entered as the search text. Selecting **Find Next** initiates the search from the current cell and then moves the cell cursor to the first cell storing the search text. To continue searching the spreadsheet, the **Find Next** button is selected again. A dialog box is displayed if the search text is not found.

When the Find/Change command is used it searches only cell contents; the value displayed by a formula will not be included in a search. A more specific search can be specified by using the **Whole word** and **Case sensitive** options in the Find/Change dialog box. Clicking on the Close box closes the dialog box.

9.8 The Go To Cell Command

The Go To Cell command from the Options menu (⌘**G**) can be used to move the cursor directly to a particular cell. Executing the command displays a dialog box where a cell name can be typed:

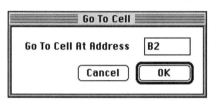

Selecting OK moves the cell cursor to B2

Typing a cell name and selecting **OK** moves the cell cursor to the indicated cell. This can be faster than scrolling when moving long distances in a spreadsheet.

9.9 The MAX and MIN Functions

ClarisWorks includes two functions which determine either the maximum or minimum value stored in a range of cells. These functions are useful to the Ivy University accounting department for determining the highest and lowest employee salaries. The MAX function takes the form:

=MAX(<range of cells>)

For example,

=MAX(C2..C9)

displays the maximum value stored in the range C2 to C9. The MIN function takes the form:

=MIN(<range of cells>)

For example,

=MIN(B2..F3)

displays the minimum value stored in the range B2 to F3.

An Introduction to Computing Using ClarisWorks

9

Practice 4

In this Practice you will search a large payroll spreadsheet and compute the maximum and minimum gross pays. Display the Shortcuts palette is if is not already shown.

1) OPEN IVY PAYROLL

Open IVY PAYROLL which calculates the payroll for 25 Ivy University employees.

2) GO TO CELL G34

a. From the Options menu, execute the Go To Cell command. The Go To Cell dialog box is displayed.

b. Type G34 and select **OK**. The cell cursor is placed directly on cell G34.

3) DETERMINE THE MAXIMUM GROSS PAY

a. Enter the label Max pay:

b. Format the label as bold.

c. Move the cursor to cell H34. From the Edit menu, select Paste Function. Press the M key once to scroll the list of functions. MAX(number1,number2,...) is displayed.

d. Click on MAX(number1,number2,...) in the list of functions. Select **OK**. The Entry bar displays an equal sign in front of the function to create a formula.

e. On the Entry bar, highlight everything between the function's parentheses.

f. Place the mouse pointer on cell H30. Drag from cell H30 upward to H6. If H6 is not currently displayed, the screen scrolls automatically as the mouse pointer is dragged upward.

g. Stop dragging when cells H30 through H6 have been highlighted. The cell range is inserted into the function. Note that the cell range is entered as H6..H30; the order in which the cells were highlighted makes no difference. Click on the Check box to enter the formula. The gross pay of J. Sowers, 348.25, is displayed as the maximum salary in the cell range used in the function.

h. Format the value as currency with 2 decimal places.

4) DETERMINE THE MINIMUM GROSS PAY

a. Select cell G35.

b. Enter the label Min pay:

c. Format the label as bold.

d. Select cell H35. From the Edit menu, select Paste Function.

e. Highlight the MIN(number1,number2,...) function. Select **OK** to enter the function into a formula.

f. On the Entry bar, highlight everything between the function's parentheses.

g. Highlight cells H6 through H30 and then click on the Check box. S. Munger's gross pay of 75 has been calculated as the minimum value in the cell range used in the function.

h. Format the value as currency with 2 decimal places.

5) SEARCH FOR THE TEXT "BALL"

a. From the Edit menu, drag down to the Find/Change command. In the submenu, select Find/Change to display the dialog box.

b. Type Ball and select **Find Next**. The cell cursor is placed in cell A7 which contains the name Ball, R. Note that Ball is highlighted on the Entry bar as well.

c. Remove the Find/Change dialog box by clicking on its Close box.

6) SEARCH FOR ALL OCCURRENCES OF THE LETTER P

   a. Press ⌘**G** to display the Go To Cell dialog box. Type A1 and select **OK** to move the cell cursor to cell A1.

   b. Press ⌘**F** to display the Find/Change dialog box. The previous search text is highlighted in the dialog box.

   c. Type a P to replace the old search text. Select **Find Next**. The cell cursor moves to the label "Ivy University Payroll" which is the first cell after cell A1 to contain a "p."

   d. Select **Find Next** again to repeat the search. The cursor moves to the label "Employee Name," which is the next cell to contain a P.

   e. Continue using **Find Next** until cell D1 is found again.

   f. Type XYZ to replace the search text. Select **Find Next**. A dialog box is displayed with the message: The text "XYZ" could not be found. Select **OK** to remove the box.

   g. Close the Find/Change dialog box.

7) SAVE THE MODIFIED IVY PAYROLL

9.10 Expanding a Spreadsheet

Data can be added to a spreadsheet by simply making entries into unused rows and columns, but this should be done with care. If data is added without thought to the overall plan, the spreadsheet will quickly become a jumble of unrelated data.

Expanding a spreadsheet requires the same careful planning as the initial spreadsheet. The four steps for planning a spreadsheet should again be used so that the modified spreadsheet can easily support further modification and expansion.

The Ivy University accounting department has determined that the IVY PAYROLL spreadsheet would be more useful if it could calculate and deduct taxes and social security from each employee's gross pay. The four steps for planning are used to determine how the spreadsheet should be modified to incorporate these changes:

1. New data generated is the taxes, social security, and net pay (the actual pay an employee receives after deductions have been made).

2. The modified spreadsheet will need to include the tax rate, which is 15%, and the social security rate, which is 6%.

3. The deductions and net pay need to be calculated. These calculations are performed by multiplying the tax and social security rates by the gross pay to generate the deductions. Net pay is computed by subtracting the deductions from gross pay.

4. The spreadsheet format is important—careful planning makes the spreadsheet easy to use and modify. To display this data, we add three columns titled Taxes, Soc. Sec., and Net Pay. To allow the social security rate to be easily changed, it is stored in a single cell that may be referenced in a formula. By doing this, it will only be necessary to change the value in one cell whenever a rate changes, rather than the formulas for each employee.

An Introduction to Computing Using ClarisWorks

9.11 Absolute Copying

Relative copying enables formulas to be copied to other cells, with ClarisWorks changing cell references automatically. In some situations we will want to copy formulas in which certain cell references do not change. For example, if all the employees of Ivy University were to receive a bonus, the bonus amount could be stored in cell A3. Then the following formula could be entered into cell I6 to compute the pay for one employee by adding his or her gross pay and the bonus:

=H6+A3

If the Fill Down command was used to copy this formula into cells I7 and I8, A3 would become A4 and A5. To avoid this problem ClarisWorks allows cell references to be kept constant by placing a dollar sign in front of both the column letter and row number (A3). When copies are now made, the cell reference A3 does not change. This is called *absolute copying*.

The Command (⌘) and Option keys can be used to place dollar signs in front of a cell reference. For example, to enter the above formula in a selected cell with an absolute reference to cell A3, an equal sign is first typed. Next, clicking on cell H6 enters its name into the formula. A plus sign is then typed. To enter the absolute reference A3, the Command and Option keys are pressed and held down while the mouse is used to click on cell A3.

9.12 Copy, Cut, and Paste

Often the same label, value, or formula needs to be stored in a number of different cells. We can type it over and over again, or duplicate it with the Copy command from the Edit menu (⌘C).

Duplicating a block of cells is a four step process:

1. Highlight the cells to be copied.
2. Execute the Copy command from the Edit menu (⌘C). A copy of the cell contents, including any applied formatting, is copied to the Clipboard.
3. Place the cell cursor where the data is to appear.
4. Execute the Paste command from the Edit menu (⌘V).

The Cut command from the Edit menu (⌘H) removes a selected cell's contents and any applied formatting and places it on the Clipboard. Paste can then be used to paste the contents into other cells.

The Cut, Copy, and Paste buttons on the Shortcuts palette can also be used to execute the editing commands.

The Clipboard contents are viewed by using the Show Clipboard command from the Edit menu. Executing this command displays a window containing the cell values that have been Cut or Copied to it. Although cell formatting options are placed on the Clipboard as well, they are not used in the Clipboard window. The Clipboard contents cannot be changed from this window, only viewed.

Practice 5

In this Practice you will add columns to IVY PAYROLL which calculate taxes, social security, and net pay for each of the Ivy University employees. Start ClarisWorks and open IVY PAYROLL if you have not already done so. Display the Shortcuts palette if it is not already shown.

1) ENTER HEADINGS FOR COLUMNS I, J, AND K

a. Select cell I5. Type `Taxes` and press the tab key to move the cursor to cell J5.
b. In cell J5 enter the label `Soc. Sec.`
c. Select cell K5 and enter `Net Pay` as the label.

2) RIGHT ALIGN THE HEADINGS

a. Highlight the block of cells I5 through K5.
b. Use the Shortcuts palette to right align the headings.

3) ADD SOCIAL SECURITY RATE LABEL

a. From the Options menu, use the Go To Cell command to move the cell cursor to cell A3.
b. Enter the label `Soc. Sec. rate:`

4) ENTER SOCIAL SECURITY RATE

a. Select cell B3.
b. Enter `6%` for the Social Security rate. Because the cell has not been formatted to display percent, ClarisWorks automatically converts the percent value to its equivalent decimal value, 0.06.
c. Be sure the cell cursor is still on B3. On the Shortcuts palette, click on the Percent button (🔳). The cell has been formatted to display percentages with 2 decimal places.

5) ENTER FORMULAS FOR TAXES COLUMN

a. Select cell I6.
b. Enter the formula `=H6*15%` to calculate the taxes as 15%. 28.8 is displayed in cell I6.
c. Cell I6 should still be selected. On the Shortcuts palette, click on the Currency Format button.
d. With the cell cursor on cell I6, highlight the block from cell I6 through I30.
e. From the Calculate menu, select Fill Down to copy the formula into cells I7 through I30. A 15% tax is now calculated for each employee.

6) ENTER FORMULAS FOR SOCIAL SECURITY COLUMN

a. Place the cell cursor on cell J6.
b. Type an equal sign (=).
c. Click on cell H6 to enter it into the formula.
d. Type an asterisk (*).
e. If necessary, click on the scroll arrows until cell B3 is visible. Press and hold down the Command and Option keys. Click on cell B3. The absolute reference B3 is entered into the formula.
f. Click on the Check box to enter the formula to calculate the social security deduction as 6% of the gross pay, 11.52.

g. Cell J6 should still be selected. On the Shortcuts palette, click on the Currency Format button.
h. Highlight cells J6 through J30.
i. From the Calculate menu, select Fill Down to copy the formulas into cells J7 through J30. A 6% social security deduction is now calculated for each employee.
j. Move the cell cursor to cell J7. Note how ClarisWorks used relative copying for the cell reference that does not use the dollar signs (H7) and absolute copying for the cell reference using the dollar signs (B3).

7) ENTER FORMULAS TO CALCULATE NET PAY

a. Select cell K6.
b. Enter the formula =H6-I6-J6 to calculate the net pay (gross pay minus the taxes and social security deductions). 151.68 is displayed.
c. Cell K6 should still be selected. On the Shortcuts palette, click on the Currency Format button.
d. Highlight cells K6 through K30.
e. Press ⌘D to execute the Fill Down command. The formula from cell K6 is copied into cells K7 through K30.

8) CHANGE THE SOCIAL SECURITY RATE

a. Move the cell cursor to cell B3.
b. Type 6.5% to replace the current value and click on the check box. If necessary, scroll so that columns J and K are visible. Note how ClarisWorks automatically recalculated all the values in the columns.

9) SAVE IVY PAYROLL

Check - Your IVY PAYROLL should look similar to the following:

	F	G	H	I	J	K
5	Thu	Fri	Gross Pay	Taxes	Soc. Sec.	Net Pay
6	3.0	7.0	$192.00	$28.80	$12.48	$150.72
7	5.5	3.0	$156.00	$23.40	$10.14	$122.46
8	7.0	6.0	$153.00	$22.95	$9.94	$120.11
9	5.0	6.0	$130.50	$19.58	$8.48	$102.44
10	6.0	7.5	$203.55	$30.53	$13.23	$159.79
11	5.0	7.5	$173.25	$25.99	$11.26	$136.00
12	8.0	3.5	$247.10	$37.06	$16.06	$193.97
13	7.0	7.5	$157.98	$23.70	$10.27	$124.01
14	8.0	7.0	$149.62	$22.44	$9.73	$117.46

9.13 Inserting and Deleting Columns and Rows

It is possible to insert or delete whole rows or columns in a spreadsheet. This is especially helpful to Ivy University when a new employee has been hired and a row must be inserted, or an old employee leaves and a row must be deleted. It is also useful when columns must be inserted between existing columns. For example, a new column to deduct pension plan contributions can be inserted between the Soc. Sec. and Net Pay columns in IVY PAYROLL.

Calculate
Move...
Fill Right   ⌘R
Fill Down   ⌘D
Fill Special...
Sort...   ⌘J
Insert Cells... ⇧⌘I
Delete Cells... ⇧⌘K
Calculate Now ⇧⌘=
✓Auto Calc

To insert a new row, first click on the row number where the new row is to appear, then execute the Insert Cells command from the Calculate menu (⇧⌘I). The selected row and all those below it move down to accommodate the newly inserted row. When a column has been selected, executing the Insert Cells command inserts a new column. The selected column and all those to the right are moved over. Newly inserted rows and columns are empty and contain no data, formulas, or formatting.

To delete a row, first select it by clicking on its row number and then execute the Delete Cells command from the Calculate menu (⇧⌘K). All rows below the deleted row move up to fill its position. A column is similarly deleted by first selecting it and then executing the Delete Cells command. The columns to the right of the deleted column then move to the left. Immediately executing the Undo command restores a deleted row or column.

When cells are inserted or deleted, ClarisWorks automatically changes the range of any formulas that are involved. For example, if row 3 is deleted, the formula `=SUM(C1..C9)` changes to `=SUM(C1..C8)`. If instead a row is inserted between rows 1 and 10, the formula becomes `=SUM(C1..C10)`.

· ·

Practice 6

In this Practice, cells will be deleted and inserted into the IVY PAYROLL spreadsheet. Employee H. Crane has quit, so her information will be deleted and a new employee's information will be added. Start ClarisWorks and open IVY PAYROLL if you have not already done so.

1) DELETE THE ROW CONTAINING EMPLOYEE CRANE, H.

    a. Use the Find/Change command (⌘F) to locate the cell storing the name Crane. Close the Find/Change dialog box.

    b. Select the row containing H. Crane's data by clicking on its row number.

    c. From the Calculate menu, select the Delete Cells command. The row is deleted and all rows below move up to fill the space.

2) INSERT ROW AND DATA FOR NEW EMPLOYEE

    a. Select row 22.

    b. From the Calculate menu, select Insert Cells. A new row is inserted at row 22 and the rows below move down.

    c. Enter the following data into the inserted row:

        Nitrate, A.   5.5   6.5   7   8   2   1.5

    d. Format cell B22 as currency with 2 decimal places. Format cells C22 through G22 as fixed with 1 decimal place.

3) TRANSFER FORMULAS TO THE NEW ROW

The new row will require the copying of the four formulas into columns H through K to calculate A. Nitrate's salary and deductions. We can copy all of the formulas at once by highlighting them together as the source.

    a. Highlight the block of cells H21 through K22.

    b. From the Calculate menu, select Fill Down. The new formulas are copied into A. Nitrate's row and the values are automatically calculated.

9

Gross Pay	Taxes	Soc. Sec.	Net Pay
$137.50	$20.62	$8.94	$107.94

4) SAVE THE MODIFIED IVY PAYROLL

9.14 Using the IF Function

It is sometimes desirable to have a simple decision made based upon the data stored in a spreadsheet. In ClarisWorks such a decision is made using the IF function and is based on a comparison entered into the function. If the comparison is true, one value is displayed in the cell; if not, a second value is displayed. The IF function has the form:

=IF(<comparison>, <true value>, <false value>)

For example, assume cell B2 contains the following formula:

=IF(C4<E7,10,20)

A 10 is displayed in cell B2 if the value in C4 is less than the value in E7. If the value in C4 is greater than or equal to the value in E7, 20 is displayed in B2. What will be displayed if C4 contains the value 35 and E7 contains the value 30?

The comparison part of the IF function can contain one of the following *relational operators*:

=	equal to
<	less than
>	greater than
<=	less than or equal to
>=	greater than or equal to
<>	not equal to

The following are examples of valid IFs:

```
=IF(N1<=25,50,100)
=IF(B2<K25,0,B2*15%)
=IF(C9>MIN(C2..C7),C11,C14)
=IF(D22<>F25,0,SUM(E1..E10))
```

The IF function can be used in the IVY PAYROLL spreadsheet by the accounting department to calculate two tax brackets rather than one. For example, if an employee's gross pay exceeds $250, 25% is deducted for taxes. If the gross pay is less than or equal to $250, 10% is deducted. Calculating all of the salaries separately for the two tax brackets would be time consuming. The IF function can be used to automatically determine which tax bracket the employee's gross pay falls into and then calculate the correct taxes. Another advantage of the IF function is that when the taxes are recalculated the net pay will also be recalculated automatically.

To calculate B. Attis' taxes, taking into account the two tax brackets, we could replace the formula in cell I6 with:

```
=IF(H6>250,H6*25%,H6*10%)
```

This formula states that if the gross pay stored in cell H6 is greater than 250, multiply it by 25% and display that value. If the value stored in H6 is less than or equal to 250, multiply it by 10% and display that value.

9.15 Changing the Way a Spreadsheet is Printed

The number of cells printed on each page of a spreadsheet can be changed by either using a different print orientation or by changing a document's margins. The Document command from the Format menu displays the following dialog box:

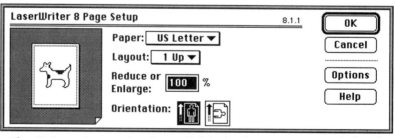

Changing the margins affects the number of cells printed on each page

Reducing the left, right, top, and bottom margins allows more cells in a spreadsheet to fit on each page.

The Page Setup command from the File menu displays a dialog box that contains the **Orientation** option:

The Orientation option is available in the Page Setup dialog box

Clicking on the rightmost **Orientation** option (⊞) prints the spreadsheet across the widest part of the page in *landscape orientation*. This is useful because more columns fit on a page.

An Introduction to Computing Using ClarisWorks

9

Practice 7

In this Practice you will further expand the IVY PAYROLL spreadsheet to allow for two tax brackets. Start ClarisWorks and open IVY PAYROLL if you have not already done so.

1) ENTER NEW TAX FORMULA

   a. Move the cell cursor to cell I6.
   b. Enter the formula `=IF(H6>250,H6*25%,H6*10%)`. Because the value in H6 is less than 250, the taxes are 10% and therefore the value displayed changes to $19.20.

2) COPY THE NEW FORMULA TO CELLS I6 THROUGH I30

   a. Highlight the block of cells from I6 through I30.
   b. From the Calculate menu, select Fill Down to copy the new tax calculation. Notice how the cells in column I have automatically been recalculated and the new values displayed.
   c. Click anywhere in the spreadsheet to remove the highlight.

<u>Check</u> - Your spreadsheet should be similar to:

	F	G	H	I	J	K
	F	**G**	**H**	**I**	**J**	**K**
5	Thu	Fri	Gross Pay	Taxes	Soc. Sec.	Net Pay
6	3.0	7.0	$192.00	$19.20	$12.48	$160.32
7	5.5	3.0	$156.00	$15.60	$10.14	$130.26
8	7.0	6.0	$153.00	$15.30	$9.94	$127.75
9	5.0	6.0	$130.50	$13.05	$8.48	$108.97
10	5.0	7.5	$173.25	$17.33	$11.26	$144.66
11	8.0	3.5	$247.10	$24.71	$16.06	$206.33
12	7.0	7.5	$157.98	$15.80	$10.27	$131.91
13	8.0	7.0	$149.62	$14.96	$9.73	$124.94
14	8.0	8.0	$125.62	$12.56	$8.17	$104.90

3) VIEW THE SPREADSHEET AS IT WILL APPEAR WHEN PRINTED

   a. From the View menu, select Page View. The spreadsheet is displayed in page-sized sections.
   b. If necessary, click on the right scroll arrow once to view part of page 2. Note how the columns storing Taxes, Soc. Sec., and Net Pay appear on page 2.
   c. From the File menu, select Page Setup. A dialog box is displayed.
   d. Click on the landscape **Orientation** option (⊞). Select **OK**.
   e. If necessary, click on the appropriate scroll arrow until the right edge of page 1 is displayed and click on the down scroll arrow until the bottom edge of the page is displayed. All of the spreadsheet data now fits on one page.
   f. Save IVY PAYROLL and then print a copy.
   g. From the View menu, select Page View again to deselect it.

4) SAVE AND CLOSE IVY PAYROLL

Studies have shown that people remember more information when it is presented graphically. For this reason, data is often better displayed in the form of a chart or graph. *Charts* show the relationships between the different pieces of data. ClarisWorks can produce two general styles of charts from spreadsheet data: pie charts and series charts.

Pie charts are used to show the relation between the fractional parts that make up a whole amount:

Pie

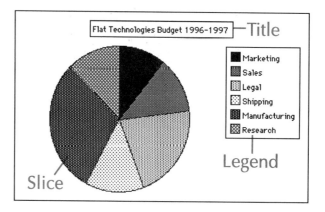

In a pie chart, each *slice* represents one fractional part of the whole. The size of a slice varies with its percentage of the total.

There are four types of series charts: bar, stacked bar, line, and hi-low. Series charts are used to show changes in data, either over time or in different categories.

In a bar chart each piece of data is represented by a bar, with taller bars representing larger numbers:

Bar

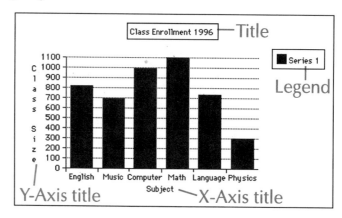

Bar charts are useful for comparing the differences between values. Titles and legends may be used to identify what is charted, as shown above.

Stacked charts show the parts of a total:

Stacked Bar

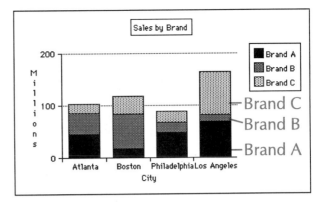

Line charts, or *graphs*, are normally used to show changes in a value over time. For example, this chart shows two cities' average temperature for each month over the period of a year:

Line

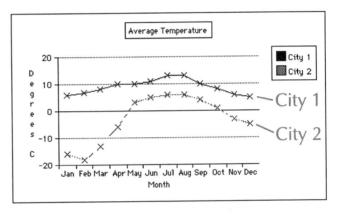

Hi-Low charts show changes in several categories over a period of time. They are used primarily with stock prices to show what the highest and lowest selling prices were for a single day.

Hi-Low

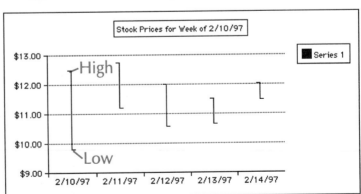

Just as with a spreadsheet, a chart should be carefully planned. You must first decide what information the chart is to contain, and in what order. Next, consider what type of chart to use. Finally, decide what titles and legends will make the chart easier to read and understand.

Pie charts are created by selecting the Make Chart command from the Options menu (⌘M) which displays the Chart Options dialog box. **Bar** is the default chart type. When **Pie** is selected from the **Gallery** section, the following options are available:

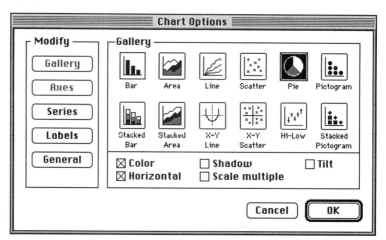

Charts are created using this dialog box

The buttons in the **Modify** section change the options that are displayed in the dialog box.

Clicking on the **Labels** button changes the Chart Options dialog box to display the **Labels** section:

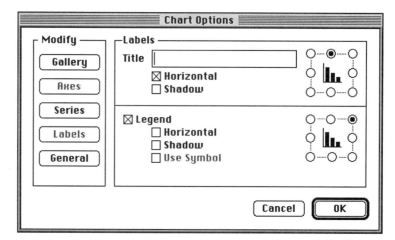

The chart title can be entered when the Labels options are displayed

The name of the chart is typed in the **Title** box. This label will appear centered above the chart as indicated by the selected radio button to the right of the box.

Clicking on the **General** button displays options to define the chart data. For example, to produce a pie chart of the following data

	A	B
1	North	120
2	South	66
3	East	85
4	West	73

first **Pie** is selected from the **Gallery** section, then the chart's title is created with the **Labels** section. Next, the data is defined using the **General** section:

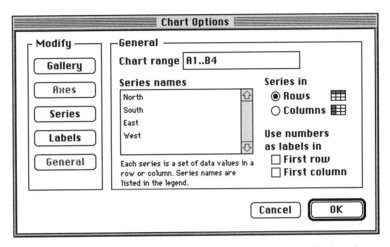

The data range to be charted is entered in this dialog box

When the **Chart range** is typed, labels appear in the **Series names** list. Each *series* represents a set of data to be displayed in the chart. The names appear as *legends* in the chart to identify the data. The **Series in** radio buttons are used to indicate whether the chart data is stored in rows or columns. In this case, **Rows** is selected. Selecting **OK** produces the pie chart:

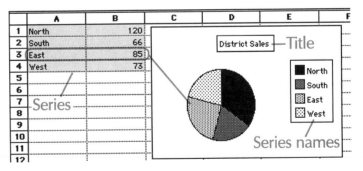

Once created, a chart is linked to the spreadsheet data so that if a number is changed, the chart automatically changes.

Charts are saved when the spreadsheet containing them is saved. Therefore, it is important to save a spreadsheet each time a chart is created or modified.

9.18 Selecting, Moving, and Sizing Charts

Clicking on a chart selects it and displays *handles* at each of its corners. Dragging a chart (but not on a handle) moves it. This is often necessary to display data stored in cells located behind the chart.

Sometimes it is desirable to display a chart and its associated spreadsheet data on screen at the same time. This may require reducing the size of the chart by dragging one of its handles inward. As the chart is reduced, more of the spreadsheet is visible. A chart is enlarged by dragging one of its handles outward:

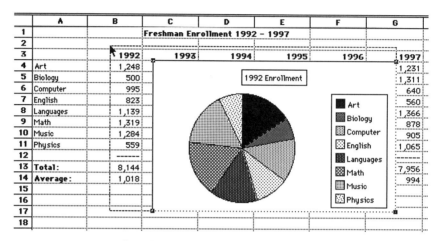

Dragging a handle changes the size of a chart—the new size is indicated by dotted lines

9.19 Modifying and Deleting a Chart

An existing chart can be modified to include new rows or columns, a different title, and so on. To modify a chart, it must first be selected. Next, the Modify Chart command from the Options menu is executed to display the Chart Options dialog box, which is the same dialog box used when creating a chart. Any changes can be made using the options in the dialog box, then **OK** is selected to apply the modifications.

To delete an existing chart it must first be selected. Executing the Clear command from the Edit menu removes it from the spreadsheet. The Delete key may also be pressed to remove a selected chart. If a chart is mistakenly deleted, immediately executing the Undo command will restore it.

Practice 8

In this Practice you will create a chart using the data stored in the IVY ENROLLMENT spreadsheet. Start ClarisWorks if you have not already done so.

1) OPEN IVY ENROLLMENT

IVY ENROLLMENT contains data on the Freshman course enrollment for Ivy University over a period of years.

2) CREATE A PIE CHART

   a. From the Options menu, select the Make Chart command. The Chart Options dialog box is displayed.

   b. In the **Gallery**, click on the **Pie** icon.

   c. In the **Modify** section, click on the **Labels** button. The Chart Options dialog box changes to display a **Labels** section.

   d. In the **Title** box, type: `1993 Enrollment`

   e. In the **Modify** section, click on the **General** button. The Chart Options dialog box changes to display a **General** section.

   f. The current range in the **Chart range** box should be highlighted. Type `A4..B11` to replace the current entry. Note the labels displayed in the **Series names** list.

   g. Select **OK** to create the chart.

3) RESIZE AND MOVE THE CHART

   a. The newly created chart should already be selected as denoted by the handles visible on all four corners. If it is not, select the chart by clicking on it.

   b. If the chart obscures columns A and B, move the pointer to the handle in the upper-left corner of the chart. Drag the handle toward the lower-right corner of the chart to reduce the chart size until columns A and B are visible.

   c. Place the pointer anywhere on the chart, being careful not to place the pointer on a handle. Drag the chart so that it is below the spreadsheet data.

4) CHANGE A VALUE IN THE SPREADSHEET

   a. Place the pointer on cell B4. Click to activate the spreadsheet. The cell cursor should now be on B4.

   b. Enter a new value of 500. Note how the chart is automatically updated to reflect this change:

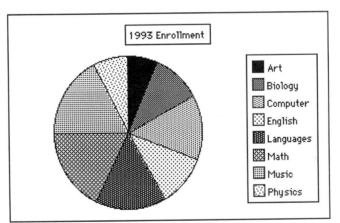

5) SAVE IVY ENROLLMENT

9

A series chart is created by selecting the Make Chart command from the Options menu. The Chart Options dialog box is displayed with **Bar** as the default series chart type:

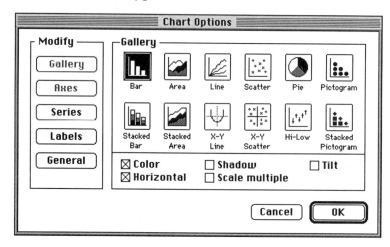

A series chart may be defined using this dialog box

Other series chart types (line, stacked, or hi-low) may be selected from the **Gallery** section.

Clicking on the **Axes** button displays the **Axis** section. Axis labels are entered here to make a series chart more informative:

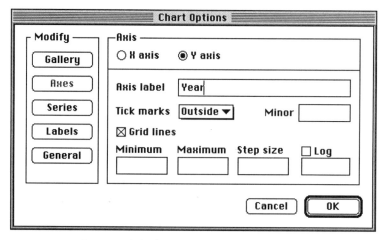

X and Y axis labels are entered in this dialog box

After typing the Y axis label, clicking on the **X axis** radio button clears the **Axis label** box so that the X axis label can be typed.

Series charts normally display data from columns instead of rows, but either can be selected using the **Series in** option in the **General** section. The number of columns included in the **Chart range** determine how many different sets of data will be displayed on a single chart.

As with the pie chart created in Practice 8, labels that appear in the **Series names** list are used as the chart legends.

9.21 Creating Data Labels

Data in a spreadsheet usually includes labels that identify the contents of a row or column. If the row or column storing these labels is included as part of the chart range they are automatically used as the X axis data labels. However, numeric labels such as dates or years are not automatically included and must be defined as labels using the Chart Options dialog box. For example, to create a line chart of the spreadsheet data

	A	B	C	D
1		**1995**	**1996**	**1997**
2	North	120	125	100
3	South	66	70	88
4	East	85	80	90
5	West	73	90	95

the **General** section of the Chart Options dialog box would appear like the following:

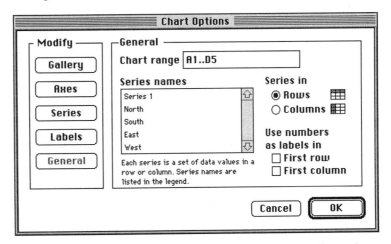

The Chart range has been typed and Rows selected

Because the first row of the chart range stores numbers, ClarisWorks has included it as a series (Series 1) in the **Series names** list. Selecting **First row** from the **Use numbers as labels in** options deletes the series from the list and designates the data as X axis data labels. The data in the first row of the range is now used as the X axis data labels:

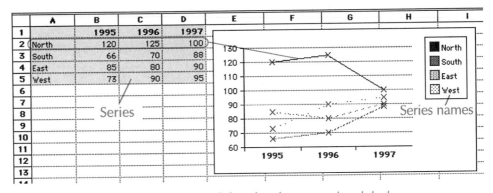

The first row of data has been used as labels

9

In this Practice you will create a line chart that graphs the changing enrollment in three of Ivy's academic departments. Start ClarisWorks and open IVY ENROLLMENT if you have not already done so.

1) CREATE A NEW CHART

    a. From the Options menu, select the Make Chart command.

    b. In the **Gallery**, click on **Line**.

    c. In the **Modify** section, click on the **Axes** button. The **Axis** section is displayed.

    d. Note that the **Y axis** option is selected. In the **Axis label** box, type: Enrollment

    e. Click on the **X axis** radio button. The **Axis label** box is cleared.

    f. In the **Axis label** box, type: Year

    g. In the **Modify** section, click on **General**. The **General** section is displayed.

    h. In the **Chart range** box, type A3..G6. Click on **Rows** for **Series in**. Note the labels in the **Series names** list.

    i. In the **Use numbers as labels in** options, click on **First row**. Series 1 is deleted from the series list and will be used as the X axis data labels.

    j. In the **Modify** section, click on **Labels**. The **Labels** section is displayed.

    k. In the **Title** box, type: Student Enrollment

    l. Select **OK** to create the chart.

2) MODIFY THE ENROLLMENT CHART

    a. Click on the Student Enrollment chart to select it, if it is not already selected.

    b. From the Options menu, select the Modify Chart command.

    c. In the **Modify** section, click on **General**.

    d. Modify the **Chart range** to A3..G7. Note that an additional series is displayed in the **Series names** list.

    e. Select **OK** to view the modified chart. A fourth line representing English enrollment is now displayed on the chart.

3) MOVE AND RESIZE THE LINE CHART

    a. From the View menu, select Page View. The spreadsheet is divided into page-sized portions.

    b. Drag the chart, being careful not to drag on a handle, to the bottom of the screen, and continue dragging until it is below the pie chart. Note how ClarisWorks automatically scrolls the screen if necessary as the chart is being dragged.

    c. Be sure that both charts fit on the same page as the spreadsheet data. If necessary, drag the handles to resize the charts so they fit within the page.

4) SAVE IVY ENROLLMENT AND PRINT THE CHART

    a. Save IVY ENROLLMENT. The Enrollment chart is saved with the spreadsheet.

    b. From the File menu, select the Print command. Select **Print** in the dialog box to print the spreadsheet. The printout will include the charts. Because charts are complex, some printers may require several minutes to print a single chart.

Check - Printed charts vary depending on the printer used, but yours should be similar to:

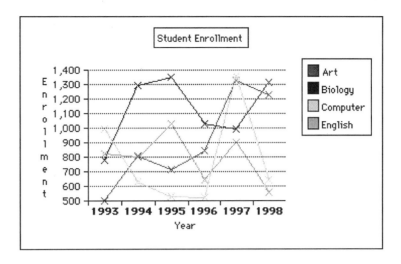

5) CLOSE IVY ENROLLMENT AND QUIT CLARISWORKS

Chapter Summary

It is important to carefully plan a spreadsheet before using ClarisWorks. This is best done by first deciding what new information the spreadsheet will produce, what data it will store, how that data could be produced without a computer, and what the spreadsheet should look like when displayed on the computer. A sketch of a spreadsheet should be created to plan its format. The sketch should indicate column headings and the type of data each column will store.

The cell names that define a range can be entered into a formula by pointing to the cells using the mouse. An alternative to typing a function name is to select one using the Paste Function command from the Edit menu.

To copy a cell's contents into a row or column of cells, the cells are highlighted and the Fill Right command used in a row or the Fill Down command in a column. Both commands are in the Calculate menu. One of their most useful applications is in copying formulas. When this is done ClarisWorks automatically changes the cell names in the copies to reflect the new rows or columns they are in. This process is called relative copying. To view the formulas in a spreadsheet the Show Formulas button on the Shortcuts palette is clicked.

Cell contents can be searched using the Find/Change command from the Edit menu. The Go To Cell command from the Options menu may be used to move the cell cursor directly to a specified cell.

The MAX and MIN functions display the maximum or minimum value stored in a specified range of cells.

When expanding a spreadsheet, the four steps for planning a spreadsheet should be used once again so that the modified spreadsheet can easily support further expansion.

To keep cell references from changing when cells are copied, dollar signs ($) are placed in front of the column letter and row number (i.e., A3). This is called absolute copying. The Command (⌘) and Option keys can be used when pointing to place dollar signs in a cell reference.

The Cut command removes a cell's contents and places it on the Clipboard and the Copy command places a copy of the cell's contents on the Clipboard. The Clipboard contents can then be placed in selected cells using the Paste command. All three commands are located in the Edit menu.

Rows or columns can be inserted into a spreadsheet using the Insert Cells command or deleted using the Delete Cells command from the Calculate menu. The point of insertion or deletion is indicated by clicking on the appropriate row number of column letter. ClarisWorks automatically changes the ranges of any involved formulas when a column or row is deleted or inserted.

A decision can be made based on data in a spreadsheet by using the IF function. If a comparison is true the first value in the function is displayed in the current cell, if false the second value is shown. For example, when the formula `=IF(A5>B4,30,15)` is evaluated, 30 is displayed if the value in A5 is greater than the value in B4, and 15 is displayed if the value in A5 is less than or equal to the value in B4.

The way a spreadsheet is printed can be changed by modifying the margins and printing orientation. The margins of a spreadsheet can be changed using the Document command from the Format menu. The printing orientation can be changed to landscape using the Page Setup command from the File menu.

ClarisWorks can use the data stored in a spreadsheet to produce pie charts and series charts. Series charts include bar, line, stacked bar, or hi-low. Generally, a bar chart is used to compare different items, a line chart to track values over time, a stacked bar chart to show the parts of a total in a bar, and a pie chart to show the relationship in percent between different parts of a whole quantity. A new chart is created using the Make Chart command from the Options menu.

A chart is selected by clicking on it. Once selected, a chart may be resized, moved, or deleted. The Modify Chart command from the Options menu is used to modify an existing chart. Data labels in the spreadsheet can be used as labels in a chart. Legends and chart titles may also be added to a chart.

Vocabulary

Absolute copying - Copying formulas that contain cell references that will not change because dollar signs have been used with the cell name (i.e., A5).

Bar chart - Data graphed as a series of bars.

Chart - A graphical representation of numeric data.

Delete Cells command - Removes rows or columns from a spreadsheet.

Document command - Used to change the margins of a spreadsheet.

Fill Down command - Copies a cell's contents to adjacent highlighted cells in a column.

Fill Right command - Copies a cell's contents to adjacent highlighted cells in a row.

Find/Change command - Moves the cursor to the next cell containing specified text.

Go To Cell command - Used to move the cursor to a specified cell.

Graph - A chart that shows changes in values over time.

Handles - Black rectangles displayed around a selected chart.

Hi-Low Chart - Shows changes in several categories over a period of time.

Insert Cells command - Adds rows or columns to a spreadsheet.

Landscape orientation - A printing orientation that indicates the document is to be printed across the widest part of the paper.

Legend - Identifies data in a chart.

Line chart - Data graphed using a continuous line.

Make Chart command - Used to create a new chart from spreadsheet data.

Modify Chart command - Used to change an existing chart.

Page Setup command - Used to change the printing orientation on a spreadsheet.

Paste command - Transfers a copy of a cell's contents from the Clipboard to a selected cell.

Paste Function command - Used to supply function names so that they need not be entered from the keyboard.

Pie chart - Data graphed as segments of a circular pie.

Placeholders - Part of a newly inserted function used to remind the user of what is to be placed in the function.

Pointing - Clicking on a cell to specify its name in a formula.

Relative copying - Copying formulas in a spreadsheet so that the cell names reflect the new rows and columns they are in. The Fill Right and Fill Down commands are used to make relative copies.

Relational operators - Used to compare two values. Operators include =, <, >, <=, >=, <>.

Series - A set of data displayed in a chart.

Show Formulas button - Button on the Shortcuts palette that displays the formulas in the cells of a spreadsheet, instead of the values.

Slice - Part of a pie chart that represents one fractional part of a whole.

Source cell - Cell or cells where data to be copied is taken from.

Reviews

9

1. What four questions should be answered when planning the layout of a large spreadsheet?

2. Sketch the layout for a spreadsheet that will contain the inventory for an automobile dealership. The spreadsheet should include the names of the different automobile models, the quantity of each model, and the price of each model. Tell what type of data each column stores.

3. a) What is usually the best method to use when entering field references in a formula in a large spreadsheet?
   b) What is the primary advantage of using this method?

4. Explain how you can have ClarisWorks enter a function name so that it does not have to be typed.

5. What is meant by the term relative copying? Give an example.

6. What steps must be taken to copy the formula =AVERAGE(C5..C9) stored in cell C22, into the range of cells D22 to G22 so that the formula correctly calculates the average for each column?

7. How can the formulas stored in the cells of a ClarisWorks spreadsheet be displayed instead of the values they calculate?

8. a) What steps must be taken to find each cell in a spreadsheet that contains the label Harry?
   b) What is displayed when a search is performed for a label that does not appear in a spreadsheet?

9. Which of the following labels would be found in a repeated search for the characters PO if the **Whole word** and **Case sensitive** options are not selected?

Position	Port
Operation	PO Box
Opinion	policy

10. What is the fastest way to move the cell cursor from cell A1 to cell Z14?

11. Write formulas that calculate:
    a) the maximum value stored in the range of cells D4 to Y5.
    b) the minimum value stored in the range of cells C1 to C9.

12. Why is it usually not a good practice to keep adding data to a spreadsheet without careful planning?

13. a) When copying formulas how is it possible to keep one cell reference constant while allowing others to change?
    b) Give two examples of when you would need to do this.

14. How can the Clipboard contents be viewed?

15. List the steps required to copy the contents of cell B4 into cell A9, B11, and C15.

16. List the steps required to delete the Net Pay column from IVY PAYROLL.

17. What steps must be taken to insert a column titled Tue into a spreadsheet that follows a column titled Mon and comes before a column titled Wed?

18. a) The formula =SUM(C3..C22) is used to sum the values in cells C3 to C22. If a row is inserted directly above row 20, what must be done to include the new cell in the sum?
    b) If a row is inserted directly above row 23, what must be done to include the new cell in the sum?

19. What will be displayed in the cell containing the following formulas if cell D4 stores a value of 30 and E7 a value of –12?
   a) =IF(D4<=E7,10,20)
   b) =IF(E7*D4<-5,E7,D4)
   c) =IF(D4-42=E7,D4*2,E7*3)

20. Write formulas that perform each of the following:
   a) Store 50 in the current cell if the value stored in D20 equals the value in C80, or 25 if they are not equal.
   b) Store the value contained in B40 in the current cell if the sum of the range of cells C20 to C30 exceeds 1000, otherwise store a 0.
   c) Store the value of R20*10 in the current cell if R20 is less than 30; otherwise store just R20's value.

21. What must be done to print a spreadsheet across the widest part of the paper?

Sections 9.16 — 9.21

22. Would a bar chart, line chart, or pie chart best be suited to display:
   a) a student's GPA over four years at college
   b) the percentages spent on different parts of Ivy University's budget
   c) the number of faculty members in each department at Ivy
   d) the number of books sold each day for a month at the college bookstore
   e) the percentage of Ivy's students from each state in the United States

23. What happens to a chart stored with a spreadsheet if the data in the spreadsheet is changed?

24. Explain the steps required to create a bar chart from the IVY PAYROLL spreadsheet displaying each employee's net pay.

25. Explain how to display a previously created chart and move it to the right of spreadsheet data.

26. How is a series chart created?

27. Explain the steps required to modify a chart to include an additional series.

28. Explain how to include a chart title and axes labels on an existing chart.

Exercises

1. The Ivy University Alumni Association has decided to use a spreadsheet to determine how much it must charge each member attending its annual Homecoming Dinner Dance so that it will not lose money. Below are the costs of each item based upon 50 members attending:

	A	B
1	Expenses	50 Members
2	Band	$1,500.00
3	Decorations	$185.00
4	Print Tickets	$73.15
5	Electricity	$50.00
6	Advertising	$182.00
7	Clean up	$78.00
8	Appetizers	$56.00
9	Entrees	$111.00
10	Dessert	$34.50
11	Beverages	$150.00
12		
13	Cost/Member	$48.39

a) Create a new spreadsheet with the information shown above that calculates the cost per member when 50 members attend. All of the costs are summed and the total divided by the number of members attending to produce the cost per member. Format the column widths and cells appropriately. Save the spreadsheet naming it Dance.

b) In columns C, D, and E calculate the cost per ticket when 100, 150, or 200 members attend. Consider the following when adding these columns:

- The expenses for Band through Clean up remain the same no matter how many members attend. Be careful to set up these values in the new columns so that if the value in column B is changed it will also change in the other columns. For example, if Band is changed to $785.50 in column B, it should also appear as $785.50 in the three new columns.
- The values for Appetizers through Beverages change depending on how many members attend. Therefore, the cost for Dessert for 50 members must be multiplied by 2 to calculate the cost for 100 members, by 3 to calculate the cost for 150 members, and so on. The values for Appetizers, Entrees, and Beverages are calculated similarly.

c) Save the modified Dance and print a copy. Your spreadsheet should be similar to:

	A	B	C	D	E
1	Expenses	50 Members	100 Members	150 Members	200 Members
2	Band	$1,500.00	$1,500.00	$1,500.00	$1,500.00
3	Decorations	$185.00	$185.00	$185.00	$185.00
4	Print Tickets	$73.15	$73.15	$73.15	$73.15
5	Electricity	$50.00	$50.00	$50.00	$50.00
6	Advertising	$182.00	$182.00	$182.00	$182.00
7	Clean up	$78.00	$78.00	$78.00	$78.00
8	Appetizers	$56.00	$112.00	$168.00	$224.00
9	Entrees	$111.00	$222.00	$333.00	$444.00
10	Dessert	$34.50	$69.00	$103.50	$138.00
11	Beverages	$150.00	$300.00	$450.00	$600.00
12					
13	Cost/Member	$48.39	$27.71	$20.82	$17.37

d) Produce the following charts using the data in Dance:

- A pie chart that displays the percent amounts of each cost when 50 members attend. Title the chart `Dance Expenses for 50 Members`, as shown below:

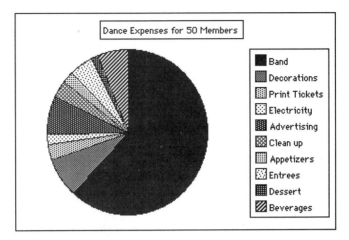

- A bar chart that displays the cost per member when 50, 100, 150, and 200 members attend. Title the chart `Homecoming Dance Ticket Cost`, as shown below:

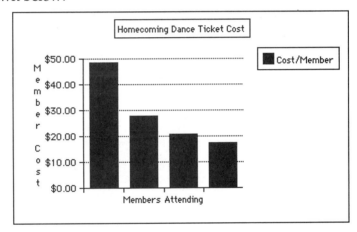

- A bar chart that displays the costs when 50, 100, 150, and 200 members attend. Title the chart `Expenses`, as shown below:

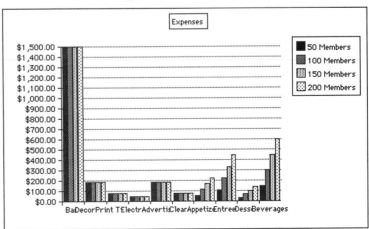

e) Display the spreadsheet in Page View. Move and resize the charts as necessary so that the spreadsheet data and all the charts are displayed on two pages. Save the modified Dance and print a copy.

2. Mr. Hernandez, owner of the Aztec Café, would like to expand the spreadsheet created in Chapter Eight, Exercise 5 to compute the gross and net pay of each employee.

   a) Open AC Employees. The pay rate per hour needs to be in the spreadsheet. In column J, enter an appropriate label and the following pay rates. Format the label and values appropriately.

Employee	Pay Rate
H. Berry	$2.80
G. Diez	$3.60
K. Martin	$2.80
D. Romani	$10.40

   b) Gross pay is computed by multiplying the total number of hours worked by pay rate. In column K, enter an appropriate label and the formulas necessary to compute the gross pay for each employee. Format the labels and values appropriately.

   c) Net pay is computed by making the necessary deductions from the gross pay. Taxes are 12% and social security is 6%. In column L, enter the label Taxes and formulas to compute 12% of each employee's gross pay. In column M, enter the label Soc. Sec. and formulas for the deductions. In column N, enter the label Net Pay and formulas to deduct the taxes and social security from the gross pay of each employee.

   d) Save the modified AC Employees.

   e) Mr. Hernandez has hired two more employees. Insert the data shown below into the spreadsheet so that the employee names remain in alphabetical order by last name. Add the necessary formulas to the spreadsheet.

   | D. Roberts | 8 | 8 | 6 | 0 | 10 | 12 | 0 | $4.20 |
   | P. Jorge | 0 | 0 | 8 | 8 | 8 | 8 | 8 | $3.60 |

   f) Bold and right align titles as appropriate. Resize columns I, J, K, L, M, and N so that they are just wide enough to completely display their titles. The expanded spreadsheet should look similar to the one shown below:

	G	H	I	J	K	L	M	N
1								
2								
3	Fri	Sat	Total Hours	Pay Rate	Gross Pay	Taxes	Soc. Sec.	Net Pay
4	8	4	40	$2.80	$112.00	$13.44	$6.72	$91.84
5	10	0	42	$3.60	$151.20	$18.14	$9.07	$123.98
6	8	8	40	$3.60	$144.00	$17.28	$8.64	$118.08
7	0	4	20	$2.80	$56.00	$6.72	$3.36	$45.92
8	12	0	44	$4.20	$184.80	$22.18	$11.09	$151.54
9	10	0	47	$10.40	$488.80	$58.66	$29.33	$400.82

   g) Decrease the left and right margins to 0.44" each. Change the print orientation so that the spreadsheet will print across the widest part of the paper. Save the modified AC Employees and print a copy.

9

3. The STOCK2 spreadsheet stores the names, purchase price, and number of shares of stocks owned by Grace van Ivy, a relative of Ivy University's founder. You are to assist her by expanding the spreadsheet to produce calculations. Open STOCK2.

   a) Ms. van Ivy wants to know how much money she has made or lost on each stock. In column D add the label `Current Price` and enter the current price per share:

Campbell's Soup	$41.38	Ford Motor Co.	$50.63
Chrysler	$40.88	General Motors	$31.88
Coca Cola	$40.63	Heinz	$41.50
Disney	$47.00	Hershey	$41.13
Eastman Kodak	$51.88	McDonald's	$14.00
Federal Express	$58.88	Pepsi Co.	$40.63

   Format the label in column D as right aligned and bold. Increase the column width until all data is displayed. Format the values as currency.

   b) Add the label `Original Value` to column E, then bold and right align it and widen the column to display it. The original value of each stock is calculated by multiplying the shares bought by the purchase price. Enter formulas to compute the original value of each stock. Format the values as currency with commas.

   c) At the bottom of column E calculate the total paid for all of the stock. Include a label for the total and be sure the label and values are formatted appropriately.

   d) Add the label `Current Value` to column F. Current value is found by multiplying the number of shares by the current price. Enter formulas to compute the current value of each stock. Sum column F to find the current total value of the stocks. Format the label and values appropriately.

   e) Ms. van Ivy wants to know what stocks have gained in value and which ones have lost in value. In column G enter the label `Gain or Loss` and calculate the gain or loss of each stock by subtracting the original value from the current value. Format the label appropriately. Format the cells for currency with commas, and have negative numbers appear in parentheses.

   f) Produce a bar chart to show Ms. van Ivy how her stocks are performing. Chart the Purchase Price and the Current Price. Title the chart `Stock Comparisons`:

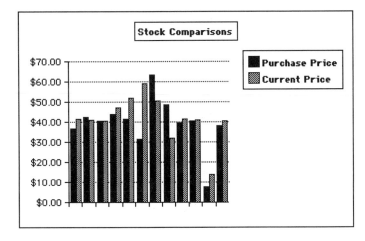

   g) Display the spreadsheet in Page View. Move and resize the chart as necessary so that the spreadsheet data and chart are displayed on one page. Save the modified STOCK2 and print a copy.

4. Fantasy Wheels Used Cars wants to use a spreadsheet to keep track of the value of its inventory. The spreadsheet should record the year and model of each car for sale, and the price Fantasy paid for it. In addition, Fantasy typically sells their cars at a 15% markup, and would like to include this information in the spreadsheet.

a) Carefully plan the Fantasy spreadsheet. Take into consideration all of the ways the spreadsheet might be used. In your plan, include a column for the selling price. The year should also be in its own column.

b) Using the plan from part (a), enter the following data into a new spreadsheet file:

1972 Corvette, price paid: $8,500	1989 Ferarri, price paid: $22,340
1990 Porsche, price paid: $31,000	1955 Studebaker, price paid: $950
1957 Bel Aire, price paid: $1,250	1980 Aston-Martin, price paid: $56,700
1978 Triumph, price paid: $4,560	1958 Thunderbird, price paid: $14,000
1983 Rolls Royce, price paid: $34,460	1967 Mustang, price paid: $11,230
1958 Cadillac, price paid: $8,895	1948 Bentley, price paid: $49,500
1993 Jaguar, price paid: $24,650	1968 GTO, price paid: $12,000
1985 DeLorean, price paid: $28,999	1978 Bricklin, price paid: $36,200

Be imaginative and add three of your own cars to the inventory. Format all labels and values appropriately. Change the width of any columns if appropriate.

c) Save the spreadsheet naming it Cars.

d) Add labels and formulas to calculate the following in your spreadsheet:

- Total of prices paid for inventory
- Average price paid per car
- The minimum price paid for a car
- The maximum price paid for a car
- Profit for each car when it sells at the 15% markup price
- Total profit if all of the cars were to sell at the 15% markup price

Format all labels, data, and column widths appropriately.

e) The 1972 Corvette has been sold. Delete its row from the spreadsheet. Be sure to modify any formulas that might need to be changed.

f) Fantasy has acquired two new cars. Add the following data to the spreadsheet, being sure to modify any formulas that might need to be changed:

1991 Honda, price paid: $6,500   1989 Jeep, price paid: $5,350

g) Fantasy is having a sale on all cars built before 1970. Create a properly formatted column titled Sale which displays only a 7.5% markup on the price paid if the car is on sale, and a 15% markup if it is not.

h) Create a properly formatted column titled Sale Profit which displays the profit that Fantasy would earn if all of the pre-1970 cars were sold at the 7.5% markup price described in part (e). Total this column and format the entire column appropriately.

i) Save the modified Cars and print a copy.

9

5. Your best friend, Mike Entrepreneur, is opening a lawn mowing service and wants you to set up a spreadsheet for his business.

   a) Plan the spreadsheet so that Mike can enter his customers' names, and the lengths and widths of their lawns in meters. In your plan, include a column for calculating lawn area and the price of cutting the lawn if Mike charges $0.08 per square meter. Also include calculations and labels for the total income Mike receives from mowing all his customer's lawns and the average income per lawn. Be sure to include proper labels for all data.

   b) Using the design from part (a), create the spreadsheet on the computer. Include data for a minimum of 15 customers. Format all data and labels appropriately. Change the width of any columns if appropriate.

   c) Save the spreadsheet naming it Lawns.

   d) Mike wants to include his expenses in the spreadsheet so that he can determine his profits. He has determined that his fuel and maintenance costs are $.07 per 10 square meters of lawn area. Title the next column Expense and use formulas to compute the expense for each lawn. Include formatted calculations and labels for the total and average expenses as well.

   e) Profit is computed by deducting the expense from the price. Title the next column Profit and use formulas to compute the profit made on each lawn and the total and average profit.

   f) Create a bar chart titled Mike's Lawn Service that displays the price, expense, and profit for each of the first five customers in the spreadsheet. Your chart should be similar to the following:

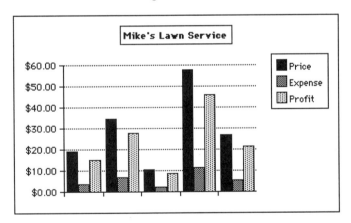

   g) Display the spreadsheet in Page View. Move and resize the chart as necessary so that the spreadsheet data and the chart are displayed on one page. Save the modified Lawns and print a copy.

6. You have decided to record the average yearly temperature for your city for a 50 year period. You can find this information in an almanac, at the town library, or use the example data given below:

Year	Temp	Year	Temp	Year	Temp	Year	Temp	Year	Temp
1947	18	1957	20	1967	22	1977	18	1987	22
1948	18	1958	19	1968	23	1978	14	1988	18
1949	14	1959	22	1969	21	1979	19	1989	18
1950	19	1960	18	1970	22	1980	20	1990	22
1951	23	1961	18	1971	23	1981	22	1991	21
1952	22	1962	14	1972	22	1982	23	1992	22
1953	23	1963	19	1973	23	1983	19	1993	19
1954	20	1964	20	1974	19	1984	22	1994	22
1955	22	1965	23	1975	22	1985	23	1995	19
1956	23	1966	23	1976	18	1986	19	1996	22

a) Create the spreadsheet, including proper labels and the year and average temperature for a 50 year period. To save typing use a formula to calculate and display the year. Format all data and labels appropriately. Change the width of any columns if appropriate.

b) Save the spreadsheet naming it Temp.

c) Add labels and formulas to calculate the following in your spreadsheet:

- The average temperature over the past 50 years.
- The average of the first 25 years only.
- The average of the last 25 years.
- The minimum and maximum temperatures for the first 25 years.
- The minimum and maximum temperatures for the last 25 years.

Format all labels, data, and column widths appropriately.

d) Create a chart titled `Average Temperature` which is a line graph of the temperature for the years 1960 to 1965. Include X and Y axis labels as shown:

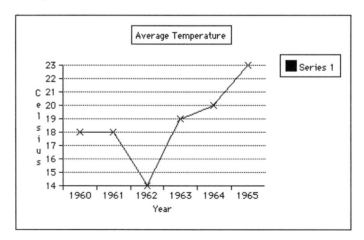

(In the Chart Options dialog box, you will have to indicate that the first column contains labels.)

e) Modify Average Temperature to chart all of the yearly data. Display the spreadsheet in Page View. Move and resize the chart as necessary so that the spreadsheet data and the chart are displayed on two pages. Save the modified Temp and print a copy.

9

7. Dorothy Sophocles would like to modify the Expenses spreadsheet created in Chapter Eight, Exercise 3 to determine her monthly savings.

  a) Open Expenses. Below the monthly totals, add a row with the label `Income` and monthly net income of $1,420.00 for June, July, and August. Bold the label.

  b) Savings is computed by subtracting total expenses from income. Below the income row, add a row that computes the savings for each month. Include a bold label.

  c) Create a pie chart titled `June Expenses` that displays June's expenses as percentages of the overall expenses. The chart should be similar to:

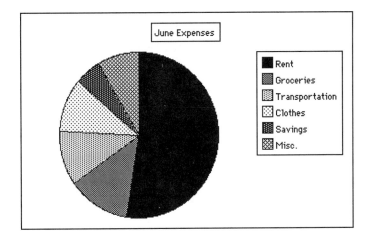

  d) Display the spreadsheet in Page View. Move and resize the chart as necessary so that the spreadsheet data and chart are displayed on one page. Save the modified Expenses and print a copy.

8. The following figures represent the data for the last 10 years for Flat Technologies, a one-product manufacturer:

Year	Expenses	Units Sold	Price/Unit
1	$50,000.00	6,000	$14.50
2	$60,000.00	7,500	$15.50
3	$65,000.00	8,000	$16.00
4	$75,000.00	10,000	$17.00
5	$77,500.00	15,000	$17.75
6	$70,000.00	14,000	$19.00
7	$65,000.00	11,500	$19.00
8	$63,500.00	10,250	$18.50
9	$60,000.00	10,750	$18.25
10	$62,500.00	11,000	$18.50

  a) In a new spreadsheet, enter the above data. Include proper labels, and format all data and labels appropriately. Change the width of any columns if appropriate.

  b) Save the spreadsheet naming it Flat.

  c) Add a column titled `Profit` which calculates the profit (income minus expenses) for each year. Income is computed by multiplying Units Sold by Price/Unit. Format the label and all data appropriately.

d) Add a row to the bottom of the spreadsheet which calculates the average of the yearly expenses, unit sales, price, and profit columns. Include a proper label and format the label and all data appropriately. Change the width of any columns if appropriate.

e) Produce a line chart titled `Flat Technologies Years 1 to 10` which graphs expenses for years 1 to 10. Include X and Y axis labels as shown:

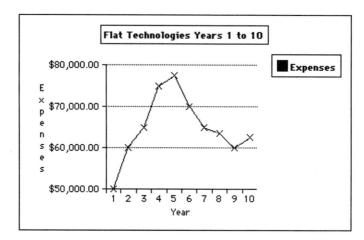

(In the Chart Options dialog box, you will have to indicate that the first column contains labels.)

f) Display the spreadsheet in Page View. Move and resize the chart as necessary so that the spreadsheet data and chart are displayed on one page. Save the modified Flat and print a copy.

9. You have been asked to get price quotes from several printers to have a small newsletter printed for your club:

Printer A:	$0.25 per copy up to 1000 copies
	$0.23 per copy for every copy over 1000
Printer B:	$0.27 per copy for up to 900 copies
	$0.15 per copy for every copy over 900
Printer C:	$0.28 per copy for up to 500 copies
	$0.20 per copy for every copy over 500

a) Create a new spreadsheet that shows the cost for printing 500, 1000, and 1500 copies of the newsletter for each of the three printers. Use the IF function in a formula to calculate the prices.

b) Save the spreadsheet naming it Printing Costs.

c) Add a column to the spreadsheet which shows the minimum cost for printing each of the three numbers of copies.

d) The club president would also like quotes for 750 and 1250 copies. Add two rows to the spreadsheet which calculate and display the costs for these numbers of copies. Be sure to copy the appropriate formulas. Save the modified Printing Costs and print a copy.

e) Produce a bar chart titled `Price Quotes` that displays the cost each printer charges for the different numbers of copies. Include X and Y axis labels as shown:

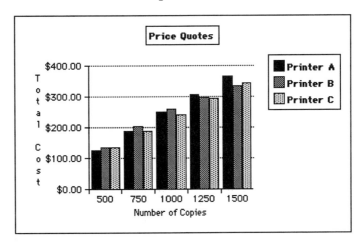

(In the Chart Options dialog box, you will have to indicate that the first column and the first row contain labels.)

f) Printer C has heard about the other printer's prices and has decided to change his quote to the following:

$0.27 per copy for up to 500 copies
$0.21 per copy for every copy over 500

Change the formulas for Printer C to reflect this new price. Display the spreadsheet in Page View. Move and resize the chart as necessary so that the spreadsheet data and chart are displayed on one page. Save the modified Printing Costs and print a copy.

An Introduction to Computing Using ClarisWorks

Chapter 10

Advanced Spreadsheet Techniques

Sort

CHOOSE

VLOOKUP

Lock Title Position

PMT

Set Print Range

Objectives

After completing this chapter you will be able to:

1. Answer What If? questions using a spreadsheet.

2. Sort the data in a spreadsheet.

3. Use text in functions.

4. Use the CHOOSE and VLOOKUP functions.

5. Create an amortization table using the PMT function.

6. Print a specified range of cells.

10

In Chapter Nine a large spreadsheet was created. The four steps of planning were used to make the spreadsheet easy to modify and expand. In this chapter you will use these skills to ask and answer "What If?" questions by making predictions based on spreadsheet data.

10.1 Asking "What If?"

One of the most powerful features of a spreadsheet is its ability to answer *What If?* questions. A What If? question is simply a concern or question the user may have. For example, a cookie manufacturer may wonder: What if the price of sugar increases? How will this affect the cost of my cookies? These questions can be easily answered by substituting numbers in a spreadsheet model.

A spreadsheet containing data relating to a particular situation is called a *model*. Financial predictions can be made based on such a spreadsheet model. For example, consider the cookie manufacturer. Factors involved in producing cookies include the cost of the ingredients, packaging, and labor. A spreadsheet model would need to include these factors in order to make financial predictions. If the cost of sugar were to increase, the new price could be entered into the spreadsheet to see how the overall cost of production would be affected. A decision to raise or not raise the price of cookies could then be made based on this model. Because spreadsheets perform calculations rapidly, a number of different situations can easily be tested. Many businesses use this spreadsheet modeling technique to help make decisions.

Another example of a What if? question concerns the Ivy University payroll. The employees of Ivy University have demanded a wage increase. Because the budget at Ivy is very tight, the administration is concerned about how much the raises will cost. To determine the effects of a wage increase on Ivy's budget, the IVY PAYROLL spreadsheet will be modified to calculate various possibilities. The employees want a 15% increase of their gross pay. Ivy plans to offer a 5% increase, but may have to compromise at 10%. To see how much each of these percentages will cost, three new columns will be added to the spreadsheet.

Practice 1

In this Practice you will answer the "What If?" question described in Section 10.1 by adding three columns to the IVY PAYROLL spreadsheet that calculate raises of 5%, 10%, and 15%.

1) START CLARISWORKS AND OPEN IVY PAYROLL

Display the Shortcuts palette if it is not already shown.

2) ENTER HEADINGS FOR THE RAISES

a. In cell L5, enter the heading: `5% Raise`
b. In cell M5, enter the heading: `10% Raise`
c. In cell N5, enter the heading: `15% Raise`
d. Highlight cells L5 through N5. Right align the block of cells.

3) ENTER FORMULAS FOR THE RAISES

a. In cell L6, enter the formula: `=H6*105%`
   This formula multiplies the gross pay in H6 by 105% to calculate a new gross pay which is 5% higher than the original.
b. In cell M6, enter the formula `=H6*110%` to calculate a 10% raise.
c. In cell N6, enter the formula `=H6*115%` to calculate a 15% raise.
d. Highlight cells L6 through N6. Format the block as currency.

4) COPY THE RAISE FORMULAS AS A BLOCK

a. Highlight cells L6 through N30 as a block.
b. From the Calculate menu, select Fill Down.
c. Select cell L30. Note how relative copying was used to change cell names.

5) SUM THE NEW GROSS PAYS

a. Select cell K32. Enter the label: `New pay:`
b. Select cell L32. Enter the formula: `=SUM(L6..L30)`
c. Use the Shortcuts palette to format cell L32 to display dollars and commas.
d. Copy the formula in cell L32 into cells M32 and N32. The model now includes the sums of each of the pay increase columns.

6) CALCULATE THE INCREASED COST OF RAISES

a. In cell K33, enter the label: `Raise cost:`
b. In cell L33, enter the formula: `=L32-$H$32`
   Cell H32 contains the current total pay. We want to make copies of this formula, but we do not want the cell reference H32 to change when copied. This requires the dollar signs in the cell name.
c. Use the Shortcuts palette to format cell L33 for dollars.
d. Copy the formula in cell L33 into cells M33 and N33. Because of the dollar signs, the cell reference H32 does not change when copied.

Check - The last rows of the new columns should be similar to:

	K	L	M	N
32	New pay:	$5,118.70	$5,362.45	$5,606.20
33	Raise cost:	$243.75	$487.50	$731.24

7) SAVE THE MODIFIED IVY PAYROLL

10.2 Using Sort to Organize a Spreadsheet

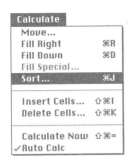

The cell contents of a spreadsheet can be organized in alphabetical or numerical order by first highlighting a block of cells and then using the Sort command from the Calculate menu (⌘J). For example, consider the following highlighted block:

	A	B
1	Produce	Current Stock
2	garlic	49
3	head lettuce	20
4	potatoes	16
5	apples	50
6	bananas	29

The block of cells to be sorted must first be highlighted

Executing the Sort command from the Calculate menu displays the Sort dialog box:

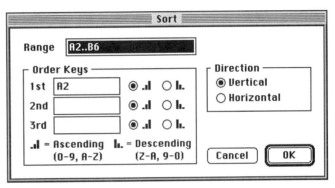

Selecting OK sorts rows 2 through 6

The cell name in the **1st** box identifies the *key sort column* that will be used to sort the highlighted block. In this case, the highlighted cells in column A will be used because we want the names of the produce displayed in alphabetical order. Radio buttons to the right of the **1st** box are used to select ascending (low to high) or descending (high to low) as the sort order. Ascending (.∎∎) is the desired option in this case because descending (∎∎.) would display the produce items in reverse alphabetical order. Because we want the highlighted data sorted by row, the **Direction** option needs to be **Vertical. Horizontal** is used to sort columns.

When **OK** is selected, the highlighted block is sorted based on the values in the key sort column. It is important to realize that an entire row is not moved, only the contents of the highlighted block. Therefore all related data must be included within the highlighted block:

	A	B
1	Produce	Current Stock
2	apples	50
3	bananas	29
4	garlic	49
5	head lettuce	20
6	potatoes	16

The highlighted block has been sorted by row

Sorting the same block of cells with B1 as the **Order Key** produces the following:

	A	B
1	Produce	Current Stock
2	potatoes	16
3	head lettuce	20
4	bananas	29
5	garlic	49
6	apples	50

Column B was used to sort the data in ascending order

Practice 2

In this Practice, IVY PAYROLL will be updated and sorted. Start ClarisWorks and open IVY PAYROLL if you have not already done so.

1) INSERT DATA FOR TWO NEW EMPLOYEES

a.   Select row 30 by clicking on its row number.
b.   From the Calculate menu, select Insert Cells. A new row is inserted. Repeat this procedure to insert a second new row.
c.   In the appropriate cells of rows 30 and 31, enter the following data for the two new employees:

```
Hadriano, L.    7.5     8    7.5     8    8.5     9
Caxton, C.      4.25   4.5     6    6.5     7     8
```

d.   Format cells B30 and B31 as currency displaying two decimal places. Format cells C30 through G31 as **Fixed** with 1 as the **Precision**.

2) COPY FORMULAS FOR NEW EMPLOYEES

a.   Highlight cells H29 through N31.
b.   From the Calculate menu, select Fill Down.

3) SORT THE DATA

Adding rows can result in a randomly ordered list of employees. Specific employees would be hard to find, so it is best if the employee rows were in order alphabetically by last name.

a.   Place the pointer on the row number for row 6 and drag to the row number for row 32 to highlight all the rows containing employee data.
b.   From the Calculate menu, select the Sort command. A6 is displayed in the **1st** box, the order is **Ascending**, and **Vertical** is the **Direction**. Select **OK** to accept these default options. After a slight pause, the highlighted rows are sorted alphabetically.
c.   Scroll through the spreadsheet so that the new employee rows are visible. Employee names are now in alphabetical order.
d.   Click anywhere in the spreadsheet to remove the highlight.

<u>Check</u> - Your spreadsheet should look similar to that shown on the next page:

	A	B	C	D	E	F	G	H
5	Employee Name	Rate/Hr	Mon	Tue	Wed	Thu	Fri	Gross Pay
6	Attis, B.	$8.00	6.0	4.0	4.0	3.0	7.0	$192.00
7	Ball, R.	$4.00	9.5	12.0	9.0	5.5	3.0	$156.00
8	Bickle, R.	$6.00	5.0	7.0	0.5	7.0	6.0	$153.00
9	Cambell, M.	$4.50	5.0	6.0	7.0	5.0	6.0	$130.50
10	Caxton, C.	$4.25	4.5	6.0	6.5	7.0	8.0	$136.00
11	Esser, C.	$5.50	5.0	8.0	6.0	5.0	7.5	$173.25
12	Gilman, J.	$7.00	8.0	7.8	8.0	8.0	3.5	$247.10

4) SAVE IVY PAYROLL AND CLOSE THE SPREADSHEET

10.3 Using Text in Functions

Text can be used in some functions. Like a label, text can contain letters and numbers. However, the entire label must be enclosed in quotation marks ("). Of the functions discussed so far, the IF function is the only one that can use text. For example, the following formula is valid in ClarisWorks:

=IF(B3>=70,"Above average","Below average")

This formula displays Above average if the value in cell B3 is greater than or equal to 70. Otherwise, Below average is displayed.

The cell name of a cell storing a label can also be used in the IF function. For example, suppose Above average was stored in cell C1, and Below average in cell C2. The following formula produces the same result as the formula above:

=IF(B3>=70,C1,C2)

Text can also be used in the comparison part of the IF function. When compared, the alphabetical order of the text is determined. For example, the following formula displays True because apple comes before orange alphabetically:

=IF("apple"<"orange","True","False")

Cells that store labels can also be compared. For example, if the label apple was stored in cell B3, and the label orange stored in cell B5, the formula =IF(B3<B5,B3,B5) displays apple.

....

Practice 3

In this Practice, the Grades spreadsheet created in Chapter Eight will be modified to determine a student's status and display the appropriate label. Start ClarisWorks if you have not already done so.

1) OPEN GRADES

2) ENTER A LABEL AND FORMAT IT

    a. Move the cell cursor to cell G1.
    b. Enter the label: Status
    c. Format the label as right aligned and bold.

3) ENTER FORMULA TO DETERMINE A STUDENT'S STATUS

    a. Select cell G3.
    b. Enter the formula: `=IF(F3>=70,"Passing","Failing")`
        Since the value in cell F3 is less than 70, `Failing` is displayed in cell G3.
    c. Right align the label displayed in cell G3.

4) COPY THE FORMULA TO CELLS G4 THROUGH G8

    a. Highlight cells G3 to G8.
    b. From the Calculate menu, select Fill Down.
    c. Click anywhere in the spreadsheet to remove the highlight.

<u>Check</u> - Your spreadsheet should be similar to:

	A	B	C	D	E	F	G
1	Name	Test 1	Test 2	Test 3	Test 4	Student Average	Status
2		9/12/97	10/17/97	11/14/97	12/12/97		
3	C. Bowser	50	82	68	64	66.0	Failing
4	D. Warheit	86	89	78	88	85.3	Passing
5	M. Porter	78	100	90	89	89.3	Passing
6	B. Presley	45	78	66	78	66.8	Failing
7	D. Sophocles	66	76	78	55	68.8	Failing
8	T. Hogan	85	74	83	66	77.0	Passing
9	Test Average:	68.33	83.17	77.17	73.33		

5) SAVE GRADES AND CLOSE THE SPREADSHEET

10.4 CHOOSE

The IF function can be used to create a formula that displays one value if a comparison is true, and another value if the comparison is false. Sometimes it is necessary to select one value from a list of many values. The CHOOSE function can be used to do this.

CHOOSE has the form

$$\text{=CHOOSE(<choice>, <option}_1\text{>, <option}_2\text{>, ..., <option}_N\text{>)}$$

where <choice> is a numeric value between 1 and N. CHOOSE displays the value in the list which corresponds to <choice>. If <choice> is 1, CHOOSE displays <option$_1$>, if it is 2 then <option$_2$> is displayed, and so on. For example, given the formula

    `=CHOOSE(A1,10,15,20,25)`

10 is displayed if the value stored in cell A1 is 1, 15 if the value stored in A1 is 2, 20 if the value is 3, and 25 if it is 4. If <choice> is less than 1 or greater than N (the number of possible values) `#ARG!` is displayed, meaning that a corresponding value is not available.

Only the integer portion of <choice> is used to determine which value to display. For example, if A1 stores 2.6, 15 is displayed because only the integer portion of the value, 2, is used. The options (<option$_1$>, <option$_2$>, etc.) in the CHOOSE function can be values, formulas, cell names, or text.

Practice 4

In this Practice you will modify the IVY PAYROLL spreadsheet to include a retirement deduction which allows employees to contribute different percentages of their salaries. This will be calculated using the CHOOSE function. Start ClarisWorks if you have not already done so.

1) OPEN IVY PAYROLL AND DISPLAY THE SHORTCUTS PALETTE

2) INSERT COLUMNS TO CALCULATE RETIREMENT CONTRIBUTION

   a. Select column I by clicking on its column letter.
   b. From the Calculate menu, select Insert Cells. A new column is inserted. Repeat this procedure to insert a second new column. Taxes is now column K.

3) ENTER TITLES

   a. Select cell I5.
   b. Enter the title: `Retire Code`
   c. In cell J5, enter the title: `Retirement`
   d. Highlight cells I5 and J5. Format the cells as right aligned.

4) ENTER THE RETIREMENT CODES

There are five retirement codes numbered 1 through 5 which determine the percentage of gross pay that will be deducted for each employee. Enter the following numbers into column I as indicated:

Cell	Code	Cell	Code	Cell	Code
I6	2	I15	4	I24	2
I7	3	I16	2	I25	3
I8	1	I17	1	I26	1
I9	4	I18	3	I27	4
I10	2	I19	2	I28	3
I11	2	I20	1	I29	2
I12	5	I21	5	I30	2
I13	3	I22	2	I31	5
I14	3	I23	4	I32	1

5) ENTER THE FORMULA TO CALCULATE RETIREMENTS

Each of the codes above corresponds to the following percentages which are used to calculate the retirement deduction:

Code	Percentage
1	0%
2	3%
3	5%
4	8%
5	10%

   a. In cell J6, enter the formula: `=CHOOSE(I6,0,H6*3%,H6*5%,H6*8%,H6*10%)`
   The CHOOSE function first looks in cell I6 which contains the retirement code 2 to determine the value of <choice>. Because the value in cell I6 corresponds to <option$_2$> in the CHOOSE function, ClarisWorks multiplies the gross pay in cell H6, $192.00, by 0.03 to compute the retirement deduction. Cell J6 displays 5.76, the result of the calculation.

b. Format cell J6 as currency.
c. Highlight cells J6 through J32.
d. From the Calculate menu, select Fill Down to copy the formula.

6) RECALCULATE THE NET PAY

a. Select cell M6.
b. Edit the existing formula so that the cell stores the formula =H6-J6-K6-L6
   The amount of $154.56 is displayed. Net pay is now computed by subtracting taxes, social security, and retirement from the gross pay.
c. Highlight cells M6 to M32. From the Calculate menu, use Fill Down to copy the formula.
d. Click anywhere in the spreadsheet to remove the highlight.

7) SAVE IVY PAYROLL

Check - Your spreadsheet should be similar to:

	H Gross Pay	I Retire Code	J Retirement	K Taxes	L Soc. Sec.	M Net Pay
5	Gross Pay	Retire Code	Retirement	Taxes	Soc. Sec.	Net Pay
6	$192.00	2	$5.76	$19.20	$12.48	$154.56
7	$156.00	3	$7.80	$15.60	$10.14	$122.46
8	$153.00	1	$0.00	$15.30	$9.94	$127.75
9	$130.50	4	$10.44	$13.05	$8.48	$98.53
10	$136.00	2	$4.08	$13.60	$8.84	$109.48
11	$173.25	2	$5.20	$17.33	$11.26	$139.47
12	$247.10	5	$24.71	$24.71	$16.06	$181.62

10.5 VLOOKUP

VLOOKUP is a function similar to CHOOSE except that the values to be displayed are stored in cells in the spreadsheet, not listed in the function itself. As an example of this function's usefulness, consider calculating tax withholdings using different tax rates based on gross pay. In Chapter Nine, two different rates were used to calculate taxes: 25% for those employees earning over $250 and 15% for all others. The two-way decision was naturally represented by the IF function. Suppose, however, there were 10 or 15 different tax rates. Multiple possibilities are often better represented by the VLOOKUP function.

The VLOOKUP function requires the values it uses to be stored in a table in the spreadsheet. This is an advantage because the values used are always displayed and can be included in spreadsheet printouts. In addition, the values are easily changed by modifying only the VLOOKUP table.

VLOOKUP has the form

=VLOOKUP (<value>, <range>, <columns>)

where <value> is a numeric expression and <range> is the cell range where the values to be displayed are stored. When evaluated, ClarisWorks finds the largest number in the first column of <range> which is less than or equal to <value>, and then displays the value that is stored in the cell <columns> over. The value of <columns> is usually 1 to indicate that the cells adjacent to the first column of <range> store the values to be displayed.

An Introduction to Computing Using ClarisWorks

This is similar to the manual operation of looking up a value in a two column table: the desired data is searched for in the first column, then the value read from the second column.

As an example, examine the following spreadsheet fragment:

C2			=VLOOKUP(B2,A8..B11,1)	
	A	**B**	**C**	**D**
1	Jockey	Number of Wins	Salary per Race	
2	Sam	105	$200.00	
3	Rhonda	38	$75.00	
4	Franklin	77	$125.00	
5				
6				
7	Salary Based on Wins			
8	0	$75.00		
9	50	$125.00		
10	100	$200.00		
11	1000	$200.00		
12				

With the formula =VLOOKUP(B2,A8..B11,1) in cell C2, Claris-Works looks in cell B2 for its value, which is 105. ClarisWorks then looks in cells A8 through A11 for the largest value which is less than or equal to 105, in this case 100 (stored in A10). The value of the cell to the right, in this case cell B10, is then displayed in cell C2. Since the value of B10 is $200.00, then $200.00 is displayed in C2. In a similar manner, the function displays $75.00 in cell C3 because cell A8 stores the largest value in <range> which is less than or equal to 38 (the value in B3).

The values in <range> must be in ascending order for VLOOKUP to work correctly. If the <value> is less than the first value stored in <range>, #N/A! is displayed. For this reason it is important to make the first value stored in <range> less than any value that will be looked up. If <value> is larger than the last value in <range>, #N/A! is displayed. To prevent this, the last value in the VLOOKUP table must be larger than any value that will be looked up. VLOOKUP differs from CHOOSE in that the <value> can be negative or zero as long as it falls within the values stored in <range>.

When using the VLOOKUP function, absolute references should be used to define <range>. This guarantees that the cell references in the table will not change if the Fill Down or Fill Right commands are used to copy a formula containing a VLOOKUP.

VLOOKUP is used in a spreadsheet when a table of information is needed to make calculations. An example of this is when a store needs to calculate tax deductions for the payroll. The tax deduction for each employee is based on their gross pay:

Gross Pay	Tax Rate
under $100	0%
$100–$299	8%
$300–$499	10%
$500–up	12%

To create the VLOOKUP table based on the tax information shown above, you must first determine what the contents of the table must be in order to work with a VLOOKUP function. The table is then created in an existing spreadsheet, and the necessary VLOOKUP function is placed in an appropriate formula. For the tax information listed on the previous page, the spreadsheet would look similar to:

C2	x ✓	=B2*VLOOKUP(B2,B8..C12,1)	
	A	**B**	**C**	**D**

	A	B	C	D
1	Employee	Gross Pay	Taxes	
2	Brown, T.	$365.87	$36.59	
3	Raucher, D.	$98.30	$0.00	
4	Jefferson, P.	$499.23	$49.92	
5				
6				
7			Tax Table	
8		$0	0.00%	
9		$100	8.00%	
10		$300	10.00%	
11		$500	12.00%	
12		$5000	12.00%	

The first and last rows of the VLOOKUP table are included as the lower and upper limits of the possible VLOOKUP values. For example, since cell B3 stores the value $98.30, $0.00 is calculated because the VLOOKUP function returns 0% which is then multiplied by the value in cell B3.

10.6 Locking Titles

A problem encountered when working with a large spreadsheet is that as you scroll, rows and columns containing labels that describe the data scroll off the screen. This makes it difficult to determine what columns or rows the displayed cells are in. ClarisWorks solves this problem by enabling you to *lock* selected rows and columns so that they cannot be scrolled.

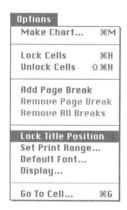

Executing the Lock Title Position command from the Options menu designates the row and column containing the cell cursor as well as every row above the cell cursor and every column to the left of the cell cursor as locked. For example, selecting cell A6 and executing Lock Title Position locks every cell in column A and rows 1 through 6. The cell cursor is then automatically moved to cell B6 because it is the first selectable cell:

	A	B	C	D
1				Ivy Univer
2				
3	Soc. Sec. rate	6.50%		
4				
5	Employee Name	Rate/Hr	Mon	Tue
6	Attis, B.	$8.00	6.0	4.0
7	Ball, R.	$4.00	9.5	12.0
8	Bickle, R.	$6.00	5.0	7.0
9	Cambell, M.	$4.50	5.0	6.0
10	Caxton, C.	$4.25	4.5	6.0

Locked cells are displayed with solid borders

When rows are scrolled, locked columns remain on the screen. Locked rows remain on the screen when columns are scrolled. Selecting the Lock Title Position command again unlocks affected cells. When a spreadsheet is printed, any rows or columns with locked cells are printed on each page.

Practice 5

The IVY PAYROLL spreadsheet will be modified to allow for seven tax rates using the VLOOKUP function. Cells will be locked to keep the employee names and column titles on the screen. Start ClarisWorks and open IVY PAYROLL if you have not already done so.

1) ADD A VLOOKUP TABLE TO THE SPREADSHEET

The following tax rates will be used in calculating taxes:

Salary	Tax Rate
under $100	0%
$100-$149	8%
$150-$199	10%
$200-$249	12%
$250-$299	17%
$300-$599	28%
$600-up	33%

a. The tax table will be stored in cells C40 through D47. Enter the title `Tax Table` in cell D39.
b. Bold the title.
c. Enter the following values into the indicated cells to create the tax table:

Cell	Salary	Cell	Tax Value
C40	0	D40	0%
C41	100	D41	8%
C42	150	D42	10%
C43	200	D43	12%
C44	250	D44	17%
C45	300	D45	28%
C46	600	D46	33%
C47	10000	D47	33%

d. Format cells C40 through C47 for **Currency** with 0 **Precision**.
e. Format cells D40 through D47 for **Percent** with 0 **Precision**.

2) LOCK TITLES

a. Select cell A5.
b. From the Options menu, select the Lock Title Position command. Frozen cells are designated by solid borders.
c. Click on the right scroll arrow to scroll columns. Column A remains on the screen while cells not locked are scrolled off the screen.
d. Click on the down scroll arrow to scroll rows. Rows 1 through 5 remain on the screen.

3) CALCULATE TAXES USING THE VLOOKUP FUNCTION

a. In cell K6, replace the existing formula with =H6*VLOOKUP(H6,C40..D47,1) The gross pay stored in H6, $192.00 is multiplied by 10% to compute the tax deduction of $19.20. Dollar signs ($) are needed in the function to keep the cell references for the VLOOKUP table from changing when Fill Down is used.
b. Highlight cells K6 to K32.
c. From the Calculate menu, select Fill Down. The old formulas are replaced and new calculations are performed.
d. Click anywhere in the spreadsheet to remove the highlight.

Check - The modified spreadsheet should look similar to:

| K6 | ×✓ | =H6*VLOOKUP(H6,C40..D47,1) |

	A	G	H	I	J	K	L
1							
2							
3	Soc. Sec. rate:						
4							
5	Employee Name	Fri	Gross Pay	Retire Code	Retirement	Taxes	Soc. Sec.
6	Attis, B.	7.0	$192.00	2	$5.76	$19.20	$12.48
7	Ball, R.	3.0	$156.00	3	$7.80	$15.60	$10.14
8	Bickle, R.	6.0	$153.00	1	$0.00	$15.30	$9.94
9	Cambell, M.	6.0	$130.50	4	$10.44	$10.44	$8.48
10	Caxton, C.	8.0	$136.00	2	$4.08	$10.88	$8.84
11	Esser, C.	7.5	$173.25	2	$5.20	$17.33	$11.26
12	Gilman, J.	3.5	$247.10	5	$24.71	$29.65	$16.06
13	Graham, T.	7.5	$157.98	3	$7.90	$15.80	$10.27
14	Hadriano, L.	9.0	$307.50	3	$15.38	$86.10	$19.99

4) SAVE AND CLOSE IVY PAYROLL

a. Save IVY PAYROLL and print a copy.
b. Deselect Lock Title Position from the Options menu and save IVY PAYROLL again.
c. Close IVY PAYROLL.

10.7 Using Text in CHOOSE and VLOOKUP

As with the IF function, text can be used in the CHOOSE and VLOOKUP functions. The actual text enclosed in quotation marks or a cell name which stores a label can be used. The following formula includes a CHOOSE function which uses text:

=CHOOSE(C3,"Freshman","Sophomore","Junior","Senior")

In this function, the word Freshman is displayed if the value stored in cell C3 is 1. If C3 stores the value 2 then Sophomore is displayed, etc.

The VLOOKUP function can be used to display text by storing labels in the range. As an example, examine the following spreadsheet fragment:

| C2 | ×✓ | =VLOOKUP(B2,B8..C11,1) |

	A	B	C	D
1	Student	GPA	Status	
2	Jones, H.	3.8	Dean's List	
3	Gruvnurt, L.	1.2	Probation	
4	Werner, S.	2.9	OK	
5				
6				
7		Student Status		
8		0.0	Probation	
9		2.0	OK	
10		3.5	Dean's List	
11		4.0	Dean's List	
12				

The formula =VLOOKUP(B2,B8..C11,1) in cell C2 displays Dean's List because cell B10 stores the largest value in <range> less than or equal to the value in cell B2 (which is 3.8).

Practice 6

In this Practice, the Grades spreadsheet will be modified to display each student's letter grade. Start ClarisWorks if you have not already done so.

1) OPEN THE GRADES SPREADSHEET

Open Grades and display the Shortcuts palette if it is not already visible.

2) ENTER AND FORMAT A GRADE LABEL

a. Select cell H1. Enter the label: Grade
b. Center align and bold the label.

3) ADD A VLOOKUP TABLE

a. In cell B12, enter the label: Letter Grade Table
b. Enter the following data into the indicated cells to create the grade table:

Cell	Score		Cell	Grade
B13	0		C13	F
B14	60		C14	D
B15	70		C15	C
B16	80		C16	B
B17	90		C17	A
B18	100		C18	A

Note that the scores in the grade table must be in ascending order for the VLOOKUP function to work properly.

4) ENTER A FORMULA TO DETERMINE A STUDENT'S GRADE

a. Select cell H3.
b. Enter the formula =VLOOKUP(F3,B13..C18,1)
   Since the value in cell F3 is less than 70, but greater than 60, D is displayed in cell H3.
c. Center align the grade in cell H3.

5) COPY THE FORMULA TO CELLS H4 THROUGH H8

a. Highlight cells H3 to H8.
b. Use the Fill Down command to copy the formula to the highlighted cells.
c. Click anywhere in the spreadsheet to remove the highlight.

Check - Your spreadsheet should be similar to:

H3	×✓	=VLOOKUP(F3,B13..C18,1)	
	F	G	H
1	Student Average	Status	Grade
2			
3	66.0	Failing	D
4	85.3	Passing	B
5	89.3	Passing	B
6	66.8	Failing	D
7	68.8	Failing	D
8	77.0	Passing	C

6) CHANGE C. BOWSER'S SCORE ON TEST 1

C. Bowser has taken a makeup test that replaces Test 4. Select cell E3 and enter `90`, the new score. ClarisWorks automatically recalculates any formulas that refer to the cell containing the test score. Note how C. Bowser's average has been recalculated, the status has changed to `Passing`, and the grade is now a C. This example demonstrates the computing power of the spreadsheet.

7) SAVE, PRINT, AND CLOSE GRADES

a. From the File menu, select Page Setup. Click on the landscape **Orientation** option and then **OK**.
b. Save Grades, print a copy, and then close Grades.

10.8 Amortization Tables

One of the most useful applications of a spreadsheet is to produce an amortization table. *Amortization* is a method for computing equal periodic payments for a loan. *Installment loans* are repaid in a series of periodic payments and are often computed using this method. Car loans and mortgages are examples of this type of loan. Each installment, or payment, is the same and consists of two parts: a portion which goes to reducing the principal and the remainder to pay interest due on the principal for that period. *Principal* is the amount of money owed. Therefore, the principal decreases as a loan is repaid.

An *amortization table* displays how much interest and principal make up each payment of an installment loan. Interest is computed as a percentage of the current principal. The principal portion of the payment goes toward reducing the amount owed. For example, the payment made each month on a 30 year loan of $100,000 borrowed at an interest rate of 12% is $1,028.61. On the first payment made, $1,000.00 goes toward interest and $28.61 to reduce principal (i.e., the amount owed). On the 60th payment, $977.15 pays interest and $51.47 reduces principal. The final payment is $10.18 interest and $1,018.43 principal.

The PMT function is used to calculate the periodic payment for an installment loan. The interest rate, the number of payments to be made, and the amount of the loan (principal) are needed by the PMT function. A formula using the PMT function takes the form

=PMT (<rate>, <term>, <present value>)

where <rate> is the interest rate per period, <term> is the number of payments to be made, and <present value> is the amount to be paid back. As an example, if you borrow $100,000 to purchase a house at an interest rate of 12% for 30 years, the formula would be:

=PMT(12%/12,360,-100000)

Since the payments are monthly, the interest rate must also be monthly. This is computed by dividing the annual rate of interest, 12%, by 12. The number of payments is 360, 30 years × 12 months. The present value of the loan, –100000, is negative to indicate a borrowed amount of money. When entered into a cell, the formula displays a value of 1028.612596. This means that the monthly payment for this loan is $1,028.61.

10.9 Printing a Selected Spreadsheet Area

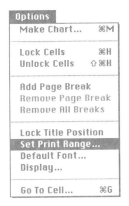

The Set Print Range command from the Options menu can be used to change the printable spreadsheet area. It is often easier to first highlight the desired block of cells before executing Set Print Range:

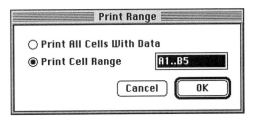

Cells A1 through B5 will become the print range when OK is selected

The displayed **Print Cell Range** can be changed by typing in a new range. Selecting **OK** designates the printable spreadsheet area. Executing the Print command then prints only those cells in the range.

To be able to print the entire spreadsheet, execute the Print Range command again, then select the **Print All Cells With Data** option and **OK**.

. . . .

Practice 7

In this Practice you will complete an amortization table which displays the interest and principal paid on each payment of a loan. Start ClarisWorks if you have not already done so.

1) OPEN THE LOAN SPREADSHEET

Open LOAN. Notice that the loan information will be stored in cells that can be referenced in formulas. By storing the data in cells, it is easy to answer What If? questions. For example, what if a $20,000 loan at an interest rate of 10% to be re-paid over 5 years was obtained? To answer this, 10% is entered into the cell storing the interest rate, 20000 is the principal, and 60 is the number of payments. Any formulas referencing these cells are automatically recalculated and display the new values, including the payment amount.

2) ENTER THE LOAN'S INFORMATION

a. In cell C3, enter the principal: `100000`
b. In cell C4, enter the yearly interest rate: `12%`
c. In cell C5, enter the number of payments: `360` (30 years × 12 monthly payments)

3) CALCULATE THE MONTHLY PAYMENT

In cell C7, enter the formula: `=PMT(C4/12,C5,-C3)`. The division by 12 is needed to convert the yearly interest rate in cell C4 to a monthly value. $1,028.61 is displayed.

4) CALCULATE TOTAL PAID AND TOTAL INTEREST

a. In cell C9, enter the formula: `=ROUND(C5*C7,2)`. This formula computes the total paid for the loan, including principal and interest.
b. In cell C10, enter the formula: `=C9-C3`. The total interest paid over 30 years is calculated.

5) ENTER THE FIRST PAYMENT DATA

   a. In cell A13, enter: 1
   b. In cell B13, enter: =C3
   c. In cell C13, enter =B13*(C4/12) to calculate one month's interest on the loan. $1,000.00, which is 1% (12%/12) of the principal, is displayed. The cell reference C4 contains dollar signs because the interest rate will be the same for each payment.
   d. In cell D13, enter the formula =IF(C13<0.01,0,C7-C13) to calculate the amount of the payment which is applied to the principal, $28.61. If the value in cell C13 is less than 0.01, then 0 is displayed. This comparison must be made because it is not possible to pay less than a penny.
   e. In cell E13, enter the formula =B13-D13 to calculate the new principal owed.

6) ENTER FORMULAS FOR THE SECOND PAYMENT

   a. In cell A14, enter the formula =A13+1.
   b. To display the new principal, enter =E13 in cell B14.
   c. Highlight cells C13 to E14.
   d. Use Fill Down to copy the formulas in cell C13 through E13 into cells C14 through E14. This completes the data for the second payment and the principal owed, $99,942.49 is displayed in cell E14.

7) COMPLETE THE TABLE USING FILL DOWN

   a. Highlight cells A14 to E372.
   b. Use the Fill Down command to copy cells A14 through E14 into rows 15 through 372. Because of the large number of cells and formulas involved, it will take a moment for the computer to recalculate the spreadsheet. Note the value in cell E372. The principal owed is $0.00 which indicates the loan has been paid in full.

Check - Your spreadsheet should be similar to:

	A	B	C	D	E
1			Loan Amortization		
2					
3	Principal =		$100,000.00		
4	Interest rate =		12.00%		
5	No. of payments =		360		
6					
7	Monthly payment =		$1,028.61		
8					
9	Total paid =		$370,300.53		
10	Total interest =		$270,300.53		
11					
12	Payment	Principal	Pay to Interest	Pay to Principal	Principal Owed
13		1	$100,000.00	$1,000.00	$28.61	$99,971.39
14		2	$99,971.39	$999.71	$28.90	$99,942.49
15		3	$99,942.49	$999.42	$29.19	$99,913.30
16		4	$99,913.30	$999.13	$29.48	$99,883.82
17		5	$99,883.82	$998.84	$29.77	$99,854.05

8) PRINT A PORTION OF THE SPREADSHEET

   a. Highlight cells A1 through E15.
   b. From the Options menu, select the Set Print Range command. The Print Range dialog box is displayed with the highlighted range as the **Print Cell Range**.
   c. Select **OK**.

d. From the View menu, select Page View. Note that only the cells designated as the print range are displayed. This is because Page View displays a spreadsheet as it will appear when printed.

e. Save LOAN and then print a copy.

f. From the Options menu, select Set Print Range.

g. Select the **Print All Cells With Data** option and then select **OK**. The entire spreadsheet is displayed.

h. From the View menu, select Page View to deselect it.

9) CREATE AN AUTO LOAN MODEL

The present values in LOAN represent a house loan. By changing the interest rate and the number of payments, payment amounts can be compared for a car.

a. In cell C3, enter the new principal : 10000

b. In cell C4, enter the new yearly interest: 10%

c. The car loan is a 5 year loan; therefore, the number of monthly payments will be 5×12. In cell C5, enter the new number of payments: 60

d. Note how the spreadsheet has been recalculated. Scroll down to row 72 which contains the last payment. The spreadsheet can easily model loans with less than 360 payments.

e. Save LOAN.

10) ENTER YOUR OWN VALUES INTO THE LOAN SPREADSHEET

a. Experiment by changing the principal and interest of the LOAN spreadsheet to any values you like. Change the number of payments to see how that affects the interest paid for the loan.

b. From the File menu, select Close. Click on **Don't Save** in the dialog box when prompted to save the file.

c. Quit ClarisWorks.

10.10   Where can you go from here?

The last three chapters introduced you to the concepts of a spreadsheet: how one is designed, created on the computer, and used to produce calculations. There are other ClarisWorks spreadsheet options we have not discussed which you may want to learn. Reading the spreadsheet sections in the *ClarisWorks User's Guide* supplied by Claris is a good place to start.

Spreadsheets can be used to store laboratory data to produce scientific and statistical calculations as well as financial calculations. Larger and more powerful spreadsheet programs such as Lotus 1-2-3 and Excel include many advanced calculating features. These spreadsheet programs are similar to ClarisWorks and should look familiar to you in many ways. Having learned the ClarisWorks spreadsheet, you will be able to easily learn and use other spreadsheet software.

Chapter Summary

A spreadsheet can be used to answer What If? questions. By including factors that relate to a particular situation, a spreadsheet model can be produced which may then be used to make financial decisions.

The Sort command from the Calculate menu can organize the cells in a spreadsheet in alphabetical or numerical order.

Text can be used in functions such as the IF function. For example, the formula =IF(A5<30,"Cheap","Expensive") displays Cheap if A5 is less than 30 and Expensive if A5 is greater than or equal to 30. The cell name of a cell storing a label can also be used in the IF function.

Relational operators can be used to compare text in the IF function. For example, if cell A5 contains George and B12 Andrews then the formula =IF(A5<B12,"Yes","No") displays No since George is greater than Andrews.

The CHOOSE function can select one value from a list of many. When given a choice, 1 to N, the CHOOSE function displays the appropriate option.

The VLOOKUP function selects values from a VLOOKUP table that is stored in range of cells. When given a numeric expression, <value>, and the cell range where values are stored, <range>, VLOOKUP finds the largest number in <range> which is less than or equal to <value>. It then displays the value stored in the cell to the right of the cell range. Both the CHOOSE and VLOOKUP functions can be used to display text.

ClarisWorks allows rows and columns to be locked using the Lock Title Position command from the Options menu. This feature is especially useful in keeping rows and columns containing labels from scrolling off the screen.

An amortization table displays how much interest and principal make up each payment of an installment loan. The PMT function is used to calculate the periodic payments of an installment loan.

The Set Print Range command can be used to print only a portion of a spreadsheet.

Vocabulary

Amortization - A method for computing equal periodic payments for a loan.

Amortization table - Displays the interest and principal paid on each payment of a loan.

Ascending values - Increasing in value from low to high.

Descending values - Decreasing in value from high to low.

Installment loan - Loan that is repaid in a series of periodic payments.

Key sort column - Column containing the data used in a sort.

Lock Title Position command - Used to designate rows and columns so that they cannot be scrolled off the screen.

Model - A spreadsheet containing data relating to a particular situation.

Principal - The amount of money borrowed.

Set Print Range command - Used to designate a specific range of cells to be printed.

What If? question - Question or concern a spreadsheet user has. Can be answered with a model.

10 Reviews

Sections 10.1 — 10. 5

1. a) Explain what is meant by a "What If?" question.
    b) How can a spreadsheet be used to answer "What If?" questions?

2. Make a list of 5 "What If?" questions that could be answered using the IVY PAYROLL spreadsheet.

3. Explain how the data in the IVY PAYROLL spreadsheet could be sorted in ascending order based on employee per-hour pay.

4. Write formulas using the IF function for each of the following:
    a) If B3 is less than or equal to C12 display Low, if greater than display High.
    b) If A5 is equal to Z47 display Jonathan, if not equal to display Judith.
    c) If C25 is greater than D19 display Great!, otherwise display Terrible!

5. Give three situations in which the CHOOSE function could be used.

6. Write a CHOOSE function which displays 100 if cell B20 contains a value of 1, 500 if a 2, 900 if a 3, and 1200 if a 4.

7. Describe three situations in which a VLOOKUP table could be used.

8. The Lawrenceville Widget Company uses the following discount rates when large numbers of widgets are ordered:

Number of Widgets	Discount
100 - 149	10%
1000 - 1999	30%
2000 or over	70%

    Convert this into a VLOOKUP table, and make a sketch of the VLOOKUP table.

9. Write a formula that uses the VLOOKUP function to display the proper discount percent if cell C12 stores the number of widgets. Use the VLOOKUP table created in Review question 8.

Section 10.6 — 10.10

10. Explain the steps required to keep the row containing the labels that identify the columns in IVY PAYROLL from scrolling off the screen.

11. Write a CHOOSE function that displays Excellent if cell B20 contains a value of 1, Good if a 2, Fair if a 3, and Poor if a 4.

12. Briefly explain what an amortization table is and how it might be used.

13. a) How much interest is paid in the first month of a loan of $5,000 borrowed for 5 years at 12% per year interest?
    b) Show what PMT function is used to calculate the monthly payments on the above loan.

14. Describe the steps needed to print only the values displayed in the cell range A3..D17.

Exercises

1. The Ivy alumni are unhappy about plans for their annual dance. Perform the following What If? questions using the Dance spreadsheet created in Chapter Nine, Exercise 1.

   a) Open Dance. The alumni have decided against using the band *The Poison Ivys*. Many of the younger alumni want the *Dreadful Greats* instead, but they will cost $3,500. Update the spreadsheet to calculate the cost per member with the new band.

   b) Many alumni want better desserts. Update the spreadsheet with the cost of desserts doubled.

   c) A group of alumni do not want to hold the dance in Ivy Hall which the University will let them use if they pay for electricity and clean up. These members want to hold the dinner dance at the Leaf County Inn which will cost $7,000. Insert a row that includes the new hotel cost and then delete the rows for Electricity and Clean up because these costs are included in the Inn's fee.

   d) Save the modified Dance and print a copy.

2. The STOCK2 spreadsheet modified in Chapter Nine, Exercise 3 contains Grace van Ivy's stock portfolio information. She would like it modified to help her evaluate the portfolio.

   a) Open STOCK2. Ms. van Ivy has decided that it would be best to sell those stocks which have lost more than 30% of their original value. In column H, add the label Stock Status and make it bold. Use the IF function in a formula to display Sell for stock that should be sold or Retain for stock that should be held. Be careful when creating the IF functions. Format the column so that all text is displayed and is right aligned.

   b) Grace van Ivy must pay a commission to her stockbroker when she sells stock. The commission is based on the following scale:

Number of Shares	Commission
0 - 29	5%
30 - 69	4%
70 - 99	2%
100 - 149	1%
150 and over	0.5%

   The dollar amount of the commission is calculated by multiplying the current value of the stock by the appropriate commission percent. In column I, enter the label Commission and make it bold. In this column, use the VLOOKUP function in a formula to calculate and display the sales commission on each of Ms. van Ivy's stock.

   c) Save the modified STOCK2 and print a copy.

3. Fantasy Wheels Used Cars would like to have the Cars spreadsheet created in Chapter Nine, Exercise 4 modified to determine the markup of its cars based on each car's condition.

   a) Open Cars. A rating system of 1 to 5 will be used. The rating for each car is:

Rating	Cars
1	Studebaker, Thunderbird, DeLorean, Bricklin
2	Mustang, Jaguar, Honda, Jeep
3	Ferarri, Aston-Martin, Triumph, GTO
4	Bel Aire, Rolls Royce, Cadillac
5	Porsche, Bentley, all other makes

   In column H, enter the label `Rating`. Format the label as right aligned and bold. Enter each car's rating as listed above. Decrease the column width.

   b) The percent (%) markup for each rating is as follows:

Rating	Markup
1	10%
2	20%
3	35%
4	50%
5	75%

   In column I, enter the label `Rating Markup`. Format the label as right aligned and bold. Widen the column to accommodate the label. Use a formula that includes the CHOOSE function to compute the price of each car after its markup. Format the column appropriately.

   c) Save the modified Cars and print a copy.

4. Mike Entrepreneur wants to ask What If? questions about raising his prices for his lawn service. This can be done by modifying the Lawns spreadsheet created in Chapter Nine, Exercise 5.

   a) Open Lawns. Modify the spreadsheet so that only one entry needs to be changed to raise the price per square meter. Make any necessary changes to formulas that use this value. Determine what happens to his total profits when he doubles and triples his price per square meter.

   b) Mike's customers with large lawns are complaining bitterly about his prices. In response to the complaints he has decided that all customers with lawns of less than 1,500 square meters will pay $0.06 per square meter and those with larger lawns will pay $0.04 per square meter. Modify the spreadsheet so that there is one charge for lawns greater than 1,500 square meters and another charge for lawns with an area under 1,500 square meters. Use an IF statement in a formula to calculate the price for each customer.

c) Mike must pay taxes on the price he charges so he wants the following tax information built into the Lawns spreadsheet:

Price	Tax
$0 - $14	0%
$15 - $39	5%
$40 - $59	7%
$60 - $99	12%
$100 - $199	15%
$200 and above	30%

Add a column titled Taxes that displays the taxes Mike must pay for each of his customers. Use a VLOOKUP table to produce the calculations. Display the total and average tax amounts as well.

d) Save the modified Lawns and print a copy.

5. Mr. Hernandez, owner of the Aztec Café is planning to give his employees a bonus based on their position. He would like to use the AC Employees spreadsheet modified in Chapter Nine, Exercise 2 to compute the bonuses.

a) Open AC Employees and insert a new column after the column that stores the employee names. In the new column enter the label Position. Format the label as bold. D. Romani and D. Roberts are managers. The other employees are servers. Enter the employee positions into the new column. Right align all the positions and label. Format the column widths appropriately.

b) In column P enter the label Bonus. Format the label as right aligned and bold. Mr. Hernandez wants to give managers a bonus of 10% of their gross pay and servers 5% of their gross pay. Use the IF function in a formula to compute the bonuses.

c) Save the modified AC Employees and print a copy.

6. Anna Silver needs to borrow $10,000 to purchase a car and would like to ask What If? about different car loans.

a) Open LOAN2 which contains the formulas to compute the monthly payment, total paid, and total interest of an amortized loan. Enter 10000 as the principal in cell C3, 8% as the interest in cell C4, and 48 as the number of payments in cell C5.

b) Copy cells C3 through C10 into columns D, E, and F. Change the interest rate in column C to 7%, column D to 8%, column E to 9%, and column F to 10%.

c) Create a bar chart that shows the monthly payment at different interest rates.

d) Display the spreadsheet in Page View. Move and resize the chart as necessary so that it will fit on the same page as the spreadsheet data.

e) Save the modified LOAN2 and print a copy.

Chapter 11

Integrating the Word Processor, Database, and Spreadsheet

Close

Mail Merge

Show Tools

Make Chart

Objectives

After completing this chapter you will be able to:

1. Open multiple files and switch between them.

2. Copy text between word processor files.

3. Copy data between database files.

4. Copy data between spreadsheet files.

5. Copy data between the database and spreadsheet.

6. Integrate database and spreadsheet data with a word processor document.

7. Copy data into a new file.

8. Use the word processor to create a mail merge document for use with the database.

9. Use application frames to create compound documents.

ClarisWorks is an *integrated* software package. This means that the word processor, database, and spreadsheet can be used by running only one program. There are two important reasons for using integrated packages: data can be copied between applications, and it is easy to learn and use each application because they have similar commands. For example, the Save command from the File menu always saves the current file whether you are using the word processor, database, or spreadsheet.

11.1 Using Multiple Windows

ClarisWorks allows many files to be open at the same time. This can include any combination of word processor, database, and spreadsheet files, but the number of files that can be open may be limited by the amount of memory your computer has available.

In the Open dialog box, ClarisWorks displays a list of existing files. A file can be opened by highlighting its name and selecting **Open**, which places a copy of the file into the computer's memory. The Open command can then be used again to open a second file. Each file is placed in its own *window*, which is the area on the screen displaying the file. ClarisWorks displays a list of the open files in the View menu:

View	
New View	
Open Frame	
✓Page View	⇧⌘P
Slide Show...	
Show Styles	⇧⌘W
Show Tools	⇧⌘T
Hide Rulers	⇧⌘U
Tile Windows	
Stack Windows	
IVY ENROLLMENT (SS)	
IVY PAYROLL (SS)	
✓IVY PROMO (WP)	
Student (DB)	

Open files

The View menu displays the names of all open files

The *active file* is designated by a check mark and is the one currently displayed on the screen, usually with a highlighted Title bar. When a file is selected from the View menu, ClarisWorks automatically switches to the proper application and displays that file making it active. The letters in parentheses after the file's name indicate the type: WP for word processor, DB for database, and SS for spreadsheet.

There are many reasons for switching between files. For example, you may be writing a letter in the word processor and wish to refer to some figures stored in a spreadsheet. With both files open, you could use the View menu to switch to the spreadsheet, view the figures, and then switch back to the word processor letter. Other reasons include sharing data between applications as described later in this chapter.

ClarisWorks maintains the current status of each open file, including any changes made, in that file's window. This includes the position of the cursor and any options set so that it is possible to work with one file, switch to another, and return to the first file, picking up exactly where you left off. An option set in one window has no effect on any other. For example, a database can be displayed in Browse view in one window, and another database displayed in Layout view in a different window.

An open file does not have to be saved until you have finished working with it. However, it is a good idea to save modified files from time to time as a precaution. Selecting the Save command from the File menu saves only the active file.

Practice 1

In this Practice you will open several Ivy University files and switch between them.

1) BOOT THE SYSTEM AND START CLARISWORKS

2) OPEN THREE FILES

    a. From the File menu, select the Open command and open IVY CONGRAT. The IVY CONGRAT word processor file is placed in a window and displayed on the word processor screen.

    b. Open IVY STUDENT. The IVY STUDENT database is placed in a second window and displayed on the database screen. IVY CONGRAT is still open, but may be obscured by the second window.

    c. Open IVY PAYROLL. The IVY PAYROLL spreadsheet is placed in a third window.

    d. Move the cell cursor to cell A5.

3) SWITCH TO THE IVY STUDENT DATABASE

    a. Display the View menu. There are three open files listed at the bottom of the menu. Note the active file is denoted by a check mark.

    b. From the View menu, select IVY STUDENT. The database screen is displayed with the IVY STUDENT window.

4) SWITCH TO THE IVY CONGRAT DOCUMENT AND BACK TO IVY PAYROLL

    a. From the View menu, select IVY CONGRAT. The word processor is displayed with the IVY CONGRAT window.

    b. From the View menu, select IVY PAYROLL. The spreadsheet is displayed. Note that the cell cursor is still on cell A5, where it was placed in step 2 above.

11.2 Close - Removing Files from Memory

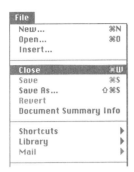

When work on an open file is complete, the file should be closed by selecting the Close command from the File menu (⌘W). Closing a file frees some of the computer's memory which allows ClarisWorks to perform certain operations faster. Closing windows also avoids accidental changes. When a file is closed, its window is removed from the screen, and Claris-Works automatically switches to the next open window.

If changes have been made to a file, it should be saved on disk before it is closed. If you attempt to close a file that has been edited but not saved, ClarisWorks warns you before proceeding.

11.3 Displaying Multiple Windows

Each window can be resized to allow other windows to be viewed. While this is not necessary, it is sometimes helpful to see the contents of more than one file on the screen at the same time. The Adjust box in the lower-right corner of a window is used to change its size:

Dragging the Adjust box changes the window's size

Dragging this box towards the upper left makes the window smaller. A window is moved to a new location by dragging its Title bar. The Zoom box in the upper-right corner of the window can be clicked to expand the window to full-screen size:

Clicking on the Zoom box expands a window to full screen size

In the Practices that follow, it is your choice as to whether to display more than one window on the screen at the same time or not. Unless you are specifically directed, you may perform the Practice in the manner that is most convenient for you.

11.4 Copying Data Between Applications

In previous chapters you duplicated data by first placing it on the Clipboard using the Copy command then executing Paste to put a copy of the data elsewhere in the document. This method can also be used to copy data from one file to another. When the Copy command is executed, Claris-Works places a copy of the highlighted data onto the Clipboard. ClarisWorks has only one Clipboard, no matter which file is currently active. Therefore, by then making a different file active and executing the Paste command, a copy of the Clipboard contents is pasted into a different file.

The ability to copy text from one word processor document to another can save typing and can help to maintain consistency between documents. ClarisWorks allows you to do this using the editing commands from the Edit menu.

To copy text from one word processor document to another, four steps are required:

1. Highlight the text to be copied.
2. Execute the Copy command from the Edit menu.
3. Make the file to receive the copied text active.
4. Place the cursor where the text is to be inserted and execute the Paste command.

Copying the text simply transfers a copy of the highlighted block to the Clipboard; the original file remains unchanged. However, pasting data into the receiving file modifies that file, and before it is closed it must be saved to retain the changes.

Practice 2

In this Practice you will copy a paragraph from one word processor document into another. The three files IVY CONGRAT, IVY STUDENT, and IVY PAYROLL should still be open from the last Practice. We will first close IVY STUDENT and IVY PAYROLL, and then copy a paragraph from the IVY HANDBOOK document into the IVY CONGRAT letter.

1) CLOSE THE UNNEEDED FILES

a. From the File menu, select the Close command to close the currently displayed file, IVY PAYROLL. IVY PAYROLL is closed and the previous window displayed.

b. From the View menu, select IVY STUDENT and then Close it. The window containing IVY CONGRAT is again displayed.

2) OPEN IVY HANDBOOK

IVY HANDBOOK is a word processor file containing a passage from the Ivy University student handbook that is to be copied into IVY CONGRAT. From the File menu, select Open and open IVY HANDBOOK. IVY HANDBOOK is opened and placed in another window. Two word processor files are currently open.

3) COPY TEXT TO THE CLIPBOARD

a. Move the cursor to the first paragraph which begins "One of the most..." if it is not already there.

b. Highlight the entire paragraph by clicking four times in rapid succession. This ensures that the paragraph marker is included in the highlight.

c. From the Edit menu, select Copy. A copy of the highlighted text is placed on the Clipboard.

d. Because IVY HANDBOOK is no longer needed, select Close from the File menu to remove it from the screen. IVY CONGRAT is now displayed.

4) PASTE THE CLIPBOARD CONTENTS INTO THE IVY CONGRAT LETTER

a. From the Edit menu, select Show Clipboard. A window is opened which displays the Clipboard. Note that although IVY CONGRAT is the only open file, the Clipboard contains text copied from IVY HANDBOOK.

b. Click on the Clipboard window's Close box to remove it from the screen.

c. Place the cursor at the position where the text should be inserted, the second blank line after the sentence which reads "To quote the student handbook:"

d. From the Edit menu, select Paste. The paragraph from IVY HANDBOOK is copied from the Clipboard and placed at the current cursor position.

e. Save IVY CONGRAT.

<u>Check</u> - The file should be similar to:

> Dear·Faculty·and·Staff:↵
> ↵
> I·am·proud·to·announce·the·Dean's·List·awards·for·this·semester.··Each·of·these·students·should·be·congratulated·for·their·exceptional·academic·achievement.↵
> ↵
> As·you·know,·only·students·with·an·exceptional·GPA·are·included·in·the·Dean's·List.··To·quote·the·student·handbook:↵
> ↵
>   One·of·the·most·coveted·academic·honors·is·to·be·included·in·the·Dean's·List.··To·qualify·for·the·Dean's·List,·a·student·must·possess·a·GPA·greater·than·3.6.↵
> ↵
> The·following·students·are·recipients·of·this·semester's·Dean's·List·award:↵

5) CLOSE IVY CONGRAT

11.6 Copying Data Between Two Spreadsheets

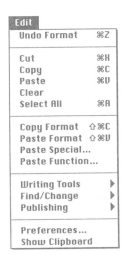

Data can be copied from one spreadsheet to another in the same way text is copied between word processor documents. This can save you from retyping data and can be very useful when making spreadsheet models to answer What If? questions.

To copy data between two open spreadsheets, four steps are required:

1. Highlight the cells to be copied.
2. Execute the Copy command.
3. Make the spreadsheet to receive the copied data active.
4. Place the cell cursor where the data is to appear and execute the Paste command.

The pasted cells automatically include all formulas and formatting that they had in the original spreadsheet.

Copied cells can be inserted between already existing cells by first making room for the new data. For example, to copy a row from one spreadsheet into the center of another you must first insert a blank row in the receiving spreadsheet. If blank space is not created in the receiving spreadsheet, the pasted data will overwrite existing data.

Practice 3

In this Practice you will copy a group of cells from one spreadsheet to another, adding the data for a group of new employees to the IVY PAYROLL spreadsheet. Start ClarisWorks if you have not already done so.

1) PREPARE THE WINDOWS

    a. Open IVY NEW EMPLOYEE. These are four new employees who need to be added to the IVY PAYROLL spreadsheet.
    b. Open IVY PAYROLL.

2) INSERT EMPTY ROWS IN THE RECEIVING SPREADSHEET

    a. Highlight row 32 by clicking on its row number.
    b. From the Calculate menu, select Insert Cells. A new row is inserted above the one highlighted.
    c. Use the Insert Cells command to insert 3 more rows.

3) COPY DATA TO THE CLIPBOARD

    a. From the View menu, select IVY NEW EMPLOYEE.
    b. Highlight the four rows containing data.
    c. From the Edit menu, select Copy to place a copy of the highlighted data on the Clipboard.
    d. Close IVY NEW EMPLOYEE.

4) PASTE THE CLIPBOARD CONTENTS IN THE PAYROLL SPREADSHEET

    a. Select cell A32.
    b. From the Edit menu, select Paste. The new employee data is copied into the empty rows.
    c. The formulas need to be copied for the new employees. Highlight cells J31 through P35.
    d. From the Calculate menu, select Fill Down. The formulas are copied into the new rows and recalculated.

5) SORT THE EMPLOYEE DATA

    a. After the insertion, the employee names are no longer in alphabetic order. Highlight rows 6 through 36.
    b. From the Calculate menu, select Sort. In the dialog box, select **OK** to accept the default options.
    c. Scroll through the data and note how the employees are now in alphabetical order.
    d. Save IVY PAYROLL.

<u>Check</u> - The new employees inserted into the spreadsheet automatically change the payroll totals displayed at the bottom of the spreadsheet:

	M	N	O	P
38	New pay :	$6,344.24	$6,646.34	$6,948.45
39	Raise cost :	$302.11	$604.21	$906.32

11.7 Copying Records Between Two Databases

Records can be copied from one database to another. This can be helpful when two similar databases need the same data.

To copy records between two open databases, four steps are required:

1. Highlight the records to be copied.
2. Execute the Copy command.
3. Make the database to receive the copied records active and display the appropriate Layout in Browse view.
4. Execute the Paste command.

To highlight a record from any Layout in Browse view, click on a field name. More records can be highlighted by either dragging or by holding down the Command key while clicking on a field name in each record. Records can be highlighted in List view by clicking on the box to the left of the record. Every record in a database can be selected at once by executing the Select All command from the Edit menu (⌘A).

When records are copied to the Clipboard, only the fields displayed in the current Layout are copied regardless of how many fields are in the database.

Pasted records are added to the end of the receiving database. If the database has previously been sorted, it will need to be resorted after the new records are added.

When records are pasted into a database that has different fields from the original, the entries from the first field in the original file are copied to the first field in the second file and so on, regardless of the field names as long as corresponding fields are of the same type.

Practice 4

In this Practice you will transfer records between two database files. Start ClarisWorks if you have not already done so.

1) PREPARE THE WINDOWS

    a. Close any open files.
    b. Open IVY STUDENT. Display Layout 1 in Browse view if it is not already displayed.
    c. Open IVY NEW STUDENT.

2) HIGHLIGHT THE RECORDS TO BE COPIED

We want to copy all of the records in IVY NEW STUDENT. From the Edit menu, execute the Select All command.

3) COPY THE HIGHLIGHTED RECORDS TO THE IVY STUDENT DATABASE

    a. From the Edit menu, select Copy.
    b. Close IVY NEW STUDENT. IVY STUDENT is again displayed.
    c. From the Edit menu, select Paste. The highlighted records from IVY NEW STUDENT are added as new records to the end of IVY STUDENT.

d. Use the Bookmark to display record 83. David Gould's record has been copied from the IVY NEW STUDENT database. Scroll up to view the two other new records.

e. Sort the database on the Last Name field. The records are again in order by last name.

f. Save IVY STUDENT.

11.8 Copying Spreadsheet Data into a Word Processor Document

Businesses sometimes send memos or letters that contain the data from a spreadsheet. ClarisWorks allows you to copy spreadsheet data into a word processor document.

To copy cells from an open spreadsheet to an open word processor document, four steps are required:

1. Highlight the spreadsheet cells to be copied.
2. Execute the Copy command.
3. Make the word processor document active.
4. Place the cursor where the data is to be inserted and execute the Paste command.

Cells copied into a document are automatically separated by tabs. Tab stops can be set to better align the data.

Practice 5

In this Practice, part of a spreadsheet will be copied into a word processor document. Start ClarisWorks if you have not already done so.

1) PREPARE THE WINDOWS

a. Close any open files.
b. Open the IVY CONGRAT word processor file.
c. Open Grades. (You created the Grades spreadsheet in the Practices of Chapter Eight.)

2) COPY THE CELLS TO THE CLIPBOARD

a. In Grades, highlight cells A1 through E9.
b. From the Edit menu, select Copy.
c. Close Grades. IVY CONGRAT is displayed.

3) PASTE THE CELLS INTO THE DOCUMENT

a. From the Edit menu, select Show Clipboard. Although a word processor document is the active file, the Clipboard displays the contents of the spreadsheet cells. Close the Clipboard.
b. Move the cursor to the second blank line after the paragraph which begins "Dr. Sulfuric's Chemistry class…."
c. From the Edit menu, select Paste. The Clipboard contents, the cells from Grades, are placed at the current cursor position. Note how tabs are used to separate the different columns.

An Introduction to Computing Using ClarisWorks

d. Highlight the spreadsheet data and then set left-aligned tab stops at the 2.5, 3.5, 4.5, and 5.5 inch marks.

e. Save IVY CONGRAT.

<u>Check</u> - Your document should be similar to:

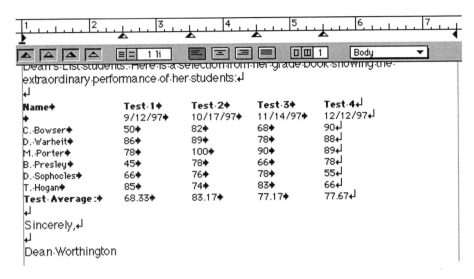

11.9 Copying Database Records into a Word Processor Document

Businesses sometimes include data from databases in letters and memos. ClarisWorks allows records from a database to be copied into a word processor document.

To copy data from an open database into an open word processor document, four steps are required:

1. Highlight the records to be copied.
2. Execute the Copy command.
3. Make the word processor document active.
4. Place the cursor where the data is to be inserted and execute the Paste command.

Each record copied into a word processor document is placed in a separate paragraph. The fields in each record are automatically separated by tabs. Tab stops can be set to better align the data.

Practice 6

In this Practice selected fields from a database will be copied into a word processor document. A report will be displayed to limit the number of records and fields. Start ClarisWorks if you have not already done so.

1) PREPARE THE WINDOWS

IVY CONGRAT should still be displayed from the last Practice. Open IVY STUDENT. Display the Dean's List Report.

2) COPY THE DATA TO THE CLIPBOARD

    a. From the Edit menu, execute the Select All command.
    b. From the Edit menu, select Copy.

3) PASTE THE DATA INTO IVY CONGRAT

    a. From the View menu, select IVY CONGRAT.
    b. Move the cursor to the second blank line after the paragraph which begins "The following students are recipients...."
    c. From the Edit menu, select Paste. The records from the Clipboard have been inserted into the word processor document. Note how tabs are used to separate the fields.
    d. Highlight the table of database records and set the following tab stops: left aligned at 2 inches and decimal aligned at 3.25 inches.

Check - Your document should be similar to:

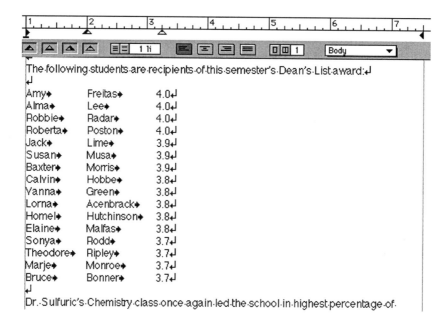

4) SAVE IVY CONGRAT AND PRINT A COPY

    Save the modified letter and print a copy of it.

5) CLOSE ALL OPEN FILES

    a. Close IVY CONGRAT.
    b. Close IVY STUDENT. A warning dialog box is displayed. Select **Don't Save** to close the file without saving changes.

11.10 Copying Data Between the Database and Spreadsheet

What If? questions can be performed on the data in a database by copying the records into a spreadsheet model. In addition, spreadsheet data can be copied into a database so that reports can be generated.

To copy data between an open spreadsheet and an open database, four steps are required:

1. Highlight the data to be copied.
2. Execute the Copy command.
3. Make the receiving document active.
4. Place the cursor where the data is to appear and execute the Paste command.

When records are copied from a database into a spreadsheet, each record is placed in a row and each column corresponds to a field. This means that entries in the first field are placed in the first column, the entries in the second field in the second column, and so on.

When cells are copied from a spreadsheet into a database, the data in the first column of cells is copied to the first field, the second column to the second field, and so on. However, formulas are not copied—only the values of each cell.

11.11 Copying Data into a New File

So far, we have used the Copy command to copy data into a previously created file. Copy can also be used to transfer data to a new file. When this is desired, the new file is created and then the Clipboard contents pasted into it. For example, to create a new spreadsheet from a database file, four steps are required:

1. Highlight the records to be copied.
2. Execute the Copy command.
3. Execute the New command to create a new, empty spreadsheet.
4. Place the cursor where the data is to be inserted and execute the Paste command.

A new database can be created from a spreadsheet in a similar manner. However, the new database must have fields of the appropriate types for each column of data copied.

Practice 7

In this Practice you will create a new spreadsheet named Books using the information from the IVY BOOKSTORE database. Start ClarisWorks if you have not already done so.

1) PREPARE THE WINDOWS

   a. Close any open files.
   b. Open IVY BOOKSTORE. Display Layout 1 in Browse view.

2) COPY THE RECORDS TO THE CLIPBOARD

   a. We want to copy all of the records into the new spreadsheet, so highlight all the records in the database.
   b. From the Edit menu, select Copy.

3) PASTE THE RECORDS INTO THE NEW SPREADSHEET

    a. From the File menu, select New.

    b. Double-click on the **Spreadsheet** option. A new, empty spreadsheet is shown on the screen.

    c. Select cell A2. From the Edit menu, select Paste. The records from IVY BOOKSTORE are copied starting at the current cursor position, each field in a separate column.

4) FORMAT THE NEW SPREADSHEET

    a. Widen column A until all data is completely visible.

    b. Add appropriate titles for each of the columns storing data. Bold the titles and format the titles in columns C and D as right aligned.

    c. Format the prices in column D as currency.

5) COMPUTE THE AVERAGE PRICE OF THE ITEMS

    a. Select cell C28.

    b. Enter the label: `Average Price:`

    c. Select cell D28.

    d. Enter the formula `=AVERAGE(D2..D26)` to determine the average price of the merchandise.

    e. Format cell D28 for currency displayed to 2 decimal places.

6) SAVE AND PRINT THE SPREADSHEET

    Save the new spreadsheet naming it Books and print a copy.

11.12 Copying a Chart into a Word Processor Document

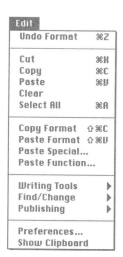

Businesses sometimes include charts of data in letters and memos. ClarisWorks allows you to paste spreadsheet charts into a word processor document.

To copy a chart from an open spreadsheet into an open word processor document, four steps are required:

1. Select the chart to be copied.
2. Execute the Copy command.
3. Make the word processor document active.
4. Place the cursor where the chart is to be inserted and execute the Paste command.

Clicking on the inserted chart selects it and displays a handle, which can then be dragged to resize the chart. Paragraph alignment, indents, tabs, and tab stops can be used to position the chart in a document.

An Introduction to Computing Using ClarisWorks

Practice 8

In this Practice you will insert a chart into a word processor document. Start ClarisWorks if you have not already done so.

1) PREPARE THE WINDOWS

    a. Close any open files.
    b. Open IVY REPORT.
    c. Open IVY ENROLLMENT.
    d. Scroll the spreadsheet so that the line chart is displayed.

2) COPY THE CHART TO THE CLIPBOARD

    a. Click on the line chart to select it. Handles are displayed.
    b. From the Edit menu, select Copy.
    c. Close IVY ENROLLMENT.

3) PASTE THE CHART INTO THE LETTER

    a. Place the cursor in the second blank line after the paragraph that begins "Proof of our continuing…."
    b. From the Edit menu, select Paste. The chart is placed at the cursor position.

4) CENTER THE CHART

    a. The cursor should be just to the right of the chart, in the same paragraph as the chart.
    b. In the Format bar, click on the Center alignment control. The chart is centered.

5) RESIZE THE CHART

    a. Place the I-Beam pointer on the chart and click once. The chart is selected as indicated by the handle in the lower-right corner.
    b. Drag the handle in the lower-right corner of the chart up and to the left until the chart size is reduced slightly.

6) SAVE AND THEN PRINT IVY REPORT

11.13 Mail Merge

One of the most powerful applications provided by an integrated package is the ability to use *mail merge* to create personalized form letters. For example, businesses sometimes send letters or advertisements in the mail that include the recipient's name throughout the letter. This is an example of a mail merged form letter.

Mail merge takes advantage of the computer's ability to integrate the information stored in a database with a word processor letter, and print the result. To create such a letter, the letter is first typed into the word processor with special markers where field data should be inserted. Any data stored in the database can be included in the letter. When complete, executing the appropriate command prints one copy of the letter for each record in the database, printing the indicated field's data from that record in the letter.

The position of merged data in a letter is specified by inserting *field markers* into the document. Executing the Mail Merge command from the File menu (⇧⌘M) displays a dialog box with a list of database files:

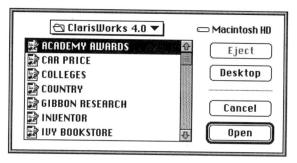

Database files are displayed in this dialog box

Scrolling through the list, highlighting IVY STUDENT, and then selecting **Open** opens the database and then displays the word processor document with the Mail Merge palette:

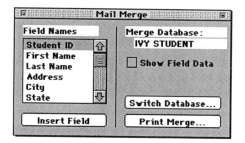

Fields for the selected database are displayed in this palette

The **Field Names** list displays the fields for the selected database. Highlighting a field name and clicking the **Insert Field** button places a marker for that field in the word processor document at the current cursor position. The field marker can then be formatted in the word processor document just like any other text.

Clicking the **Print Merge** button on the Mail Merge palette displays the Print dialog box. Selecting **Print** prints the actual information from the database in place of the markers. To print a document that shows the markers instead of data, select the Print command from the File menu. This can be useful for reviewing the document before printing the mail merged letters.

To mail merge a letter, four steps are required:

1. Open or create the word processor document.
2. Execute the Mail Merge command and select the desired database to open the file and display the Mail Merge palette.
3. Add field markers to the letter using the Mail Merge palette.
4. Select the **Print Merge** button from the Mail Merge palette to print the merged documents.

When **Print Merge** is selected, ClarisWorks generates and prints a personalized copy of the word processor document for each visible record in the database. If there are 50 records in the database, 50 personalized documents will be printed. Since ClarisWorks merges data only from visible records, queries or reports can be used to limit the number of letters printed. For example, Ivy University could print mail merge letters for only those students with unpaid tuition.

Practice 9

In this Practice you will modify and print a mail merged letter. Although this letter will contain data from only two fields, it is possible to create a mail merged document that contains data from any field in the open database. Start ClarisWorks if you have not already done so.

1) PREPARE THE WINDOWS

    a. Close any open files.
    b. Open the IVY TUITION letter.

2) OPEN STUDENT AND DISPLAY THE MAIL MERGE PALETTE

    a. From the File menu, select Mail Merge. The dialog box is displayed.
    b. Select Student from the list, then select **Open** to open the Student database and display the Mail Merge palette.
    c. Drag the palette's title bar to move it. Place the palette so that it obscures as little text as possible.

3) INSERT THE FIELDS INTO THE LETTER

    a. Place the cursor after the r in "Dear" and type a space.
    b. On the Mail Merge palette, highlight First Name in the **Field Names** list if it is not already highlighted. Click on the **Insert Field** button. A marker for the First Name field is inserted into the document.
    c. Type a space. Highlight Last Name in the list and then click on **Insert Field**. The Last Name marker is inserted into the document.
    d. Type a colon (:).

Check - The First Name and Last Name markers should be inserted into the letter so that the line appears on the screen as:

Dear·«First·Name»·«Last·Name»:↵
↵

4) PRINT PLAIN AND MERGED COPIES OF THE TUITION LETTER

    a. Save the modified letter on disk.
    b. From the File menu, select Print. Select **Print** to print a plain (non mail-merged) copy of the letter. Note the position of the field markers in the text. Only one copy of the letter is printed and the word processor screen is again displayed.
    c. On the Mail Merge palette, click on the **Print Merge** button to display the Print dialog box.
    d. Select **Print** to print a personalized copy of the letter for each record in the database. In the printed copies, the markers have been replaced by the different names from the database.
    e. Close the Mail Merge palette by clicking on its Close box.

In the previous Practice you created and printed a simple mail merge document. While this document contained the data from only two fields, it is important to realize that any field from the open database may be included in a mail merge. In addition, it is possible to reuse fields. For example, the recipient's first name could appear in the mail merged letter twice; once in the address and once in the greeting. Also, data from fields may be printed inside other text. That is, a field marker may be inserted inside a sentence and ClarisWorks will adjust any text following the marker to make room for the merged data.

Another powerful mail merge technique involves using queries or reports to limit the number of mail merged documents produced. It is not usually the case that a mail merge document will be printed for every record in a database. Normally a query will first be used to limit the number of records displayed. When **Print Merge** is then selected, documents are produced for only those records which meet the query's criteria.

Practice 10

In this Practice you will modify and print a more complex mail merged letter. A query will be used to limit the number of letters printed.

1) PREPARE THE WINDOWS

    a. Close all open files.
    b. Open the IVY GPA letter.

2) INSERT TWO FIELD MARKERS INTO THE LETTER

    a. From the File menu, execute the Mail Merge command. Select the IVY STUDENT database, then select **Open** to open the database and display the Mail Merge palette.
    b. Place the cursor on the second blank line below the date.
    c. On the Mail Merge palette, double-click on First Name in the **Field Names** list. A marker is inserted into the letter.
    d. Type a space. On the Mail Merge palette, double-click on Last Name in the **Field Names** list. A marker is inserted into the letter.

3) INSERT THE NEXT FIELDS INTO THE LETTER

    a. Move the cursor to the line below the First and Last Name markers.
    b. Insert an Address field marker.
    c. Move the cursor to the line below the Address marker and insert a City field marker.
    d. Type a comma (,) followed by a space and then insert a State field marker.
    e. Type a space and then insert a Zip field marker.
    f. Place the cursor after the r in "Dear" and type a space.
    g. Insert a First Name field marker and type a colon (:).

4) INSERT A GPA FIELD MARKER INTO THE LETTER

a. Move the cursor into the middle of the letter, between the two spaces after "Your GPA of...."

b. Insert a GPA field marker.

Check - Your letter should be similar to:

```
1/11/97↵
↵
«First·Name»·«Last·Name»↵
«Address»↵
«City»,·«State»·«Zip»↵
↵
Dear·«First·Name»:↵
↵
It·is·with·the·greatest·pleasure·that·I·inform·you·of·your·selection·as·an·
Ivy·Scholar.·Your·GPA·of·«GPA»·makes·you·an·academic·winner·eligible·for·
a·tuition·reduction·next·term.↵
↵
Do·not·consider·transferring·to·another·college.·We·need·you·here·at·old·
Ivy!↵
↵
↵
Yours·truly,↵
↵
↵
Steven·C.·Munger↵
Assistant·Dean↵
```

5) APPLY A QUERY TO THE DATABASE

a. From the View menu, select the IVY STUDENT database.

b. Note the Mail Merge palette is still visible. Like any palette, it may be rolled-up to use less space. Click on the Mail Merge palette's Roll-up box in the upper-right corner to display its Title bar in the upper-right corner of the screen.

c. From the Layout menu, use the Find command to display only those student records with a GPA of 4.0.

6) PRINT PLAIN AND MERGED COPIES OF THE TUITION LETTER

a. From the View menu, select IVY GPA.

b. Save IVY GPA.

c. Print a plain (non mail-merged) copy of the letter using the Print command from the File menu. Note the position and number of the field markers.

d. On the Mail Merge title bar, click the Roll-up box to again display the palette.

e. On the Mail Merge palette, click on **Print Merge** to display the Print dialog box. Select **Print** to print a personalized copy of the letter for only the records which meet the query's criteria (GPA of 4.0).

11.15 Compound Documents

A *compound document* is a powerful form of integration in which a single document contains more than one application. For example, a spreadsheet can exist as part of a word processor document. It is also possible to have a word processor document in a spreadsheet or database like the following:

	A	B	C	D	E	F
8	H. Crane	66	76	78	55	68.8
9	M. Lui	85	74	83	66	77.0
10						
11	**Test Average**	68.33	83.17	77.17	77.67	
12						
13			⋆→ Final·grades·**must**·be·turned·in·by·January·6th↵			
14			⋆→ Students·eligible·for·honors·are·to·be·notified·by·			
15			January·4th↵			
16			⋆→ Those·students·who·are·failing·are·also·to·be·			
17			notified·by·January·4th↵			
18						

The word processor was used to add text to a spreadsheet

The word processor portion of the document above is called a text *frame*. Previously we have seen how text or data can be copied from one type of document and pasted into another. Once pasted, the data has the same properties as the other data in the document. For example, data copied from a spreadsheet and pasted into a word processor document is no longer numeric data. The numbers are now simply text characters and can no longer be used in calculations. However, by using frames the data may be added to a document without changing its type. In the spreadsheet above, the text frame displays text with hanging indents and superscripted text. This kind of formatting is not possible in a spreadsheet document.

When the cursor is placed in the text frame, the word processor screen's Menu bar is displayed. When the cell cursor is in the spreadsheet document, the spreadsheet screen's Menu bar and Entry bar are available. In this way, text may be entered and formatted using all the features of the word processor while data in the spreadsheet retains its properties. When a compound document is saved, its frames and the data they contain are stored with the document.

11.16 Using Application Tools

A compound document can contain multiple text, spreadsheet, and paint frames. The Tool panel contains the tools needed to create an application frame and is displayed by selecting the Show Tools command from the View menu (⇧⌘T). Clicking the Show Tools button in the lower-left corner of the screen (▣) also displays the Tool panel:

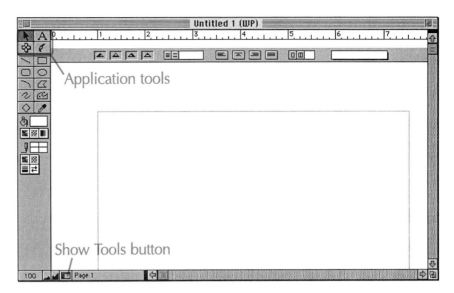

Application tools are used to create frames

The Spreadsheet tool, which is used to create a spreadsheet frame, is selected by clicking on it in the Tool panel. Moving the pointer to the Work area of the displayed document and then dragging creates the spreadsheet frame, as shown below:

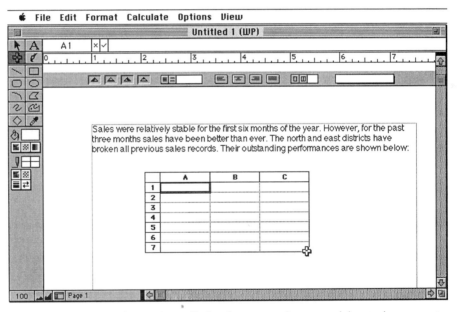

A spreadsheet frame has all the features of a spreadsheet document

The spreadsheet Entry bar and Menu bar displayed in the file above indicate that the spreadsheet frame is currently active. Data may be entered or copied into the spreadsheet frame the same as in any spreadsheet document. All the spreadsheet functions and formatting options are also available in a spreadsheet frame.

A frame can be made *active* by selecting the corresponding application tool and then clicking the mouse pointer in the frame. When a frame is active, the cursor is displayed in the frame and the appropriate Menu bar shown. For example, to move the cursor from the Work area of a word processor document to a spreadsheet frame, select the Spreadsheet tool and then click on the spreadsheet frame. The cell cursor is displayed in the frame and the spreadsheet Menu bar and Entry bar are available. Selecting the Text tool and clicking in the word processor Work area moves the cursor back to the word processor document and displays its Menu bar. The cursor may also be moved between a frame and the document that contains it by simply double-clicking the mouse pointer in the desired area.

The Pointer tool from the Tool panel can be used to *select* an existing frame. When selected, a frame displays handles that can be dragged to resize it:

11	Test Average	68.33	83.17	77.17	77.67		
12							
13			Final grades **must** be turned in by January 6th↵				
14			Students eligible for honors are to be notified by				
15			January 4th↵				
16			Those students who are failing are also to be				
17			notified by January 4th↵				
18							
19							

When a handle is dragged, a dashed line is displayed to indicate the frame size

Resizing a text frame allows more or less text to be displayed. When a spreadsheet frame is resized, the number of cells displayed changes.

Dragging on the frame (not on a handle) moves it. Pressing the Delete key or executing the Cut command from the Edit menu removes the selected frame and it contents from the document.

Practice 11

In this Practice you will modify a letter to include a spreadsheet frame.

1) PREPARE THE WINDOWS

    a. Close all open files.
    b. Open the IVY DIVERSITY word processor file. This letter will go to Ivy U students to inform them of the diverse student body.

2) CREATE A SPREADSHEET FRAME

    a. Scroll until the blank space between the second and third paragraphs is visible.
    b. Click on the Show Tools button in the lower-left corner of the screen (▣) to display the Tool panel. Note the application tools at the top of the panel.
    c. Click on the Spreadsheet tool to select it (▦).
    d. Move the mouse pointer onto the Work area of the word processor document. The pointer changes to the plus sign shape of the spreadsheet pointer.

e. Place the pointer in the blank part of the document below the second paragraph. Drag the pointer down and to the right. Releasing the mouse button creates a spreadsheet frame. The Menu bar changes and an Entry bar is displayed.

Check: Your screen should look similar to:

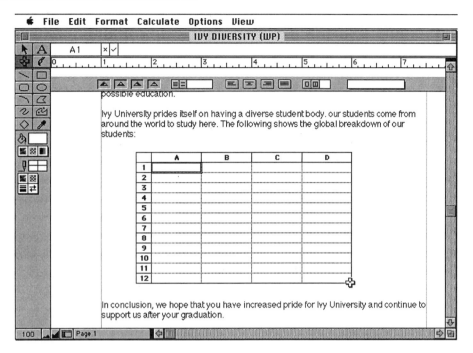

3) CHANGE THE FRAME SIZE AND MOVE IT

a. In the Tool panel, click on the Pointer tool.

b. Click on the spreadsheet frame. Handles are displayed indicating that it is selected.

c. Drag the lower-right corner of the spreadsheet to resize it. Continue resizing the frame until only columns A and B and rows 1 through 9 are visible.

d. Drag the frame (do not drag on a handle) so that it is on the left side of the page, below the second paragraph, similar to the following:

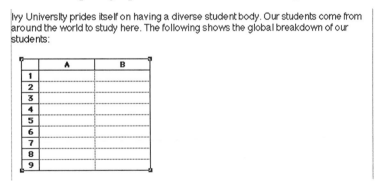

4) ENTER DATA INTO THE SPREADSHEET FRAME

a. Select the Spreadsheet tool and click on the spreadsheet frame to make it active. Note that the menus at the top of the screen have changed to the spreadsheet application menus and the Entry bar is displayed.

b. Enter the data shown below into the spreadsheet. Format the titles as bold, right align the `Students` label, and format the numbers as **Fixed** with **Commas** and 0 as the **Precision**:

	A	B
1	**Area**	**Students**
2	Africa	213
3	Asia	471
4	Europe	689
5	North America	3,503
6	South America	576
7	Other	49
8		
9		

c. Select cell B9. Enter the formula `=SUM(B2..B7)` to determine the total number of students. Format the cell as fixed with commas and 0 precision.
d. In cell A9, enter the label `Total:` and make it right-aligned and bold.
e. Select cell B2. Enter `100`. Note how the sum in cell B9 changes to reflect the new value in cell B2. If this data were not stored in a spreadsheet frame, it would not be possible to manipulate it this way.
f. Change the value in cell B2 to `213`. The sum in cell B9 reflects the change.

5) ***SAVE IVY DIVERSITY AND PRINT A COPY OF IT***

a. Save IVY DIVERSITY.
b. From the File menu, select Print. Select **Print** to print a copy of the document. Note the spreadsheet frame printed in the word processor document.

11.18 Creating Charts in a Compound Document

In Section 11.12 we learned how to copy a chart from a spreadsheet to a word processor document. The copied chart will not change to reflect new data in the spreadsheet. However, a chart *created* in a word processor document from a spreadsheet frame is linked to its data. When a value in the spreadsheet frame changes, the chart is updated as well.

Charts are created from data in a spreadsheet frame in the same way they are created in a regular spreadsheet document. However, after the chart has been created, it is automatically placed in the document, not in the spreadsheet frame.

A chart created from a spreadsheet frame may be selected by clicking on it. When selected, the chart displays handles that are used for resizing it. A selected chart may also be dragged to a different position in the document or deleted by pressing the delete key or using the Cut command.

Practice 12

In this Practice, you will create a chart from a spreadsheet frame. Mail merge will be used to print form letters from the modified letter. Start ClarisWorks and open IVY DIVERSITY if it is not already displayed.

1) CREATE A PIE CHART

   a. In the Tool panel, click on the Spreadsheet tool if it is not already selected.

   b. Place the pointer on cell A1 in the spreadsheet frame and click the mouse. Cell A1 is selected.

   c. From the Options menu, select the Make Chart command. The Chart Options dialog box is displayed.

   d. In the **Gallery**, select **Pie**.

   e. Click on **General**. Type A2..B7 as the **Chart range**.

   f. Click on **Labels**. Type Ivy Student Diversity in the **Title** box.

   g. Select **OK** to display the chart. Note the handles indicating the chart is selected.

2) RESIZE AND MOVE THE CHART

   a. Drag one of the chart handles inward to reduce the chart size.

   b. Drag the chart to move it (do not drag on a handle). Place it to the right of the spreadsheet frame. Continue to move and resize the chart until the letter appears similar to the following:

Ivy University prides itself on having a diverse student body. Our students come from around the world to study here. The following shows the global breakdown of our students:

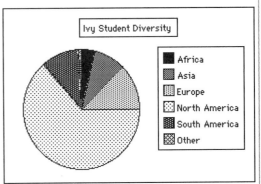

	A	B
1	**Area**	**Students**
2	Africa	213
3	Asia	471
4	Europe	689
5	North America	3,503
6	South America	576
7	Other	49
8		
9	**Total:**	5,501

In conclusion, we hope that you have increased pride for Ivy University and continue to support us after your graduation.

3) MODIFY THE SPREADSHEET FRAME

   a. Double-click on cell B5 to select it.

   b. Enter 975 as the new number of students. The chart changes to correspond to the spreadsheet data.

4) SAVE IVY DIVERSITY AND PRINT A COPY

5) CLOSE IVY DIVERSITY AND EXIT CLARISWORKS

Chapter Summary

This chapter presented the commands necessary to copy data between the applications. The ability to copy data between applications is one of the primary reasons for using an integrated package such as ClarisWorks.

In ClarisWorks, more than one file can be open at the same time, each in its own window. This can include any combination of word processor, database, and spreadsheet files. An open file can be made active by selecting the filename from the View menu. When work has been completed on a file, it can be saved and closed using the Save and Close commands.

Multiple windows can be displayed at one time using the Adjust box to resize them. The window can be repositioned by dragging on its Title bar. The Zoom box can be used to expand a window to full-screen size.

To transfer data between two open files, four basic steps are required:

1. Select the data to be copied.
2. Execute the Copy command.
3. Make the receiving file active.
4. Place the cursor where the data is to be inserted and execute the Paste command.

This chapter explained how data can be copied between:

- two word processor documents (Section 11.5)

- two spreadsheets (Section 11.6)

- two databases (Section 11.7)

- a spreadsheet and word processor document (Section 11.8 and Section 11.12)

- a database and word processor document (Section 11.9)

- a database and spreadsheet (Section 11.10)

- an open file and a new file (Section 11.11)

- a database and word processor document for mail merge (Sections 11.13 and 11.14)

One of the most powerful abilities of an integrated package is producing mail merge documents. In mail merge, a word processor document and database are both opened. The Mail Merge palette is used to place markers in the document identifying where data from the database fields is to be inserted. When the document is printed, the markers are automatically replaced with information from the database, creating a different copy of the document for each visible record. In this way, the computer can produce personalized form letters. Queries and reports can be used to limit the number of visible records, which affects the number of mail merged documents printed.

A compound document contains more than one application. For example, a word processor document can contain a spreadsheet. An application within a compound document is displayed in a frame created with an application tool. Application tools are displayed by selecting the Show Tools command from the View menu. A frame can be selected using the Pointer tool. Once selected, frames can be moved, resized, and deleted. A frame's corresponding application tool is used to make it active.

A chart created from data in a spreadsheet frame is displayed in the document, not in the frame. Changing a value in a spreadsheet frame updates any corresponding charts.

Vocabulary

Active file - The file currently being worked on.

Active frame - The frame currently containing the cursor.

Application tools - The four tools at the top of the Tool panel. The Text, Spreadsheet, and Paint tools are used to create frames. The Pointer tool is used to select an existing frame.

Compound document - A form of integration in which a document contains more than one application. See also frame.

Field marker - Used for a mail merge document, they are placed in a word processor document to refer to a field in a specified database.

Frame - An application area in a document created using application tools from the Tool panel. See also compound document.

Integrated - A software package that contains different applications. Because ClarisWorks is integrated, data can be copied between its three applications areas.

Mail merge - Using the contents of a database file and a word processor document to have the computer produce personalized form letters.

Selected frame - Frame with handles displayed. The Pointer tool is used to select a frame.

Window - An area on the screen where an open file is displayed.

Reviews

Sections 11.1 — 11.7

1. a) What is meant by an integrated software package?
    b) What are two advantages of using such a package?

2. What is the purpose of having more than one file open at the same time?

3. a) What is a window?
    b) What steps are required to switch from one window to another window?

4. What is meant by the "active" file when using windows?

5. Give two examples of when you might want to switch between windows. Explain what files would be stored in the different windows.

6. Why should files be closed after you are finished working with them?

7. Explain how three windows can be displayed simultaneously.

8. The word processor file IVY NEWS contains a paragraph that describes the inauguration of Ivy University's new president. Explain the steps required to copy this paragraph into a word processor file named ALUMNI that contains a letter to be sent to all Ivy alumni.

9. List the steps required to copy two columns from a spreadsheet named OWED and insert them between two existing columns in a spreadsheet named ASSETS.

10. Fantasy Cars has just bought out Luxury Autos and wants to add the records from Luxury Autos' inventory database into their own database. List the steps required to do this.

Sections 11.8 — 11.14

11. Give three examples of when you might want to copy part of a spreadsheet into a word processor document.

12. List the steps required to copy part of a spreadsheet to a word processor document.

13. List the steps required to copy the records of a database to a word processor document.

14. Give three examples of where you might want to copy information from a database into a spreadsheet. For each example explain what the spreadsheet would be used for.

15. List the steps required to copy a spreadsheet chart into a document.

16. What does "mail merge" mean?

17. a) Explain the steps required to mail merge the names and addresses of customers from Fantasy Cars' customer database into a letter sent to each customer.
    b) What additional steps would be required to send the letters to only customers living in Boca Raton, Florida?

18. When printing a mail merge letter, what is printed if the Print command from the File menu is used?

Sections 11.15 — 11.18

19. a) What is a compound document?
    b) Give two examples of what a compound document is used for.

20. How is a spreadsheet frame created?

21. a) How can a text frame be made active?
    b) How is a text frame selected?
    c) Explain how a text frame is resized and moved.

22. Explain how a chart is produced from the data in a spreadsheet frame.

11 Exercises

1. Ivy University must raise next semester's tuition in order to cover its increasing labor costs.

   a) Create a letter using the word processor which notifies students of the upcoming tuition increase. The letter should be similar to the following:

   > Dear Student:
   >
   > We are sorry to inform you that due to rising costs we are forced to raise your tuition by $1,000. This increase is effective next semester.
   >
   > Sincerely,
   >
   > The Administration

   b) Save the letter naming it Increase.

   c) The administration has decided that students might take the news of a tuition increase better if it came in a personalized letter. Using the IVY STUDENT database, modify the Increase letter to mail merge the students' first name in place of the word "Student."

   d) Save the modified Increase. Print mail merged letters for all students from Texas (TX).

   e) In order to keep its better students from transferring to less expensive schools, the Ivy administration has decided that the tuition increase should be on a sliding scale based on the student's GPA. Every student's tuition will increase by $500, and an additional $100 will be charged for each tenth of a GPA point below 4.0:

GPA	Increase
4.0	$500.00
3.9	$600.00
3.8	$700.00
	...
0.1	$4,400.00
0.0	$4,500.00

   Modify the IVY STUDENT database to contain a calculation field named `Increase` that displays the amount of the tuition increase. Add the new field to the Student GPAs layout and format it to display dollar values.

   f) Modify the Increase letter to merge the actual tuition increase in place of the "$1,000."

   g) Save the modified Increase and IVY STUDENT. Using the new Increase, print mail merged letters for all students with last names beginning with K.

2. The Fantasy Wheels preowned car company would like to transfer their inventory database Wheels into a spreadsheet so that they can perform "What If?" questions with the data. This database was created in Chapter Five, Exercise 10.

a) Create a new spreadsheet that contains the year, make, amount paid, and asking price for each car copied from the Wheels database. Format the spreadsheet, adding titles and labels where necessary. Save the spreadsheet naming it What If.

b) Add two columns to the spreadsheet. Have the first new column calculate a new asking price which is a 10% increase of the current asking price. The second new column should display the additional profit gained by selling the cars at these new prices. Save the modified What If spreadsheet.

c) Acting as Fantasy's sales manager, use the word processor to write a letter to the owner of Fantasy Wheels describing your plan to raise prices. Save the letter naming it New Price.

d) Place a copy of the What If spreadsheet data into the New Price letter. Save the modified New Price and print a copy.

3. In Chapter Eight, Exercise 6 Mr. Horatio von Money used a spreadsheet named STOCKS to calculate his donation to Ivy University. Copy the spreadsheet data into a new word processor letter informing the IU Board of Trustees of the donation. Save the letter naming it New Donations and print a copy.

4. Use the IVY STUDENT database to display the students who have not yet paid their tuition bills and have a GPA less than 1.5. Create a new mail merge letter warning them to pay the bill or face expulsion from Ivy U. Save the letter naming it Expel and print a merged copy of the letter for each student.

5. Your friend Jill is searching for a new car and has written to you for information.

a) Using the CAR PRICE database, display all cars with air conditioning that cost less than $9,000. Copy those records into a new spreadsheet. Include proper labels and formatting in the spreadsheet. Save the spreadsheet naming it Cars For Jill.

b) Create a letter informing Jill of her choices. Include the Cars For Jill spreadsheet data in the letter. Save the letter naming it Letter To Jill and print a copy.

6. You have been asked to gather some statistics about car prices for your economics class.

a) Create a new spreadsheet that contains all of the data about new car prices from the CAR PRICE database. Use proper labels and formatting. Save the spreadsheet naming it Prices.

b) Modify the Prices spreadsheet to calculate each of the following:
    • average base price of a new car
    • average price for a new car with air
    • average price for a new car with stereo
    • average price for a new car with sunroof
    • maximum base price of a new car
    • minimum price of a new car with air

c) Using the word processor, create a report detailing your findings for the class. Include the actual calculated figures from Prices in the report. Save the report naming it Car Stats and print a copy.

7. Use the word processor to create the following memo:

> Memo to: Steve Munger, Asst. Dean
> From: Bob Doucette, Dean
>
> Steve:
>
> The following students have received Dean's List status:
>
> Please update their records. Thank you.

Copy the table of Dean's List students from the IVY CONGRAT letter modified in Practice 6 into this memo. Save the file naming it Dean List Memo and print a copy.

8. You have moved. Using the Address database created in Chapter Five, Exercise 1, prepare a personalized mail merged letter to each of your friends which gives your new address. Save the letter naming it New Address and print merged copies. An example is shown below:

> Amy Eppelman
> 713 Graisbury Avenue
> Haddonfield, NJ 08033
>
> Dear Amy:
>
> This is just a short note to let you know I have a new address:
>
> 1389 Southwest Drive
> Atlantic, FL 33800
>
> Of course, we'll still get together on your birthday. Call me at (213) 555-1324.
>
> See you soon,
>
> A. Friend

9. In Practice 7 you created a spreadsheet named Books by transferring records from the Ivy Bookstore database file. Open Books and make the following changes to it:

a) In column E create a formula that displays the value of the items in stock for each item (price per item multiplied by the number of items in stock). Title the column appropriately, and format the title.

b) At the bottom of column E calculate and display the average value of all items available.

c) Format column E to display dollar values with commas.

d) Save the modified Books spreadsheet and print a copy.

10. Ivy Bookstore has decided to have a sale on every item in the Clothing department.

   a) Using the word processor, create a new letter that notifies students of the upcoming sale. The letter should be similar to the following:

   > Dear Student:
   >
   > Ivy Bookstore is pleased to announce its annual year-end clearance sale. Next Friday and Saturday, come to the Ivy Bookstore for unbelievable savings on everything in our Clothing department:

   b) Save the letter naming it Clothing Sale.

   c) Create a spreadsheet frame below the text in the letter. Size the frame so that it contains seven rows and four columns. Center the frame below the text.

   d) Open IVY BOOKSTORE and display Layout 1. Copy all those records from the Clothing department to the spreadsheet frame in Clothing Sale.

   e) It is not necessary to display the department names or number of items in stock. Delete columns B and C of the spreadsheet frame.

   f) Widen column A so that the item names are shown entirely, and format the values in column B as currency. Insert a row at the top of the spreadsheet and enter appropriate names for each of the columns. Format the titles.

   g) All those items priced higher than $30 are on sale at 20% off, otherwise the sale price is 10% off. In column C, enter formulas to compute the sale price for each of the items. Title the column appropriately.

   h) Resize the spreadsheet frame so that column D is not displayed. Save and then print a copy of the letter.

   i) Using the Student database, modify the Clothing Sale letter to mail merge the student's first name in place of the word "Student." Save the modified Clothing Sale and print the mail merged letters.

Chapter 12
An Introduction to Desktop Publishing

Show Rulers

Select All

Align Objects

Object Info

Cut, Copy, Paste, Show Clipboard, Undo

Print

Page View

Move To Front

Move To Back

Frame Links

Show Tools

Objectives

After completing this chapter you will be able to:

1. Explain what desktop publishing is.

2. Create objects in a Draw document and images in a Paint document.

3. Describe the differences between objects and images.

4. Describe and use the Draw tools and Paint tools.

5. Use the Fill and Line palettes to modify objects and images.

6. Rotate objects in a draw document.

7. Create and use linked text frames in a draw document.

8. Use graphics to enhance word processor, database, and spreadsheet documents.

12

ClarisWorks' desktop publishing capabilities allow you to manipulate text and graphics using the draw and paint applications. This chapter presents these two applications and how they can be employed to create professional-looking documents.

12.1 What is Desktop Publishing?

Combining text and graphics into one document is called *desktop publishing*. With desktop publishing you can create advertisements, brochures, invitations, newsletters—you are limited only by your imagination. Desktop publishing can easily be done in ClarisWorks using the drawing application. In a *draw document* you can create graphics and add text.

12.2 The Draw Document

A new draw document is created by selecting the **Drawing** option in the New Document dialog box and then selecting **OK**. A blank draw document is displayed, as indicated by (DR) after the filename in the title bar:

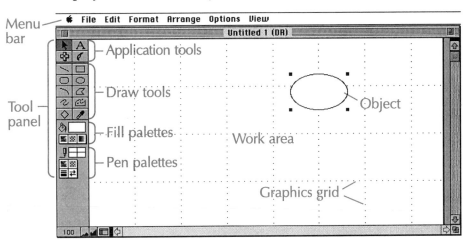

A ClarisWorks draw document

The *graphics grid* is composed of dotted lines in the Work area that can be used to position objects in the document. The grid does not appear on the document when printed. The Tool panel consists of four sections: Application tools, Draw tools, Fill palettes, and Pen palettes. The Pointer is the default tool as indicated by the highlighted button in the Applications tools section. The Draw tools are used to produce *objects* such as ovals, rectangles, lines, and polygons. Each object is a separate element that can be selected, moved, resized, copied, and deleted from a draw document. The Fill and Pen palettes are used to change the appearance of objects.

As with other ClarisWorks applications, the scroll bars are used to view different portions of the page.

12.3 The Draw Tools

The Draw tools are used to create different objects. In a draw document, the Draw tools are displayed in the Tool panel below the Application tools:

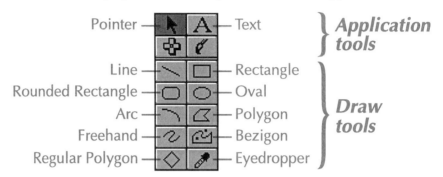

Application Tools

Draw Tools

- **Pointer** - select, move, and resize objects.
- **Text** - add text to a drawing.

- **Line** - draw lines at different angles.
- **Rectangle** - draw rectangles and squares.
- **Rounded Rectangle** - draw rectangles with rounded corners.
- **Oval** - draw ovals and circles.
- **Arc** - draw segments of an oval.
- **Polygon** - draw open and closed polygons.
- **Freehand** - draw irregular lines.
- **Bezigon** - draw shapes with smooth curves.
- **Regular Polygon** - draw closed polygons with a specified number of sides.
- **Eyedropper** - set pen and fill attributes quickly.

Most of the Draw tools are used in the following manner:

1. Select the desired graphics tool by clicking on it in the Tool panel. The pointer changes to cross-hairs.
2. Place the cross-hairs at the starting position for the graphic.
3. Drag the cross-hairs to display an outline of the object as it is created.
4. Release the mouse button to place the object on the page.

The Polygon tool (⬚) is used to draw closed and open shapes:

A closed and an open shape

Unlike most of the other tools, the Polygon tool is not used by dragging the pointer. To draw a polygon, first select the Polygon tool, then move the cross-hairs to where you want to start drawing and click once. Next, draw each side of the polygon by moving the cross-hairs to the location of the next corner and click once. Each time you click, a line will be drawn connecting that position with the last place you clicked. The last side that closes the shape completes the object. An open shape is created in the same manner, except the mouse is double-clicked when the object is completed.

When creating graphics, holding down the Shift key acts to constrain the drawing to a "perfect" shape. For example, holding down the Shift key while creating a rectangle forces the rectangle to be a square, and holding the Shift key when creating an oval draws a circle. Holding the Shift key when using either the Line or Polygon tool constrains lines to 45 degree angles only. When using the Shift key it is important to release the mouse button first to ensure that the shape drawn remains "perfect."

As with other ClarisWorks applications, the last drawing action can be undone by executing the Undo command (⌘Z) from the Edit menu.

12.4 The Show Rulers Command

Executing the Show Rulers command from the View menu (⇧⌘U) displays horizontal and vertical Rulers that are used to align and measure objects. Dotted lines called *guidelines* appear on both Rulers and move with the mouse pointer to show its current position. In this example, the pointer is at the 1¾" horizontal, 2¼" vertical mark:

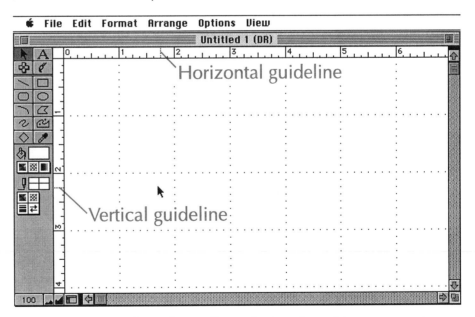

Guidelines on the Rulers indicate the location of the mouse pointer

The Rulers and Guidelines are useful when an object must be drawn to a specific size, and when the placement of the object needs to be precise.

In this Practice you will create objects of different shapes in a new draw document. A newsletter for Ivy University will be developed over the next few Practices.

1) CREATE A DRAW DOCUMENT AND DISPLAY THE RULERS

    a. Following the steps given in Chapter Two, boot the System and start ClarisWorks.

    b. From the New Document dialog box, select **Drawing** and then **OK**. A blank draw document is displayed.

    c. From the View menu, select the Show Rulers command. Locate the different parts of the screen: the Tool panel, Draw tools, graphics grid, Rulers, and guidelines.

2) SELECT THE RECTANGLE TOOL FROM THE TOOL PANEL

    a. In the Tool panel, click once on the Rectangle tool (▢).

    b. Move the pointer into the Work area. The pointer shape changes to cross-hairs and the guidelines in the Rulers move with the pointer, showing its position.

3) POSITION THE POINTER AND DRAW A RECTANGLE

    a. Using the guidelines on the Rulers, position the pointer at the ½" horizontal, ¼" vertical mark:

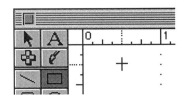

    b. Press and hold down the mouse button and then drag down and to the right. Note the outline of the rectangle and that the guidelines indicate the pointer's position.

    c. Using the guidelines, continue to drag the pointer to the 7" horizontal, 2" vertical mark and then release the mouse button. ClarisWorks places the rectangle on the draw document, and the pointer returns to the default arrow shape.

4) DRAW A TRIANGLE AND A CIRCLE

    a. Select the Polygon tool (◿) and position the pointer at the 1" horizontal, 3" vertical mark.

    b. Click once and then move (do not drag) the pointer to the 1½" horizontal, 4" vertical mark. Remember that when drawing a polygon, dragging is not necessary.

    c. Click once, move the pointer to the 2" horizontal, 3" vertical mark, and click again.

    d. Move the pointer back to the 1" horizontal, 3" vertical mark and click once to complete the triangle, a closed polygon.

    e. Select the Oval tool (⬭) and move the pointer to the 4" horizontal, 3" vertical mark.

    f. Hold down the Shift key and then drag the pointer to the 5" horizontal, 4" vertical mark. Release the mouse button and then the Shift key. ClarisWorks places a circle in the document.

5) DRAW TWO LINES

    a. Select the Line tool (◥) and move the pointer to the 3" horizontal, 3" vertical mark.

    b. Drag the pointer down and to the left and release the mouse button at the 2" horizontal, 5" vertical mark.

    c. Select the Line tool again and move the pointer to the 6" horizontal, 3" vertical mark.

d. Hold down the Shift key and then drag the pointer in a circular motion. Notice that the line moves only at 45 degree angles because the Shift key is being held down. When the pointer is at the 7" horizontal, 4" vertical mark, release the mouse button and then the Shift key.

<u>Check</u> - Your document should be similar to:

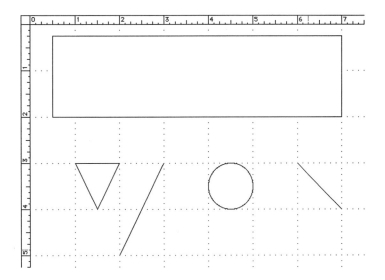

6) SAVE THE DRAW DOCUMENT

From the File menu, select the Save command. Type Fitness as the filename, then select **Save**.

12.5 Selecting Objects

An object must first be *selected* before any formatting or other commands are applied to it. To select an object, click the mouse pointer on it. When selected, an object is displayed with *handles* that indicate its size. A rectangular object has a handle at each corner while other objects, such as the oval and polygon, have handles that indicate their width and height:

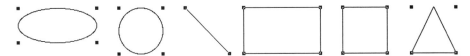

Handles are displayed when an object is selected

A currently selected object can be deselected by clicking once on any blank area of the document.

More than one object can be selected at a time by holding down the Shift key when clicking once on each of the objects. This allows multiple objects to be cut, moved, or formatted at the same time. When several objects are selected, it is possible to *deselect* one by holding down the Shift key and clicking on it.

Multiple objects can also be selected using *marquee selection*. Dragging the Pointer tool in the draw document creates a box that is visible until the mouse is released. Creating this box around several objects selects all of the objects that are completely surrounded by the marquee:

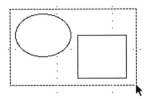

Releasing the mouse button selects all objects within the marquee

All of the objects in a draw document may be selected at the same time by executing the Select All command from the Edit menu (⌘**A**).

12.6 Positioning Objects in a Draw Document

A selected object can be moved by dragging. A lighter-colored outline of the object appears while it is being dragged; when the mouse button is released the object appears in its entirety:

Releasing the mouse button places the object in a new location

When moving an object, it is important not to drag one of the handles because this will change the object's shape. If a handle is dragged by mistake, immediately executing the Undo command (⌘**Z**) will return the object to its original size and shape.

A selected object may also be *nudged* to a new position by pressing an arrow key. Each time the arrow key is pressed, the object moves a fraction of an inch in the direction of the arrow.

Objects can be aligned with respect to other objects. To align several objects, first select them and then execute the Align Objects command from the Arrange menu (⇧⌘**K**). A dialog box is displayed:

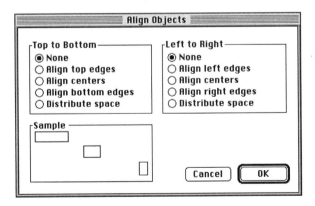

A group of selected objects can be aligned in various ways

Then, select the desired alignments from the **Top to Bottom** options and from the **Left to Right** options. As options are selected, a representation of aligned objects is displayed in the **Sample** area. When the desired alignment is chosen, select **OK** to apply the options to the selected objects.

An Introduction to Computing Using ClarisWorks

Several buttons on the Shortcuts palette can also be used to align a group of selected objects:

Align bottom edges

Align left edges

Align right edges

Align top edges

Align horizontal centers

Align vertical centers

12.7 Changing an Object's Shape

An object can be reshaped by first selecting it and then dragging one of its handles with the pointer tool. For example, a rectangle could be made wider by dragging a handle on its right side to the right:

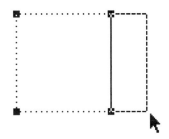

The dashed line indicates the new size of the object

This action is called *stretching*. Dragging handles in other directions can make the rectangle taller, shorter, or more narrow. Dragging a handle at an angle stretches both the height and width of an object at the same time:

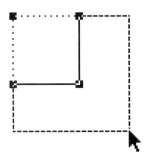

Objects can be stretched in both directions by dragging at an angle

12.8 Using the Info Palette

The size and position of a selected object can be changed with precision by using the *Info palette*. Executing the Object Info command from the Options menu displays the Info palette which shows the position of the object on the page, as well as its width and height:

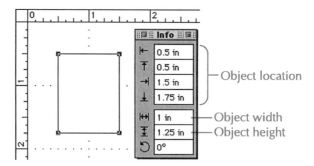

The Info palette displays all of the selected object's dimensions

The measurements in the palette above indicate that the left side of the rectangle runs along the horizontal 0.5 inch mark, the top edge along the vertical 0.5 inch mark, the right side along the horizontal 1.5 inch mark, and the bottom edge along the vertical 1.75 inch mark. The object's size is indicated as 1 inch wide and 1.25 inches tall. For non-rectangular shapes, ClarisWorks displays the outermost location of each side. In the example below, the leftmost part of this polygon is at the horizontal 0.5 inch mark:

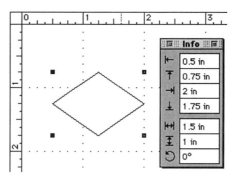

The Info palette displays the location of the outermost measurement for each side of a selected polygon

A selected object can be moved to an exact location or sized to exact dimensions by changing the values in the entry boxes of the Info palette. For example, to stretch the polygon above to a height of 2 inches, type 2 in the Object height box and press Return.

Practice 2

You will select, move, and resize some of the objects you created in the last Practice. Start ClarisWorks and open Fitness if you have not already done so.

1) SELECT A LINE AND MOVE IT

   a. If it is not already selected, place the mouse pointer over the line that has an endpoint at the 7" horizontal, 4" vertical mark and click. Handles appear on each end.

b. Press the right-arrow key. The selected object is "nudged" to the right.
c. Place the pointer on the middle of the line (away from the handles) and drag the line upwards. Note the outline showing the new position of the line.
d. When the top endpoint of the line is at the 6" horizontal, ¼" vertical mark, release the mouse button. The line is placed in the new location, inside the large rectangle.

2) SELECT AND STRETCH THE CIRCLE

a. Place the pointer over the circle and click. The circle is selected and handles are shown.
b. Place the pointer on the handle in the lower-right corner of the circle.
c. Drag straight to the right to the 6" horizontal mark and release the mouse button. The circle becomes longer, forming an oval.

3) RESIZE THE OVAL USING THE INFO PALETTE

a. From the Options menu, select the Object Info command to display the Info palette. Drag the palette's title bar and place the palette to the right of the oval.
b. Select the oval if it is not already selected. The Info palette indicates that the object is currently 2 inches wide and 1 inch tall.
c. We will change the oval back into a circle. Double-click on the 2 in the width box, highlighting it. Type 1, replacing the old value. Press the Return key and note how the shape of the oval changes to a circle.

4) MARQUEE SELECT OBJECTS AND ALIGN THEM

a. Place the pointer above and to the left of the triangle.
b. Hold down the mouse button and drag the pointer down, until it is below and to the right of the long line. Be sure that both the line and triangle are completely surrounded by the marquee.
c. Release the button. Both objects are selected.
d. From the Arrange menu, select the Align Objects command.
e. Select the **Align bottom edges** option. Note the appearance of the three objects in the **Sample** area of the dialog box.
f. Select **OK** to align the bottom edges of the triangle and the long line.
g. Click the pointer on a blank area in the document to remove the selections.

Check - Your document should be similar to the following:

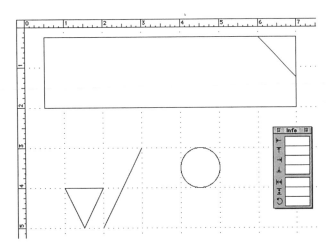

5) SAVE THE MODIFIED FITNESS

12.9 The Editing Commands

Objects can be copied, deleted, and added to a document using commands from the Edit menu. The Cut command from the Edit menu (⌘H) removes a selected object from a draw document and places it on the Clipboard. The Clipboard contents can be placed in the draw document using the Paste command from the Edit menu (⌘U). Executing the Clear command deletes a selected object without placing it on the Clipboard. The Copy command (⌘C) places a copy of the selected object on the Clipboard and leaves the original in the document.

The effect of the last drawing operation can be reversed using the Undo command from the Edit menu (⌘Z). For example, undoing a Clear places the deleted object back onto the draw document. Undoing a stretch returns the object to its original size and shape.

The Undo, Cut, Copy, and Paste buttons on the Shortcuts palette can also be used to execute these editing commands.

12.10 Printing and Viewing a Draw Document

Before printing a document it is important to save it on disk. Selecting the Print command from the File menu displays the Printer dialog box. Selecting Print in the dialog box prints the document. As with other ClarisWorks applications, the Print button in the Shortcuts palette can be used to Print one copy of a document.

In order to see a ClarisWorks draw document as it will look when printed, the document must be in page view. To do this, execute the Page View command from the View menu (⇧⌘P). The page controls in the lower-left corner of the screen can then used to change the magnification of the view. Clicking on the Zoom-out control displays a smaller version of the document. This is useful for viewing an entire page. Zoom-in can be used to enlarge the current view.

12.11 The Fill and Pen Palettes

The *Fill palettes* and *Pen palettes*, located in the Tool panel, allow you to change the appearance of an object. Each group of palettes has an accompanying *sample* area that displays the currently selected Fill or Pen options:

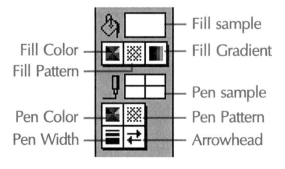

The Fill and Pen palettes

Options are chosen from the Fill and Pen palettes by moving the pointer over the desired palette's button and holding the mouse button down. This displays the palette of options. Dragging the pointer to the desired option and releasing the mouse button applies that option to the selected object. For example, the Fill Pattern button displays the Fill Pattern palette:

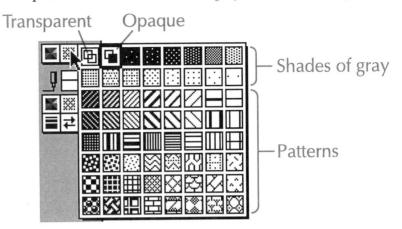

The Fill Pattern palette

Dragging the pointer into the palette and releasing the mouse button applies the highlighted fill pattern to the selected object. Choosing the Opaque pattern fills the selected object with the current Fill Color (the default is white), and choosing Transparent removes the object's fill, allowing objects and the graphics grid behind it to be seen.

The Fill Color palette has options for changing the color of a selected object's fill, and the Fill Gradient palette has options for gradient fills. Using the Fill Pattern palette, shown above, a selected object can be filled with an opaque color, different shades of gray, patterns, or made transparent.

The width of lines drawn and the outlines of objects can be changed using the Pen Width palette. The Pen Color and Pen Pattern palettes function similarly to the corresponding Fill palettes, except their options apply only to the lines and outlines. Arrowheads can be added to lines using the Arrows palette.

All of the Fill and Pen palettes can also be displayed in moveable palettes, similar to the Shortcuts palette or Info palette. Selecting the desired button and then dragging into the Work area causes the palette to "tear away" from the Tool panel:

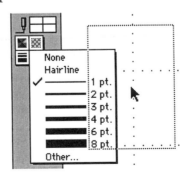

This list of options is being "torn away" from the Tool panel

When the mouse button is released, a palette is displayed:

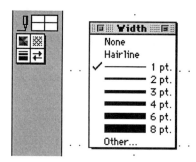

A tear-away palette can be moved and closed

Practice 3

In this Practice you will change the appearance of objects, view the draw document, and print a copy of it. Start ClarisWorks and open Fitness if you have not already done so. Display the Info palette if it is not already displayed.

1) DELETE THE LONG LINE

    a. Click on the long line that is next to the triangle to select it.

    b. Press the Delete key. The line is removed from the document permanently.

2) COPY AND PASTE THE CIRCLE

    a. Press ⇧⌘H to display the Shortcuts palette.

    b. Click on the circle to select it.

    c. On the Shortcuts palette, click on the Copy button. A copy of the circle is placed on the Clipboard.

    d. On the Shortcuts palette, click on the Paste button. A copy of the circle is placed in the draw document on top of the original.

    e. Move the new circle to the left so that the original circle is visible.

    f. Press the Delete key to delete the new circle.

    g. Click on the Close box of the Shortcuts palette to remove it.

3) CHANGE THE CIRCLE'S LINE WIDTH

    a. Click on the circle to select it.

    b. Place the mouse pointer over the Pen Width button (▤) in the Pen palettes section of the Tool panel.

    c. Click and hold the mouse button to display the Pen Width options.

    d. With the mouse button still pressed, drag down the list of choices and release the button when the check mark is next to the 6 pt. option. The circle's outline increases.

4) DISPLAY THE FILL PALETTE

    a. Place the pointer over the Fill Pattern button (▦) in the Fill palettes section of the Tool panel.

    b. Click and hold the mouse button to display the options and then drag all the way over to the right side of the Work area. Release the mouse button to place the palette.

5) FILL THE CIRCLE AND TRIANGLE

    a. Select the circle if it is not already selected and then click on the last fill pattern in the first row of the Fill palette (▦). The circle is filled with a medium shade of gray.

b. Select the triangle and then click on the next to last fill pattern in the second row of the Fill palette (□). The triangle is filled with a light shade of gray.

c. Close the Fill Pattern palette by clicking on its Close box.

6) MOVE THE SHAPES INTO THE LARGE RECTANGLE

a. Select the triangle if it is not already selected, then on the Info palette type 2 in the Object bottom location box (⊥). Type 0.5 in the Object left side location box (⊢). Press the Return key to move the triangle into position.

b. Select the circle, then on the Info palette type 1.25 in the Object bottom location box (⊥), and type 0.75 in the Object left side location box (⊢). Press the Return key to move the circle into position.

7) VIEW THE DRAW DOCUMENT

a. From the View menu, select the Page View command. Blank margins appear around the Graphics grid area of the document.

b. Click twice on the Zoom-out control (▣). The view scale changes to 50 percent and the edges of the draw document page can be seen.

c. Click on the Zoom-in control (▣) until the view scale indicates 100. Scroll to the top of the document.

Check - Your document should be similar to:

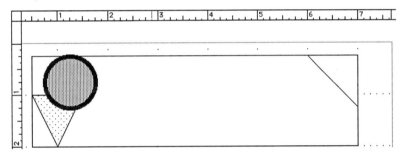

8) SAVE AND PRINT FITNESS

a. Save the document.

b. From the File menu select the Print command. The Print dialog box is displayed. Click on the **Print** button to accept the defaults.

12.12 The Move To Front and Move To Back Commands

As you have discovered, it is possible to move objects on the draw document by dragging them. It is also possible to place an object over another. Because ClarisWorks keeps track of the order in which objects are created, an item drawn after another will block or cover the first object if it is dragged over the first. It is helpful to think of these objects as being "stacked" on top of each other:

Arrange	
Move Forward	⇧⌘+
Move To Front	
Move Backward	⇧⌘-
Move To Back	
Align To Grid	⌘K
Align Objects...	⇧⌘K
Reshape	⌘R
Free Rotate	⇧⌘R
Transform	▶
Group	⌘G
Ungroup	⇧⌘G
Lock	⌘H
Unlock	⇧⌘H

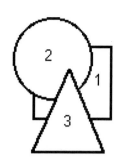
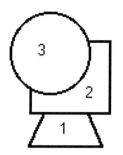

The triangle on the right has been moved to the back of the stack

The order in which objects are stacked can be changed by using the Move to Front and Move to Back commands from the Arrange menu. The Move to Front command moves a selected object to the top of the stack and the Move to Back command moves a selected object to the bottom.

12.13 Creating Text Frames

Text can be entered into a draw document with the Text tool. A text object is created by first selecting the Text tool and then clicking the I-beam pointer on the draw document, displaying a dotted-line *text frame* with a blinking cursor. Any text typed is inserted into the frame:

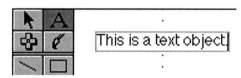

Clicking the mouse pointer anywhere outside the text frame removes both the cursor and the border and the object is displayed with its handles.

A text object may be selected by clicking anywhere in the text with the pointer tool. Once selected, text objects can be moved, deleted, copied, and resized. As with any object, handles are used for adjusting the frame's size. When the frame is resized, the text automatically adjusts:

This is a text object. It has a blinking cursor and a border.

This is a text object. It has a blinking cursor and a border.

Line length is automatically adjusted when the frame is resized

To edit or format text in a text frame, click once anywhere within the selected text frame to display the I-Beam, then format the text as desired. Note that when the I-Beam pointer is in a text object, the Menu bar changes to the word processor menus.

12.14 Rotating Objects

Any selected object, including text frames, can be rotated around its center by typing the number of degrees to be rotated in the Rotation box on the Info palette and pressing Return:

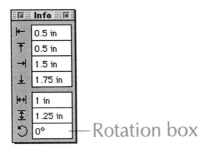

—Rotation box

Entering a positive number rotates the object counterclockwise, and entering a negative number rotates the object clockwise. For example, rotating a triangle 45° resembles the following:

before rotating   after rotating

Practice 4

In this Practice you will create text frames, move objects, and rotate objects. The title area of the newsletter will be completed. Start ClarisWorks and open Fitness if you have not already done so. Display the Info palette if it is not already displayed.

1) REARRANGE THE OBJECTS

a. Select the circle. Note how it partially covers the triangle.
b. From the Arrange menu select the Move to Back command. The circle almost disappears, with only its handles and a small portion of its top indicating its location. The circle has been moved to the bottom of the stack, behind all objects including the large opaque rectangle.
c. Select the large rectangle, then from the Arrange menu select the Move to Back command. Now the Rectangle is on the bottom of the stack and the triangle is on the top.

2) CREATE A TEXT FRAME

a. Select the Text tool (A) from the Tool panel and click in the blank space below the large rectangle. A blinking cursor appears in a box with a dotted-line frame border.
b. Type Free! then click the pointer in any blank space in the draw document. The text frame is displayed with handles.

3) ROTATE THE TEXT

a. In the Rotation box on the Info palette, type −45 and press Return to rotate the text object 45° clockwise.

b. Drag the text object to the upper-right corner of the large rectangle, and position it within the triangular area:

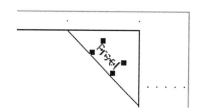

4) CREATE A TEXT FRAME AND FORMAT THE TEXT

    a. Select the Text tool from the Tool panel and click in the blank space below the large rectangle and near the left side of the Work area. A blinking cursor appears in a box with a dotted-line frame border.

    b. Type SHAPES then press Return. The cursor moves to a new line.

    c. Type The Ivy University Fitness Newsletter.

    d. Move the I-Beam pointer to the word "SHAPES" and double-click to highlight the word. From the Size menu, select 72. The word "SHAPES" is now very large.

5) FORMAT MORE TEXT

    a. Highlight the entire line that begins "The Ivy University…."

    b. From the Size menu, select 18, then from the Style menu, select Italic.

    c. Click once outside of the text frame to display the frame's handles. Stretch the frame to the right until all of the text is visible if it is not already visible.

    d. Use the Info palette to position the frame's left side at 2 inches, and the top of the frame at 0.5 inches.

<u>Check</u> - The title area of the newsletter is now complete and should be similar to:

6) SAVE FITNESS AND PRINT A COPY

12.15 Adding Text from Word Processor Documents

With the same four step process that you used to copy text between applications in Chapter Eleven, text from word processor documents can be copied to draw documents:

    1. Highlight the text to be copied.

    2. Execute the Copy command from the Edit menu.

    3. Display the draw document.

    4. Execute the Paste command from the Edit menu.

The text is transferred into a text frame in the draw document. The text frame may then be moved, formatted, and resized as necessary. Note that the copied text retains all formatting from the word processor document.

12.16 Linked Text Frames

Sometimes you may need to have parts of the same story in two locations of the same draw document. For example, a newsletter is made up of many separate stories, some that are divided into different columns. For this purpose, ClarisWorks allows you to break apart text frames into multiple text frames that are *linked* to each other. When text in a linked frame is edited, the text automatically adjusts by either flowing into or taking text from the frames it is linked to.

Linked text frames have *indicators* at the tops and bottoms of the frames:

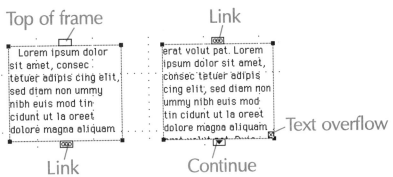

Indicators appear at the tops and bottoms of linked text frames

The Top of frame indicator appears at the top of the first frame in the story. The Link indicators can be at the top or the bottom of a frame, and appear when there is text linked before or after that frame. The Continue indicator appears on the last text frame. The Text overflow indicator appears in the bottom-right corner of the last text frame if there is more text in the story that is not displayed. Linked text frames, like unlinked text frames, can be resized by dragging on their corner handles.

To designate a text frame as a linked frame, first select the frame and then execute the Frame Links command from the Options menu (⌘L). The selected frame is then displayed with a Top of frame indicator and a Continue indicator. Additional frames can then be created by first clicking once on the Continue indicator, then clicking the I-Beam pointer once anywhere in the draw document to create a new frame, linked to the first. This new frame can then be resized as desired. More frames can be made by clicking once on the Link indicator or Continue indicator that is at the location in the story where the new frame is to be linked.

12.17 Desktop Publishing: Layout

The placement of graphics and text on a published page is not arbitrary. The size and location of each element in the document should be carefully planned; this is called the *layout*. The designer creating the document makes these initial decisions by first sketching the document on paper, then creating it on the computer. A copy of the document is then printed and reviewed. Parts of the design may then be changed if necessary.

The designer considers three concepts when making the initial sketches of the document: audience, balance, and consistency. The contents of the document must be appropriate for the audience—the people who will receive the final product. For example, it would not be appropriate to use an elegant, script font in a newsletter about sumo wrestling. Balance refers to how the text and graphics on the page relate to each other. For example, having all the pictures at the bottom of the page is not as effective as having them placed throughout the page. Consistency is an important concept in longer documents. It refers to repetitive items such as page numbers. It would not be wise to place the page number in a different location and different font on each page.

Through experience and training, designers know what layout techniques are most effective for each type of document. For example, 12 point type is usually not used for the text of a newsletter; 11 point or 10 point type is better. Such details can make the difference between a professional-looking document and one that is amateurish. One way to gain insight into effective layout techniques is to look around you. Open a magazine to an advertisement and scrutinize the ad. What fonts and sizes are used? Where are the graphics placed on the page in relation to the text? What audience is the ad intended for and is it appropriate for them? To fully understand the basics of design, it may help to make sketches of the newsletter pages and advertisements you find around you.

Practice 5

In this Practice you will add text from word processor documents and create linked text frames. The newsletter will be completed. Start ClarisWorks, open Fitness, and display the Info palette if you have not already done so.

1) ADD TEXT FROM A WORD PROCESSOR DOCUMENT

    a. Open News Story, a document created in the practices of Chapter Two.

    b. Highlight the title of the story and the first two paragraphs, then from the Edit menu select Copy to place a copy of the block onto the Clipboard.

    c. Close News Story.

2) PASTE THE TEXT INTO THE NEWSLETTER AND BOX IT

    a. Display Fitness if it is not already displayed.

    b. From the Edit menu, select Paste. The story is placed in the draw document in a text frame. Handles are displayed on the text frame because it is selected.

    c. Use the Info palette to place the text frame so that the top of the frame is at 5" and the right side of the frame is at 7".

    d. Select the Rectangle tool and draw a box 3.25" wide and 4.75 inches tall.

    e. Use the Info palette to position the box so that the top is at 4.25" and the right side is at 7.25".

    f. With the box still selected, from the Arrange menu select the Move to Back command. The story is now visible.

3) ADD ANOTHER STORY

    a. Open LEAD STORY. Notice the large, bold title of the story and the smaller text in the rest of the story.

    b. From the Edit Menu, execute the Select All command. The entire story, including the title, is selected.

    c. Execute the Copy command to place a copy onto the Clipboard.

    d. Close LEAD STORY.

4) PASTE THE TEXT INTO THE NEWSLETTER AND LINK THE FRAME

    a. Display Fitness if it is not already displayed and scroll to the top of the document.

    b. Execute the Paste command. The story is placed in the draw document in one long text frame. Handles are displayed on the text frame because it is selected.

    c. From the Options menu, select the Frame Links command. The frame is changed to a linked text frame, and the Top of frame indicator is visible.

5) RESIZE AND MOVE THE TEXT FRAME

    a. Scroll the document until the bottom of the linked text frame is visible. Note the Continue indicator at the bottom of the frame.

    b. Drag straight up on one of the frame's corner handles to resize the frame. Stop when the bottom of the frame is near the 7¼" vertical mark.

    c. Check the Info palette to be sure that the frame's size is 2.78 inches wide and 7.13 inches tall. Adjust the frame's size using the Info palette if necessary.

    d. Scroll up so that the top of the linked text frame is visible.

    e. Use the Info palette to position the frame so that the top is at 2.5" and the left side is at 0.5".

6) BREAK THE LINKED FRAME APART

    a. Scroll the document until the bottom of the linked text frame is visible. Note the Continue indicator and the Text overflow indicator at the bottom of the frame.

    b. Click once on the Continue indicator. The pointer changes to an I-Beam shape.

    c. Use the scroll bar to scroll back to the top of the document.

    d. Click once in the blank area to the right of the current text frame and below the title area of the newsletter. A tiny text frame appears.

    e. Using the Info palette, resize the text frame to 2.78 inches wide and 1.6 inches tall. Note the Link indicator at the top of the text frame, because it is linked to the frame before it.

    f. Use the Info palette to position the frame so that the top is at 2.5" and the right side is at 7".

Check - The newsletter should be similar to that shown on the next page:

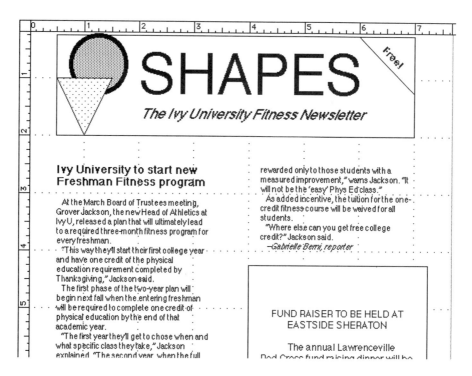

7) SAVE, PRINT, AND CLOSE FITNESS

12.18 The Paint Document

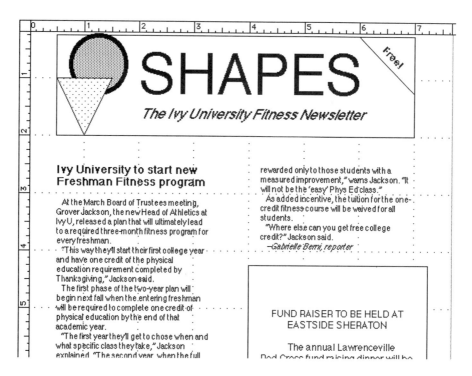

You have learned how to draw, move, and modify objects in a draw document. Now you will learn how to paint *images* using the paint application. A new paint document is created by selecting the **Painting** option in the New Document dialog box and then selecting **OK**. A blank paint document is displayed, as indicated by (PT) after the filename in the title bar. The paint screen looks similar to the draw screen with the addition of eight painting tools:

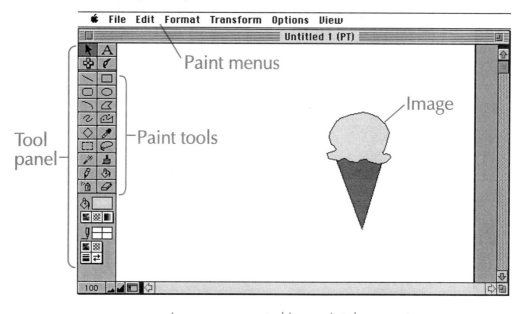

Images are created in a paint document

An Introduction to Computing Using ClarisWorks

Paint images are made up of tiny *pixels* (picture elements) that are either filled with "paint" or empty:

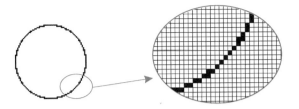

Images are made up of individual pixels
(grid shown to help identify individual pixels)

When grouped together, a number of adjacent pixels make up a recognizable image, such as a circle or square. Individual pixels can be filled or erased, giving the artist control over the shape and appearance of the image. However, each pixel remains independent of any other.

There are other differences between a draw object and a paint image. For example, a draw object can be selected and then dragged to a new location or resized using the handles. Paint images, because they are made of independent pixels, cannot be selected by simply clicking with the mouse pointer.

Another difference between the two applications is how they are placed in a document. Remember that in a draw document multiple objects can be "stacked" on top of each other. The object on the bottom of the stack can be moved or edited. However, all paint images are created on one layer and are not "stackable." When an object is drawn over another, it permanently covers the first image and creates a new, single image. For example, if a solid gray square is painted over a solid gray circle, it permanently covers the circle:

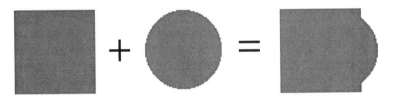

When images overlap, a new image is created

Neither the circle nor the square can be selected separately because they are now combined into one image.

12.19 The Paint Tools

The Paint tools are used to create different shapes, lines, and fills and to select specific areas of images. Many of the Paint tools work the same as the Draw tools, like the Rectangle tool and the Oval tool. However, some tools are available only in a paint document:

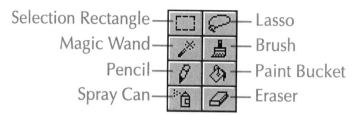

- **Selection Rectangle** - used to select a rectangular section.
- **Lasso** - used to select an irregular shape.
- **Magic Wand** - selects adjacent pixels of the same color.
- **Brush** - paints with the current fill color and pattern.
- **Pencil** - draws fine lines.
- **Paint Bucket** - fills an enclosed area.
- **Spray Can** - simulates a can of spray paint.
- **Eraser** - erases whatever it is dragged over.

A Paint tool can be selected by clicking on it in the Tool panel. The button is highlighted and the pointer changes to an appropriate shape. To paint, drag the pointer in the Work area. The Paint Bucket tool is the only exception: it is used to fill a closed shape with color by placing the Paint Bucket pointer inside the enclosed shape and clicking the mouse button once. Unlike the Draw tools, a Paint tool remains selected after using it.

As with other ClarisWorks applications, the last painting action performed can be undone by executing the Undo command (⌘Z) from the Edit menu.

12.20 Using the Selection Rectangle and Lasso Tools

The Selection Rectangle is used to select a rectangular section of an image. Once selected, the piece can be moved, modified, copied, or cut. To select part of an image, click once on the Selection Rectangle tool on the Tool panel and place the cross-hairs at one corner of the area that is to be selected. Drag the mouse, creating a dotted-line around the image, and release the mouse button. Everything within the rectangle is selected. The selected area can then be moved by dragging or nudged with the arrow keys. In the example below, a selection has been made and moved out of the circle:

Use the Selection Rectangle tool to select rectangular areas

To select a non-rectangular shape the Lasso tool is used. With the Lasso, you are able to guide the selection pointer around and in between shapes and select only the needed image:

Lasso tool

The Lasso is used to select irregular shapes

Only the painted image inside the Lasso's line is selected, not the blank space between the line and the image.

Practice 6

In this Practice you will create a new paint document and paint several images. Start ClarisWorks if you have not already done so.

1) CREATE A PAINT DOCUMENT

a. From the File menu, select New. The New Document dialog box is displayed.
b. Double-click on **Painting**. A new paint document is displayed. Locate the Paint tools and note that the Pencil tool is already selected and the Fill sample is black. These are the defaults for a new paint document.
c. From the View menu, select the Show Rulers command. The Rulers are displayed.

2) PAINT A CIRCLE

a. Select the Oval tool from the Tool panel. Using the guidelines shown in the Rulers, position the pointer at the 1" horizontal, 1" vertical mark.
b. Hold down the Shift key, then drag the pointer to the 2" horizontal, 2" vertical mark. Release the mouse button and then the Shift key. A solid black circle is created. Note that the pointer is still a cross-hairs and that the Oval tool is still highlighted.
c. Select the Pointer tool and position the pointer over the circle you just painted.
d. Click the mouse button once. The circle is not selected because in a paint document, images cannot be selected by clicking on them. Note that the Pencil tool has become the active tool because it is the default.

3) PAINT A SQUARE

a. Select the Rectangle tool and position the cross-hairs at the center of the circle you just painted.
b. Hold down the Shift key, then drag the cross-hairs near the 3" horizontal, 3" vertical mark. Release the mouse button and then the Shift key. The paint image is now shaped like a square partially positioned over a circle.

4) *PAINT A CLOSED SHAPE*

Select the Brush tool (🖌) from the Tool panel and paint a closed shape that resembles a mountain to the right of the "buildings" you just created by dragging the pointer:

Note: Be sure the line is continuous and has no breaks in it.

5) *CHOOSE A FILL PATTERN AND FILL THE SHAPE*

a. Display the Fill Pattern palette and select a pattern. Notice that the Fill sample area on the Tool panel displays the new fill pattern.
b. Select the Paint Bucket tool (🪣) from the Tool panel.
c. Move the pointer onto the paint document. The pointer is shaped like a paint bucket.
d. Position the pointer inside the closed shape you just painted and click once. The enclosed area is filled with the fill pattern you just selected.

Note: If the entire screen fills with the pattern, select the Undo command (⌘Z). Then, using the Brush tool, fix any breaks in the outline line painted in step 4. Select the Paint Bucket again, and make sure that you place the pointer inside the shape's outline.

6) *WRITE YOUR NAME WITH THE PENCIL TOOL*

a. Select the Pencil tool (✏) and write your name in the space below the painted images by dragging the pointer as if you were writing on a piece of paper.
b. Select the Eraser tool (▨). Erase the last letter in your name by placing the pointer over the letter and dragging the mouse over the lines.
c. From the Edit menu, select the Undo command. Your name is restored.

7) *SELECT YOUR NAME USING THE SELECTION RECTANGLE*

a. Choose the Selection Rectangle (▢) from the Tool panel.
b. Place the cross-hairs pointer above and to the left of your name. Drag the cross-hairs down and to the right, so that your entire name is enclosed by a dotted line. Do not include any part of the other images in your selection.
c. Release the mouse button. The dotted line remains, indicating the selected area.

8) *MOVE THE IMAGE*

a. With the image still selected, place the mouse pointer inside the selection. The pointer changes to an arrow shape.
b. Drag the image downward a little. The entire image moves because it is selected. Notice that it is still selected when you stop dragging it.
c. Press the Delete key to remove your name.

12 Check - The document should be similar to:

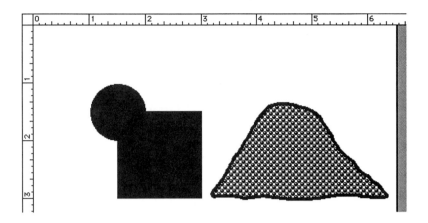

9) SAVE AND PRINT THE PAINT DOCUMENT

    a.   From the File menu, select the Save command. Type `My Scenery` as the filename and then select **Save**.

    b.   From the File menu, execute the Print command and select **Print**.

12.21 Using Draw and Paint with Other Documents

Now that you have learned the basics of using the draw and paint applications, you can apply these skills to enhance the appearance of word processor documents, database layouts and reports, spreadsheets, and charts. For example, lines and boxes can draw attention to important information in spreadsheets or database reports:

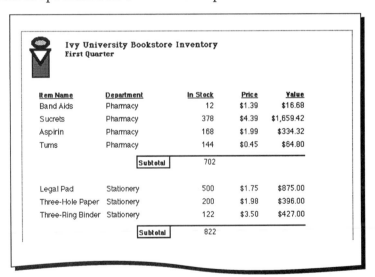

Graphics help to draw attention to important information

One way to add drawings to another application is to just draw on the current application's screen. To do this, select Show Tools from the View menu (⇧⌘T) or click on the Show Tools button (▣) at the bottom of the screen. The Draw tools appear along the left side of the screen. Enhancements can then be made by selecting a tool and drawing in the existing document. Note that you do not have to create a draw document first—the Draw tools are available in all of the other applications.

To add paint images from a paint document or complex graphics created in a draw document, first select the image or items to be copied then Copy them to the Clipboard. The image or graphic can then be pasted into the desired document.

When using the Draw tools and paint images to enhance other documents, keep it simple. Too many graphic elements can make a document busy-looking, confusing, and hard to read.

Practice 7

In this Practice you will add the mountain image you created in My Scenery to the poem you wrote in the Practices of Chapter Two. Start ClarisWorks and open My Scenery if you have not already done so.

1) OPEN POEM

Open Poem, which contains a short poem about two people and a hill.

2) COPY AN IMAGE TO THE CLIPBOARD

a. From the View menu, select My Scenery to display the paint document.
b. Select the Selection Rectangle tool (▦), if it is not already selected, and place the cross-hairs to the right and below the mountain shape.
c. Drag the cross-hairs up and to the left, just until the entire mountain shape is enclosed by a dotted line. Do not include any other images in the selection.
d. Release the mouse button. The dotted line remains, indicating what is selected.
e. From the Edit menu, select Copy. A copy of the selected image (the mountain) is placed on the Clipboard.
f. Close My Scenery without saving it. Poem is again displayed.

3) ADD THE IMAGE TO THE POEM

a. Place the I-Beam pointer at the end of the last line in the Poem.
b. Press Return twice to make a blank paragraph and start a new one.
c. From the Edit menu, select Paste. A copy of the mountain image is placed in the word processor document at the current cursor position.

4) DRAW A LINE BETWEEN THE TEXT AND THE MOUNTAIN

a. Select the Show Tools command from the View menu. The Draw tools are displayed.
b. Select the Line tool.
c. Place the cross-hairs below the first word in the last line of the poem and above the mountain. Note that the cross-hairs change back to the pointer when it is moved outside of the page guides. Be sure that the cross-hairs is just inside the page guides.
d. Hold the Shift key down and drag the cross-hairs straight to the right until the pointer is near the 5" ruler mark. Release the mouse button and then the Shift key.

<u>Check</u> - Your document should be similar to:

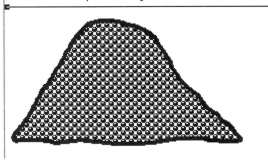

Jack and Jill went up the hill
to fetch a BIG pail of gold.
Jack fell down and broke his arm,
and Jill stood up and laughed.

5) SAVE AND CLOSE POEM

    a. Save Poem and print a copy.
    b. Close Poem and quit ClarisWorks.

12.22 Where can you go from here?

This chapter has presented the basics of using ClarisWorks to create graphics. There are many other commands and options available in both the paint and draw applications. The best way to learn about them is by reading the appropriate sections of the ClarisWorks manual supplied by Claris. The Macintosh is a powerful graphics tool and many graphics programs exist for it: Adobe Illustrator and SuperPaint are two of the most popular "illustration" programs. All graphics programs are either paint or draw applications and because you have learned the basics in Claris-Works you should be able to use other graphics programs easily.

Chapter Summary

This chapter described what desktop publishing is and how you can use the Draw tools to create professional-looking documents. It also described how to use the Paint tools to create images. A draw document is created by selecting the **Drawing** option from the New Document dialog box. The draw document's Tool panel contains tools that are used to produce different objects. Both horizontal and vertical Rulers can be displayed along with guidelines that show the pointer's current position. These help place and position elements on the drawing grid.

ClarisWorks has over a dozen drawing tools including a pointer, Text, Line, Rectangle, Oval, and Polygon tools. Objects can be resized by stretching, moved by dragging, nudged with the arrow keys, and edited in various ways. An object must be selected first before it can be edited. Selected objects are displayed with handles. Editing commands such as Cut, Copy, and Paste can also be used to modify objects.

Multiple objects can be selected using three different methods: by holding down the Shift key and clicking on objects, by using marquee selection, or by using the Select All command from the Edit menu.

The Info palette displays the current position and size of a selected object. The precise position and size of a selected object can be changed by typing new values into the Info palette.

Draw documents can be viewed as they will appear when printed using the Page View command and Zoom tools.

The Pen palettes are used to change the weight (thickness) of a selected object or add arrowheads to selected lines. The Fill palettes are used to fill an object, such as a polygon, with a selected pattern or color.

Objects that overlap one another can be described as stacked. The order of stacking can be changed using the Move To Front and Move To Back commands from the Arrange menu.

Text is entered into a draw document by creating a text frame with the Text tool. The font, size, and style of this text can be changed using commands in the Format menu. Any object, including text frames, can be rotated using the Info palette.

Text from word processor documents can be added to a draw document by cutting and pasting. The pasted text is in a text frame that can be linked and then broken apart into linked text frames using the Frame Links command from the Options menu.

The three main concepts to consider when determining the layout of a desktop publishing project are audience, balance, and consistency.

Paint images are created in a paint document. There are several Paint tools including the Brush, Pencil, and Paint Bucket. Paint images are composed of pixels (picture elements) and not separate objects as in a draw document. However, the Selection Rectangle and Lasso tools can be used to select paint images. Images can be filled, moved, and rotated.

Draw tools may be used in other ClarisWorks applications such as the word processor by using the Show Tools command from the View menu. Both draw and paint graphics can be copied and then pasted into another application such as a database.

Vocabulary

Align Objects command - Aligns selected objects as indicated by the options chosen.

Deselect - To make a selected object unselected. A deselected object is not displayed with handles.

Desktop publishing - Combining text and graphics into one document.

Fill palettes - Used to change the fill pattern of an object or image.

Fill sample - Area on the Tool panel that shows the current fill options including color, pattern, and gradient.

Frame Links command - Makes the selected text frame a linked text frame.

Graphics grid - Non-printing grid displayed in a draw document. Used to align objects.

Guidelines - Lines that appear on the Ruler indicating the pointer's current position.

Handles - Black rectangles displayed around a selected object. Used to adjust the size of an object.

Image - Collection of pixels in a paint document.

Indicators - Displayed at the top and bottom of linked text frames.

Info palette - Used to position an object and change an object's size.

Layout - The size and location of each element in a document.

Linked text frames - Multiple frames that contain one story.

Marquee selection - Selecting multiple objects by dragging to create a box around them.

Move to Back command - Moves the selected object to the bottom of the stack.

Move to Front command - Moves the selected object to the top of the stack.

Nudge - To move either a draw object or a paint selection a short distance by pressing an arrow key while the object is selected.

Object - Element in a draw document such as a rectangle or line.

Object Info command - Displays the Info palette.

Pen palettes - Used to change a line's weight and add arrowheads.

Pen sample - Area on the Tool panel that shows the current line options including color, width, and pattern.

Perfect shape - An exact shape drawn by pressing the Shift key while dragging the mouse (such as a square or circle).

Pixel - Individual elements that make up a paint image.

Polygon - A shape with many sides.

Selected object - An object that is displayed with handles.

Show Rulers command - Displays rulers along the top and left side of the Work area.

Show Tools command - Displays the Tool panel.

Stretching - Reshaping a selected drawing by dragging one of its handles.

Text frame - Box in which text may be typed.

Reviews

Sections 12.1 — 12.8

1. List the steps required to produce a draw document and then draw a rectangle from the 1" horizontal, 1" vertical mark to the 3" horizontal, 5" vertical mark.

2. How can the rectangle drawn in Review 1 be resized so that the lower-right corner is at the 4" horizontal, 6" vertical position?

3. What is meant by a "perfect shape" and how can one be drawn?

4. What steps are required to move the rectangle created in Review question 2 to the bottom of the screen?

5. What information is displayed in the Info palette?

6. How could the rectangle moved in Review question 4 be placed at an exact location on the screen?

7. List two ways that a group of objects can be selected.

Sections 12.9 — 12.13

8. List the steps necessary to create three copies of an already drawn square object.

9. Explain how to change the line weight of a previously created object.

10. Explain how to fill an object with a pattern.

11. If a circle is drawn over a square, how can the objects be reversed so that the square is in front of the circle?

12. Explain how the text Today is the greatest day!   can be entered into a draw document.

13. List the steps necessary to bold the text entered in Review question 12.

Sections 12.14 — 12.21

14. List the steps required to rotate a text frame.

15. How can text from a word processor document be added to a draw document?

16. What are Link indicators and where do they appear?

17. How can more linked frames be created from a linked text frame?

18. When designing a document, what three concepts are considered?

19. Give two reasons for adding draw objects or paint images to another type of document, such as a word processor document

20. Explain the two ways that draw objects can be added to another type of document, such as a word processor document.

21. List three differences between a paint image and a draw object.

22. What tool is used to fill a paint image?

23. a) What two tools may be used to select paint images?
    b) Explain how to use the two selection tools in part (a).

24. How can a drawing be created directly on a word processor document screen?

Exercises

1. You have decided to make a page-sized poster for your wall that includes special information about you and the year you were born.

    a) In the new draw document, create a text frame and write a short paragraph about yourself. Include your favorite food, music, hobbies, etc. Format the paragraph using different character styles and sizes. Change the paragraph alignment.

    b) Save the file naming it My Birth Year.

    c) Open ACADEMY AWARDS. In this database, display the record for the year you were born. Copy the record and paste it into the draw document in a new text frame. Format and label the information in the text frame. Add a title at the top of the text frame, then bold and center the title.

    d) Open COUNTRY and display the record for the country you were born in. Copy the record and paste it into the draw document in a new text frame. Format and label the information in the text frame. Add a title at the top of the text frame, then bold and center the title.

    e) Create a spreadsheet frame. Enter your birthdate in cell B2 and then label it appropriately. ClarisWorks has a NOW function that computes the current date in days. Enter the formula =ROUND(NOW()-B2,0) in cell B3 to display the number of days that have elapsed since your birthday. Resize the spreadsheet frame as necessary.

    f) Arrange the frames to create an attractive document. Use the Draw tools to enhance the document. Save the modified My Birth Year and print a copy.

2. Ivy University would like to have its student database look more attractive. Open IVY STUDENT, display Layout 1, and display the Tool panel.

    a) In Layout view, draw a box around the student name and address information. Use the Move To Back command so that the fields are visible.

    b) Draw a line below the GPA and Tuition fields to separate each record. Save the modified IVY STUDENT and print a copy of the first record.

3. The Memo word processor document was created in Chapter Eleven, Exercise 7. Open Memo and display the Tool panel so that a letterhead can be added to it.

    a) Open IVY-U NEW LOGO. Place a copy of the graphic at the top of Memo.

    b) Emphasize the list of students who have made the Dean's List by creating a box around the names. Save the modified Memo and print a copy.

4. Modify the Address database created in Chapter Five, Exercise 1 by adding graphics in Layout view. Include your own logo and at least two other objects that enhance the form. Save the modified Address and print a copy of one record.

5. The IVY PROMO word processor document could be made more interesting by adding graphics to it. Open IVY PROMO and display the Tool panel.

   a) Open IVY LEAF. Place a copy of the graphic into the footer of IVY PROMO. Place it to the left of the page number. Resize the graphic as necessary.

   b) Use the Draw tools to draw a box around the table that contains the global breakdown of the students attending Ivy University. Use the Move To Back command so that the figures are visible. Draw a line above the sums at the bottom of the table.

   c) Save the modified IVY PROMO and print a copy of page 4.

6. The STOCK2 spreadsheet modified in Chapter Ten, Exercise 2 contains Grace van Ivy's stock portfolio information. Open STOCK2 so that it may be enhanced with graphics and display the Tool panel.

   a) Ms. van Ivy's favorite stocks are Disney and Hershey. Draw boxes around the rows containing the data for these stocks. Use the Move To Back command so that the data is visible. Change the line weight of the boxes so that they appear more bold.

   b) Use the Oval tool to create an oval around the cell containing the total value of the stock. Use the Transparent fill pattern so that the data behind the oval is visible.

   c) Draw at least two other objects to enhance the spreadsheet. Save the modifed STOCK2 and print a copy.

7. Open LOAN, a spreadsheet, so that it may be enhanced with graphics. Display the Tool panel.

   a) Use the Oval tool to create an oval around the cell that contains the Monthly payment. Use the Move To Back command so that the Monthly payment is visible.

   b) Create an arrow that points to the Interest rate.

   c) Draw at least two other objects to enhance the spreadsheet. Save the modified LOAN and print a copy.

8. Bonster Enterprises, a large, new company that produces suntan products and beach chairs, has asked you to create a new logo for them. Create a new paint document and make a logo for Bonster Enterprises. The logo must include a sun and a palm tree, in addition to anything else that you decide to add. Save the paint document naming it Bonster and print a copy.

9. Dr. Jessica A. Nenner, a veterinarian, has asked you to create her letterhead stationery.

   a) In the new draw document, create a text frame with the Doctor's full name. Format the text using a different font and larger size.

   b) Save the file naming it Nenner Letterhead.

   c) Display the document in Page View. Move the text frame to the upper-left corner of the page.

d) In a new text frame, enter Dr. Nenner's information:

> 32 Glastonbury Avenue
> Whately, MA 02433
> phone (413) 555-8876
> fax (413) 555-9820
> e-mail nenner@petdoc.lvp

Format the information in the same font that you used in part (a), but leave the size as 12 point. Move the text block so that it is in the bottom-left corner of the page.

e) Display the rulers and draw a line starting at the ½" horizontal, ½" vertical mark down to the 8¾" horizontal, ½" vertical mark. Change the line's width to 3 pt.

f) Save the modified Nenner Letterhead and print a copy.

10. In a new draw document, create a two-page newsletter on any topic that you wish. The newsletter must contain the following features:

- A box around the title of the newsletter.
- At least four different stories.
- A table of contents.
- At least two advertisements.
- Bold all headlines.
- Correct spelling.
- At least one object rotated.
- Multiple columns per page (like a newspaper).

Save the newsletter naming it First Issue and print a copy.

An Introduction to Computing Using ClarisWorks

Chapter 13

Telecommunications and the Social and Ethical Implications of Computing

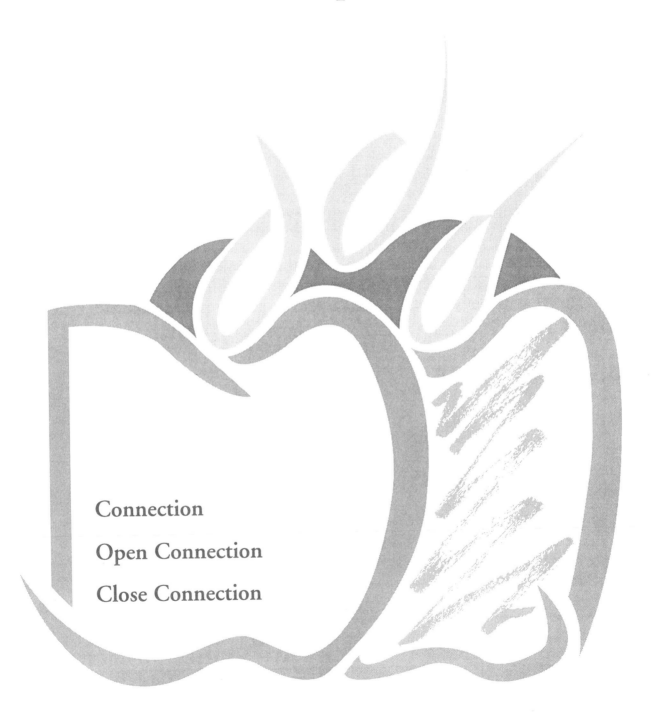

Connection

Open Connection

Close Connection

Objectives

After completing this chapter you will be able to:

1. Define telecommunications and describe its uses.

2. Use the ClarisWorks Communications application to connect to an information service.

3. Describe Networks.

4. Understand the Internet.

5. Understand what a Gopher is.

6. Understand what the World Wide Web is.

7. Understand Internet addresses.

8. Understand what TCP/IP, HTTP, and HTML are used for.

9. Describe artificial intelligence and its use in expert systems and natural language processing.

10. Understand how robots may be used to automate tasks.

11. Describe different careers in computing and their educational requirements.

12. Understand virtual reality and CD-ROMs.

13. Understand the ethical responsibilities of computer use and programming.

14. Understand the uses of desktop publishing.

13

In this concluding chapter we discuss our future with computers, computer-related career possibilities, and the social and ethical consequences of living in a computerized society. After having studied the previous chapters you should have a good understanding of how useful and powerful a computer is. In the first chapter of this text we stated that computers, unlike people, could not actually think but could store huge amounts of data and process it at very high speeds. This chapter describes these capabilities and how they are being exploited to perform an ever increasing and varied number of tasks.

13.1 Telecommunications

Telecommunications means the sending and receiving of data over telephone lines. With a *modem* a computer is capable of transmitting and receiving data between any two locations connected by phone lines. To send data to another computer (*transmit*), a modem converts the computer's binary data into tones which are then sent over phone lines. To *receive* data, a computer's modem converts the tones from the phone line back into binary form. This process involves what is called signal <u>mo</u>dulation and <u>dem</u>odulation, hence the name modem. In addition to the modem, special telecommunications software is required.

Modems can be "external" (outside the computer)
or "internal" (built in)

The rate at which data is sent over the phone lines is measured in *bits per second* (bps), sometimes referred to as *baud rate*. As discussed in Chapter One, a bit is the smallest unit of information in the binary system. Each ASCII character is composed of 8 bits, or one byte. Currently the most common modem rates are 14,400 and 28,800 bps. However, newer modems are being developed that are capable of communicating at even higher speeds.

Any type of data that a computer is capable of storing can be sent and received by modem. Using a modem it is possible to access and search very large databases which might store financial data, news reports, travel information, or a company's sales data. If you go to a travel agent to book an airplane ticket, the agent will most likely use a computer to check the availability of flights and then make your reservation. The agent's computer is connected by modem to a large computer that contains a database of flight information. This database is similar to the ones you created using ClarisWorks, only much larger.

Because of telecommunications it is now possible for many people to work at home rather than in an office. This is referred to as *telecommuting*. Writers and news reporters often write their stories at home on a word processor and then transmit their word processor files to their office which may be many miles away. Financial consultants, accountants, and travel agents are sometimes able to work at home accessing databases and other information using a computer and modem. Telecommunications also makes access to the Internet possible as explained later in Section 13.5.

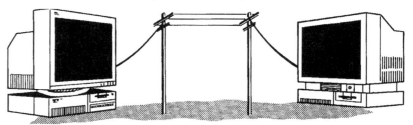

Telecommunications allows two computers to exchange information over telephone lines

13.2 Bulletin Board Systems and E-Mail

A popular form of telecommunication is the electronic *bulletin board system* or *BBS*. People who subscribe to a bulletin board service can call another computer and transmit messages which are then stored. This is called *posting* a message. When other subscribers of the service call the bulletin board they can list posted messages. Many companies and other organizations maintain bulletin boards to keep their employees aware of important events. For example, the Ivy University Alumni Association could have an electronic bulletin board which lists upcoming events such as athletic competitions and alumni reunions. Some BBSs are run by individual users and are normally free. Others called *information services* are controlled by large companies and offer for a fee a variety of different services such as shopping or international weather forecasts. CompuServe, Prodigy, and America Online are three popular information services.

Electronic mail or *e-mail* is used to send and receive messages meant for one person or a small group. Members of information services and bulletin board systems can send and receive e-mail. The person sending the message types in the name of the recipient and the message. When the recipient connects to the electronic mail service he or she is notified of any mail. The primary advantage of this system is speed. When an e-mail message is sent, it can be received in a matter of seconds even to recipients half way around the world.

To keep electronic mail private a password system is usually employed. When first calling to receive messages, a person is asked to enter a secret password which must then be verified by the computer before the messages are transmitted.

Messages, files, and graphics can be copied from a BBS or information service to your computer. This is called *downloading* and involves having the system's computer send a copy of the file to your computer, where it will be stored on disk. Once downloaded, you can print or edit the file. Similarly, the process of sending files from your computer to a BBS or information service is called *uploading*.

13.3 Telecommunicating with ClarisWorks

ClarisWorks has a communication application. If your computer is equipped with a modem, this application allows you to contact electronic bulletin boards and information services to send and receive data.

Telecommunicating can be complex, involving many different options such as baud rates. In order for telecommunications to take place, both computers must use the same options. New subscribers to an information service normally receive a packet describing the options which must be used to access that particular service. Fortunately, ClarisWorks allows the options for each different service to be saved in a communications file. Once the options are saved, the user does not have to be concerned about setting the proper options again.

Selecting **Communications** from the New Document dialog box displays the communications screen:

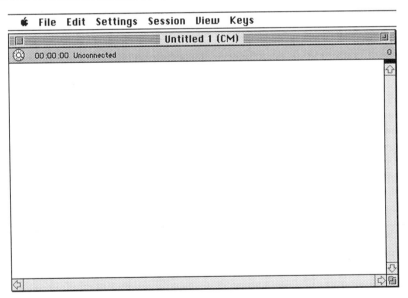

The ClarisWorks communications screen

Communications files are noted by the letters CM in parentheses after the filename in the Title bar.

For two computers to communicate, they both must use the same option settings. The four most important options are:

Baud Rate: The speed at which each computer will send and receive data. 14,400 and 28,800 are common values.

Data bits: The number of bits (binary digits) that make up one piece of data. This is normally 7 or 8.

Parity: How the receiving computer will determine if an error occurred in the transmission of data. Common parity choices are named None, Odd, and Even.

Stop bits: The number of bits, normally 1 or 2, sent to indicate the end of a piece of data.

These four items are so important that bulletin board Systems (BBS) and information services are classified by the settings that they expect. For example, a BBS may list itself as "14400, 8, None, 1" or "144, 8, N, 1" meaning that its computer communicates using 14,400 baud, 8 data bits, no parity, and 1 stop bit. In ClarisWorks, these settings are made using the Connection command. Executing the Connection command from the Settings menu displays the following dialog box:

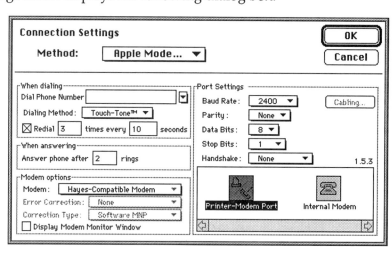

*Telecommunications options can be set in the
Connection Settings dialog box*

It is here that baud rate, data bits, stop bits, and parity options are set. The telephone number is also entered into the Connection Settings dialog box.

The options for **Baud Rate, Dial Phone Number**, etc. are saved in a communications file by selecting the Save command from the File menu. Opening a previously saved communications file recalls these options. This way, a communications file for each information service you contact can be created to simplify the process of telecommunicating.

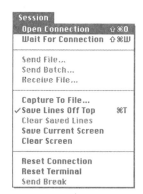

After the options have been set and saved, ClarisWorks can be used to contact the information service by selecting the Open Connection command from the Session menu (⇧⌘O). When executed, Open Connection dials the phone number you supplied and attempts to contact the other computer. If a connection is made, ClarisWorks displays a dialog box alerting you. The other computer then takes control of your computer, and anything that you type is sent to it. For this reason, the computer that you are connected to is often called the *host*. Executing the Close Connection command from the Session menu (⇧⌘0) terminates communications with the host and hangs up the phone.

Practice 1 - Connecting to a BBS

In this Practice you will set options to access a BBS, and create a communications file for that BBS's options. If you do not have a modem attached to your computer you will not be able to perform this Practice.

Make sure that your modem is connected to a phone line and is turned on. As examples for this exercise we will use the options 2400, 7, Even, 1 and the telephone number 800-346-3247. You may be able to get actual information about a local BBS from your computer dealer.

1) BOOT THE SYSTEM AND START CLARISWORKS

2) OPEN A NEW COMMUNICATIONS FILE

    a. Select the **Communications** option from the New Document dialog box.
    b. Select **OK**. The communications screen is displayed.

3) SET THE COMMUNICATIONS OPTIONS

    a. From the Settings menu, execute the Connection command. Note the default options for **Baud Rate** (2400), **Parity** (None), **Data Bits** (8), and **Stop Bits** (1).
    b. Click on the triangle in the **Parity** box to display a submenu. Select the Even option.
    c. Change the **Data Bits** option to 7.
    d. The "port" is the location of the modem in your computer. Normally, this is Modem Port, but your computer may be different.
    e. In the **When dialing** section, type the phone number `1-800-346-3247` in the **Dial Phone Number** box.
    f. Select **OK** to remove the dialog box.

4) SAVE THE OPTIONS IN A FILE NAMED BBS TEST

    a. From the File menu, select Save.
    b. Type the name `BBS Test` and select **Save**. ClarisWorks saves the communications options, including the phone number, in a file named BBS Test.

5) INITIATE COMMUNICATIONS

    a. From the Session menu select the Open Connection command. ClarisWorks initializes the modem and displays a message:

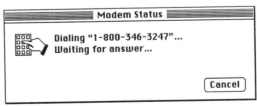

Depending on the type of modem that you have, you may be able to hear the phone as it is dialed.
    b. When the host computer answers the phone and establishes communications with your modem, ClarisWorks displays a connect message and may beep.

Note: If the host is already connected to another computer, or if your communications options are not set correctly ClarisWorks displays a message such as, Error, Busy, or No Carrier. If this occurs, check your options and tell ClarisWorks to dial again by selecting the Open Connection command from the Session menu.

c. The connect dialog box appears briefly:

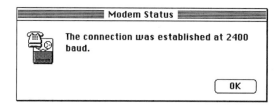

d. Press the Return key to initiate communications.

Check - When communications have been established, the host computer transmits a welcome message. Messages differ from service to service, but most ask for a name or account number. Your screen should be similar to:

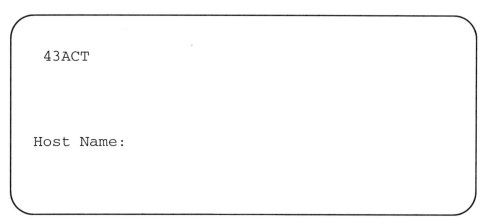

Because you are connected, anything typed on your keyboard will be sent to the host computer. You will next enter a host name and receive information by following the instructions that the host computer sends to your machine.

6) ENTER PHONES AS THE HOST

At the "Host Name" prompt, type PHONES and press Return. The other computer responds with a message. You are telecommunicating: your computer sent the message "PHONES" over the modem to the other computer which has now responded.

7) TERMINATE COMMUNICATIONS AND EXIT CLARISWORKS

a. From the Session menu, select the Close Connection command to terminate communications. ClarisWorks displays the message:

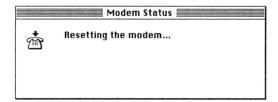

b. Quit ClarisWorks.

13.4 Networks

Business, government agencies, and universities often *network* their microcomputers. Networked computers can communicate with each other using a transmission medium such as telephone lines, fiber optics, satellites, and digital microwave radio. They can be in the same building, many miles apart, or on different continents. A network allows applications software, files, and devices, such as printers, to be shared.

Networks usually employ an e-mail system so that users can communicate with each other. To maintain privacy and provide security, network e-mail systems require a password for access.

To share data on a network a file server is used. A *file server* is a computer containing large disk storage to which all other computers on the network have access. A computer on the network can access a file on the server as easily as if it were stored on its hard drive. There are a number of advantages to using a file server including reduced cost. It is cheaper to maintain one computer with a very large hard disk than several computers with smaller hard disks.

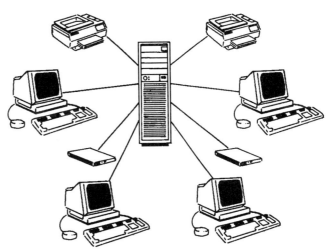

Networked computers can share files and send messages

A good example of the benefits of networking is a business that has computers in different departments. Suppose that you, as an employee, are preparing a report with a co-worker. If you are not using networked computers, the report file must be saved on a diskette and carried to the co-worker. On a network, you could both have access to the file at the same time. This is especially helpful for large projects which require, for example, a spreadsheet from the accounting department, a database from the marketing group, and a letter from the advertising department.

A common network type is the *LAN* or Local Area Network. The computers and other hardware devices in a LAN are usually within a short distance of each other. Rapid developments are being made in the area of the *wireless LAN*, using technologies such as lasers, radio waves, and cellular phones to network the computers. Wireless telecommunications technology, combined with portable computers, will allow users to access their computer data from anywhere in the world.

13.5 The Internet

The *Internet* is a network of networks. It is comprised of business networks, university networks, government networks, and other networks all over the world. Through this vast global network, users are able to access an almost unlimited variety of resources from the most current scientific data to movie reviews. Scientists even host conferences online, where they join from many countries to discuss a topic without ever leaving their laboratories. Researchers currently working on the Human Genome Project, the massive effort to identify all the genes in human DNA, are pooling their findings into a single huge database available to anyone with access to the Internet. There are currently more than 5,000 special interest groups available on the Internet, ranging from bungee jumping to particle physics, as well as 2,500 electronic newsletters.

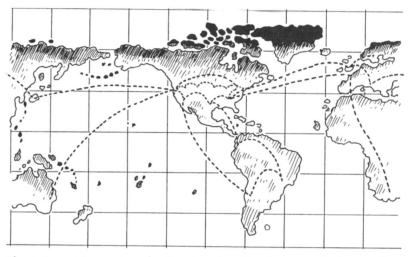

The Internet is a network of networks allowing people from all over the world to communicate

Originally, the Internet was established by the U.S. government and research institutions so that their members could communicate with each other, but soon many others realized its usefulness and started to access it. In the 1970s the United States developed regional and national computer networks, with other countries doing the same. By the 1980s connections were established between the various national networks. Now almost every country is linked to the Internet. What makes the Internet unique is that no one is in charge of it; it is not run by a company or country. The Internet depends on the cooperation of all its interconnected networks. Each local network is responsible for its own financing and connection to the nearest larger network. Currently most universities, many businesses, and a growing number of high schools have connections to the Internet. Many individuals, including members of information services, connect to the Internet using telecommunications.

How do the thousands of networks comprising the Internet communicate with one another? They use a standardized method of communication called a *protocol* that allows different computer networks and computers to talk to one another. The protocol, *TCP/IP* (Transmission Control Protocol/Internet Protocol), is a worldwide standard for the packaging and addressing of computer data so that data can be transmitted to any computer running the protocol software. For example, when e-mail is sent, it is first divided by the Transmission Control Protocol (TCP) into data packets. TCP then adds two pieces of information to each packet. First, data is added that allows the receiving computer to determine that the data packet has not been altered in transmission, a kind of packing list. Second, the address of the receiving computer is added by the Internet Protocol (IP). With this TCP/IP information, data packets can take different routes and still reach the correct destination. Computers called *routers*, located at the intersections of networks, determine which path is best for a packet's journey.

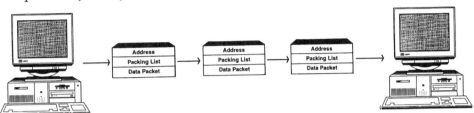

Data transmitted over the Internet is divided into packets

13.6 Internet Addresses

Internet protocol requires that users have an address. This address is used by TCP/IP for the transmission of data so that other Internet users can communicate. An Internet address takes the form:

username@host.subdomain.domain

The username refers to the person that holds the Internet account. The host refers to the name of the computer running the TCP/IP software. This name was selected when the software was installed. The subdomain refers to the company, organization, educational institute, etc. that owns the computer host. The domain refers to the type of institution. For example, the address:

zmalfas@circa.ufl.edu

is the Internet address for Zoe Malfas whose account is on a host computer named circa located at the University of Florida which is an educational institution.

The following is a list of common domains:

Identifier	Meaning
int	international organization
com	commercial organization
mil	US military facility
net	networking organization
edu	educational institution
org	nonprofit organization
gov	government facility

Because the resources of the Internet are so vast it is impossible to know where all of the resources are located. Therefore it can be rewarding to *surf* the Internet. When surfing you have no particular resource in mind and no idea of what you might discover; you just access different locations and see what's there. This process is similar to going into a library and just browsing through the books. It is also similar to channel surfing where you switch from one television channel to another to see what is being broadcast.

One way to surf the Internet is with a Gopher. *Gopher*, developed at the University of Minnesota, makes information on the Internet easily accessible. Gopher displays menus of options. Selecting a menu item may take you to another menu or display a file. By selecting menu items, you are able to travel around the Internet without needing to know the addresses at which the resources are located.

Gopher is based on the client/server concept. A *client* is a program that requests information. A *server* is a program that provides the information. Gopher servers are now located at many Internet sites.

A typical Gopher menu looks like the following:

```
            Internet Gopher Information Client

                     Ivy University


 --> 1.   About the Athletics Department.
     2.   About the Education Department.
     3.   About the Liberal Arts Department.
     4.   About the Minor Skin Injury Department.
     5.   Gopher Servers at Ivy University.
     6.   Ivy University Catalog.


 Press ? for Help, q for quit, u to go up a menu Page: 1/1
```

To determine if a Gopher client is available through your Internet connection, type gopher and press Return. Other Gophers are accessed by typing gopher followed by a space and the address of the gopher. For example, typing gopher consultant.micro.umn.ed connects to the CIA World Factbook gopher. Other Gophers include the following:

Gopher	Address	Provides access to:
Academic BBSs	yaleinfo.yale.edu	Other Internet sites dedicated to academics
Business Statistics	infopath.ucsd.edu	General business indicators, commodity prices, real estate statistics, etc.
CIA World Factbook	consultant.micro.umn.edu	Information about every country and territory in the world
Physics Gopher	granta.uchicago.edu	Vast amounts of information pertaining to physics

Gopher	Address	Provides access to:
Stock Market	lobo.rmhs.colorado.edu	Stock market closing quotes and comments for recent dates
The White House	gopher.well.sf.ca.us	Information on various policies, including Internet access to other government information.

13.8 The World Wide Web

One of the most popular areas of the Internet is the *World Wide Web* (WWW), originally developed at the CERN laboratories in Switzerland to disseminate scientific data. As with Gopher, the Web can be used to surf the Internet. However, on the Web, users explore Internet resources graphically. Connecting to a Web site displays its *Web pages.* A Web page can contain graphics, fancy text, and easy access to other Web sites.

Because there is so much information on the Web, indexes of Web pages exist. These indexes are search tools that contain databases of Web pages. *Yahoo* is one such tool for searching the Web. When a company adds a Web page to a Web site, it can request that the page be added to the Yahoo database. Other programs such as *Lycos* follow links in Web pages all over the Web and automatically add new links to its database. This type of program is called a *robot program.*

Internet sites that provide Web access run HTTP software. *HTTP* is Hyper Text Transfer Protocol. Each Web site, or *Web server*, has an address called a *URL* (Uniform Resource Locator). To connect to a Web site a Web browser and a URL must be used. A *Web browser* understands HTTP to properly display the graphics and text of Web pages. A common Web browser is Netscape.

After connecting to a Web site, the first page displayed is called the *home page*. For example, Ivy's home page provides access to information about the University including admissions, athletic schedules, events, and a message from Ivy's president:

Web pages are written in a language called *HTML* (Hypertext Markup Language). *Hypertext* is text that contains links to other text. Web pages contain links, usually indicated by highlighted words, to other Web addresses. For example, in Ivy University's home page **A Message from the President** is a link to a page that displays a picture of Ivy's president and a letter written by her. There is a URL associated with the **A Message from the President** link. When the link is clicked, the Web browser displays the page at that address.

HTML documents can be created using any word processor. Special codes, or *tags*, are placed inside brackets. The Web browser uses these tags to determine how the Web page should be displayed and what should be displayed for each link. A portion of Ivy's home page is shown below:

```
<HTML>
<HEAD>
<TITLE>ivyweb</TITLE>
</HEAD>
<BODY>

<H2><CENTER>Ivy University<CENTER></H2><P>
<IMG SRC="ivy.gif"><P>
<IMG SRC="ivyleaf.gif">
<A HREF ="http://www.ivyu.edu/president/
letter.html"><B>A Message from the President
</B></A><P>

...
```

In the document above, the <H2> tag indicates a heading will follow. A slash (/) is used to indicate the completion of a tag. For example, in the text above </H2> indicates the end of the heading. The ivy leaves below the Ivy University heading are placed using an image tag. The <A HREF tag tells the Web browser that when the user clicks on the phrase **A Message from the President** the Web page at http://www.ivyu.edu/president/letter.html should be displayed.

There are many tags that can be used in an HTML document. Tags must be used to control every aspect of the Web page including text formatting, graphics, and links.

Currently, the Web makes surfing the Internet fun and easy through interesting and attractive Web pages. However, developments are being made that will allow animation and special effects to be incorporated into Web pages. One such development is a programming language called *Java*. Developed at Sun Microsystems, Java programs can run on any computer. This makes it possible for programs to be sent over the Internet as easily as e-mail. A Web browser called *HotJava*, also by Sun Microsystems, will allow users to create customized Web pages according to their specifications.

Many businesses, schools, and government facilities have Web sites. They often publish their home page address in advertisements, commercials, and printed materials. Popular Web sites include the following:

Web Site	Address
Apple computer	http://www.apple.com
ESPN sports	http://espnet.sportszone.com

Web Site	Address
USA Today	http://www.usatoday.com
The Library of Congress	http://www.loc.gov
The White House	http://www.whitehouse.gov/
Internet College Exchange	http://www.usmall.com/college
The Rock and Roll Hall of Fame	http://www.rockhall.com
Yahoo directory	http://www.yahoo.com

13.9 Networks of the Future

In the future, every house will be able to have a direct link to the Internet. The high-speed cable that comes into your house and is connected to your computer will be able to transmit voice, data, image, and video information to your PC. This high-speed access will allow you to receive a full color copy of a painting from a far away museum or the sounds of a concert being held on another continent.

Networks of the future will transmit and receive voice, data, image, and video information in *digital* form. Digital information is 0s and 1s (bits) that can be sent over a carrier such as a wire, fiber optics, or radio wave. For example, a photographic image can be scanned to convert it to digital form and then transmitted as digits to a computer. The receiving computer then translates the data back into a copy of the original photograph. Such technology is currently used to send pictures to Earth from space probes billions of miles away and by news photographers thousands of miles from their newspapers.

Networks of the future will be *interactive* so that users can send as well as receive information. For example, it will be possible to shop in a virtual store. The word *virtual* in this case means "existing in effect though not in actual fact." A virtual store therefore, exists only on the computer screen. In a virtual store, you can shop using an input device that enables you to roam through the store and request information on a selected item. An order can be placed and then the item will be delivered to your home. It no longer matters whether the user lives in an isolated part of the country or in a large city; the store will be available to everyone.

13.10 Improved Microprocessors and Software

In Chapter One we traced the history of computing and discovered that as technology improved, computers increased in speed, decreased in size, stored more data, and most importantly became less expensive. The trend has continued with the development of smaller, more powerful microprocessors. Microprocessors can already be found in telephone answering machines, watches, CD players, cameras, television sets, refrigerators, washing machines, and other appliances:

Ordinary household appliances have microprocessors

One example of the use of a microprocessor is in the anti-lock braking system (ABS) found on many cars. As the brakes are applied, a computer connected to sensors on the car's wheels detects when the car begins to skid. The computer then takes control of the brakes, pumping them rapidly to keep the wheels from locking. Other microprocessors are now used to increase the efficiency of an automobile engine or control how safety devices will perform in case of an accident.

One of the most useful areas of microprocessor development is in the diagnostic systems of complex electronic devices. Many devices such as computers and car engines have become so complicated that it is difficult to determine what is wrong when they malfunction. Therefore, microprocessors have been developed which pinpoint the component that is not working properly and then alert the user. These types of systems are commonly found in automobiles, aircraft, or any device that contains a large number of complicated parts.

Besides the development of better microprocessors, software has continued to improve. Most software developers are attempting to make their software more *user friendly*, which means easier to use. In learning the different applications in ClarisWorks you learned a number of commands. By having similar commands in each application, the program was easier to learn and use.

13.11 Supercomputers and Neural Networks

Because computers are asked to perform increasingly difficult tasks, considerable effort and money has been committed to developing supercomputers. These computers can perform one trillion (1,000,000,000,000) calculations per second. By comparison the UNIVAC built in 1951 could perform only 1,000 calculations per second. Some supercomputers achieve such speed using a technique called *parallel processing* in which a number of high-speed microprocessors are combined. A problem is first broken into parts and they are then solved simultaneously, or in parallel, on separate microprocessors. Why are such high speeds needed? Because computers are being asked to produce solutions in an acceptable amount of time for problems requiring billions of calculations. In the next two sections we discuss two such problems: the analysis of the data in very large databases and the production of sophisticated graphics to create motion picture effects.

In addition to hardware techniques such as parallel processing, there is software being developed which can substantially increase a computer's ability. Neural-network software, designed to be similar to the pattern of cells in the human brain, can "learn" from analyzing large sets of data. The software is capable of producing a statistical model describing important relationships and patterns in the data. This technique in combination with parallel-processing is especially useful for working with the information stored in large databases.

13.12 Database Marketing

In Chapters Five through Seven you learned how to create and manipulate a ClarisWorks database. A major problem that confronts the computer industry is how to work with extremely large databases with millions of records. Any time you make use of a credit card or fill out a product warranty card you are supplying information that will be stored in a database. For example, the Blockbuster Entertainment Corporation has a database of nearly forty million households and two million daily rentals of its videotapes. This database contains information on the rental habits of Blockbuster's customers. Does a customer prefer children's films or action movies? Based on such information Blockbuster is testing a computerized system that recommends ten movies the customer has not previously rented. The data is also useful in promoting new businesses for Blockbuster such as its Discovery Zone play center subsidiary.

Credit card companies have vast databases which are difficult to store and search because of their size. Marketers developing sales campaigns want to be able to sift through such data in order to discover patterns that will predict personal behavior. For example, what combination of income, credit-card spending, investments, and geographical location identifies a person most likely to purchase a new automobile? The answer can produce a list of potential customers that is impossible to generate in any other way. Such sophisticated database searches require multiple and interrelated criteria. Currently, this kind of computing ability can only be supplied by very powerful computers which employ advanced technologies such as parallel-processing.

13.13 Computer Generated Motion Picture Effects

Many of the special effects we see in motion pictures are computer generated. By scanning each separate frame from a motion picture into a computer, each part of the image is digitized and stored as a byte of information called a *pixel*. Once in this form the image can be manipulated pixel by pixel to produce a new image. This technique can be used, for example, to combine images into a film that shows dinosaurs running through a park. Small models of the dinosaurs and the outdoor setting are filmed separately and then combined on the computer:

Computers can generate images of models and manipulate them

Another example is a film that requires an actor to be suspended on wires to give the illusion of flying. Obviously, if the audience sees the supports the effect will be ruined, but by digitizing the film the wires can be removed frame by frame.

One of the most exciting computer generated effects is *morphing*, a process by which a photographic image slowly turns into a second image. This technique is especially startling when done with faces. For example, a human face can be changed into that of a wolf by digitizing a picture of each face and then changing each part of one face into the other, pixel by pixel.

13.14 Artificial Intelligence

Although computers cannot think, one of the major areas of research continues to be the development of programs that are capable of making increasingly complex decisions. Using computers to make decisions which would normally be made by human beings is called *artificial intelligence*. Herbert Schorr, a computer scientist at IBM, has declared that the development of artificial intelligence is the second wave of the information revolution. The first wave was the development of automated data processing which you studied when producing databases and spreadsheets. According to Schorr "the second wave will automate decision making."

The Internal Revenue Service (IRS) has defined artificial intelligence as "the science of making machines do things that would require intelligence if done by man." As an example, there are currently computers which can play chess so well that they can beat all but the best human players. Universities actually challenge each other's computers to play chess to determine which has the best chess playing program. Are these computers really intelligent? Most computer scientists would say no. They are simply programmed to make a series of decisions in response to the moves made by their opponents. It is merely their speed and ability to access huge amounts of stored data that make them appear to be intelligent.

In 1950 the brilliant English mathematician Alan Turing wrote a paper entitled "Computing Machinery and Intelligence" in which he raised the question "Can machines think?" To answer that question he invented the "Imitation Game." Briefly summarized, the game involves placing a person and a computer in separate rooms and an interrogator in a third room. Communicating by typed questions and answers, the interrogator questions the human and computer to determine which is the computer. If the interrogator cannot tell the difference between the responses then, according to Turing, the machine has human thought capabilities. Since not even psychologists can agree on a definition of intelligence, this is probably as good a test as any. Currently, no computer or software program has been shown to be capable of consistently passing the *Turing test*. However, when limited to a specific topic, say sports, several programs have fooled their human interrogators into thinking that they were communicating with another human.

An Introduction to Computing Using ClarisWorks

13.15 Expert Systems

One promising area of research into artificial intelligence is the development of *expert systems*. An expert system is programmed to produce the same solution a human expert would if asked to solve the same problem. An example of such a system is the one installed by the credit card division of American Express. In the past when a store called to get approval for a large charge, a trained credit expert would have to decide if approval should be given. By asking a series of questions about the amount being charged, the type of item being purchased, and so on, the expert would then make a decision. Now if an American Express card holder wants to make a large purchase, for example a $10,000 oriental rug, in many cases a computer will decide whether or not to approve the purchase.

One of the more secretive uses of expert systems is that used by U.S. intelligence agents to avert terrorist acts. Programmed with the knowledge of a handful of terrorism agents, the system has proven surprisingly accurate in its ability to predict when and where terrorist activities will occur. Another similar system is used by the FBI to predict the activities of criminals. Both systems have been programmed with rules that human experts have developed based on decades of experience in dealing with terrorists.

We earlier referred to the IRS definition of artificial intelligence. They have developed an expert system which analyzes tax returns to determine if a person is correctly reporting income or making improper deductions. Programmed to look for suspicious patterns, the IRS computer decides when a human agent should consider initiating an audit.

The IRS uses expert systems to find improper tax deductions

Currently there are thousands of expert systems in use, with the number increasing each year. To date, the expert systems that work the best are those for which a series of rules can be used to make a decision. When specific rules do not apply, as when intuition must be used, expert systems are usually not successful.

13.16 Speech Recognition Software

Designing a computer system that can recognize human speech has long been a goal of computer scientists. Advancements in computer processors and *speech recognition software* have made many such systems available. Speech recognition software uses *natural language processing*, a field of artificial intelligence which translates spoken words into text.

Today speech recognition software has been developed for dictation and command and control. *Dictation systems* can be used for voice mail, in the medical field for creating transcriptions, and in many different fields for data entry. *Command and control systems* are often used by those with physical handicaps, including carpal tunnel syndrome, to control their computers by spoken words. Other applications for command and control systems are voice activated car phones and navigating through phone menus. For example, many companies today allow you to choose from their menu of choices by saying or pressing the number of the desired menu choice ("Please press or say one."). Another interesting application of speech recognition software is at the medical center of the University of Virginia. There, a robot has been equipped with speech recognition software so that technicians can give it a specimen for delivery and then tell it where to go. The robot then delivers its package.

Another form of speech recognition software that is being developed is for continuous speech. Continuous speech refers to normal speaking patterns. However, there are difficulties in producing natural language processing systems for continuous speech. First, many words have different meanings based upon the context in which they are used. The word "change," for example, could mean money as in "Here's your change" or a different order as in "Change my order to a hot dog." Second, there are almost an unlimited number of ways of giving the same instructions. Finally, a speech-recognizing computer needs to be able to understand many different voice patterns and accents.

In the future, speech recognition software will be used in telecommunications. As discussed in Section 11.1, telecommunications is the sending and receiving of data over the telephone lines. Advancements in speech recognition software will allow a person to retrieve information from a database by simply asking for it over the phone. In the same way, the status of credit card or bank accounts can be checked. Telecommuting is another area where advancements in speech recognition software will be used. Employees will be able to call the office and log on to their computer and update schedules, etc. by talking over the phone.

13.17 Robotics

Another application of artificial intelligence is in *robotics*. To be defined as a robot a machine must be able to both be programmed and move. Most robots, unlike those seen in the movies, are simply moveable arms that can be directed to perform a task. Because they can be programmed, robots can make simple decisions and then act upon them. Of the robots currently "employed," many are used in the automobile industry to spot weld and spray paint cars. As robots become capable of performing increasingly complicated tasks, they will undoubtedly be used in many more industries.

There are a number of advantages to using robots. One is their ability to perform tasks too dangerous for humans. Robots have been developed which can remove and defuse bombs, work in highly radioactive environments, or under conditions of extreme noise or temperature. Their use in aiding the physically challenged is also a very promising area of research. A major advantage of robots is that they can perform their tasks tirelessly, willing to work 24-hour days without rest or vacations.

Robots can work 24 hours a day with no rest

However, a task as simple as picking up an egg has proven difficult for a robot to perform. The hand-eye coordination which we take for granted requires an extremely complex set of actions which are difficult to duplicate mechanically. Even a task as simple as moving through a room without hitting objects can be difficult for a robot.

We have all seen science fiction movies where a robot becomes so humanlike that it exhibits emotions and temperament, but so far no real robot has been developed which has any of these traits. In all probability such a robot is a very long way off, if indeed one can ever be created.

When natural language processing and artificial intelligence programs are perfected, the use of robots will undoubtedly increase. The dream of having a machine you can order around like a personal servant may then become a reality.

13.18 Virtual Reality

One of the most exciting applications of computing is in creating *virtual reality*. The word virtual is defined as "existing in effect though not in actual fact" while virtual reality is "using a computer to create a world that does not exist." To enter this world the user usually wears special gloves and a helmet containing small computer screens, both of which contain motion sensors. This system is *interactive* which means that the actions of the user determine what the computer displays.

Wonderful interactive games can be created using virtual reality. In one popular game the player enters a room displayed in the helmet and moves his or her head looking for a villain. When the villain is spotted a finger in the glove is used to shoot at the villain. The player has the sensation of stalking the villain through different rooms, up and down stairs, in a world that appears startling real. Obviously the types of games that such technology can create is nearly endless.

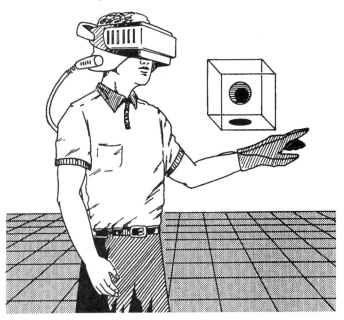

The helmet and glove contain motion sensors that communicate the movements of the wearer to the computer

The worlds created through virtual reality need not be limited to games, but can be used for many practical purposes. For example, computers are now used to create a virtual world that allows a pilot to train landing a jet airliner in a variety of weather conditions without risking a real plane or the pilot's life. Medical students perform simulated operations on patients created by the computer, and architects design buildings through which clients are able to journey without anything being built. Such technology allows customers to experience a "hands-on" demonstration of products or services before they have been actually developed.

It is the convergence of powerful imaging and computing technology that has made virtual reality possible. Major improvements in the way that people interact with the computer are expected to make the virtual experience more realistic. Experiments have been performed using whole body suits similar to wet suits to monitor the motion of most body parts and stationary bicycles which allow the user to pedal through a virtual world. Voice recognition software will also allow the virtual world to respond to voice commands. This is a field that has only began to demonstrate its considerable potential. What worlds might you enjoy experiencing in virtual reality?

13.19 CD-ROM

As computer applications have grown to include the use of graphics, sound, and very large amounts of text, a technology has been needed to store vast quantities of data in an easily usable format. This need has been fulfilled by the CD-ROM (an acronym for compact disc, read-only memory) which stores data so that it can be read by a laser but cannot be changed. CD-ROMs can store 600 megabytes of data on a small disc which is approximately equal to the storage capacity of 400 diskettes—enough space to store the text of 100 books each containing 1,000 pages.

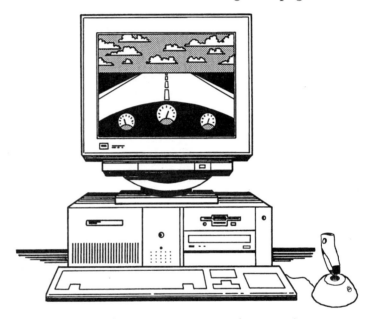

CD-ROMs allow users to run sophisticated programs

Libraries make use of CD-ROMs to store all types of text and graphics including encyclopedias and magazine articles. Because they are stored in digital form it is easy to search them in a manner similar to searching a large database. Since a CD-ROM used by a computer is almost identical in format to a CD used to produce high fidelity sound recordings, the computer can be used with headphones and software to listen to music CDs. In later sections we will discuss multimedia, home computing, and desktop publishing, all of which can make use of the CD-ROM.

13.20 Hypermedia / Multimedia

Technologies such as computing, communications, and imaging (print and video) are merging so that we will no longer be able to identify one from the other. *Hypermedia* or *multimedia* is an example where text, graphics, video, and sound are accessible together through a computer:

A multimedia computer system often includes speakers, a joystick, a CD-ROM drive, earphones, and a microphone

An exciting application of hypermedia is a computerized encyclopedia where the user can access an entry that includes different types of linked information. When accessing an entry on Ludwig von Beethoven, the user might be asked if she would like to see a picture of Ludwig, hear a selection from his ninth symphony, or take a video tour of his house in Vienna. The possible applications of hypermedia are boundless and include computerized repair manuals where the user could, for example, ask for information on an automobile transmission and then access different videos that demonstrate how a certain type of repair is performed. Educational training includes instruction in a foreign language where the student reads a word, hears how the word is pronounced, and then asks to see a person holding a conversation that includes the word.

13.21 Computing at Home

Personal computers are now inexpensive enough that many people have powerful machines at home. As such, software has been specifically created for the home user. Below we discuss several personal applications for home use.

Games and Entertainment

A popular use for home computers is in the field of entertainment. For example, software is now available that produces graphics which can be recorded on a VCR. This allows the home user to produce professional-looking titles and animation for home videos.

Many people enjoy playing computer games at home. There are several different types available, but they generally fall into two categories: *simulations* and *role-playing*. In simulations, the computer graphically simulates an action such as driving a car. A popular simulation is Microsoft's Flight Simulator in which the computer is used to fly a plane. By giving different commands, the "plane" can be made to takeoff, accelerate, turn, land, etc. while the cockpit is displayed on the screen. Flight Simulator is so realistic that pilots use it to practice flying techniques at home. There are other forms of simulations available such as card games, sports, or arcade games.

Role-playing or fantasy games involve solving a complex puzzle by directing the actions of a character described on the screen. This is similar to reading a book, but being able to tell the character what to do. In role-playing games the user enters commands such as "go west" or "open the door" which the character follows. The player could be looking for treasure, or seeking information about a crime. The sense of player involvement will become even greater as virtual reality games become available to the home user.

Arts

The computer can be used by artists to draw and paint pictures. Input devices called *scanners* can convert drawings and pictures into a file, which can then be modified using the computer. Photographers can use similar software to retouch photographs and produce special effects.

Today's musicians are using a special type of computer output called *MIDI*—Musical Instrument Digital Interface. MIDI permits a computer to control synthesizers, allowing entire scores to be composed, edited, and performed using the computer.

Productivity

Other software helps personal computer users to be more productive. For example there are several packages for managing home finances. These help develop a budget, keep track of expenses, prepare taxes, and print checks to pay bills. Some allow you to pay bills using a modem. Software can provide opportunities for home study in a variety of different fields: math, science, reading, and for specialized courses such as the SAT or real estate examination. This is called *computer aided instruction*. Some students find that the ability to work at home at their own pace increases their understanding of the topic.

13.22 Mobile Computing

Advancements in computer technology have caused computer components to become smaller and smaller. This trend is especially true of processing chips which can now contain millions of components in an area as small as a fingernail. Because of this reduction computers the size and weight of a 5 pound book are now being manufactured with the power of a large desktop model, including the monitor. Usually called *laptops*, these small computers can be powered by batteries and therefore operated anywhere including in airplanes and automobiles. Business people, newspaper reporters, and students are among the many users who find laptop computers convenient.

The miniaturization of parts through advances in technology has lead to the development of the *personal digital assistant* or PDA. Often using cellular telephone technology and a built-in modem, the PDA creates a computing environment that is *mobile* or *nomadic*:

PDAs are small enough to fit into a shirt pocket

No longer encumbered by either size or wires, the PDA allows its user to travel anywhere and yet have access to e-mail, the Internet, or any information that can be transmitted over a modem. Electronic news, including traffic, weather, or stock data, can be sent to a PDA based on the users profile. Such technology is of obvious advantage to a salesperson traveling around the world.

13.23 Careers in Computing

Doctors, artists, educators, farmers, and almost any profession you can think of are currently using or will soon make use of computers. As computers have become more powerful they play an ever increasing role in the world we live in. Consequently most people, no matter what field they are employed in, use computers in some way at work. It is estimated that by the year 2000 over 90% of all office personnel will have a computer terminal or PC at their desks.

If you have become interested in computers you might consider a career in computing. According to recent government projections, the computer field will continue to hire people at an increasing rate. In this section we discuss some computer careers that you might consider and the education required to enter them.

The area of computing that employs the largest number of people is *data processing*. Data processing involves the electronic entry, storage, manipulation, and retrieval of data. Businesses, governments, educational institutions—almost any organization—require the management of large amounts of data and therefore need employees capable of data processing. Careers in data processing are usually divided into five categories: data-entry operator, system analyst, system developer, system manager, and computer scientist. We will consider each area separately, outlining the qualifications expected of a person entering the field. After that we will discuss three careers related to the manufacture and sale of computer hardware (computer engineer, manufacturing worker, and computer sales representative.)

Data-Entry Operator

A *data-entry operator* types data into a computer. Data-entry operators may work for banks entering cancelled checks, department stores entering inventory figures, or educational institutions entering student records. A data-entry operator should possess a high school diploma and the ability to type quickly and accurately.

System Analyst

Before a data processing system can be set up a *system analyst* must first analyze and design the system. The analyst must determine how an organization will use their computer system, what data they will store, how they will access it, and how they expect the system to grow in the future. The same planning used in the database chapters of this text have given gave you an introduction to what a system analyst does.

A system analyst should possess a comprehensive knowledge of data-processing methods, currently available software and hardware, and programming languages. Most system analysts are college graduates who have majored in computer science or business administration or both.

System Developer/Programmer

After the system analyst has determined what type of system should be installed, the *system developer* provides the necessary software. A programmer should possess a detailed knowledge of the programming language or languages being used as well as an ability to reason analytically and pay close attention to details.

The education required to be a programmer is usually determined by the needs of the employer. Many businesses employ programmers who have taken technical school or community college programming courses. Large or specialized companies, which need highly sophisticated programming, usually require college graduates. A good way to start in preparing for a career as a programmer is to take programming and computer science courses, as well as mathematics.

System Manager

Companies with large data processing requirements usually employ a manager who is responsible for running the Management Information Systems department (MIS). The *MIS manager* must organize the computer and human resources of the department in order to best achieve the organization's goals.

A system manager should possess a detailed understanding of data-processing methods, hardware, and software. A college degree in business administration with a concentration in information systems is usually required.

Computer Scientist

The study of computer science is a very broad field involving many disciplines including science, electronics, and mathematics. A *computer scientist* often works in research at a university or computer manufacturer developing new computer applications software and hardware. It is computer scientists who first design and develop robots, natural language processors, or any of the other many applications that we have mentioned.

A computer scientist usually has both undergraduate and graduate school degrees. To prepare to be a computer scientist it is advisable to take science courses, especially physics, mathematics courses including calculus, and programming and computer science courses.

The computer industry careers previously discussed primarily involve working with software. The computer hardware industry also offers a number of career opportunities including the design, manufacture, service, and sale of computers.

Computer Engineer

Computer engineers design and manufacture computers. This field is broad and includes engineers who develop new computer applications. Other engineers translate ideas produced by researchers into manufactured products.

A computer engineer usually possesses both undergraduate and graduate degrees in engineering. To prepare to be a computer engineer it is important to take science and mathematics courses including physics and calculus, as well as programming courses.

The people who help build computer systems usually possess a number of talents including the ability to work with their hands. Specifically, manufacturing workers are adept at handling tools.

Manufacturing Worker

Manufacturing workers have usually earned a high school or community college degree. Good preparation for such a career includes taking courses in mechanical arts as well as science and mathematics.

A very large number of people sell computers either as representatives who travel and visit clients or as salespeople in computer stores. It is important that they possess a thorough knowledge of the equipment they sell and be able to explain how it may be used by each customer.

Computer Sales Representative

Preparation for a *computer sales representative* should include courses in business as well as computer science. The level of education required will depend on the sophistication of the equipment being sold. Often a high school or community college degree will be sufficient. To sell large computer systems, a sales representative may be required to have a four-year college degree.

13.24 The Social and Ethical Consequences of Computers

The society in which we live has been so profoundly affected by computers that historians refer to the present time as the *information age*. This is due to the computer's ability to store and manipulate large amounts of information (data). Computers have become such a dominant force that if all of them were to disappear much of our society would be unable to function. Because of computers we are evolving out of an industrial and into an information society, much as over a hundred years ago we evolved from an agricultural society into an industrial one. Such fundamental societal changes cause disruptions which must be planned for. For this reason it is crucial that we consider both the social and ethical consequences of our increasing dependence on computers.

We have already mentioned the impact of telecommunications. By allowing people to work anywhere that telephones or satellite communications are available, we are likely to become a more diversified society. Large cities with their centralized offices will no longer be as necessary. In fact, after the Los Angeles earthquakes in 1994 a computer newspaper had the headline "A not-so-gentle push for telecommuting." Such decentralization could reduce traffic congestion, air pollution, and many of the other consequences of an urban society. Because of this, Alvin Toffler in his book *The Third Wave* called this the age of the "electronic cottage."

In our discussion of robots we mentioned their ability to work 24-hour days without vacations. While this is obviously a major benefit to an employer, it could have a negative impact on employees. Manufacturers are increasingly able to replace factory workers with machines, thereby increasing efficiency and saving money. This trend, however, also leads to increased unemployment of those factory workers who lack technical skills.

The argument is often used that new technologies such as robotics create jobs for the people who design, build, install, and service them. While this is true, these new jobs require well educated, highly trained people. For this reason it is important to think carefully about the educational requirements needed for employment. As we become an increasingly "high-tech" society, those properly prepared for technical jobs will be the most likely to find employment. In response to this problem many states have instituted programs to train laid-off factory workers so that they may enter technical fields.

Another concern is that the widespread dependence on information services such as the Internet will create two groups; those with access to information and those without. The *National Information Infrastructure Act* is a government sponsored version of the Internet, with business (commercial) participation. One of the goals of the NII is to provide access to the information highway at every school, hospital, and public library.

13.25 The Right to Privacy

With computers impacting on our lives in an ever increasing number of ways, serious ethical questions arise over their use. By ethical questions we mean asking what are the right and wrong ways to use computers. As human beings we want to insure that our rights as individuals are not encroached upon by the misuse of these machines.

Probably the most serious problem created by computers is in invading our right to privacy. Because computers can store vast amounts of data we must decide what information is proper to store, what is improper, and who should have access to the information. Every time you use a credit card, make a phone call, withdraw money from the bank, reserve a flight on an airplane, or register to take a course at school a computer records the transaction. Using these records it would be possible to learn a great deal about you—where you have been, when you were there, and what you have done. Should this information be available to everyone?

Computers are also used to store information about your credit rating, which determines your ability to borrow money. If you want to buy a car and finance it at the bank, the bank first checks your credit records on a computer to determine if you have a good credit rating. If you purchase the car and then apply for automobile insurance, another computer will check to determine if you have traffic violations. How do you know if the information being used is accurate? To protect both your privacy and the accuracy of data stored about you, a number of laws have been passed.

The **Fair Credit Reporting Act of 1970** deals with data collected for use by credit, insurance, and employment agencies. The act gives individuals the right to see information maintained about them. If a person is denied credit they are allowed to see the files used to make the credit determination. If any of the information is incorrect, the person has the right to have it changed. The act also restricts who may access credit files to only those with a court order or the written permission of the individual whose credit is being checked.

The **Privacy Act of 1974** restricts the way in which personal data can be used by federal agencies. Individuals must be permitted access to information stored about them and may correct any information that is incorrect. Agencies must insure both the security and confidentiality of any sensitive information. Although this law applies only to federal agencies, many states have adopted similar laws.

The **Financial Privacy Act of 1978** requires that a government authority have a subpoena, summons, or search warrant to access an individual's financial records. When such records are released, the financial institution must notify the individual of who has had access to them.

The **Electronic Communications Privacy Act of 1986** (ECPA) makes it a crime to access electronic data without authorization. It also prohibits unauthorized release of such data.

Laws such as these help to insure that the right to privacy is not infringed by data stored in computer files. Although implementing privacy laws has proven expensive and difficult, most people would agree that they are needed.

13.26 Protecting Computer Software and Data

Because computer software can be copied electronically it is easy to duplicate. Such duplication is usually illegal because the company producing the software is not paid for the copy. This has become an increasingly serious problem as the number of illegal software copies distributed by computer *pirates* has grown. Developing, testing, marketing, and supporting software is an expensive process. If the software developer is then denied rightful compensation, the future development of all software is jeopardized.

Software companies are increasingly vigilant in detecting and prosecuting those who illegally copy their software. In recent years, software companies have actually made "raids" on businesses and educational institutions to search their computers. An organization found guilty of using illegally copied software can be fined, and its reputation damaged. Therefore, when using software it is important to use only legally acquired copies, and to not make illegal copies for others.

Another problem that is growing as computer use increases is the willful interference with or destruction of computer data. Because computers can transfer and erase data at high speeds, it makes them especially vulnerable to acts of vandalism. Newspapers have carried numerous reports of home computer users gaining access to large computer databases. Sometimes these *hackers* change or erase data stored in the system. These acts are usually illegal and can cause very serious and expensive damage. The Electronic Communications Privacy Act of 1986 specifically makes it a federal offense to access electronic data without authorization.

One especially harmful act is the planting of a *virus* into computer software. A virus is a series of instructions buried into a program that cause the computer to destroy data when given a certain signal. For example, the instructions to destroy data might wait until a certain time or date is reached before being executed. Because the virus is duplicated each time the software is copied, it spreads to other computers, hence the name virus. This practice is illegal and can result in considerable damage. Computer viruses have become so widespread that there are now computer programs that can be used to detect and erase viruses before they can damage data.

Contaminated disks are one way that viruses are spread from computer to computer

Most people are becoming aware that the willful destruction of computer data is no different than any other vandalization of property. Since the damage is done electronically the result is often not as obvious as destroying physical property, but the consequences are much the same. It is estimated that computer crimes cost the nation billions of dollars each year.

13.27 The Ethical Responsibilities of the Programmer

It is extremely difficult, if not impossible, for a computer programmer to guarantee that a program will *always* operate properly. The programs used to control complicated devices contain millions of instructions, and as programs grow longer the likelihood of errors increases. A special cause for concern is the increased use of computers to control potentially dangerous devices such as aircraft, nuclear reactors, or sensitive medical equipment. This places a strong ethical burden on the programmer to insure, as best he or she can, the reliability of computer software.

The Department of Defense (DOD) is currently supporting research aimed at detecting and correcting programming errors. Because it spends billions of dollars annually developing software, much of it for use in situations which can be life threatening, the DOD is especially interested in having reliable programs.

As capable as computers have proven to be, we must be cautious when allowing them to replace human beings in areas where judgement is crucial. Because we are intelligent, humans can often detect that something out of the ordinary has occurred and then take actions which have not been previously anticipated. Computers will only do what they have been programmed to do, even if it is to perform a dangerous act.

We must also consider situations in which the computer can protect human life better than humans. For example, in the space program astronauts place their lives in the hands of computers which must continuously perform complicated calculations at very high speeds. No human being would be capable of doing the job as well as a computer. Computers are also routinely used to monitor seriously ill patients. Since computers are able to work 24 hours a day without becoming distracted or falling asleep, they probably perform such tasks better than most humans would.

DESKTOP PUBLISHING AND GRAPHICS

The popularity of computers has produced a new generation of software geared to the presentation of information. Computers can now be used to manipulate art work, pictures, and text. These applications allow an organization, educational institution, or individual to produce professional looking documents without the use of artists, designers, or typesetters.

13.28 Printers

Probably the most important advance which made desktop publishing possible was the creation of a low-cost, dependable printer. A *laser printer* uses a beam of light to draw each character on the page, employing a process similar to a photocopier. This allows for smooth characters. A close examination of a character produced by a laser printer illustrates this:

T

A character produced by a laser printer is smooth

Laser printers are also able to produce graphics such as pictures and diagrams with a similar level of clarity. Color laser printers are also available for printing images in full color.

An *inkjet printer* contains an ink catridge and places very small dots on the paper to form characters and graphics. The output from an inkjet printer is also high quality, but not quite as smooth as the output from a laser printer. Color inkjet printers are also available. They are very inexpensive compared to color laser printers and produce very good color output.

13.29 Desktop Publishing

One of the most popular uses for laser printers is in the field of *desktop publishing*, or DTP. As discussed in Chapter Twelve, special software allows persons not trained in art or layout to create professional looking documents using a personal computer and a laser printer. It is the purpose of desktop publishing software to combine text (created in a word processor) with illustrations (created by a graphics program) to produce the final document. Before desktop publishing existed, creating a document such as a brochure was a complicated procedure, involving many people:

1. A writer to create the text of the brochure.
2. An artist to produce the illustrations.
3. A typesetter to print the text.
4. A layout person to combine the text and illustrations into the completed brochure using scissors and glue.
5. A printer to produce the brochure.

Now a single person can perform all of these tasks using a computer. A major advantage of using desktop publishing software is that changes can easily be made to a document instead of cutting and pasting with glue. Illustrations and text can be added or deleted, changed in size, or the whole layout redone—all on a computer screen.

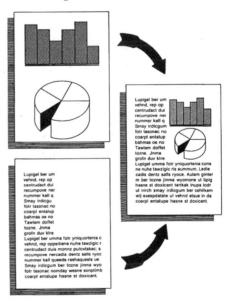

DTP software combines graphics and text into one file

By laying out a document on the computer screen instead of on paper different layouts can be created and printed until the desired combination is found. Once completed, the final version can be printed and the document saved on disk so that it can be edited or reprinted at a later time.

Three of the most commonly used desktop publishing programs are PageMaker, FrameMaker, and QuarkXPress. Less powerful and inexpensive programs such as Publish It!, Microsoft Publisher, and PrintShop allow DTP documents to be created and printed on dot matrix printers. Most of these packages contain collections of prepared illustrations called *clip art* which can be included in documents, often eliminating the need for an artist.

13.30 Graphics and Illustration Software

Using specialized software it is possible to create graphic images on the computer. Graphic images are non-text items such as drawings, photographs, charts, logos, etc. The advantage of using a computer rather than drawing on paper is that the image can then be manipulated; resized, rotated, etc. and the image can then be stored in the computer's memory. When the final version is created, it can be printed in black and white using a laser printer, or in color using a color printer. The graphics you created in Chapter Twelve are simple examples of what can be accomplished using graphics software.

Stock Prices Last Week

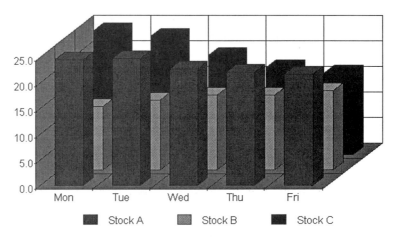

Sophisticated graphics programs can easily produce three-dimensional objects, charts, and graphs

There are several powerful programs available for creating and editing graphic images. Two of these are Adobe Illustrator and CorelDraw. Most require the use of a specialized input device to aid in the drawing. The most popular of these devices are the mouse and the drawing tablet.

In addition to allowing the easy modification of a graphic, illustration software often has a variety of advanced tools that can quickly manipulate a graphic in ways that would be difficult manually. For example, suppose a business hires an artist to design a logo. Using pen and paper, the artist can then sketch the logo and add any colors using paint. If the company then wants to see what the logo looks like in a different color, the artist must redraw the logo and apply the different color. If the logo is instead prepared using illustration software, the artist can move the cursor to the desired location on the screen, execute a command which says to change the color, and print the new version. Other examples of editing options include changing line widths, erasing lines and objects in a diagram, and changing the size or position of objects. Once complete, the final graphic can be saved in a file on disk so that it could be edited or reprinted at a later date.

Another advantage to using illustration software is that any graphics produced can easily be placed in a desktop-published document. Most DTP software packages can read the files produced by illustration software, and place a graphic directly into a DTP document. Some DTP packages can even perform basic editing on the image, allowing it to be scaled (resized), rotated, or cropped (only part of the graphic is displayed).

13.31 Where can we go from here?

In this text we have presented the history of computing, showed you how to word process, use a database and a spreadsheet, and have considered the future of computing. Our hope is that you are excited by computers and realize the tremendous potential they have to serve us in a wide variety of ways. We also hope that you have been made aware of how computers might be misused. It is therefore the duty of each one of us to ensure that the awesome power given to us by computers be used only to benefit humankind.

Chapter Summary

One of the most important advances in the field of computing has been in telecommunications, which means the sending of computer data over phone lines. Modems are used both to transmit and receive computer data. Because of telecommunications many people may be able to work at home.

A popular form of telecommunications is the electronic bulletin board (BBS) which allows users to transmit and receive messages. A similar form of telecommunications is electronic mail (e-mail) where individual users are able to receive messages meant only for them.

ClarisWorks has a Communications application that allows access to information services. Using the Connection command from the Settings Menu, options are entered for the telephone number, baud rate, data bits, parity, and stop bits. These settings can then be stored in a file. The Open Connection command from the Session menu dials the number and attempts to establish communications with the other computer. To terminate the communications, Close Connection is used.

Networks allow computers to communicate with each other over telephone lines, fiber optics, satellites, and digital microwave radio. Each computer connected to a network is called a node. The most common network is the Local Area Network (LAN) which allows files to be shared between a number of computers. These files are usually stored on a file server.

The Internet is a large network of networks linking computers all over the world. Through the Internet personal computer users have access to information resources worldwide. Searching through the vast quantities of information is assisted by specialized software, services, and search tools, including indexes to the numerous databases. Graphics as well as text are available on the World Wide Web, a popular area of the Internet.

In the future all voice, data, image, and video information will be transmitted and received in digital form. Networks are being developed throughout the world capable of carrying such digital information to almost any spot on earth.

The continued development of microprocessors has affected many products including automobiles and home electronics devices. With their ability to make simple decisions, microprocessors can automate many of the functions performed by these devices. Software will be increasingly user friendly.

Supercomputers are being built that can perform up to one trillion calculations per second. Neural-network software is designed to be similar to the pattern of cells in the human brain and "learn" by analyzing large sets of data. Two problems requiring large amounts of computer power are database marketing and computer generated motion picture effects.

Using computers to make decisions normally made by human beings is called artificial intelligence. Although computers cannot think, they can be programmed to make decisions which, for example, allow them to play chess. Expert systems are a form of artificial intelligence where a computer is programmed with a set of rules that can solve a problem, producing the same solution a human expert would. Credit card companies, the IRS and hospitals are a few of the organizations currently using expert systems.

Recognizing spoken words and translating them into digital form is called speech recognition which involves natural language processing, a field of artificial intelligence that translates a sentence into its separate parts to understand its meaning. Numerous problems face the successful development of language processing systems.

A robot is a machine that can be programmed and also move. Robots are currently used to perform manufacturing tasks. When natural language processing and artificial intelligence programs are perfected, the use of robots will increase.

Virtual reality is using the computer to create a world that does not exist. To enter this world the user usually wears a helmet containing small computer screens and gloves with motion sensors. CD-ROMs can store up to 600 megabytes of data on a small disk and can be used in creating virtual reality or hypermedia. Hypermedia combines text, graphics, video, and sound together on a computer.

The use of personal computers in the home, including laptops and personal digital assistants, has become popular and will grow with the increased availability of telecommunications and networks. Home computers are often used to play games, assist in hobbies, and to run productivity applications such as ClarisWorks.

Careers in computing and the educational requirements needed to pursue them were discussed in this chapter. Careers which require only a high school education as well as those requiring a college education were presented.

Historians refer to the present time as the information age due to the computer's ability to store and manipulate large amounts of data. As the use of computers increases they will profoundly affect society including what jobs will be available and the length of the work week.

A problem created by computers is their potential for invading our right to privacy. Laws have been passed to protect us from the misuse of data stored in computers.

Because computer software is easy to copy, illegal copies are often made, denying software manufacturers of rightful compensation. Another problem has been the willful destruction of computer files by erasing data or planting a virus into programs that can spread when the programs are copied.

As computers are increasingly used to make decisions in situations which can threaten human life, it becomes the responsibility of programmers to do their best to insure the reliability of the software they have developed. We must continue to be cautious not to replace human beings with computers in areas where judgement is crucial.

Desktop publishing software has made it possible for computers to produce and manipulate art work, pictures and the layout of documents. Laser printers, which employ a beam of light to draw characters on a page, are often used in desktop publishing applications.

Special software is used to create graphics images such as drawings, photographs, charts, etc. on the computer. This software allows the images to be easily manipulated and modified.

Vocabulary

Artificial intelligence - Computers used to make decisions which would normally be made by a human being.

Baud rate - Rate at which characters of data are transmitted in telecommunications. Also called bits per second (bps).

BBS - Electronic bulletin board system where subscribers can post and read messages using telecommunications.

Bulletin board system (BBS) - Telecommunications service which allows subscribers using a computer and modem to transmit messages that can be received by all the other subscribers.

CD-ROM (Compact Disc Read-Only Memory) - An aluminum plastic-coated disc, capable of storing up to 600 megabytes of data, which is read by a laser.

Clip art - Collection of previously prepared graphics for use in desktop publishing.

Client/Server - A program requesting information on the Internet / A program that provides requested Internet information.

Command and Control systems - Computer systems that can be controlled by spoken words.

Computer aided instruction - Using specialized software to learn at home, at your own pace.

Database marketing - Searching a very large database in order to extract marketing information.

Data processing - Electronic entry, storage, manipulation, and retrieval of information using a computer.

Desktop publishing - Using special software to create professional looking documents on a computer.

Dictation systems - A oomputer system that converts spoken words to text.

Digital - Information expressed as a series of binary digits.

Download - To transfer a message or computer file from a bulletin board system or information service to your computer.

Electronic mail (e-mail) - Telecommunications service which allows a person using a computer and modem to send a private message to another person's computer.

Expert system - System programmed to produce the same solution a human expert would if asked to solve the same problem.

File server - A computer containing large disk storage that provides file access to other computers in a network.

Gopher - A tool that can be used to access information on the Internet.

Hacker - Person who uses a modem to enter a computer system without authorization.

Home page - The first page displayed after connecting to a Web site.

Host - The computer running a bulletin board or information service.

HotJava - A Web browser that can be used to create customized Web pages.

HTML - Hypertext Markup Language. The language that is used to create Web pages.

HTTP - Hypertext Transfer Protocol. The protocol used by Web sites.

Hypermedia - Graphics, video, text, and sound accessed together. Also called multimedia.

Information age - Current historical time characterized by increasing dependence on the computer's ability to store and manipulate large amounts of information.

Information highway - Nickname for a large, publicly accessible computer network, the full name is the National Information Infrastructure. Often applied to the Internet.

Information service - A company that provides different telecommunications services, usually for a fee.

Interactive - Sending information to and receiving information from a computer, which often reacts to your actions.

Internet - A large network linking computers located around the world.

Inkjet printer - A printer that uses an ink cartridge to place small dots on a page to form text and images.

Java - A programming language that will allow programs to be easily sent over the Internet.

Laptop computer - A small computer usually powered by batteries allowing it to be operated in almost any location.

Laser printer - A printer that employs a beam of light to draw characters.

Local Area Network (LAN) - Networking nearby microcomputers so that they can share data.

MIDI (Musical Instrument Digital Interface) - Using computers to control synthesizers.

Mobile computing - A computing environment in which a computer uses cellular phone technology and a modem to send and receive information. Also called nomadic.

Modem - Device which translates binary data into tones and tones back into binary data so that computer data can be sent over telephone lines.

Morphing - A process by which a digitized image turns into a second image.

Natural language processing - Using a computer to determine the meaning of words in sentence form. Often used with speech recognition to control the actions of a computer.

Neural network software - Software designed to simulate the pattern of cells in the human brain allowing it to "learn" from analyzing large sets of data.

Network - Computers that are connected so that data can be transmitted between them.

Parallel processing - A computer containing a number of high-speed microprocessors which solves a problem by breaking it into parts and solving the parts simultaneously.

Personal digital assistant (PDA) - A very small computer usually containing a modem to allow its user to receive or send electronic information.

Pirate - Person who illegally copies or distributes computer software.

Pixel - A byte of information from a graphic that has been digitized.

Posting - Leaving a message on a BBS.

Protocol - A standardized method of communication that allows computer networks and computers to talk to one another.

Robot - Machine which can be programmed and is also capable of motion.

Robot program - A program such as Lycos that follows links in Web pages and automatically adds new links to its database.

Robotics - The study and application of robots to perform tasks.

Scanner - Input device that can be used to convert drawings and pictures into digital format.

Simulation - Where a computer produces information similar to that produced by a real world situation (i.e., flight simulation).

Speech recognition - Using a computer to recognize individual spoken words. See also natural language processing.

Supercomputer - A computer capable of performing billions of calculations per second.

Surfing - Accessing different Internet locations to see what information is there.

Tags - HTML codes used to determine how a Web page is displayed and what will be displayed.

Telecommunications - Sending and receiving computer data over telephone lines.

Telecommuting - Using telecommunications to work at home.

Turing Test - "Imitation Game" used to determine how advanced an artificial intelligence program or system is.

Upload - To transfer a message or computer file from your computer to a bulletin board system or information service.

URL - Uniform Resource Locator. The address required to connect to a Web site.

User friendly - Software that is easier to use.

Virtual reality - Using the computer to create a world that does not exist.

Virus - Program which hides within another program for the purpose of destroying or altering data.

Web browser - A program that understands HTTP to display the graphics and text of Web pages.

Web page - Information at a Web site that can include graphics, fancy text, and easy access to other Web sites or pages.

Web server - A Web site.

Wireless LAN - Networking nearby microcomputers without physically connecting them.

World Wide Web (WWW) - A graphical user interface to surf the Internet.

Yahoo - A tool for searching the Web which contains indexes of Web pages.

Reviews

Sections 13.1 — 13.3

1. Describe four databases that you would like to be able to access using telecommunications. State why each of them would be useful to you.

2. Besides those listed in the text, list three occupations where people would be able to work at home rather than in an office using telecommunications.

3. What is the difference between an electronic bulletin board and electronic mail?

4. If all of the students in your class had computers and modems at home, in what ways could they be used by your classmates and instructor?

5. What is meant by the term "host"?

6. Explain how the baud rate is changed in a ClarisWorks communications file.

Sections 13.4 — 13.8

7. Describe how 3 different organizations might make use of computer networks.

8. Explain how an automobile dealership might use a computer network.

9. Explain what type of files might be stored on the file server in a school computer network.

10. Describe how a Shakespearean scholar might make use of Internet.

11. List 3 different ways in which you might use Internet.

12. Your friend's Internet address at work is `cesser@hostl.cia.gov`. What type of employer does she work for?

13. What is a gopher?

14. How could you use a gopher to find information about Newton's Law?

15. What do the letters HTTP stand for?

16. What do the letters HTML stand for?

17. How could you use the Web to find information that appeared in *USA Today*?

Sections 13.8 — 13.14

18. Discuss some of the advantages of transmitting voice, data, image, and video information in digital form.

19. What tasks do microprocessors perform in automobiles?

20. What is artificial intelligence?

21. a) What devices owned by your family contain microprocessors and what are they used for?
    b) What devices would you like to see include microprocessors? Why? What tasks would the microprocessors perform?

22. List three types of problems that would require a supercomputer to solve.

23. Describe a problem that you believe could be solved using neural-network software. Explain how the software will "learn."

24. Describe a marketing problem that can be solved by making use of a very large database. Include a description of the database.

25. List three movies you have seen recently that make use of computer generated effects.

26. State three questions you would ask to determine which was the human and which the computer when playing Turing's Imitation Game. Asking "Are you the computer?" is not fair!

Sections 13.15 — 13.22

27. List four jobs where you think expert systems could be used to help the people performing the jobs. Explain why the systems would be helpful.

28. List four jobs where expert systems could probably not be used, and explain why.

29. Would an expert system be helpful to you in selecting clothes to buy? Explain why or why not.

30. What are some of the difficulties being encountered in the development of natural language processing systems?

31. Why should we be careful in trusting expert systems? What do they lack that humans possess?

32. If you could have a robot built to your own specifications, what would you have it be capable of doing?

33. Describe 3 ways in which Ivy University might use virtual reality in educating its students.

34. Briefly describe a game you would enjoy playing in virtual reality.

35. What kind of data would you like to have stored on a CD-ROM? How would you make use of it?

36. Describe how hypermedia might be used by Ivy University's English Department.

37. Describe some of the changes that you believe will occur in the way computers are used in the home over the next ten years.

38. How could you make use of a personal digital assistant that includes a cellular telephone?

Section 13.23

The nine computer careers mentioned in this chapter include:

(1) data-entry operator
(2) system analyst
(3) system developer/programmer
(4) system manager
(5) computer scientist
(6) computer engineer
(7) manufacturing worker
(8) sales representative

39. Which of the listed careers require only a:
   a) high school diploma
   b) college diploma
   c) college and graduate school degrees

40. For each of the following students list the careers above that he or she should consider:
   a) a student who likes mathematics.
   b) a student who wants to be involved in the management of a business.
   c) a student who wants to work in the development of rocket guidance systems.
   d) a student who likes to think through problems in a methodical, logical way.
   e) a student who likes to work with their hands.

Sections 13.24 — 13.27

41. Alvin Toffler named his book "The Third Wave." What were the first two waves?

42. What is meant by the term "high-tech" society?

43. a) How do you believe society will benefit from the information age?
   b) What might be the negative aspects of the information age?

44. How can a computer be used to invade your privacy?

45. What can you do if you are turned down for credit at a bank and believe that the data used to deny credit is inaccurate?

46. What is necessary for a federal government authority to access an individual's financial records? What must the authority do after accessing the records?

47. What ethical responsibilities does a programmer have when writing a program that will be used to design a bridge? Can the programmer absolutely guarantee that the program will operate properly? Why?

48. How does a laser printer differ from a dot matrix printer?

49. a) What are 4 advantages of using desktop publishing?
    b) Describe 3 organizations that might make use of desktop publishing.

50. Describe 3 uses you might make of graphics and illustration software.

A | Appendix A
ClarisWorks Functions

The following is a partial list of functions that can be placed in a spreadsheet cell or in the formula for a summary or calculated field in a database. A complete list is given in the *ClarisWorks User's Guide* supplied by Claris.

Functions

In the function examples that follow,

<value> can be replaced by:

- a single number (such as 10)
- a cell reference for a cell storing a numeric value (e.g., C5)
- an expression that evaluates to a value (such as C5*2)
- a field reference enclosed in single quotes for a field storing a numeric value (such as 'GPA')

<range> can be replaced by:

- a cell reference for a cell storing a numeric value (e.g., C5)
- a list of cells separated by commas (such as A1, B12, D5)
- a continuous range (A1..A10)
- a mixture of both separated by commas (A1, B1..B5, C3, C9..C12)
- a field reference enclosed in single quotes (such as 'GPA')

Mathematical Functions

ABS(<value>**)**
Returns the absolute value of <value>: ABS(10) returns 10, ABS(–10) returns 10.

EXP(<value>**)**
Returns *e* raised to the power of <value>.

FACT(<value>**)**
Returns the factorial of <value> where <value> is a positive whole number: FACT(3) is 6 ($3! = 3 \times 2 \times 1$).

FRAC(<value>**)**
Returns the fractional portion of <value>: FRAC(12.234) returns 0.234.

INT(<value>**)**
Returns the integer closest to <value>: INT(1.9) returns 1, INT(–7.24) returns –8.

LN(<value>**)**
Returns the natural logarithm (base *e*) of <value>. <value> must be positive.

LOG10(<value>**)**
Returns the base 10 logarithm of <value>. <value> must be positive.

MOD(<value1>, <value2>**)**
Returns the remainder of <value1> ÷ <value2>. <value2> may not be 0.

PI()
Returns the constant 3.14159... (pi, π). No argument is used.

RAND(<value>**)**
Returns a random integer between 0 and <value>. <value> is optional, and if omitted the random number is a real number between 0 and 1.

ROUND(<value>, <decimals>**)**
Returns <value> rounded to <decimals> decimal places. When the <decimals> is 0, <value> is rounded to the nearest integer.

SIGN(<value>**)**
Returns 1 if <value> is positive, 0 if <value> is 0, and –1 if it is negative.

SQRT(<value>**)**
Returns the square root of <value>. <value> must be positive.

Statistical Functions

AVERAGE(<range>**)**
Returns the average of the values in <range>.

COUNT(<range>**)**
Returns the number of non-blank cells in <range>.

MAX(<range>**)**
Returns the largest value in <range>.

MIN(<range>**)**
Returns the smallest value in <range>.

PRODUCT(<range>**)**
Returns the product of the values in <range>.

STDEV(<range>**)**
Returns the standard deviation of a population based on the values (samples) in <range>.

SUM(<range>**)**
Returns the total of the values in <range>.

VAR(<range>**)**
Returns the variance of a population based on the values (samples) in <range>.

Logical Functions

AND(<range>)
Returns TRUE if every value in <range> evaluates to TRUE, and FALSE if any value in <range> evaluates to FALSE. If range stores values, 0 represents FALSE, and nonzero values are TRUE.

IF(<condition>, <true value>, <false value>)
Returns the <true value> if <condition> is true, <false value> if false.

NOT(<value>)
Returns TRUE if <value> is 0, and FALSE if <value> is nonzero: NOT(C1="Bill") is FALSE when C1 stores the label "Bill" and TRUE otherwise.

OR(<range>)
Returns TRUE if any value in <range> evaluates to TRUE, FALSE if all values in <range> evaluate to FALSE. If range stores values, 0 represents FALSE, and nonzero values are TRUE.

Trigonometric Functions

ACOS(<value>)
Returns the arc cosine of <value> in radians. <value> must be between −1.0 and +1.0.

ASIN(<value>)
Returns the arc sine of <value> in radians. <value> must be between −1.0 and +1.0.

ATAN(<value>)
Returns the arc tangent of <value> in radians.

ATAN2(<Xvalue>, <Yvalue>)
Returns the arc tangent in radians of an angle defined by the coordinates <Xvalue>, <Yvalue>.

COS(<value>)
Returns the cosine of <value> where <value> is measured in radians.

DEGREES(<value>)
Converts <value> from radians to degrees.

RADIANS(<value>)
Converts <value> from degrees to radians.

SIN(<value>)
Returns the sine of <value> where <value> is measured in radians.

TAN(<value>)
Returns the tangent of <value> where <value> is measured in radians.

Financial Functions

FV(<Rvalue>, <Tvalue>, <Pvalue>, <PVvalue>, <Evalue>**)**
Returns the future value of an investment where <Rvalue> is the interest rate per period, <Tvalue> is the term, and <Pvalue> is a periodic payment. <PVvalue> is the present value of the investment and <Evalue> is 0 if payments occur at the end of the period, or 1 if payments occur at the beginning of the period. Both <PVvalue> and <Evalue> are optional and may be left out of the function.

PMT(<Rvalue>, <Tvalue>, <Pvalue>, <Fvalue>, <Evalue>**)**
Returns the periodic payment on an installment loan where <Rvalue> is the interest rate per period, <Tvalue> is the term, and <Pvalue> is the present value of the investment. <Fvalue> is the future value of the investment and <Evalue> is 0 if payments occur at the end of the period, or 1 if payments occur at the beginning of the period. Both <Fvalue> and <Evalue> are optional and may be left out of the function.

RATE(<Fvalue>, <Pvalue>, <Tvalue>**)**
Returns the fixed interest rate required to turn an investment of <Pvalue> into <Fvalue> when <Tvalue> is the term. <Tvalue> must be positive.

Date/Time Functions

ClarisWorks stores all Dates and Times as a serial number which represents the amount of time elapsed since January 1, 1904. For example the serial number 34,000 represents 34,000 days since 1/1/04, or Saturday, February 1, 1997. Some of the functions below convert between serial numbers and Dates/Times. For more information about the internal representations for Dates/Times see the *ClarisWorks User's Guide* supplied by Claris.

SECOND(<time>**)**
MINUTE(<time>**)**
HOUR(<time>**)**
Returns the seconds, minutes, or hours portion of a <time> constant or a time stored in a cell or field.

DAY(<date>**)**
WEEKDAY(<date>**)**
MONTH(<date>**)**
YEAR(<date>**)**
Returns the day, weekday, month, or year portion of a <date> constant or a date stored in a cell or field.

DAYNAME(<value>**)**
Returns the name of the day represented by <value>. Value must be between 1 and 7, where 1 represents the label Sunday: DAYNAME(2) returns Monday.

DATETOTEXT(<serial_date>**)**
Converts a <serial_date> number to its date: DATETOTEXT(34000) returns 2/1/97.

TEXTTODATE(<text_date>**)**
Returns the serial number for <date>: TEXTTODATE("2/1/97") is 34000.

TIMETOTEXT(<serial_time>**)**
Converts a <serial_time> number to its time.

TEXTTOTIME(<text_time>**)**
Returns the serial number for <time>.

NOW()
Returns the current date and time. No argument is used.

Special Functions

CHOOSE(<value>, <option₁>, <option₂>, ...**)**
Returns <option₁> if the <value> is 1, <option₂> if the <value> is 2, and so on. <options> can be any mix of numbers, text, cell references, etc. The <value> must be greater than 0, and less than or equal to the number of <options> listed.

HLOOKUP(<value>, <range>, <rows>**)**
Horizontal look up that locates cell in first row of <range> that contains the largest value that is less than or equal to <value>. Returns contents of cell that is <rows> below that cell.

VLOOKUP(<value>, <range>, <columns>**)**
Locates cell in first column of <range> that contains the largest value thatis less than or equal to <value>. Returns contents of cell that is <columns> to the right of that cell.

A

An Introduction to Computing Using ClarisWorks

B | Appendix B
System Commands and Backups

Filenames

Every program and file on a disk is identified by a unique name. For this reason you have specified a filename each time you saved a new file. A filename may be from one to thirty-one characters long. Only the following characters are allowed to be used as part of a filename:

Letters: A, B, ¼ Y, Z
Numbers: 0, 1, ¼ 8, 9
Special Characters: Any character, including spaces and special symbols, except the colon (:).

While special characters may be used, it is usually best to limit filenames to only letters, numbers, and spaces. Examples of valid filenames are:

CHAPTER 1
Student
94 Grades
COMPUSERVE

Using the Macintosh System

ClarisWorks normally controls the creating and saving of files. There are times, however, when you will need to have access to certain Macintosh System commands to manage and organize your files. As an example, you might want to delete old data files from your disk.

The Macintosh System uses an application called *Finder* to maintain the Desktop—the area you see on the screen when the computer is turned on. Finder enables you to copy files, delete files, and initialize disks. The Finder Menu bar is displayed at the top of the screen when the computer is turned on:

🍎 File Edit View Label Special

*The Finder menu bar has pull-down menus
similar to ClarisWorks*

Deleting Files

Sometimes a file is no longer needed and should be removed from disk. Files are deleted by dragging the file's icon to the Trash icon. For example, suppose AC EMPLOYEES is no longer needed:

1. Boot the Macintosh System. Do not run ClarisWorks, but leave the Finder screen visible.
2. Insert the data disk that contains AC EMPLOYEES into the drive.
3. Double-click on the Data Disk icon to display its contents.
4. Drag the AC EMPLOYEES icon to the Trash icon:

Hard Disk

Data Disk

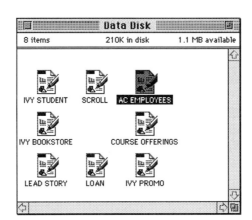

The Trash icon is highlighted when the file is dragged onto it

Caution should be used when deleting a file. Once deleted, it may be impossible to recover the file.

Trash

When files have been placed in the trash, the Trash icon bulges. To complete the deletion, select the Empty Trash command from the Finder's Special menu. When asked to permanently remove the file click on **OK** to delete the file, or select **Cancel**.

Copying Files

A copy of a file can be created using the Duplicate command from the Finder's File menu (⌘**D**). Clicking on a file's icon to highlight it and then executing Duplicate creates a copy of the highlighted file. The copy created using Duplicate is placed on the disk containing the original file. The word "copy" is appended to the copied file's name to distinguish it from the original. For example, executing Duplicate when the COURSE OFFERINGS file icon is highlighted creates an exact copy of the file with the name "COURSE OFFERINGS copy."

B | Renaming a File

A selected file can be renamed by first clicking on the filename portion of its icon. A box is displayed around the filename:

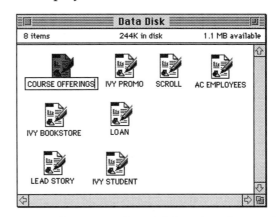

*Text may be inserted and deleted in the text box
created by clicking on a filename*

The I-Beam pointer can be clicked anywhere in the box to create an insertion point. Text may then be inserted or deleted to change the filename. Similar to the word processor, parts of the filename may be highlighted by dragging and then any text typed replaces the highlighted portion of the filename. Clicking anywhere on the white space around the icon removes the highlight and the file is renamed.

The Importance of Backups

Files that you save are stored on diskettes or on a hard disk. These files have taken time and effort to create. Businesses and other institutions that use computers have even more time invested in the data stored on their disks, and often that data is invaluable because it cannot be replaced. Chapter Two lists several sources of potential disk damage. The most common threat is the invisible magnetic radiation which surrounds us: computer monitors, electric motors, even the small magnet found in many paper clip holders. All generate sufficient magnetic radiation to destroy the files stored on a disk. Because computer disks are susceptible to different types of damage it is important to keep additional copies called *backups*, which are used if the original files become damaged.

Creating Backups with Finder

Although it is easy to create backups of a file or disk, many people do not take the time to do so. There are many stories of businesses that have lost thousands of dollars when their only copy of an important file, such as a client list database or accounts receivable spreadsheet, has been damaged. Backups are important for individual users as well.

The simplest way to create a backup of your ClarisWorks files is to make a copy of your data disk. This can be done as follows:

1. Boot the System. Do not run ClarisWorks, but leave the Finder screen visible.
2. Insert your data disk into the drive.
3. From the Special menu, select the Eject Disk (⌘E) command. The data disk's icon remains on the screen, but is dimmed:

Data Disk

An ejected disk's icon is shown dimmed on the Desktop

4. Insert a blank disk in the drive.
5. If the disk has not been formatted, follow the commands given in the dialog boxes to initialize it:

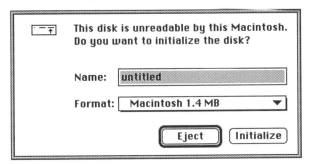

This disk is unreadable by this Macintosh. Do you want to initialize the disk?

Name: untitled

Format: Macintosh 1.4 MB ▼

Eject   Initialize

Inserting an unformatted disk displays this dialog box

Type a meaningful name such as `Backup Data` for the **Name** and then select **Initialize** to format the disk. A warning dialog box will then be displayed:

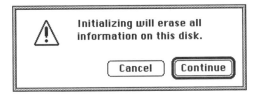

⚠ Initializing will erase all information on this disk.

Cancel   Continue

Selecting Continue starts the initialization process

Select **Continue**. The Backup Data disk icon will appear on the Desktop when initialization is complete.

6. Drag the dimmed data disk icon over top of the new disk. The following dialog box is displayed:

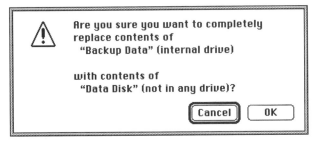

⚠ Are you sure you want to completely replace contents of "Backup Data" (internal drive)

with contents of "Data Disk" (not in any drive)?

Cancel   OK

A disk copy may be canceled by clicking on Cancel

7. Swap the disks as requested. When the copy is complete, remove the backup and store it in a safe place.

B Copying a Single File

A backup copy of a single file can be made by dragging that file's icon onto another disk. For example, suppose you want to make a copy of a ClarisWorks database file named COURSE OFFERINGS:

1. Insert the data disk containing COURSE OFFERINGS in the drive.
2. Double-click on the Data Disk icon to display its contents.
3. From the Special menu, select Eject. The data disk is ejected.
4. Insert an initialized disk in the drive for use as a backup.
5. Drag the COURSE OFFERINGS icon from the Data Disk window to the Backup Data disk icon:

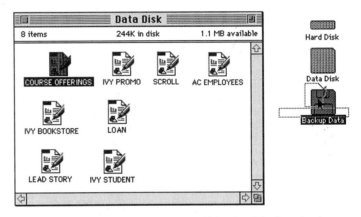

The Backup Data disk icon will be highlighted when the COURSE OFFERINGS file is dragged on to it

Swap disks as directed. When the process is complete, a copy of the COURSE OFFERINGS file has been made on the backup disk.

6. Remove the backup disk and store it in a safe place.

Making a Backup Copy with ClarisWorks

When working in ClarisWorks, executing the Save command from the File menu saves a file using its current filename. Backup copies of the same file can be saved by using the Save As command from the File menu. The Save As command allows you to save a file under a different filename, into a different folder, or onto a floppy disk. To make a backup copy of a file onto a floppy disk:

1. Open the desired file in ClarisWorks.
2. From the File menu, select the Save As command (⇧⌘**S**). The Save As dialog box is shown.
3. Insert the backup disk that will contain the backup file. ClarisWorks changes the dialog box to show the contents of the backup disk:

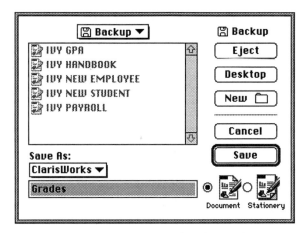

*Inserting a disk changes the dialog box to
show the contents of that disk*

4. Select **Save**. This creates a copy of the open file on the backup disk.
5. To protect the file, immediately Close (⌘**W**) the new copy.
6. Remove the backup disk and store it in a safe place.

As previously mentioned, the Save As command in ClarisWorks also allows you to save a file under another filename on the same disk. For example, use Save As to create a copy of Grades on the same disk using the filename Grades Backup. This will protect you if something happens to the original file.

It is important to keep backup disks in a different location than the original copies. That way, the chances of both copies being destroyed are minimal. For example, if you keep your ClarisWorks data diskette at school, keep a backup copy at home. Businesses often store backup disks in special fireproof safes or in safe deposit boxes at a bank. Several companies have gone into business just to provide safe "off-site storage" for important computer data.

Remember, the data stored on a diskette is not permanent and can easily be erased or damaged. Following the diskette handling rules given in Chapter Two and keeping backup copies in a safe place are the best insurance against data loss.

Appendix C
Keyboarding Skills

Learning to Touch Type

The ability to *touch type* is especially helpful in using a computer. When touch typing place your hands on the keyboard in a position that allows you to strike any of the keys without looking at the keyboard. The advantage of learning how to do this is that you can keep your eyes on the material you are typing. You will also be able to type with greater accuracy and speed than you could using the "hunt and peck" method where you must search for each key before striking it.

Before you begin to type it is important to have your hands and body in their proper positions. Your hands should be placed lightly on the keyboard with the slightly curved fingers of the left hand on the keys **ASDF** and the right hand on the **JKL;** keys. The left pinky is placed on the **A** key while the other fingers of the left hand placed on the **SDF** keys. The right pinky is placed on the semicolon (;) key and the other fingers of the right hand on the **LKJ** keys. The right thumb is placed on the spacebar. With the fingers placed as just described, this is called the "home" position.

Place the chair you are sitting in so that your arms reach out leaving the elbows loosely at your side. Sit in a relaxed but erect position with both feet flat on the floor. Maintaining proper posture will help to keep your body from tensing. Try not to slouch or bend over the keyboard. The proper posture is shown in the diagram:

Always maintain proper posture when touch typing

To touch type it is necessary to memorize the location of each of the keys on the keyboard. This is best accomplished by learning just a few keys at a time which you will do when performing the following lessons. Developing an even, smooth rhythm as you type is important. You want to strike each of the keys with the same pressure using a steady pace. To help you develop speed and accuracy a Timed Practice in most lessons asks you to keep track of how many words per minute you are typing and the number of mistakes being made.

Each of the following keyboarding lessons makes use of the ClarisWorks word processor. Therefore, we will begin by learning how to access and use the word processor. Read pages 2-1 through 2-10 in Chapter Two and performing the steps in Practices 1 and 2 on the computer to learn how to run ClarisWorks.

Lesson 1 - The Home Row: ASDF JKL;

Start ClarisWorks as described in the beginning of Chapter Two and create a new Word Processor document. A blank word processor screen is displayed. You will perform each of the typing lessons on this screen. Note the blinking line at the top left-hand side of the screen which is called the *cursor*. It indicates where characters typed into the word processor will appear.

Place your hands on the keyboard in the *home position* or on the *home row* described above with the left hand on the keys **ASDF** and right hand on the keys **JKL;**. The right thumb is placed on the spacebar.

Type the following letters and when you finish each line, press the Return key with your right pinky. The cursor will move down one line and to the left side of the screen. Note that the semicolon (;) is normally followed by a space when typing actual material. Do not look at your hands while you type, look only at the picture of the keyboard below.

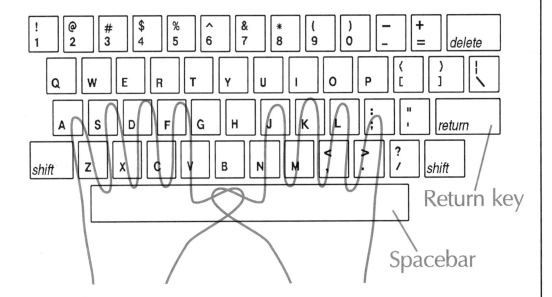

Always place your fingers on the home row when beginning to type

C

Practice 1.1

```
1   aaa ;;; aaa ;;; sss lll sss lll ddd kkk ddd kkk fff jjj fjf
2   aaa sss sas asa sss aaa sas aaa sss sas aaa sss sas sss a;a
3   ddd ada ddd daa dss dad dsd ddd sss aaa ads asd asd dad sls
4   sss aaa ddd ddd ssa dad dsd dsa dsa dss daa aaa sss dda dkd
5   fff fff faf fss fss fas fas fad ffd faa fsa ffs fsa fad fjf
6   fss saf fad sfa fss fad fsa sda fad aff fsd sff ffa sss fjf
7   jjj jjj jja jaf jfj jdj jfs jja jad jsf jja jda jaf jjj jfj
8   jad daj fja das saj jjs jsa daf sfj jad faj jjj jad jaa dkd
9   kkk kka kkk kak kjk kss kkj kak ksa ksk kfk kkf kkk kjj kdk
10  kad dak sak adk sak akk kak jak jak dak ask sak kkk kjk ala
11  lll lll lff llk lak las lad lfl lld lll lsk lfl lkl ljl lal
12  lsl sal fal dsl lsl llf jal all sal lsa fal lll lkl lal a;a
13  ; ; ; ; fa; da; sa; da; fj; sa; da; jl; ; ; ; sa; lad; jak;
14  dad dad lad lad sad sad add add lad ask dad fall fall falls
15  ask ask fad fad ads ads dad lass lass sass sass salad salad
```

Practice 1.2

```
1   ;;; aaa lll sss kkk ddd jjj fff ;a; a;a lsl sls kdk dkd jfj
2   sas saa asa asa dfd fdf ffd dfd das sad sad das las das ad;
3   jjkk kkjj jkjk kjkj jkkj l; l; jkl kjl; dakl kald jakl jakl
4   jjk jjl jj; jaj ksk lal las las kad kad laf laf la; ja; la;
5   aad aas aaf aaj aak aal aa; fad fad dad dad lad lad sad sad
6   dask jljl fafa fajk ddl; jadl lads lads dads dads sads jakl
7   asks asks dads fall lass fads lask fads lads ffjj kkll fkf;
8   asks dads fall fads lask adds lass fall alls lads dads sad;
```

Repeat the Practices above until you can type the characters without referring to the keyboard diagram.

When you have completed the lesson and want to leave ClarisWorks select the Quit command from the File menu using the mouse as described in Section 2.10, or hold down the Command key and press the Q key (⌘Q). You will then be asked if you wish to save the file. Click on the **No** button.

Lesson 2 - RTYU

In this lesson you will learn the **RTYU** keys.

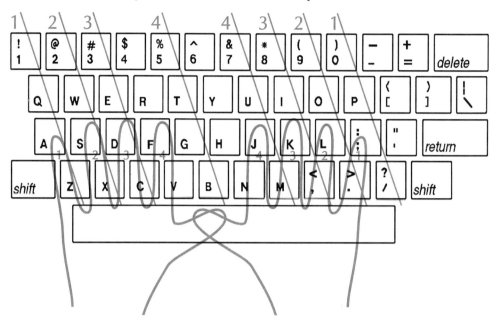

*Press **R** and **T** with the left hand, and **Y** and **U** with the right*

The letters **RT** are typed using the pointer finger of your left hand and **YU** with the pointer finger of your right hand. Note the lines that show which finger is used to type which keys: "1" for the pinky, "2" for the ring finger, "3" for the index and "4" for the pointer.

From this point on, each lesson will begin with a review of the previous lesson. Before proceeding to the new letters, practice this review several times until you feel comfortable. **Remember to press the Return key at the end of each line with your right pinky.**

Review

1   aaa ;;; aaa ;;; sss lll sss lll ddd kkk ddd kkk fff jjj fjf

2   aaa sss lll sas asa ddd das kkk jjj lkl fff fjf jfj klk jas

3   ljl kfk ldf klj kjk ljk fsd sda jkl fsd sad sad lad lad fad

4   dada fada sads jass klas fas; dad; fkal dasd jjkk jaka fada

5   asks lads lass daj; jakl kfkf ladf klds adas fjl; dads lads

Practice 2.1

```
 1  fff ffr frf frr frr rrr frr frf rrr frf frr rrr fff frf rrr
 2  fff fft ftf ftt ftt ttt ttt ftf ttf ftf ttt ttt fff tff ftt
 3  frt frt frt frt fra rta rat rat jar jar far far tar tar far
 4  jjj jju juj juu juj jju juj juj uuu juu juj jjj uuu juj juu
 5  jjj jjy jyj jyy jyy yyy jyj jyy jyy jyj yyy jyy jyj jyj yyy
 6  juu juy jju juy jyu juy jyu jyu jyy juu uuu yyy uyu yuy yuy
 7  fujy furt fryt juty rfrt sats fats jakd dar; rats rats sats
 8  krad jury safy last last jury tars tars star star duty duty
 9  yard jury duty fast just dark dust data klas jars furs yard
10  ruts says lass tar; hats sats rats yard dull tart last dad;
```

Practice 2.2

```
 1  juts furs dust suds dart rats sats just just task task fast
 2  rats ruts daft rays sats lark jars salt suds suds lads furs
 3  yard duty fast lads sad; lass tars hats data tart last dust
 4  jar ask fry lad fat dad add sad rut dad add say say far tar
 5  dart dull rut; ruts furs asks lass rust just fall star rays
 6  dusk last fast lads kart dust sass furs furs just task salt
 7  dull darts suds jars lark dusts rust data data rats salt as
 8  asks just last fur dark dart says jury task tart tars darts
 9  tar rat sally sally last yard dark try; fats lark dark data
10  ruts rudy trudy rust dart just salt dark furs say; dust tad
```

Repeat the Practices above until you can type the keys without referring to the keyboard diagram. When you are finished, exit ClarisWorks by pressing ⌘**Q**. You will then be asked if you wish to save the file. Click on the **No** button.

Lesson 3 - EGHI

In this lesson you will learn the keys **EGHI**. Rather than pressing the Return key at the end of each line we are now going to allow the computer to determine where the end of each line is. If there is not sufficient room for a word at the end of a line the word will automatically be moved to the beginning of the next line in a process called *word wrap*. Where your computer breaks a line will differ from what is shown in this text since the break is determined by where the margin is set. Just keep typing the lines on the next page without ever pressing Return:

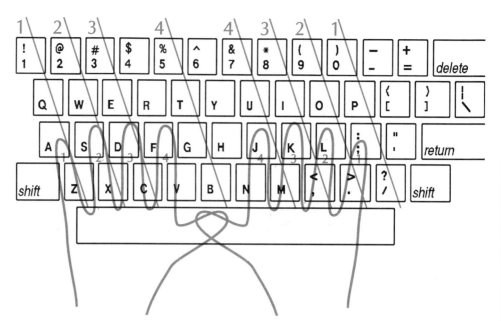

Press the **E** *and* **G** *with the left hand, and the* **H** *and* **I** *with the right*

Review

1   fff frr frf frf fft ftf ftt ftf ttt juu juj jju jju juu juj

2   jyy jyy jyj jyj fuy fuy frt fju juy jyy ftt frr jyy juy juy

3   asks jury yard jars arts judy lark rust dust just fast dark

4   trudy dark sally yard daffy salt rat tar fur rays tall fall

5   darts fats sat; us all task lad; salt dust trust last fault

Practice 3.1

1   ddd ded ded dee dde ded ded ded ddd ded dee dee dee eee ded

2   fff fgf fgf fgg fgf fgf fgg fgf fgg ggg fgg fgf fgg ggg fgf

3   fgd deg fed def fgd deg fed def deg def feg dfe eee ggg ege

4   jjj jhj jhj jhh jhj jjj hhh jhj jhh jhj jhj jjh jjh hhh jhj

5   kkk kik kik kik kii kii kik iii iii kii kik kii kii iii kik

6   jhki jhik kiik kijh kijh khij jhik kihj jhki jhki jhki jjkk

7   did tug lad the she hid set age red red did ask let age the

8   did lug tug hit age yet ask rut elk gas she she did did use

9   rake dirt sake high dirt rail jail kiss jilt hale side said

10   saddle kettle us huddle jerry jail dirt yet little rut side

11   ask rail; kiss jilt hale said elks gas hers juggle rid teds

12   the fight federal fester justify sight satisfy deride kitty

Practice 3.2

1   did lag elk yes age let rug kiss rake that said; sail hills

2   her; dig a rut age is hill high hear set sail satisfy there

3   erase refer defer agree reset sir differ legal degrees tell

4   satisfy father egret fifes fifth fly leg hedge sell his her

5   gail harsh heart thigh yalta light irish alight; ideal star

6   last jelly judge high kelly jail; kay jest hail to thee jet

7   halts the digs highest eight three furs halt judge judge as

8   lilly ladle legal aisle drill salt the these as; highest to

9   drudge tusk halt fudge last jest hail has gall deak salt as

10   hark yak said sail the less; fastest highest edge all halts

Timed Practice 3.3

The next few lessons end with a timed practice which allows you to check your speed. Type for 1 minute and then calculate your speed in words per minute by counting the words typed. Each line contains 12 words. Words in a partial line are calculated using the scale below the lines.

1   did yes let rug age rut set ted ask elk yet dad sad lads hit 12

2   sake rail jail dirt side said jails kiss rake that tug; dull 24

3   jilt just fads fife flag fall digs ages rail tell star kills 36

4   fight sight deride just father fifth kettle jelly judge ask; 48

     1   2   3   4   5   6   7   8   9 | 1   2

When you are finished, exit ClarisWorks.

Lesson 4 – CVB MNO

In this lesson the letters **CVB MNO** are added as well as capital letters. Use the finger lines in the diagram to determine which finger is used to type the new letters. To type capital letters use either your left or right pinky to depress one of the Shift keys and type the letter. If the capital letter is typed with the right hand the left pinky is used to depress the Shift key. If it is typed with the left hand the right pinky is used. As in Lesson 3, allow the computer to determine where the end of each line is by not pressing the Return key.

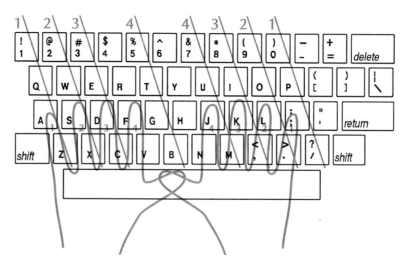

*Press the **C**, **V**, and **B** keys with the left hand, and the **M**, **N**, and **O** keys with the right. Use the pinky to press the Shift key*

....

Review

1 ded eee fgf ggg jhj hhh kik iii fge fgf jhj fgh jhi dek deg

2 digs ruts ages hill high sats fads sake rail dirt side said

3 all irish thigh gale takes legal aisle salt eight that flag

4 hail thee; fastest gail sledge haste tasks jet get hail art

....

Practice 4.1

1   ddd dcd dcc dcd ddc dcc dcc dcc ccc dcc dcd ccc dcc dcc dcd

2   fff fvf fvf fvv fvv vvv fvv fvv fvf vvv fvf fvv fvv fvv fvf

3   fff fbf fbf fbb ffb bbb fbb fbf fbb bbb fbf fbb fbb bbb fbf

4   dcv dcv cfv fvb fvb fbv fbf fvv vdc bdc bbd ccc vvv bbb bvc

5   jjj jmj jmj jmm jjm mmm jmm jmj jmm mmm mmm jmm jmj jmm jmj

6   jjj jnj jnj jnn jnn nnn jnn jnj jnj nnn jnn jnj jnj jnn jnj

7   lll lol lol loo ooo loo loo lol lol ooo loo lol lol loo lol

8   jmn jnm jnm jml jno loj ojn ooj jmn jno loj mno mno bcv bcv

9   Bill odd nod boy Bob night vent Sam avoids mad bite buried;

10 dock mint convert common bimini money none bongo volume vat

11 convince civic conic occur yucca bulb blurb member mayor to

12 ninth linen noun announce mono minds vocation victim vacate

13 kitty Gerry highly Eighty saddle kettle monies Tony convert

14 Jimmy Miami Thomas Fast Kludge Doll Rest Ernest Joan Laurie

15 Satisfy small Father; fight federal Jail tuggle yet Law Jim

An Introduction to Computing Using ClarisWorks

C

Practice 4.2

1 Lara Nina monkey said Gray is art color Has Harry come home
2 Janet will not be at school today It is too late to make up
3 Let us make haste before school starts This is not the time
4 Should you be very good or not This is the universal cReturn
5 George Ferrit was raised in Iowa John Smith in Rhode Island
6 You need to make some money; to be able to go to the movies
7 Bob Cindy Virginia Monica Nina Ollie Barbara Veronica Bruce
8 This is the time for to be verbal Robert is a very nice guy
9 Miami New York Chicago Cleveland Boston Houston Dallas Dent
10 The gain made by becoming a good typist may be considerable

Timed Practice 4.3

Type for 1 minute and then calculate your speed in words per minute by counting the words typed. Each line contains 12 words. The words in a partial line are calculated using the scale below the lines.

1 Come to my house if you need to sell a vacuum cleaner today; 12
2 This is not a good time to help you with cooking the turkeys 24
3 Bill Crane is the secretary at our local offices of the club 36
4 Virginia is a beautiful state; Its capitol city is Richmond 48

      1   2   3   4   5   6   7   8   9 | 1   2

When you are finished, exit ClarisWorks.

Lesson 5 - WQZX P,.?

In this lesson the letters **WQZX P** are added along with the period (.), comma (,), and question mark (?). The question mark is typed by pressing the left Shift key with the left pinky and the question mark key with the right. Note the finger lines for determining which finger to use for each key.

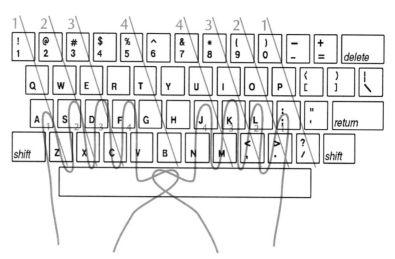

*Press the **Q**, **Z**, and **X** keys with the left hand, and the **P**, comma, period, and question mark with the right*

Review

1   dcdc fvvf fbfb jmmj jnjn Jmnj jnlo loon fvcd Fcvf jmnl Lojn

2   very task dark volt None vast many salt belt bolt none cold

3   Verbal Bimini Bahamas vacuum Nina member announce mist mold

4   members linen Venice Bob Vermont San Antonio convert Melvin

Practice 5.1

1   sss sws sww sww sws sww www sws ssw sww sws sws www sws sws

2   aaa aqa aqa aqq aqq qqq aaq aqa aqq aqq aqq aqa qqq aqa aqa

3   aaa aza azz azz zzz azz azz aza azz azz azz azz zzz azz aza

4   ;;p ;;p ;p; ;p; ;p; pp; pp; ll. ll. l.l lo. lo. la. ll. l.l

5   sss sxs sxx sxx xxx sxs sxx sxs xxx xxx ssx sxx sxs sxx sxs

6   kk, kk, kk, k, kkk, k, k, kk, ; ? ; ? ; ? ; ; ? ; ? ; ? la?

7   aqua, zap? Zeus, want; aqua. quart, extra, quilt. Zoe quill

8   quick query equip quilt quits quote Queen quality paper top

9   apple panel support append popular profess quota quail pops

10 Rudy Penn Paul, plastics proof quart quit? Walter Thomas at

11 Aztec zero, unzip. fuzzy gauze sizes Inez epitomize Prizes?

12 exact axiom vexed Felix, Exxon. Xerox, mixed index exciting

13 dozen Zeke. Brazil, William, hertz gauze dozes? lazy Zurich

14 zonal zooms seize quilt quick prime power opera? allow. Zak

15 Oprah robot Boone, Texas, Portland, Zeus Zola extremely fax

Practice 5.2

1   Jake quit his jobs. What do you want? Exit from the west.

2   Zinc is not really that pretty. Would you please be quiet?

3   I would like to go to Zurich, Brazil, Texas and Queensland.

4   Robert Roodez is a fine person whose qualities are special.

5   In which Texas cities would you like to stay at Quality Inn?

6   The Aztecs had an advanced civilization which disappeared.

7   What equipment would you like to have added to a gymnasium?

8   I have visited Washington, Texas, Arizona, Utah, Vermont.

9   Inez Zola has the qualities that will make her quite famous.

10 Do you have zebras, polar bears, and turtles at your zoo?

Timed Practice 5.3

Type for 1 minute and then calculate your speed in words per minute by counting the words typed. Each line contains 12 words. The words in a partial line are calculated using the scale below the lines. To test your accuracy count the number of letters and spaces missed.

1   There are qualities which are required to become successful. 12

2   The following will come to the front; Bob, Zelda, and Betty. 24

3   Would you please; ask your parents to allow you to visit me? 36

4   Twelve quiet students sat on the wall waiting for the twins. 48

         1   2   3   4   5   6   7   8   9 | 1   2

When you are finished, exit ClarisWorks.

Lesson 6 - :"/

In this lesson the colon (:), quote marks ("), and slash or division sign (/) are added. The colon is typed by pressing the left Shift key with the left pinky and typing the key containing the semicolon and colon. A space always follows a colon. Quote marks are typed by pressing the left Shift key with the left pinky and the key to the right of the colon key using the right pinky. The slash is typed using the right pinky.

Review

```
1   dozen unzip zesty gauze amaze wants excite explain exhausts
2   prop Perhaps?  personal, profit, operator.  Quality qualify
3   equip quest quicken, proud supports puppy Zanadu?  Exciting
4   quit extra Paul Zak?  Extra qualify pest apple quart quick.
```

Practice 6.1

```
1   : : "abcd" l: "What is that?"  "This is a quote from Jane."
2   "John is the best." The team is: Zeke, Jake, Rob and Quent.
3   ; / / ; / ; abc/de x/y; words/minute nt/m miles/hr, xyz/abc
4   These states are in the west: Utah, Oregon, and California.
5   What person said: "We have nothing to fear but fear itself"?
```

Lesson 7

The two Practices in this lesson are *timed practices*. In the first, type for one minute and then calculate your speed in words per minute by counting the words typed. Each line contains 12 words. The words in a partial line are calculated using the scale below the lines. To test your accuracy, count the number of letters and spaces missed. Record both your speed in words per minute and the number of errors per minute. Repeat the Practice a few times recording the results of each attempt. Your speed and accuracy should improve each time. Note the specific letters which appear as errors and repeat the lesson for that letter. For example, if you often type the letter R instead of T by mistake, go back and repeat Lesson 2. Note that this material is fairly difficult; you should perform all the previous lessons before attempting this one.

Timed Practice 7.1

```
1   dale rail flight word, solve draft general; writers rough at  12
2   Important: work orders going ahead; instead rise part, taken  24
3   gift week disaster creates advantage been skill oral success  36
4   sharpen your smile coal miners desire: insure achieve smiles  48
5   Press exit Zack; suspend flowers: beginning strokes reunite,  60
6   carriage blooms crowd works quite document fashion computer:  72
7   having options print transfer undo; Marcia, Melvin, Samantha  84
        1    2    3    4    5    6    7    8    9    |    1    2
```

Timed Practice 7.2

The **Tab** key is located on the upper left of the keyboard, next to the Q key. Rather than using spaces, Tab is used to indent paragraphs and to begin lines which do not start at the left margin. In the Practices below, you will press Tab once with the left pinky to indent each paragraph.

In this Practice type for five minutes and then calculate your speed in words per minute by counting the words typed and dividing by 5. The total of words is given at the end of each line. To test your accuracy count the number of letters and spaces missed. Repeat the Practice typing for ten minutes and then calculate your speed and accuracy. Repeat this Practice several times, over several days. You should note an increase in both your speed and your accuracy.

1   Many of the advances made by science and technology are 12
dependent upon the ability to perform complex mathematical 23
calculations and to process large amounts of data. It is 34
therefore not surprising that for thousands of years 44
mathematicians, scientists and business people have 54
searched for "computing" machines that could perform 65
calculations and analyze data quickly and accurately. 76

2   As civilizations began to develop, they created both 87
written languages and number systems. These number systems 99
were not originally meant to be used in mathematical 109
calculations, but rather were designed to record 119
measurements. Roman numerals are a good example of this. 130
Few of us would want to carry out even the simplest 140
arithmetic operations using Roman numerals. How then were 151
calculations performed thousands of years ago? 162

3   Calculations were carried out with a device known as 173
an abacus which was used in ancient Babylon, China and 186
Europe until the late middle-ages. Many parts of the 196
world, especially in the Orient, still make use of the 207
abacus. The abacus works by sliding beads back and 217
forth on a frame with the beads on the top of the frame 228
representing fives and on the bottom ones. After a 239
calculation is made the result is written down. 249

    1   2   3   4   5   6   7   8   9 | 1   2

Lesson 8

C

In this lesson you will make use of the top row of keys that contains both numbers and symbols. Note which finger is used to press each key. The right Shift key is used to type the symbols at the top of the keys 1 through 5 and the left Shift key for the symbols on the top of keys 6 through =.

Practice 8.1

```
1   aqa aq1 aq1 aq1 a1a a1a a11 sws sw2 sw2 sw2 s2s s2s s22 ss2
2   ded de3 de3 de3 d3d d3d d33 de3 frf fr4 fr4 f4f f4f ff4 fr4
3   fr5 fr5 fr5 f5f f5f f55 ff5 juj ju7 ju7 ju7 j7j j7j ju7 j77
4   jyj jy6 jy6 jy6 j6j j6j jy6 j66 kik ki8 ki8 k8k k8k ki8 k88
5   lol lo9 lo9 l9l l9l lo9 l99 ;p; ;p0 ;p0 ;p0 ;0; ;0; ;;0 ;p0
6   aq1! aq1! aq1! aq!! sw2@ sw2@ s2s@ Sw@@ s@@s de3# de3# d#3d
7   fr4$ fr4$ fr$$ fr$f f$4r fr5% fr5% f5%% f5%5 f%f% jy6^ jy6^
8   ju7& ju7& ju7& j&j& ju&j ki8* ki8* k**k k*8* k8*8 lo9( lo9(
9   L(990); : L( ; 0) ; )0 )) (9923) : ; 00) 19(00)   ; - - __ ;
10  ; + +567 - 342 =$45.60 + ; " ' ;+ ; + = - ; ___ -- +1895.00
11  $435.00; = 389* (873) &23 $35.89@ 380.23! 89 + 78 = $382.00
12  Mary has bought a dress that costs $145.67 plus 6.0(%) tax.
13  (A) 3^2 = 9 & $12@ for 5 items = $60.00. 89 * 34 = 3026 47%
14  If I win the Florida $10,000,000.00 lottery I must pay tax.
15  Jack & Jill went up the 3,450 m hill to fetch 12# of water.
16  23 & 79 are odd numbers! (34 + 78) / (245 * 12.8) = 0.00035
```

An Introduction to Computing Using ClarisWorks

Timed Practice 8.2

In this Practice type for five minutes and then calculate your speed in words per minute by counting the words typed and dividing by 5. The total of words is given at the end of each line. The words in a partial line are calculated using the scale below the lines. To test your accuracy count the number of letters and spaces missed.

1   Hortense Bargain has decided to reduce the price of   11
stock items #3485 (paint), #7431 (electric saws) and #2945   23
(lawn furniture) by 45%. The new prices will be $38.50@,   35
$72.95@ and $14.98@.   39

2   Ivy University is having a book fair and charging the   51
following for books and supplies: pens $0.45@, note books   62
$3.78@, and boxes of paper clips $0.67@. "An Introduction   74
to Computing Using ClarisWorks" is specially priced   85
with a 10% reduction (plus 6% sales tax). The stock number   97
of this text is #34-2578 (for paperback) and #34-2580   108
(hardcover). Heidi Crane's new novel "Old Houses in New   119
Jersey" is specially priced at $12.45 after a 25% discount.   131

3   Please be advised of the addition of the following   142
courses to the Ivy University catalog: #126 Advanced   153
Computing (2 credits), #365 Very Advanced Computing (7   164
credits), #782 Computing for the Exceptionally Intelligent   176
(12 credits). The tuition for each course is $45.00@.   187
What a bargain!   190

       1   2   3   4   5   6   7   8   9 | 1   2

Lesson 9

In this lesson type for five minutes and then calculate your speed in words per minute by counting the words typed and dividing by 5. The total of words is given at the end of each line. The words in a partial line are calculated using the scale below the lines. To test your accuracy count the number of letters and spaces missed. Repeat the Practice typing for ten minutes and then calculating your speed and accuracy.

1   One of the most important advances made in computing   11
has been in the field of "telecommunications." By   21
telecommunications we mean the sending of computer data   32
over telephone lines. To do this an additional piece of   43
hardware called a "modem" is required to translate the   54
binary data of the computer into waves which can then be   65
transmitted over phone lines. To receive data a modem   76
must also have the capability of translating the waves back   88
into binary form.   92

2   With a modem a microcomputer is capable of transmitting 104
and receiving data between any two locations connected   115
by phone lines. The rate at which each character of data   127
is sent is measured in "baud," one baud representing the   138
transmission of one character per second. Currently the   149
most common rates are 2400, 9600, and 14400 baud which means   161
2400, 9600, and 14400 characters per second. However, newer   173
modems are being created which are capable of communicating   185
at 28800 baud and higher.   190

3   In a recent newspaper article the Internal Revenue   201
Service (IRS) defined artificial intelligence as "the   212
science of making machines do things that would require   223
intelligence if done by man." As an example, there are   235
currently computers which can play chess so well that they   247
can beat all but the best players. Universities actually   258
challenge each other's computers to play chess to determine   270
which has the best chess playing program. Are these   281
computers really intelligent? Most computer scientists   292
would say no. They are simply programmed to make a series   304
of decisions in response to the moves made by their   315
opponents. It is merely their speed and ability to access   327
huge amounts of stored data which make them appear to be   338
intelligent.   341

        1   2   3   4   5   6   7   8   9 | 1   2

I Index

C

I

I

I

I

S

T

U

An Introduction to Computing Using ClarisWorks

I

I

An Introduction to Computing Using ClarisWorks